Journeys on Screen

Journeys on Screen
Theory, Ethics, Aesthetics

Edited by
Louis Bayman and Natália Pinazza

EDINBURGH
University Press

Edinburgh University Press is one of the leading university presses in the UK. We publish academic books and journals in our selected subject areas across the humanities and social sciences, combining cutting-edge scholarship with high editorial and production values to produce academic works of lasting importance. For more information visit our website: edinburghuniversitypress.com

© editorial matter and organisation Louis Bayman and Natália Pinazza, 2019, 2020
© the chapters their several authors, 2019, 2020

First published in hardback by Edinburgh University Press 2019

Edinburgh University Press Ltd
The Tun – Holyrood Road
12 (2f) Jackson's Entry
Edinburgh EH8 8PJ

Typeset in 11/13pt Ehrhardt MT Pro by
Servis Filmsetting Ltd, Stockport, Cheshire

A CIP record for this book is available from the British Library

ISBN 978 1 4744 2183 6 (hardback)
ISBN 978 1 4744 7464 1 (paperback)
ISBN 978 1 4744 2184 3 (webready PDF)
ISBN 978 1 4744 2185 0 (epub)

The right of the contributors to be identified as authors of this work has been asserted in accordance with the Copyright, Designs and Patents Act 1988 and the Copyright and Related Rights Regulations 2003 (SI No. 2498).

Acknowledgements
We would like to thank our families, friends and colleagues
for their support and encouragement.

Contents

Figures vii
Notes on the Contributors ix

   Introduction 1

Part 1a Mapping Cinematic Journeys: Chronotopes of Journeys

1 Global Visions: Around-the-World Travel and Visual Culture in Early Modernity 19
   Tiago de Luca
2 Brief Encounters: The Railway Station on Film 36
   Lucy Mazdon
3 Diasporic Dreams and Shattered Desires: Displacement, Identity and Tradition in *Heaven on Earth* 50
   Clelia Clini
4 Chronotopic Ghosts and Quiet Men: José Luis Guerín's *Innisfree* 70
   Michael Pigott
5 Memories, Notebooks, Roads: The Essayistic Journey in Time and Space 86
   Adam Ludford Freeman

Part 1b Expanding Europe: Interstitial Production and Border-crossing in Eastern European Cinema

6 Shadows of Unforgotten Ancestors: Representations of Estonian Mass Deportations of the 1940s in *In the Crosswind* and *Body Memory* 103
   Eva Näripea

7   The Holocaust and the Cinematic Landscapes of Postmemory
    in Lithuania, Hungary and Ukraine   118
    Maurizio Cinquegrani
8   Hesitant Journeys: Fugitive and Migrant Narratives in the
    New Romanian Cinema   130
    László Strausz
9   Women on the Road: Representing Female Mobility in
    Contemporary Hungarian–Romanian Co-productions   147
    Hajnal Király

Part 2a Form and Narrative in Journey Genres
10 The Sense of an Ending: Music, Time and Romance in *Before
    Sunrise*   167
    Carlo Cenciarelli
11 Moving in Circles: Kinetic Elite and Kinetic Proletariat in
    'End of the World' Films   183
    Ewa Mazierska
12 Gothic Journeys: Travel and Transportation in the Films of
    Terence Fisher   199
    Chris Fujiwara
13 Transnational Productions and Regional Funding: Border-
    crossing, European Locations and the Case of Contemporary
    Horror   215
    Stefano Baschiera

Part 2b The Politics of the Road Movie
14 Colonialism in Latin American Road Movies   235
    Natália Pinazza
15 Spaces of Failure: The Gendering of Neoliberal Mobilities in
    the US Indie Road Movie   252
    Anna Cooper
16 *Sic transit*: The Serial Killer Road Movie   270
    Louis Bayman

Index   291

Figures

1.1	Global Panoramas: the key distributed to visitors reveals the way in which the panoramic landscape implied a global spatiality	24
1.2	We Put the World Before You: this promotional logo for Charles Urban Trading Company shows the global ambitions of early cinema	30
1.3	A promotional poster for the BBC series *Planet Earth II* bears an uncanny resemblance to panorama keys by implicating a single landscape within a global space	33
4.1	Ballyglunin station, *Innisfree*	78
4.2	Ballyglunin station as 'Castletown' station in *The Quiet Man*	78
4.3	Rear projection of In(n)nisfree	84
8.1	Blocked transparency: visual barriers emphasise the viewer's activity	134
8.2	Changing the narrative's scale	137
8.3	Waiting for Behran: the space of solidarity	140
9.1	An unlikely couple travelling by horse-drawn carriage in *Katalin Varga*	153
9.2	The scarf with the curls foreshadowing the forced sexualisation of Iska	154
9.3	'Some are fifty-fifty' – Mona and Viorel in *Bibliothèque Pascal*	156
10.1	After dancing to the harpsichord and some imaginary picture-taking, Jesse and Celine hold each other tightly	173
10.2	On the train, facing forward, a tearful Celine seems to smile at the memory of her time in Vienna	174

14.1	Family pushing the broken trailer in *The Rolling Family* and close-up of the motorcycle in *The Motorcycle Diaries*	239
14.2	Journeys in *Central Station* are characterised by various precarious means of transportation	241
14.3	A series of bird's-eye shots of the Amazon forest emphasises the curves of the river	247
16.1	Automotive perception	277
16.2	Abandon to the passions	284

Notes on the Contributors

Stefano Baschiera is Senior Lecturer in Film Studies at Queen's University Belfast. His work on European cinema, material culture and film industries has been published in a variety of edited collections and journals, including *Film International, Bianco e Nero, New Review of Film and Television Studies*, and *NECSUS: European Journal of Media Studies*. With Russ Hunter, he is the co-editor of *Italian Horror Cinema*.

Louis Bayman is Lecturer in Film Studies at the University of Southampton. He is interested in questions of form, time and space in narrative cinema and has published a range of articles on form and feeling in popular genres, including horror and serial killer cinema. He is the author of *The Operatic and the Everyday in Italian Film Melodrama*, and co-editor (with Sergio Rigoletto) of *Popular Italian Cinema* and (with Natália Pinazza) of *World Cinema Directory: Brazil*, and *World Film Locations: São Paulo*.

Carlo Cenciarelli is a Lecturer at Cardiff University. His research focuses on music, sound and the moving image, and particularly on the way in which cinema provides a cultural interface for engaging with musical repertoires and audio technologies. His main publications have been on the cinematic afterlife of Western art music and on opera and digital culture, with essays published in edited collections and in journals including *Music and Letters, Twentieth-Century Music, Cambridge Opera Journal* and the *Journal of the Royal Musical Association*. He is currently editing a large volume on the history of cinematic listening (the *Oxford Handbook of Cinematic Listening*) and is working on a monograph that explores the relationship between listening cultures inside and outside the movie theatre.

Maurizio Cinquegrani is Senior Lecturer in Film at the University of Kent. Maurizio joined Kent in September 2012, having previously taught at London Metropolitan University, Birkbeck College, and King's College London. In 2011 he participated in the 'Camden Town Group in Context' research project at Tate Britain with a contribution looking at the relationship between early film practices and the work of Walter Sickert, Malcolm Drummond and other artists. In 2012 he also worked as filmic cartographer at the University of Liverpool on an AHRC-funded research project entitled 'Cinematic Geographies of Battersea: Urban Interface & Site-Specific Spatial Knowledge'. His first book, *Of Empire and the City: Remapping Early British Cinema*, was published in 2014. *Journey to Poland: Documentary Landscapes of the Holocaust* is his second monograph and follows a number of articles and book chapters on the subject of film and the Holocaust, including the present contribution to *Journeys on Screen*.

Clelia Clini is Research Associate on the 'Migrant Memory and the Postcolonial Imagination' research project at Loughborough University London, Institute of Media and Creative Industries. Prior to joining Loughborough University, she was a Research Associate at University College London, working on research projects on forced displacement and cultural interventions. Since 2012 she has worked as a Lecturer in Media and Cultural Studies at John Cabot University and at The American University of Rome. She holds a PhD in Cultural and Postcolonial Studies from the University Orientale of Naples.

Anna Cooper is Assistant Professor in the School of Theatre, Film, and Television, University of Arizona. She completed her PhD at the University of Warwick and has worked at the universities of Hertfordshire, Sussex and California (Santa Cruz). She has co-edited *Projecting the World: Representing the 'Foreign' in Classical Hollywood* and her monograph, *An American Abroad: European Travel, American Imperialism and Postwar Hollywood Cinema*, is forthcoming.

Tiago de Luca is Assistant Professor in Film Studies at the University of Warwick. He is the author of *Realism of the Senses in World Cinema: The Experience of Physical Reality* and the editor (with Nuno Barradas Jorge) of *Slow Cinema*. His new book project looks at the ways in which the whole world has been depicted in the cinema and related media.

Adam Ludford Freeman is currently completing a PhD in the School of Arts at the University of Kent. His practice as research PhD looks at place and landscape in the essay film.

Chris Fujiwara is a film critic and programmer who has written several books on cinema, including *Jacques Tourneur: The Cinema of Nightfall*, *The World and Its Double: The Life and Work of Otto Preminger* and *Jerry Lewis*. He also edited the book *Defining Moments in Movies*. He has lectured on film aesthetics and film history at Tokyo University, Yale University, Rhode Island School of Design, and elsewhere. From 2012 to 2014 he was Artistic Director of Edinburgh International Film Festival.

Hajnal Király is Senior Researcher at the Institute for Hungarian Literary and Cultural Studies, Eötvös Lóránd University of Budapest. She is a member of the research project 'Space-ing Otherness. Cultural Images of Space, Contact Zones in Contemporary Hungarian and Romanian Film and Literature'. She is also member of the project 'Rethinking Intermediality in Contemporary Cinema: Changing Forms of In-Betweenness', conducted by Ágnes Pethő at the Sapientia Hungarian University of Transylvania, Romania. Besides a cultural approach to contemporary Hungarian and Romanian cinema, her present research interests are medium theory, literary re-mediations and intermediality. Her most important publications include a book on adaptation theory and several essays in publications on intermediality, literary adaptations and cultural approaches to Eastern European Cinema, most recently in *The Cinematic Bodies of Eastern Europe and Russia. Between Pain and Pleasure* (ed. Ewa Mazierska, Matilda Mroz and Elzbieta Ostrowska).

Lucy Mazdon is Chair in Film at the University of Southampton. Her publications include *Encore Hollywood: Remaking French Cinema*, *France on Film: Reflections on Popular French Cinema*, *Je t'aime, moi non plus: Franco-British Cinematic Relations* and *Sex, Art and Cinephilia: French Cinema in Britain* (both with Catherine Wheatley).

Ewa Mazierska is Professor of Film Studies at the University of Central Lancashire. She has published over twenty monographs and edited collections on film and popular music. They include *Poland Daily: Economy, Work, Consumption and Social Class in Polish Cinema*, *Marxism and Film Activism*, with Lars Kristensen, *Relocating Popular Music*, with Georgina Gregory, *From Self-Fulfilment to Survival of the Fittest: Work in European Cinema from the 1960s to the Present* and *European Cinema and Intertextuality: History, Memory, Politics*. Mazierska's work has been translated into many languages, including French, Italian, German, Chinese, Korean, Portuguese, Estonian and Serbian. She is also principal editor of a Routledge journal, *Studies in Eastern European Cinema*.

Eva Näripea is Director of Film Archives of the National Archives of Estonia, senior researcher at the Estonian Academy of Arts, visiting professor at Tallinn University and founding co-editor of *Baltic Screen Media Review*. She has contributed book chapters to various internationally published volumes, and (co-)edited a number of special issues and anthologies on Eastern European cinemas, including *Postcolonial Approaches to Eastern European Cinema: Portraying Neighbours on Screen* (with Ewa Mazierska and Lars Kristensen). Her research interests include spatial representations in Estonian cinema, histories of Eastern European science fiction film, and reflections of neoliberalism in post-Soviet Estonian cinema.

Michael Pigott is Associate Professor of Video Art at the University of Warwick. He is co-investigator on the AHRC-funded projects 'Sensing the City' and 'The Projection Project'. He is the author of *Joseph Cornell Versus Cinema*, as well as recent articles on the image of the sleeping body in experimental film, the sonic environment of the projection box, and the uses of digital projection outside of the cinema. His album *Sounds of th0065 Projection Box* is available on vinyl and digital from Gruenrekorder.

Natália Pinazza is Lecturer in Portuguese Studies at the University of Exeter. She holds a PhD and MA from the University of Bath and a BA from the University of São Paulo. She undertook a UNESCO fellowship at the University of Ottawa, Canada. Pinazza's previous publications include *New Approaches to Lusophone Culture, Journeys in Argentine and Brazilian Cinema: Road Films in a Global Era, World Cinema Directory: Brazil*, and *World Film Locations: São Paulo*. She has published in journals such as the *Journal of Latin American Cultural Studies* and *Alphaville: Journal of Media and Film Studies*.

László Strausz is an Assistant Professor of film studies at Eötvös Loránd University (ELTE) in Budapest. His work focuses on contemporary East–Central European screen media, cultural memory, and the politics of film style. His monograph, *Hesitant Histories on the Romanian Screen*, was published in 2017.

Introduction
Louis Bayman and Natália Pinazza

It is necessary to sail, it is not necessary to live. – Plutarch

This book is about journeys. Each of its chapters concerns films that feature some kind of travel, and as a collection they reveal the journey to be less an exotic departure than a persistent presence across cinema, as well as across cultural modernity. Spanning different regions and cultures, they probe the meaning of the journey in connection with notions of belonging, memory and history, in examples that range from pre-cinema to new media and through documentary, fiction and the spaces between. They investigate film's employment of the journey as a motif for something wider, whether as metaphor for self-discovery or encounter, emblem of artistic or social transformation, and evidence of autonomy and progress, or their lack.

A principal critical intervention of the volume is to put into relief the formal and contextual frameworks that relate to purposeful movement, and to how change is symbolised in spatial terms. Rather than claiming comprehensiveness with regard to such a large topic, the book proposes to use the journey as a kind of instrument, to the extent that it inspires both formal openness and narrative purpose, describes the processes through which film circulates and responds creatively to the socio-cultural influences that give our lives significance. Diverse amongst themselves, what each chapter develops are analyses that establish the cinematic journey as inherently multi-dimensional, constituted by representational, thematic, intellectual or contextual concerns but never manifest upon just one of these axes in isolation. In this regard, as well as in its geographical scope and its refusal of binaries between US and world cinema or between genre and art cinema, the collection contributes to an integrating and polycentric approach to film.

Before introducing the individual chapters and sections comprising the book, it may be worth making a brief sketch of the significance of the journey to the study of film. Film itself of course physically moves, rolling through the camera and then the projector that illuminates its chemical imprints on screen. While the conventional model of spectatorship presents an audience transfixed within the immobility of the theatrical auditorium, exhibition is at either end of film history also determined by mobility, first in the early travelling fairground displays, and now by the contemporary proliferation of mobile devices, leading us to wonder whether it is the fixity of the cinema theatre that will in future come to be seen as the historical anomaly. Even the notion of film *going* suggests an expedition to another realm, whether as part of the urban life of the *flâneur*, the thrill of the drive-in, the trip to the mall housing the out-of-town multiplex, and so on. Film spectatorship is meanwhile enabled by activities that occur at regional, national, supra- or transnational levels, and its history is one of global trade, émigré talent, international awards and worldwide audiences; as well as of localising responses to the hegemonic tendencies of cultural imperialism.

If tales ascribing 'the first' edit, track, feature and so on should be approached with caution, it is notable how often journey narratives form the milestones of cinematic lore. We can even hazard that they present *the* method of displaying technological innovation, from the very first film the Lumières recorded, *La Sortie de l'Usine Lumière à Lyon / Workers Leaving the Lumière Factory in Lyon* (1895) and in their first exhibition, *L'Arrivée d'un train en gare de La Ciotat / The Arrival of a Train at La Ciotat* (1896). The prototype tracking shot was achieved in 1898 by George Albert Smith affixing a camera to the front of a train, inaugurating the genre that would come to be called the 'phantom ride' (Cousins 2011: 25), while narrative and editing progressed through the crosscutting of a train hold-up in *The Great Train Robbery* (Edwin S. Porter, 1903), and were further refined in the eponymous dog's repeated dash in *Rescued by Rover* (Lewin Fitzhamon, 1905). Dorothy's enchanted journey in *The Wizard of Oz* (Victor Fleming, 1939) indicates if not the first then the blockbuster establishment of the possibilities of Technicolor, and journeys continue as vehicles for the following decades' experiments in widescreen and 3D. Georges Méliès achieved the apogee of the early cinema trick film in his Jules Verne adaptation *Voyage à travers l'impossible / The Impossible Voyage* of 1904, while a full century later *Sky Captain and the World of Tomorrow* (Kerry Conran) became the first film to be entirely shot on a 'digital backlot' in 2004, taking its historical place alongside other experimental CGI voyages including *Titanic* (James Cameron, 1997), *Gravity* (Alfonso Cuarón, 2013), and many another exploration of the depths of the sea, the further reaches of space and the inner recesses of the imagination.

Such innovations are not just technological, but are artistic solutions to change in the medium. Further artistic innovations connect journeying to film history, as expanded on by Devin Orgeron in *Road Movies: From Muybridge and Méliès to Lynch and Kiarostami* (2010). The rail crash sequence in Abel Gance's *La Roue* (1922) was shown as a stand-alone sequence in film salons and cine-clubs to school a generation of interwar avant-garde impressionists and montagists, which fellow filmmaker Germaine Dulac recollected as the point when 'the art of movement and of rhythmically organised images came into its own . . . [as] a symphonic poem in which feeling explodes not in facts, not in acts, but in visual sonorities' (1932, cited in Flitterman-Lewis 1996: 93). Alternatively to such formal elaborateness, the uncertain wandering by the protagonists of Italian neo-realism through the post-war landscape led André Bazin to proclaim that film had finally realised its artistic and spiritual potential to reveal reality anew (2004). Jacques Rivette (1985) subsequently hailed *Viaggio in Italia/Journey to Italy* in 1954 with the claim that 'if there is a modern cinema, this is it', and the routes leading from it include the restless energy of the Nouvelle Vague announced in the suspension-in-movement of the freeze-frame ending of *Les quatrecents coups/The 400 Blows* (1959), the non-conformist, proto-music-video aesthetic of the journeying protagonists that pepper the New American Cinema and the landmark motorbike ride of the independent African avant-garde in the Senegalese *Touki Bouki* (Djibril Diop Mambéty, 1973).

As Dimitris Eleftheriotis summarises in his important study *Cinematic Journeys: Film and Movement* (2010), the desire to capture, harness or control movement places cinema alongside other mechanical inventions and consumer experiences of the nineteenth century. Such technologies of movement were key commodities of the modern age, and contributed to the new experiences it offered, centred on thrill and adventure. The so-called 'train effect' of reportedly panicked spectators fleeing at the sight of a locomotive moving to the foreground of the screen has been described thus by Rebecca Harrison, 'Unlike the theatre, boxing-ring, or tavern, the locomotive brought a dynamism and sensation of speed to the screen that was as new to metropolitan viewers as to fairground attendees' (2018: 66). In an example of how such novelty preoccupied contemporary commentators on modernity, the French novelist Octave Mirbeau noted that for the automobile driver 'thoughts, feelings and loves are a whirlwind. Everywhere life is rushing insanely like a cavalry charge, and it vanishes cinematographically like trees and silhouettes along a road' (1908, cited in Kern 1983: 113). Ricciotto Canudo, one of the earliest theorists of film, proclaimed in the same year an age of 'relentless detesters of slowness', in which the moving image satisfies even 'the driver who watches a cinematic spectacle after having just finished the craziest race' ([1908] 2017: 68).

The search for ever new thrills by early audiences demonstrates an apparently infinite appetite for exploration, and the coincidence of the invention of cinema with the high point of colonialism has been noted by Ella Shohat and Robert Stam in 'The Imperial Imaginary' (1994), while the vogue for travelogues in distant lands and exotic locations is discussed by Alison Griffiths in 'To the World the World We Show: Early Travelogues as Filmed Ethnography' (1999). Considering travel within the metropole itself, a fruitful partnership has been pursued between film studies and cultural and urban geography by a variety of scholars from Giuliana Bruno in *Atlas of Emotion* (2002), to Edward Dimendberg in 'The Will to Motorization' (1995), and the collection *Landscape and Film* edited by Martin Lefebvre (2006). The topic is considered on a transnational level in the collection by Ewa Mazierska and Laura Rascaroli in *From Moscow to Madrid: Postmodern Cities, European Cinema* (2003).

These studies work to understand space as not merely an inert fact or background feature, but part of the architecture of social relations, inspired not least by Michel de Certeau's interest in the strategies of institutional power structures in 'Walking in the City' (1984), and Henri Lefebvre's Marxist framework of *The Production of Space* (1991). Such analysis is also employed by the geographer David Harvey, who in *The Condition of Postmodernity: An Enquiry into the Origins of Cultural Change* (1989) understands modernity as itself a process of control of space forged through science, transport and communication technologies, colonisation and the unceasing search of capital for expansion, before a crisis of those self-same processes expressed in forms as various as the artistic avant-gardes, the explosivity of nationalist rivalries and the revolutionary implications of relativity. Harvey begins with the poet Baudelaire's claim that 'Modernity is the transient, the fleeting, the contingent; it is one half of art, the other half being the eternal and immutable' (1989: 11), for such forms of spatiality are both economic, epistemological and cultural. The restless urge to transformation encapsulated in Marx and Engels' memorable phrase that 'all that is solid melts into air' is indeed applied by Marshall Berman to the socio-cultural sphere in defining *The Experience of Modernity* (1982). Jonathan Crary in *24/7: Late Capitalism and the Ends of Sleep* (2013) and Jonathan Tomlinson in *The Culture of Speed: The Coming of Immediacy* (2007) both suggest the ongoing progression of information technologies and neoliberal social relations towards an aspiration to do away with temporal and spatial boundaries altogether. The emphasis on transformation in contemporary intellectual life itself suggests, furthermore, an epochal shift away from rationalist or Enlightenment valuations of the fixed object of categorisation, and onto those of flux, change and motion.

Cinema provides a crucial artistic reference point in these debates. For although other narrative and pictorial forms may express desires to recount or capture movement, cinema is the first to incorporate it *within* its very formal properties, through the persistence of vision, camera movement, editing and the modulation of light as it is cast across its subjects. We contend that refocusing attention onto movement has the potential to rewrite film theory, adding another dimension to its familiar story of the determining power of the gaze, for the epochs to which cinema belongs see the proliferation not only of scopic regimes (see Eleftheriotis 2010: 7–37, incorporating Foucault), but also of *mobile* ones: mobility shapes democratic ideals and dreams of national dominion, while movement determines modern forms of leisure (from the fairground, to cinema, to tourism), power (in globalisation and imperialism), warfare (see Virilio 1989), the avant-gardes (beginning with the challenges posed by Impressionism and then by Cubism), communications (from telegraphy to television and the internet), and work (from the production line to the computer screen), ultimately restructuring our consciousness of our own place within the cosmos, for the scientific revolutions that initiated the modern era established the very Earth's position as relative and mobile rather than fixed and immutable. In this, the moving pictures of cinema truly signal the arrival of the medium appropriate to its age.

Our take on journeys has its precedents, of course. Nearly two decades ago Hamid Naficy's groundbreaking book, *An Accented Cinema: Exilic and Diasporic Filmmaking* (2001), gathered the work of filmmakers in exilic and diasporic contexts under the rubric 'accented cinema', identifying key tropes while simultaneously emphasising the diversity and richness of this cinematic production. But to consider journeying means also to consider the forces that determine its obstruction, for modernity, as Zygmunt Bauman points out (2015), ushers in not only vastly increased possibilities for mobility, but the power of the nation state to choose who to exclude from its reign (something Bauman considers unthinkable in earlier eras, when all living creatures were considered to be God's children). Just as modernity extends capacities for movement, so it simultaneously implements obstacle. While it may be said that the average medieval peasant would not travel more than ten miles from their village (Newman 2017), Reece Jones's research in *Violent Borders: Refugees and the Right to Move* finds that militarily enforced state boundaries of walls and fences have increased from fifteen to seventy worldwide (Jones 2016) precisely within the period since the proclaimed triumph of globalisation, when the division of east and west fell in 1990. As Mezzadra and Nielson argue in *Border as Method, or, the Multiplication of Labor* (2013), globalisation has not brought about the promised utopia of a borderless world but a proliferation of borders that are in a continual process of renegotiation at national, supranational and local levels (a reformulation of obstacles that is covered from a different perspective in the conversation between Judith Butler and Gayatri Spivak as *Who Sings the Nation State?: Language, Politics, Belonging* (2011)).

The essays in this volume thus document epochal changes in human behaviour, from urbanisation, migration and war to tourism and shopping. Parts of this collection will demonstrate how the increasing concern with global warming and the emergence of eco-criticism in film studies have shaped spatial exploration, at times challenging the linearity and forwardness of Western journey narratives. For an interest in the social importance of the journey is also a statement of political commitment on the part of film study, dedicated to defending what is put at risk by global systems of finance and power, as it is also to the potential for liberation from the confines of national and other borders. A number of collections have connected these themes specifically to the journey narrative, most notably Wendy Everett and Peter Wagstaff (eds) *Cultures of Exile: Images of Displacement* (2005), Ewa Mazierska and Laura Rascaroli (eds) *Crossing New Europe: Postmodern Travel and the European Road Movie* (2006) and Eva Rueschmann's *Moving Pictures, Migrating Identities* (2003). The political commitment of the discipline is testified to by the blossoming of the transnational as a category of film study in the last decade, as documented by Deborah Shaw in 'Transnational Cinemas: Mapping a Field of Study' (2017). The concept of the transnational provides a way to move beyond an earlier focus in film study on the national as a counterpoint to Hollywood or other forms of cultural homogenisation. Thus 2006 saw the publication of *Transnational Cinema: The Film Reader* edited by Elizabeth Ezra and Terry Rowden, 2010 the launch of the *Transnational Cinemas* journal, and most recently of all Austin Fisher's and Iain R. Smith's 'Transnational Cinemas: A Critical Roundtable' discussion in *Frames* journal (2016) and Steven Rawle's *Transnational Cinema: An Introduction* (2018). It is these contexts that form the basis for this book.

The Structure of the Volume

Inspired by the intercultural and polycentric approach to cinematic journeys, we have structured this book into two parts. Part 1, 'Mapping Cinema Journeys', is divided into 'Chronotopes of Journeys' and 'Expanding

Europe: Interstitial Production and Border-Crossing in Eastern European Cinema'. In chapter one, Tiago de Luca examines globalising spatial and visual practices that predated, or else coincided with, the cinema in their urge to encompass the entire world as a visual spectacle in its own right. Focusing on the Cosmorama and the Georama, de Luca examines how they variously capitalised on the trope of the world and offered, in different ways, a miniaturisation of the globe within the confines of a single space. The chapter further situates the emergence and development of early cinema within this modern visual paradigm, exploring how film inherited, or else translated into filmic form, many of the functions and roles played by the world-encompassing visual practices and discourses preluding its emergence.

In chapter two, Lucy Mazdon concentrates on the cinematic representation of the railway station as both physical space and symbol or metaphor for cultural encounter of all kinds. Via discussion of a selection of films that date back to the Lumière brothers' *L'Arrivée d'un train en gare de La Ciotat* (1895), but concentrating especially on *Brief Encounter* (David Lean, 1945), Mazdon examines the different ways in which the space and iconography of the station has been used in film to represent cultural integration, transformation and/or friction.

In chapter three, Clelia Clini argues that the representation of the diasporic experience offered by Deepa Mehta's film *Heaven on Earth* (2008) acts as a complementary as well as counter-narrative to the ones offered by Bollywood cinema. Through the story of Chand, Clini investigates how Mehta addresses issues of displacement and identity and their intersection with issues of gender and class. For Clini, Mehta's film is both a critical reflection on belonging by an internationally regarded auteur, and an example of a diasporic dialogue with a popular cinematic context from which its conditions of production, however, exclude it.

Michael Pigott in chapter four examines José Luis Guerín's representation of the ghostly persistence of John Ford's *The Quiet Man* (1952) in the landscape of *Innisfree* (1990), by using Mikhail Bakhtin's concept of the chronotope to identify the lasting significance of real and imagined time-spaces in the cinematic landscape. For Pigott, just as second-generation Irishman Sean Thornton (John Wayne) returns to his spiritual homeland from Pittsburgh USA to reclaim his family land, Ford himself returns to the land of his parents' birth, and in *Innisfree* Thornton's, Ford's and Guerín's imagined Irelands all mingle and intertwine in a confusing crossroads of time, fiction, memory and landscape.

Adam Freeman, in chapter five, explores how the essay film employs spatial journeys through contemporary places in the present to uncover temporal layers of history by means of an essayistic excavation. Focusing on *Reminiscences of a Journey to Lithuania* (Jonas Mekas, 1972), *Which Way is East* (Lynne Sachs, 1994), *Content* (Chris Petit, 2010) and *6 Desires: DH Lawrence and Sardinia* (Mark Cousins, 2014), Freeman contends that such an essayistic exaction constructs a cinematic space that weaves the temporal and spatial journey together, unearthing the buried strata of place and constructing a 'thick' map or vertical reading of the landscape.

The subject matter of the book has also been shaped by political and economic changes, in particular the accession treaties through which new member states join the European Union. The EU membership of Hungary and Lithuania in 2004 and Romania in 2007 came accompanied by a body of films made in the past decade, which are the subject matter of four chapters in this book. This of course has industrial implications in terms of cross-border cooperation, as Hungarian–Romanian film co-productions show, but has also shaped how mobility and journeys have changed for individuals in those countries. Migration and, generally, journeying, are deeply connected with psychological and personal experiences, and these films portray the top-down impacts of political and economic agents. As a continuation of our mapping of journey narratives, Part 1b, 'Expanding Europe: Interstitial Production and Border-Crossing in Eastern European Cinema', explores the ways in which Eastern European representations of exilic and diasporic life use claustrophobia and temporality to engage with historical dynamisms that shape deterritorialising and reterritorialising journeys.

In chapter six, Eva Näripea focuses on recent cinematic representations of one of the most dramatic collective journeys of Estonian history – the massive Soviet deportations of Estonians in June 1941 and in March 1949. She explores how they address complex questions of collective (national) memory and identity through the portrayal of these involuntary journeys. Näripea interrogates how Ülo Pikkov's stop-motion short *Kehamälu/ Body Memory* (2011) and Martti Helde's feature-length (live-action) debut *Risttuules/In the Crosswind* (2014) relate to the contemporary post-socialist situation where the new neoliberal regime has forced many Estonians to leave their homeland for economic reasons.

Focusing on three documentaries filmed in Hungary, Ukraine and Lithuania: *Divan* (Pearl Gluck, 2003), *My Grandfather's House* (Eileen Douglas and Ron Steinman, 2003), and *Shoah par balles: l'histoire oubliée* (Romain Icard, 2008), Maurizio Cinquegrani in chapter seven explores Holocaust cinema in spatial terms and considers the place of filmic practices in relation to other ways to organise, memorialise, monumentalise and preserve the specific environments connected with the Holocaust. Cinquegrani discusses how each film addresses a journey undertaken by a member of the postgeneration to sites of memory associated with the annihilation of Eastern European Jewry, and uses particular tropes and narrative devices to establish a connection between past and present. In so doing, the chapter investigates these documentaries' use of archival material in juxtaposition with present-day filming on the same locations seen in the old photographs and footage used in the films.

While most accounts of Romanian films made since the mid-2000s approach the works from the vantage points of realism and transparency, László Strausz in chapter eight argues that films do not so much reveal a certain social world as depict the mobile, hesitant ways in which social institutions produce a reality in post-socialist society. In order to illustrate the historical-interpretive advantages of the concept of hesitation, Strausz focuses on the fugitive and migrant narratives of new Romanian cinema in *Moartea domnului Lăzărescu/The Death of Mr. Lazarescu* (Puiu, 2006), *Aurora* (Puiu, 2010), *Morgen* (Crisan, 2010) and *Periferic/Outbound* (Apetri, 2010), in which the characters physically move back and forth between various institutions such as prison, the state foster home, the hospital, various educational institutions, the police and immigration authorities. For Strausz, the films depict disorientation and hesitation as the fundamental element in the identity of the post-socialist subject, by shifting and moving their characters between these institutions and the social spaces they occupy.

In chapter nine Hajnal Király contends that despite their stylistic differences, contemporary Hungarian and Romanian films show a striking similarity in representing journeys that are aborted, delayed, interrupted, with protagonists ending up in situations of entrapment. Király focuses on three Hungarian–Romanian film co-productions: *Iszka utazása/Iska's Journey* (Csaba Bollók, 2007), *Varga Katalin balladája/Katalin Varga* (Peter Strickland, 2009) and *Bibliothèque Pascal* (Szabolcs Hajdu, 2010) and explores how they represent the incomplete, fragmented journey of female protagonists of different ages, but with similarities that link the three stories into a single, representative narrative of a quest for a home. Following an overview of the central heterotopias of these films, which are figurative of the intercultural encounter between the two countries and between East and West, Király realises a typology of their female travellers with the aim of deconstructing (Western) cultural stereotypes related to (Eastern) female mobility.

In reminding us how provisional the idea of stability can be, their accounts of journeying focus on uncertainty, liminality and marginality, rather than power, opportunity and positive transformation. By concentrating on feeling and subjective experience, these journeys contain an imaginative dimension that confuses distinctions between history, biography and fiction. At the same time, they dramatise the bureaucratic or physical enforcements through which the state is manifest in everyday interrelationships – including at the levels of exile, illegality, war and at its furthest extreme, genocide. In testifying to the journeys through which identity survives, they indicate how the final destination remains out of reach, whether it be that of the recovery of the past, the establishment of self through the attempt to participate in a wider community or the final settlement into a place called home.

To this extent, the examples above reinforce the notion that cinematic journeying promotes an undoing of conventional narrative dynamics, producing what Timothy Corrigan has called in relation to the road movie, a loosening of the 'regulating action' of narrative (1991: 142). Mazierska and Rascaroli in fact connect the postmodern to the European journey film, and their collection starts out from the observation that 'most of our examples belong to what we could define as "non-mainstream" cinema' (2006: 6). Yet any consequent assumption that journeying *necessitates* a challenge to narrative would be mistaken, as a wider historical view would show, for journey narratives recur as key turning points for various forms of literature; indeed it is hardly possible to overstate the literary importance of Homer's *Odyssey* ([8th century BCE], 2008), Dante's *Divine Comedy* ([1320] 1955), Cervantes's *Don Quixote* ([1615] 2005), Defoe's *Robinson Crusoe* ([1719] 2007), Herman Melville's *Moby Dick, or, The Whale* ([1851] 2014) and James Joyce's *Ulysses* ([1918–20] 1991). Journeys recur in tales of origin as myth, parable and legend, in *The Aeneid*, *The Lusiads*, the foundational religious texts of Judaism, Christianity and Islam alike, as well as the *Ramayana* and *Mhabharata*. In fact, departure forms the literal starting point of so many genres – the fairytale, chivalric romance, picaresque, saga, adventure – that the journey could be said to indicate something of the narrative impulse itself. Certainly, the idea that one is entering a special, sacred or imaginative realm traditionally defines the entry into the story world as a land far, far away, while the protagonist's journey provides a spatial metaphor for the story's direction towards particular goals and a specific destination.

In relation to cinema, Brian Winston argues that 'journey films solved actuality's big narrative problem – closure. How should films finish? Obviously, a journey film ends with the end of the journey', citing Roland Barthes that 'a narrative without its requisite constituent parts (a departure and an arrival) "would be a scandal"' (both cited in Bruzzi

2006: 82–3). Edward Dimendberg has succinctly judged that 'cinema gravitates towards the highway' (1995: 137). Crucial to the analyses in Part 2, 'Form and Narrative in Journey Genres' are understandings of journeying as literally moving – that is, as producing a range of affective or emotional possibilities and the dynamics that belong to the pleasure of their particular narrative structures. With this in mind, this collection seeks to address an imbalance that we see, bearing in mind that the journey narrative covers the works of Ingmar Bergman and Wim Wenders as well as films like *Dude, Where's My Car?* (Danny Leiner, 2000) and *Summer Holiday* (Peter Yates, 1963) and so hoping to establish the journey as one of the basic elements constituting popular film genres. The chapters frequently consider the struggles or imbalances over power as well as reflections upon temporality and history that tend to recur in journey narratives, but do so, crucially, in relation to the conventions and expectations opened up by their respective generic worlds.

In chapter ten, Carlo Cenciarelli relates journeying to time and romance in cinema. Considering the role of music in establishing a feeling of approaching finality in Richard Linklater's indie film *Before Sunrise* (1995), Cenciarelli argues for the 'eschatological implications of cinematic time', through analysis of the prominence of music in the closing sequences of the film and its use in establishing both plot and more meta-cinematic properties. Regarding the audiovisual nature of cinematic time, Cenciarelli discusses the use of Bach within a relatively self-aware moment of romantic closure, to expose both the illusion of permanence and the inexorability of time in ways that nevertheless add up to a sincere, and moving, final sequence.

In chapter eleven Ewa Mazierska considers science fiction, which she describes as the genre that is most invested in travel after the road movie. Mazierska argues that contemporary sci-fi sees the emergence of class as an explicit concern. This is distinct from the claims to act on the behalf of the whole of humanity made by both East and West during Cold-War sci-fi production. Through analysis of the international co-productions *Elysium* (2013) by Neill Blomkamp and *Snowpiercer* (2013) by Joon-ho Bong, she considers how the initial optimism of globalisation's utopian hopes of unimpeded mobility have turned into a sense of there being nowhere left to go, while mobility itself is stratified by class, divided into elite travel and that of the proletarian or impoverished majority, thus 'reflect[ing] existing inequalities and accelerat[ing] them'.

Chris Fujiwara in chapter twelve considers 'Gothic Journeys: Travel and Transportation in the Films of Terence Fisher'. He remarks upon the difficulty of travel in Gothic fiction, in which the feudal past continues to haunt the present, and where journeys promise both the exotic and the removal of safety. This potentially indulges in Orientalism whilst also opening up the possibility of a critique of the Enlightenment by broaching irrationality and evil, the material and the visible, the unrepresentable and taboo. Fisher's acts of transportation thus produce a complex interrelationship between conservatism and liberal critique in a context of 'British modernity in the second half of the twentieth century', in ways that test the limits of cinematic classicism.

Unlike Fujiwara, Stefano Baschiera considers travel to the unproductive de-industrialised or rural European areas in chapter thirteen. Baschiera probes the current flourishing of horror film production in Europe, where international partnerships testify to the changing forms of film funding and co-production arrangements. Elucidating how these medium- and low-budget productions get made, he explains the proliferation of horror subgenres in the developing economic imperatives to stimulate local production that are separate now from considerations of cultural prestige or quality, with the French/Belgian co-production *La meute/The Pack* (Franck Richard, 2010) as his concluding case study.

In Part 2b, 'The Politics of the Road Movie', we consider the importance of the road movie to cinematic journeying. As a way of concluding the book, however, the search is once again to undo binaries between art and genre cinema and to understand the international dimensions of the form. The three concluding chapters thus consider particularity in relation to the road movie in various ways, precisely so as to offer a widened perspective upon it.

In chapter fourteen, Natália Pinazza analyses a selected body of Latin American road movies made in the past two decades and the ways in which colonialism and its legacy inform the dramatic structure of the journey. In line with the volume's polycentric approach to cinema, Pinazza challenges notions that the road movie is a quintessentially American genre, and emphasises the contribution that Latin American film has made to the development of the road movie genre. The chapter explores how the theme of colonialism, both physical and cultural, is particularly instrumental in identifying tropes and predominant concerns in cinematic journeys set in Latin American countries whose historical experience of 'third world' and 'underdeveloped' status is negotiated in the context of a changing global economic order. The second part of this chapter will pay particular attention to the ways in which *El Abrazo de Serpiente/Embrace of the Serpent* (Ciro Guerra, 2015) uses journeys to denounce historical colonialism and engage with more contemporary and global discourses on eco-criticism that have informed recent films such as

Mad Max: Fury Road (George Miller 2015) and *The Revenant* (Alejandro González Iñárritu, 2015).

Anna Cooper shifts the focus onto gender for chapter fifteen, 'Spaces of Failure: The Gendering of Neoliberal Mobilities in the US Indie Road Movie'. Analysing contemporary road movies including *Gas Food Lodging* (Allison Anders, 1992) and *Wendy and Lucy* (Kelly Reichardt, 2008), Cooper questions the universalising assumptions of a form whose speed and mastery generically assume a male subject. In a highly original fashion, she offers an interpretation of these movies in relation to a specifically female point of view, which she argues add up to 'a form of resistant failure within US neoliberal disciplinary regimes of space and mobility'.

Finally, chapter sixteen offers Louis Bayman's '*Sic transit*: The Serial Killer Road Movie'. In tracing the common association of serial killers with mobility, Bayman stakes out a particular strand of the road movie – or set of diverse clusters around it – which feature serial killers. He outlines this as a combination of two distinct mythologies, that of the serial killer and that of the road, at the point of their common ground. The purpose of his analysis is to understand mobility in its capacity to produce a special position, one of being at odds with, yet arising from, the frame of reference that gives it meaning. The significance of this position is applied to the contrasting contexts of the American arthouse independent *Henry: Portrait of a Serial Killer* (John McNaughton, 1986) and the British comedy of manners *Sightseers* (Ben Wheatley, 2012).

Works Cited

Alighieri, Dante [1320] (1955), *The Divine Comedy*, London: Penguin.

Bauman, Zygmunt (2015), 'The Fate of the Enlightenment in the Era of Diasporisation', talk given 14 April 2015 at Bruno Kreisky Forum for International Dialogue, Vienna <https://www.youtube.com/watch?v=FaRIDSh_-lk> (last accessed 26/06/2017).

Bazin, André (2004), *What Is Cinema?*, Berkeley and Los Angeles: University of California Press, vols 1 & 2.

Berman, Marshall (1982), *All that Is Solid Melts into Air: The Experience of Modernity*, New York: Penguin.

Bruno, Giuliana (2002), *Atlas of Emotion: Journeys in Art, Architecture and Film*, New York: Verso.

Bruzzi, Stella (2006), *New Documentary: A Critical Introduction*, London: Routledge.

Butler, Judith and Gayatri Spivak (2011), *Who Sings the Nation State?: Language, Politics, Belonging*, London: Seagull House.

Canudo, Ricciotto [1908] (2017), 'The Triumph of the Cinema', in Francesco Casetti (ed.), *Early Film Theories in Italy 1896–1922*, Amsterdam: Amsterdam University Press, pp. 66–75.
Certeau, Michel de (1984), 'Walking in the City', in *The Practice of Everyday Life*, Berkeley and Los Angeles: University of California Press, pp. 91–111.
Cervantes Saavedra, Miguel de [1615] (2005), *Don Quixote*, London: Vintage.
Corrigan, Timothy (1991), *A Cinema without Walls: Movies and Culture after Vietnam*, London: Routledge.
Cousins, Mark (2011), *The Story of Film*, London: Pavilion.
Crary, Jonathan (2013), *24/7: Late Capitalism and the Ends of Sleep*, London: Verso.
Defoe, Daniel [1719] (2007), *Robinson Crusoe*, Oxford: Oxford University Press.
Dimendberg, Edward (1995), 'The Will to Motorization: Cinema, Highways and Modernity', *October*, vol. 73, Summer 1995, pp. 90–137.
Eleftheriotis, Dimitris (2010), *Cinematic Journeys: Film and Movement*, Edinburgh: Edinburgh University Press.
Everett, Wendy and Peter Wagstaff (eds) (2005), *Cultures of Exile: Images of Displacement*, New York: Berghahn.
Ezra, Elizabeth and Terry Rowden (eds) (2006), *Transnational Cinema: The Film Reader*, London: Routledge.
Fisher, Austin and Smith, Iain Robert (eds) (2016), 'Transnational Cinemas: A Critical Roundtable', *Frames Cinema Journal*, 9, April, <http://framescinemajournal.com/article/transnational-cinemas-a-critical-roundtable/> (last accessed May 2018).
Flitterman-Lewis, Sandy (1996), *To Desire Differently: Feminism and the French Cinema*, New York: Columbia University Press.
Griffiths, Alison (1999), 'To the World the World We Show: Early Travelogues as Filmed Ethnography', *Film History*, 11:3, pp. 282–308.
Harrison, Rebecca (2018), *From Steam to Screen: Cinema, the Railways and Modernity*, London: I. B. Tauris.
Harvey, David (1989), *The Condition of Postmodernity: An Enquiry into the Origins of Cultural Change*, Oxford: Blackwell.
Homer [8th century BCE] (2008), *The Odyssey*, trans. Walter Shewring, Oxford: Oxford University Press.
Jones, Reece (2016), *Violent Borders: Refugees and the Right to Move*, London: Verso.
Joyce, James [1918–20] (1991), *Ulysses*, New York: Harvester Wheatsheaf.
Kern, Stephen (1983), *The Culture of Time and Space 1880–1918*, Cambridge, MA: Harvard University Press.
Lefebvre, Henri (1991), *The Production of Space*, Oxford: Blackwell.
Lefebvre, Martin (ed.) (2006), *Landscape and Film*, London: Routledge.
Mazierska, Ewa and Laura Rascaroli (eds) (2003), *From Moscow to Madrid: Postmodern Cities, European Cinema*, London: I. B. Tauris.

Mazierska, Ewa and Laura Rascaroli (eds) (2006), *Crossing New Europe: Postmodern Travel and the European Road Movie*, London: Wallflower Press.
Melville, Herman [1851] (2002), *Moby Dick, or, The Whale*, Ware: Wordsworth.
Mezzadra, Sandro and Brett Nielson (2013), *Border as Method, or, the Multiplication of Labour*, Durham, NC: Duke University Press.
Naficy, Hamid (2001), *An Accented Cinema: Exilic and Diasporic Filmmaking*, Princeton: Princeton University Press.
Newman, Barbara (2017), 'Mercenary Knights and Princess Brides', *London Review of Books*, 39:16, 17 August, pp. 29–30.
Orgeron, Devin (2010), *Road Movies: From Muybridge and Méliès to Lynch and Kiarostami*, Basingstoke: Palgrave Macmillan.
Rawle, Steven (2018), *Transnational Cinema: An Introduction*, Basingstoke: Palgrave.
Rivette, Jacques (1985), 'Letter on Rossellini', in Jim Hillier (ed.), *Cahiers du Cinéma: 1950s: Neo-Realism, Hollywood, New Wave*, vol. 1, London: Routledge & Kegan Paul, pp. 192–202.
Rueschmann, Eva (2003), *Moving Pictures, Migrating Identities*, Jackson: University Press of Mississippi.
Shaw, Deborah (2017), 'Transnational Cinemas: Mapping a Field of Study', in Rob Stone, Alex Marlow-Mann and Pam Cook (eds), *The Routledge Companion to World Cinema*, London: Routledge, pp. 290–9.
Shohat, Ella and Robert Stam (1994), 'The Imperial Imaginary', in *Unthinking Eurocentrism: Multiculturalism and the Media*, London: Routledge, pp. 100–36.
Tomlinson, Jonathan (2007), *The Culture of Speed: The Coming of Immediacy*, London: Sage.
Virilio, Paul (1989), *War and Cinema: The Logistics of Perception*, London: Verso.

Part 1a

Mapping Cinematic Journeys: Chronotopes of Journeys

CHAPTER 1

Global Visions: Around-the-World Travel and Visual Culture in Early Modernity[1]

Tiago de Luca

Over the last two decades the world has emerged as a ubiquitous trope in our audiovisual landscape: whether we think of multinarrative films directed by global auteurs, such as *Babel* (Alejandro González Iñárritu, 2006), *360* (Fernando Meirelles, 2011) and *Mammoth* (Lukas Moodysson, 2009); the explosion of documentaries and TV series that have the planet as their focus, including *Planet Earth* (BBC, 2007 and 2016), *Home* (Yann Arthus-Bertrand, 2009), and countless others carrying Earth in their titles; the 3D variations of this genre as produced for the IMAX theatre, such as *Sacred Planet* (Jon Long, 2004) and *A Beautiful Planet* (Toni Myers, 2016); 'world symphony' films like *Samsara* (Ron Fricke, 2011), *One Day on Earth* (Kyle Ruddick, 2012) and *Life in a Day* (Kevin Macdonald, Loressa Clisby, 2011); or even a single web-environment like Google Earth. Connecting these otherwise disparate audiovisual forms and formats is a simple – though of course ultimately unattainable – goal: to depict not a world, but the world, that is to say, the entire world.

No doubt such a proliferation of world-encompassing formulations is largely connected to socio-economic globalising processes on the one hand, and an acute sense of our global environmental crisis on the other, and thus restricted to contemporary phenomena. Yet a quest to encompass the whole world certainly has precedents in media and film history. In this essay I argue that the global imaginaries surrounding the emergence of cinema provide a meaningful field against which contemporary ones can be held up and deconstructed, and vice versa. While globalising phenomena and discourses are often associated with the end of the twentieth century, a look at the media-scape within which cinema emerges reveals that grappling with the world as a – and in its – totality was deeply built into the visual culture of the time – a phenomenon that resulted in no small measure from the contemporary popularity (and feasibility) of round-the-world travels and imperialist expeditions. To investigate some of the earliest examples by which the world was visually encompassed and the respective discourses they mobilised might thus help us shed a more nuanced light on the ways we currently conceive of and perceive the Earth.

From a Panoramic to a Planetary Consciousness

As one of the most popular visual mediums of the nineteenth century, the panorama has received voluminous scholarly attention, with many authoritative histories on the subject published in English (Oettermann 1997; Comment 1999; Oleksijczuk 2011; Huhtamo 2013). Its importance for genealogies of the cinema has, likewise, been stressed by a number of scholars, whether as a means of exploring its conceptual and formal connections with early cinema and beyond (Gunning 2006; Doane 2002; Castro 2009; Miller 1996), or as a way of suggesting possible avenues through which this medium can be theorised as a precursor of contemporary manifestations in our audiovisual landscape, notably immersive realities and IMAX experiences (Roberts 1998; Grau 2003; Griffths 2013). Their many disagreements notwithstanding, however, the majority of these studies converge on one point, namely that, more than a visual spectacle and cultural phenomenon, the panorama inaugurated a novel, decidedly modern and 'particular way of seeing and looking at the world' (Castro 2009: 10). In this section, I would like to explore this idea along more literal avenues, and to take 'world' not as a mere rhetorical device or an abstract entity designating 'reality', but to explore it in terms of a specifically nineteenth-century conception and perception of the planet's scale and totality.

The nineteenth century has been examined in relation to how the profusion of panoramas engendered the formation of a 'panoramic consciousness' (Rice 1993: 70) in terms of a new mode of vision that 'aims to take in the whole' (Oettermann 1997: 22). It has also been linked to the emergence of a 'planetary consciousness' in relation to an enhanced awareness of the planet as a totality owing to a sense of confidence triggered by round-the-world travels (Chaplin 2012). I would like to forge an explicit link between these two modes of consciousness and to propose that they are, in fact, deeply entwined. My interest lies in uncovering how the panorama – and later film – was both part and parcel of a modern paradigm whereby the notion of a world totality manifested itself through different modes of visuality. Below I examine three of these modes – the metonymy, the icon and the inventory – and then move on to briefly suggest the ways in which they gained cinematic form in early cinema and beyond.

As immortalised by Jules Verne's novel *Around the World in Eighty Days* (1872), the whole world during the nineteenth century began to be perceived as being within reach, navigable and traversable: the site of utopian dreams of foreign views and exploratory quests of land possession. As Bernard Comment points out, the 'yearning for other countries, other places, for changes of scene, developed considerably during the nineteenth century ... and a thirst for discovery, for knowledge was born, not to mention the imperialistic and colonial policies that heightened people's interests in faraway lands' (1999: 132). The cultural production of this period is thus inserted within a wider perceptual and epistemological shift according to which the world was increasingly seen as an object to be encompassed and described in its totality. Not only Verne but many illustrious writers during the period attempted to carry out such a task. Already in 1848, Edgar Allan Poe had published his prose poem *Eureka: An Essay on the Material and Spiritual Universe*. Poe was inspired by the Prussian geographer and naturalist Alexander von Humboldt, to whom *Eureka* is dedicated, and who had expressed his desire to portray the entire world in a single work, an idea he subsequently carried out in his four-volume work *Cosmos: A Sketch of a Physical Description of the Universe*, published between 1845 and 1862.[2]

Within the domain of visual forms, the consolidation in the nineteenth century of the panorama (which was commended for its educative value in *Cosmos*) also testified to a quest to 'see all', as evidenced by the etymologies of its combined Greek words. Originally invented and patented by the Irishman Robert Baker in the late eighteenth century, the panorama consisted of a large-size 360-degree realistically painted surface placed inside a rotunda specifically designed for such a purpose. As one of the first mass mediums of the nineteenth century, its emergence in many European metropolises more or less coincided with the birth of the tourism industry. At first, the panorama's subject matter was often confined to the views of the cities in which they were located as a means of highlighting, by way of comparison, its impressive illusionistic qualities. However, it soon started to offer a surrogate for travel around the world in the form of exotic landscapes to which patrons could be transported in no time and at a modest price.[3]

In this respect, the panorama entertained a dual relationship with the concept of a world totality. On the one hand, as Stephan Oettermann has noted, the panorama was in many ways the antithesis of the 'ideal' landscape painting tradition, according to which 'the world in its entirety and not just a segment of it' was symbolically depicted (1997: 26). Unconcerned with realistic detail, the 'ideal landscapes' genre abided by aesthetic conventions the aim of which was an allegory of the world as centripetally enforced by the limits of the frame. The novelty of the panorama in this context resided in the way it literally disregarded the borders of the frame as the enabler of a circumscribed world, featuring no aspirations to convey a symbolic totality but only a portion of the world reproduced in painstaking topographical detail. On the other hand, the panorama participated in the consolidation of a new visual regime that, together with phenomena such as alpinism and the invention of the hot-air balloon, rescaled the perceptual stakes of the world through the experience of the horizon in the field of vision (Oettermann 1997: 7–8). To be sure, the idea that the horizon was introduced at that time has been refuted on the basis of other precedents across the history of visual arts (see Grau 2003: 62). Yet its *prevalence* in nineteenth-century visual culture is undeniable, one that is not only evidenced in the Romantic painting tradition of the sublime (as in Caspar David Friedrich's work) but also in the literature of the period.

A famous example is an extract from Goethe's *Italian Journey* diary, which both Oettermann and Comment cite as emblematic of the new ocular paradigm within which the panorama emerged and which it helped cement. Alone on the open sea, Goethe claimed that 'no one who has never seen himself surrounded on all sides by nothing but the sea can have a true conception of the world and his own relation to it' (cited in Oettermann 1997: 7–8). Although it could be argued that 'world' is employed merely figuratively in Goethe's lines, other historical evidence confirms that the panorama, as a new way of visually appropriating the world, *metonymically* implied the entire planet as an extension of the here and now of the depicted landscape. This is observed, for example, in Poe's aforementioned poem *Eureka*. Speaking of the 7,912 miles 'diameter of our own globe', Poe writes:

> If we ascend an ordinary mountain and look around us from its summit, we behold a landscape stretching, say 40 miles, in every direction; forming a circle 250 miles in circumference; and including an area of 5000 square miles. [. . .] – yet the entire panorama would comprehend no more than one 40,000th part of the mere *surface* of the globe. Were this panorama, then, to be succeeded, after the lapse of an hour, by another of equal extent; this again by a third, after the lapse of another hour [. . .] – and so on, until the scenery of the whole Earth were exhausted; and were we to be engaged in examining these panoramas for twelve hours of every day; we should nevertheless, be 9 years and 48 days in completing the general survey. (1848: 108–9; emphasis in original)

Poe's use of the word panorama to refer to a given vista, and its implication that it is co-extensive with the spherical surface of the planet makes apparent the extent to which the panoramic landscape acted as a metonymical substitute for the vastness of the world.

The frameless nature of the panorama, as the upper and lower parts of the canvas were hidden from view, further contributed to the idea of a global spatiality that extended beyond the visitor's sight, as did the keys distributed to patrons upon their visits. Initially these were single-sheet circular souvenirs meant to guide and orient the visitor, and their graphic transformation across the first twenty-five years of the panorama in many European capitals is worth noting. At their origin, these keys were drawn with an anamorphic technique that translated the 360-degree format into a two-dimensional circular figure around which a given panorama's settings and events were arranged, and within which the centrality of the spectator was implicitly or explicitly demarcated.[4] In her meticulous study of Robert Baker's circular keys from 1794 to 1816, Denise Blake Oleksijczuk has noted how the 'design shifts from locating the spectator within a flat, immersive landscape that ends at the limit of the horizon to an elevated view at the pinnacle of the globe that extends the space encompassed by pushing the horizon back into the distance' (2011: 128).

Indeed, a closer look at these anamorphic circular keys, which concurrently matured into a more or less homogeneous format across a number of countries during the panorama's first decades, suggests that the figure of the globe needs to be reckoned with as an important influence on these keys' design. In this respect, Comment's contention that 'the true panorama aspired to total illusion, [while] the circular view [of the keys] was a response to the notion of totality as perceived from a particular vantage-point' appears as less of a contradiction in terms (1999: 166). For this 'notion of totality as perceived from a particular vantage-point' was itself inscribed in the panorama as a concept, which the keys made visible by connecting a single view to a spherical spatial extension with clear global implications (Figure 1.1). As Jean-Marc Besse summarises, at its origin the panorama is informed by two organising principles: '[it] is an enclosed circular space, and one that opens itself to the contemplation of the limitless totality of the world' (2003: 183).[5]

While this 'limitless totality of the world' was often implied through metonymy, in some of the panorama's offshoots, such as the Georama, the idea to depict the planet gained quite literal contours through recourse to cartographic imagery as the *icon* of a world totality. Clearly modelled on the scale and format of panoramas, the Georama first appeared in France in 1825. Conceived by Charles Delanglard and located in Paris next to other rotundas at the Boulevard des Capucines, the attraction consisted of an enormous globe measuring one hundred feet in circumference and containing two viewing platforms inside. As with the panorama, visitors had to walk up flights of stairs in order to reach these platforms, yet here

Figure 1.1 Global Panoramas: the key distributed to visitors reveals the way in which the panoramic landscape implied a global spatiality.

they were confronted with the curious image of the map of the entire world 'inside out' rather than a single landscape. As Besse explains, the idea of reproducing a world map in a concave rather than convex surface was the main originality of Delanglard's project, the aim of which was to deliver 'a global vision . . . that remains materially inaccessible to the spectator's natural eye' (2003: 200). Besse goes on:

> [T]he Georama is not, properly speaking, a globe but a concave map which is intended to make possible a type of perception that neither the flat map nor the convex globe allow: a global, and so to speak immediate, view of the totality of the surface of the Earth. The Georama, better than the world map and the convex globe . . . fulfils the perceptual programme of the *géographie générale*: to directly see the whole. (2003: 214)

This idea was taken up in the following decades both in France (by M. Guérin) and England. Inspired by Delanglard's model, the mapmaker James Wyld built his Great Globe in Leicester Square in London in 1851, where it stayed for eleven years. More impressive than the Georama, the Great Globe measured 40 feet in diameter and 188 feet in circumference, and contained four rather than two viewing platforms inside, one above the other. It also displayed plasters in relief across the inside spherical surface depicting the Earth's continents and oceans, and painted stars on the outside. The attraction expanded its appeal so that it offered not only an iconic image of the planet, but also a tour across the world by adjoining 'halls for related objects such as small globes, atlases, maps and scenes from various places around the world' (Oettermann 1997: 90).

Another offshoot of the panorama, the Cosmorama, similarly attempted to produce a total picture of the world, though it did so in terms of an *inventory* of the world landmarks through which visitors could travel. First opened in Paris in January 1808 by Abbé Gazzera and advertised as a 'historical, geographic and picturesque voyage to different parts of the world', its model was soon imitated in other cities such as London, New York and Boston (Huhtamo 2012: 40). If the idea of travelling to different places was, for some time, the *raison d'être* of the panorama and coterminous with the rise of tourism, the Cosmorama amplified and multiplied this idea through a series of paintings of different corners of the globe. These were much smaller images painted in watercolour and placed in a semicircle within a case in front of a window. As the natural daylight illuminated the paintings from the outside, visitors could study the images through magnifying glasses set in front of the case from the inside. The paintings varied in terms of content but, as a general rule, the images often catered to an upper-class clientele with a newly acquired taste for exotic vistas. At the Regent Street Cosmorama exhibition in 1825, for example, visitors had the opportunity to walk through world landmarks as they divided their attention between two main galleries: one of Europe, which contained historical and geographical views from Brussels, Rome and Valencia, among others; and the other of Asia and Africa, in which paintings of Grand Cairo, Egyptian pyramids and the Island of Phyloe were exhibited side by side. As Erkki Huhtamo notes, 'the mode of behaviour that was built into the Cosmorama's apparatus implied bodily motion . . . Viewers had to displace themselves physically to "visit" all the sights/sites' (2012: 40).

By contrast, a moving panorama like *Whaling Voyage Round the World*, created by Benjamin Russell and Caleb Purrington in 1848, produced the opposite effect by showing a world tour of the planet's landscapes that paraded before an immobile spectator. These scenes were painted on cloth and the '8½ by 1,275-foot canvas was then mounted on upright rollers and rotated by cranks, which gave spectators the sensation of transit' (Chaplin 2012: 181). Another germane example is the *Grand voyage autour du Monde*, a moving panorama that extended for 90 metres and was exhibited at Le Théâtre Mécanique Morieux de Paris (Huhtamo 2013: 300). Moving panoramas enjoyed great success in many countries, so much so that it was this form 'that most people in Britain and in the United States would think of when the word "panorama" was mentioned', as Ralph Hyde has noted (n.d.: 63). And as the examples above demonstrate, the rolling nature of the canvas lent itself particularly well to the trope of travel, and indeed round-the-world travel.

In England, such was the popularity of travelling panoramas, and so identified with the idea of an inventory of the world had they become, that in one of the booklets commemorating 100 years of the Pooles' 'Myriorama', in 1937, the panorama is retrospectively defined in the following terms:

> And what was a panorama? It was a series of pictures, usually entitled 'A Trip Round the World', starting with a picture of London and finishing in England.
>
> Away one went, from Charing Cross, across the channel to Calais, Paris, Rome, Brindisi, North and South Africa, Australia, North and South America, and back across the Atlantic to Liverpool and home. (Poole 1937: 3)

Established in 1837 as a travelling panorama company by the showmen George and Charles Poole, and subsequently managed by several of the family successors, the Myriorama explicitly capitalised on the idea that it was a way of acquiring world knowledge for those without the means to undertake global travel. One of its programmes, entitled 'Sights of the World', for example, recognises that 'there is no more easy or agreeable way of adding to our store of knowledge than travel', but concedes that 'the desire to see the foreign parts is not always accompanied with the means of gratifying it' (Poole n.d.: 2).

In his history of the moving panorama, Huhtamo has stressed the need to differentiate it from the circular panorama: unlike the latter, moving panoramas were itinerant enterprises that travelled through the countryside, often accompanied by a lecturer and other performance and musical acts. Likewise, they failed to deliver the sense of immersive experience associated with the circular rotundas located in the big cities, and harboured tighter links with concepts such as narrativity and sequentiality. Yet, as Huhtamo also concedes, both forms shared 'features and topics, and responded to similar desires' (2013: 8). One such desire was to embrace a world totality, a desire that informed not only all panoramic forms mentioned above, but also other spectacles, such as the many world's fairs that sprouted up in Europe and the US in the second half of the nineteenth century. Displaying the latest advances in manufacturing, technology and science from a variety of countries, these fairs also comprised stands of 'exotic' spectacles of indigenous and non-Western cultures, arranged in an effort to catalogue a global humanity to be consumed in its diversity within the confines of a clearly demarcated space. As with the panorama and its variants, the trope of round-the-world travel was duly exploited in events that capitalised on the idea of a flattened and miniaturised globe through which visitors could spatially traverse. As the bastion of ethno-anthropological epistemologies, positivist beliefs and colonialist ideologies, the effect of such fairs, as Timothy Mitchell has noted, 'was to set the world up as a picture. They arranged it before an audience as an object on display – to be viewed, investigated and experienced' (1989: 220).

At the risk of conflating a wide range of forms and eclipsing their specificities, the practices and attractions mentioned above participated in a visual regime whereby the human's relation to the world and the world as a totality were redrawn along new parameters and paradigms. To varying extents, they all mobilised the trope of round-the-globe travel and attested to a quest to appropriate the world through and as images – a mode of visual appropriation that ran parallel to, and was informed by, a reconfiguration of the planet's coordinates in the context of the growing popularity and feasibility of global travels and imperialist explorations. Although colonialism was not a nineteenth-century nor a European invention, European colonialism, as Ella Shohat and Robert Stam have noted, differed from previous manifestations in terms of its 'affiliation with global institutional power, and its imperative mode, its attempted submission of the world to a single "universal" regime of truth and power' (1994: 15–16).

The images produced at this time not only reflected but also intervened in these world-encompassing discourses. As Tom Gunning has argued, if the panorama and its offshoots in the nineteenth century must be situated within 'a larger context [that] extends from the travel lecture to the postcard industry to world fair exhibits', this is because these forms are 'more than an effect' of the development of the tourism industry, new modes of travel and colonialist enterprises. They instead 'supply essential tools in the creation of a modern worldview underlying all these transformations' (2006: 30). Gunning writes:

> One cannot understand modernity without penetrating its passion for images. Images fascinate modern consciousness obsessively, and this modern sense of images comes from a belief that images can somehow deliver what they portray. Image as appropriation dominates the modern image-making industry, and travel images provide a unique perspective onto this modern phenomenon. Lynne Kirby has pointed

out that the epigraph to Burton Holmes's memoir reads: 'to travel is to possess the world'. (2006: 30)

If the recent popularity of travel provided the means by which the world was possessed, and advanced the idea that to travel the world was indeed to possess it, then the profusion of world images and images of the world not only participated in this idea but provided new means by which the planet could be visually appropriated. In so doing, these images must also be placed alongside the proliferation of increasingly refined globes, maps and other geographic and cartographic equipment, all of which showed an 'ever greater emphasis on nonlinguistic representations . . . as accurate registers of vision' (Cosgrove 2001: 207).

As Denis Cosgrove points out, an 'ability to distinguish visually the observer from the object seen (the [subject] from the globe or map) and the seen object from the reality it seeks to represent (the globe or map from the earth itself) has been fundamental to a modern Western geographical imagination' (2001: 226). This distinction was also felt in the global imaginaries and spectacles of the time, many of which capitalised on the idea of an overwhelming world that engulfed the human, while providing at the same time a distance that guaranteed some sense of control and mastery. The panorama was the embodiment of this dualism. On the one hand, its appeal was largely connected with its superlative dimensions and lack of a single perspective, which produced sensory overload and visual excess, as indicated by the many sensations of dizziness reported by patrons at the time. On the other hand, 'the central elevated viewing platform . . . gave cramped urban spectators a quick hit of immersive spectacle and momentary sovereignty over all surveyed, placing them at the heart of a simulated universe where they looked down upon the world' (Griffiths 2013: 77). Speaking of world fairs, Timothy Mitchell has similarly noted,

> [the] contradiction between the need to separate oneself from the world and to render it up as an object of representation, and the desire to lose oneself within this object-world and to experience it directly – a contradiction that world exhibitions, with their profusion of exotic detail and yet their clear distinction between visitor and exhibit, were built to accommodate and overcome. (1989: 231)

This sense of a world instrumentalised for a viewer at its centre was famously conceptualised by Martin Heidegger as the 'age of the world picture', which he deemed 'one and the same event with the event of man's becoming *subjectum* in the midst of [the world, in its entirety]'; a world thus measured 'from the standpoint of man and in relation to man' (132–3). Although it is tempting to read Heidegger's proposition literally in relation to the centrally positioned human gaze at the heart of many nineteenth-century visual spectacles, his observations relate to a wider epistemological shift whereby a number of technological, scientific and cultural phenomena radically reformulated the stakes and the scales of the world in relation to the centrality of a subject – which, of course, was often European, white and male.

'We Put the World Before You'

The emergence of photographic and cinematic images must be situated within these globalising discourses of visual appropriation and examined in terms of their relations with the forms and spectacles preceding or coinciding with their appearance. To varying extents, photography and film lent continuity to the visual expressions of a world totality examined above. In their quest for all-embracing images, both mediums cemented a panoramic mode of vision understood in terms of a metonymical quest for increasingly larger chunks of the world. As Teresa Castro has noted: 'The history of panoramism as a cultural phenomenon of the nineteenth century is inseparable from that of photography, which from its inception was interested in elongated formats' (2011: 64). The same interest is identified in early cinema, whether in the form of 'panoramic views' of landscapes that were 'elongated' in space through a moving camera (often perched on a train), or in terms of circular or half-circular descriptive camera movements that would carry the panorama in abbreviated format in its very title. All-embracing images are also produced in early cinema through the coupling between recording and aerial technology (Castro 2013:119), showing an underlying quest to contemplate the world from a distance that would culminate in the famous photographs of the Earth taken during the Apollo missions in the late 1960s.

Yet a desire to embrace the world is discerned in photography and early cinema beyond metonymy. For these forms promised more than all-encompassing images of single locales; above all they promised to show *all* corners of the globe. To the extent that many of the paintings adorning -orama spectacles attested to a quest to realistically reproduce world landscapes, photography outperformed these practices owing to its evidentiary quality. The same is true of cinema, whose mission to 'transport' viewers to faraway places was accomplished with a remarkable sense of novelty derived from its ability to record movement, with 'travel films' and 'travelogues' emerging as one of the most popular and consolidated genres, and screened in spaces that often compounded the thrill of experiencing movement by simulating means of transport.

Figure 1.2 We Put the World Before You: this promotional logo for Charles Urban Trading Company shows the global ambitions of early cinema.
Courtesy of Luke McKernan.

The ability to travel around the world and inventory its human and physical diversity was not simply programmatically embraced by the nascent film industries so much as it was often advertised as its fundamental asset: whether we look at the prevalence of trips around the world as a recurrent topic in early cinema (see Costa 2007); the Lumière brothers' widely advertised travels to exotic places; Pathé's 'World Wide Activities'; or indeed, the phrases and logos quickly adopted by film companies. Already in 1896, Méliès's Star Film promised to bring 'The Whole World within Reach', while in 1903, in the UK, the Charles Urban Trading Company vowed to 'Put the World Before You' (Figure 1.2). Later in the decade, a number of companies in Europe and the US, including RKO and the UK Korda brothers, adopted the iconic image of a globe for their logos, some of which, as in the case of Universal, still exist to this day.

Of course, this global ambition was clearly informed by colonial discourse and must be situated within the context of expansionist ideologies. As Shohat and Stam note, the 'dominant European/American form of cinema not only inherited and disseminated hegemonic colonial discourse, it also created a powerful hegemony of its own through monopolistic control of film distribution and exhibition in much of Asia, Africa and the Americas' (1994: 103). Yet a utopian impulse must also be accounted for in some globalising projects and discourses of the time. A germane example is Albert Kahn's monumental *Les archives de la planète* (1909–31), which during its two decades 'employed eleven independent cameramen and photographers . . . to record and collect life . . . in over forty countries', amassing 'a vast, multi-media, ethno-geographic visual inventory of the globe' (Amad 2010:

6). Globalism was also mobilised in the prevalent conception of film as a 'universal language' – a notion that was theorised from within different conceptual frameworks by writers as diverse as Vachel Lindsay in the USA, Ricciotto Canudo in Italy, Louis Delluc in France and Béla Balázs in Austria. In its most utopian form, the universal language idea hailed film's purely visual properties as a 'language' able to transcend cultural and national differences in the name of a global humanity.

Irrespective of the distinctive and even conflicting ideologies underlying the above forms, projects, discourses and ideas, they all attested to a conceptualisation of the film medium in terms of its ability to make the world visible, to show images of the world to the world, and to map out a newly discovered global space.

Towards a Comparative Media History

As has been noted, the dynamic media constellation within which cinema emerged offers itself as a particularly fruitful contrasting field against which to examine our contemporary audiovisual landscape, in which intermedial interactions are similarly the norm (Gunning 2007: 35–6; Elsaesser 2016: 183–4). Spurred on by the advent and proliferation of 'new media' in the early 1990s and now largely referred to as 'media archaeology', this approach, as Jussi Parikka sums up, has often focused 'on the nineteenth century as a foundation stone of modernity in terms of science, technology and the birth of media capitalism. Media archaeology has been interested in excavating the past in order to understand the present and the future' (2012: 2). Yet media archaeology has also raised its own conundrums, accused in some quarters of a certain arbitrariness in terms of how its objects of study are excavated and put in dialogue; a heterogeneous comparative model that risks lacking historiographical and contextual rigour when confronting the old and the new (see Elsaesser 2016).

With this caveat in mind, I would argue that to put the media-scape of early and late modernity on an equal footing makes especial sense when we consider the ways in which they have variously grappled with the conception of a world totality, often through recourse to the trope of global travel. This is not to say that the category of the global becomes inadequate as film matures into a narrative form and moves into the twentieth century, but only that it manifests itself with a remarkable vigour in both periods, thus allowing for a more meaningful and historicised comparative approach. Joyce E. Chaplin, for example, has noted that the planetary consciousness of our time is as pronounced as it was in the mid- to late nineteenth century, with the difference that the sense of *confidence* in round-the-world travel which characterises the consciousness of that period has been supplanted by one of *doubt* as associated with the 'growing sense that the environmental costs of planetary domination have begun to haunt us' (2012: xxi). As a result, the whole planet has reemerged as a ubiquitous theme and trope in audiovisual culture.

It is symptomatic in this respect that the self-promotional discourses surrounding many of the forms and texts I mentioned at the beginning of this chapter boast technological and technical wizardry as enabling new travels across a world whose hidden visual wonders are seemingly inexhaustible. The extremely popular BBC TV series *Planet Earth*, with its reliance on high-definition technology and new camera supports that generate 'stunning new views of the Earth' (Nicholson-Lord 2006: 6), perfectly exemplifies this phenomenon. Not coincidentally, the show has also been accompanied by a flurry of photographic and literary publications, one of which is tellingly included in the Lonely Planet series as *The Traveller's Guide to Planet Earth*. Google Earth, the internet resource which maps the planet through the superimposition of images obtained from satellite imagery, aerial photography and geographic information system (GIS) onto a 3D globe, may also be profitably understood as one more chapter in an illustrious genealogy of planetary visualisation. Seen in this light, it may be more than coincidental that a promotional poster for *Planet Earth* (Figure 1.3) bears an uncanny resemblance to the aforementioned anamorphic keys distributed to patrons upon their visits to panoramas. Similarly, the fact that viewers can zoom in to photographed street views which they can then rotate 360 degrees in a mode of vision that immediately recalls the panorama may signal the persistence of a mode of visuality whose underlying proposition is the positioning of a centralised human gaze in relation to the entire world.

However, if the world as newly imaged and imagined can be traced back to earlier images and imaginings, there is a crucial difference related to the ways in which the planet is now conceptualised as an object haunted by disappearance. In other words, if the emergence of cinema is inseparable from a fascination with its ability to record the world in movement for the first time, then recent global constructions can be said to derive their renewed visual appeal from the fact that they could be recording the Earth in its last throes. They articulate their visual urgency within holistic and ecological discourses that highlight the corporeal fragility of an interconnected though highly endangered planet. As the Earth has changed more drastically in the last fifty years than in all human history, a spectre of disappearance hovers over the planet, thus imparting a pressing urgency to its recordings. To critically engage with these imaginaries is therefore

Figure 1.3 A promotional poster for the BBC series *Planet Earth II* bears an uncanny resemblance to panorama keys by implicating a single landscape within a global space.

an urgent task of our time, yet in order to truly grasp their aesthetic, cultural and political significance, we must be prepared to situate them within a much larger history of global visions.

Notes

1 This chapter would not have been possible without a stipend I was awarded by the Bill Douglas Cinema Museum, University of Exeter, to conclude research at its archives. I am grateful to Phil Wickham and Helen Hanson for their generous help and support while I researched the museum's precious collections.
2 As Comment further points out, an 'all-knowing and all-seeing fantasy also emerged . . . in Balzac's *La comédie humaine*. Totalisation operated on a level that was logical (everything is revealed, causes as well as effects), topological

(the town and the countryside) and chronological (saturation of time and eras)' (1999: 142).
3 From early on, the panorama is also exploited for nationalist purposes, with military battles an increasingly prevalent subject matter.
4 From around 1815, the anamorphic drawing was then replaced by a rectangular horizontal print that sacrificed the circular format in the name of perspectival illusionism. Oleksijczuk attributes their transformation to a need to facilitate engagement on the part of the viewer with the keys' visual content, as the panorama became increasingly exploited in the service of national pride and interests, with military battles a recurrent trope.
5 All translations in this essay are mine.

Works Cited

Amad, Paula (2010), *Counter-Archive: Film, the Everyday, and Albert Kahn's Archives de la Planète*, New York: Columbia University Press.
Besse, Jean-Marc (2003), *Face au monde: Atlas, jardins, géoramas*, Paris: Desclée de Brouwer.
Castro, Teresa (2009), 'Cinema's Mapping Impulse: Questioning Visual Culture', *Cartographic Journal*, 46:1, pp. 9–15.
Castro, Teresa (2011), *La pensée cartographique des images: Cinéma et culture visuelle*, Lyons: Aléas Éditeur.
Castro, Teresa (2013), 'Aerial Views and Cinematism, 1898–1939', in Mark Dorrian and Frédéric Pousin (eds), *Seeing from Above: The Aerial View in Visual Culture*, London and New York: I. B. Tauris, pp. 118–33.
Chaplin, Joyce E. (2012), *Round About the Earth: Circumnavigation from Magellan to Orbit*, New York: Simon and Schuster Paperbacks.
Comment, Bernard (1999), *The Panorama*, London: Reaktion Books.
Cosgrove, Denis (2001), *Apollo's Eye: A Cartographic Genealogy of the Earth in the Western Imagination*, Baltimore and London: Johns Hopkins University Press.
Costa, Antonio (2007), 'Landscape and Archive: Trips Around the World as Early Film Topic', in Martin Lefebvre (ed.), *Landscape and Film*, New York and London: Routledge, pp. 245–66.
Doane, Mary Ann (2002), *The Emergence of Cinematic Time: Modernity, Contingency, the Archive*, Cambridge, MA and London: Harvard University Press.
Elsaesser, Thomas (2016), 'Media Archaeology as Symptom', *New Review of Film and Television Studies*, 14:2, pp. 181–215.
Grau, Oliver (2003), *Virtual Art: From Illusion to Immersion*, trans. Gloria Custance, London and Cambridge, MA: The MIT Press.
Griffiths, Alison (2013), *Shivers Down Your Spine: Cinema, Museums, and the Immersive View*, New York: Columbia University Press.
Gunning, Tom (2006), 'The Whole World Within Reach', in Jeffrey Ruoff (ed.), *Virtual Voyages: Cinema and Travel*, Durham, NC and London: Duke University Press, pp. 25–41.

Gunning, Tom (2007), 'Moving Away from the Index: Cinema and the Impression of Reality', *Differences: A Journal of Feminist Cultural Studies*, 18:1, pp. 29–52.
Heidegger, Martin (1977), 'The Age of the World Picture', in *The Question Concerning Technology and Other Essays*, translated and with an introduction by William Lovitt, New York and London: Garland, pp. 115–54.
Huhtamo, Erkki (2012), 'Toward a History of Peep Practice', in André Gaudreault et al. (eds), *A Companion to Early Cinema*, Oxford: Wiley-Blackwell, pp. 32–51.
Huhtamo, Erkki (2013), *Illusions in Motion: Media Archaeology of the Moving Panorama and Related Spectacles*, Cambridge and London: The MIT Press.
Humboldt, Alexander von [1858] (1997) *Cosmos: A Sketch of a Physical Description of the Universe*, vol. 1, Baltimore and London: Johns Hopkins University Press.
Hyde, Ralph (n.d.), 'The Artist, the Showman, and the Moving Panorama', unpublished manuscript held at the Bill Douglas Cinema Museum, University of Exeter, item number 12782.
Miller, Angela (1996), 'The Panorama, the Cinema, and the Emergence of the Spectacular', *Wide Angle*, 18:2, pp. 34–69.
Mitchell, Timothy (1989), 'The World as Exhibition', *Comparative Studies in Society and History*, 31:2, pp. 217–36.
Nicholson-Lord, David (2006), *Planet Earth: The Making of an Epic Series*, London: BBC Books.
Oettermann, Stephan (1997), *The Panorama: History of a Mass Medium*, trans. Deborah Lucas Schneider, New York: Zone Books.
Oleksijczuk, Denise Blake (2011), *The First Panoramas: Visions of British Imperialism*, Minneapolis: University of Minnesota Press.
Parikka, Jussi (2012), *What is Media Archaeology?*, Cambridge: Polity Press.
Poe, Edgar Allan (1848), *Eureka: An Essay on the Material and Spiritual Universe*, New York: Wiley and Putnam, available online at <https://books.google.co.uk/books?id=-aVkAAAAcAAJ&printsec=frontcover&source=gbs_ge_summary_r&cad=0#v=onepage&q&f=false> (last accessed January 2017).
Poole, John R. (ed.) (1937), '100 Years of Showmanship: Poole's 1837–1937', Edinburgh: Pillans and Wilson, Printers. Booklet held at the Bill Douglas Cinema Museum, University of Exeter, item number 33966.
Poole, Joseph (n.d.), 'Joseph Poole's Myriorama & Sights of the World', programme held at the Bill Douglas Cinema Museum, University of Exeter, item number 17869.
Rice, Shelley (1993), 'Boundless Horizons: The Panoramic Image', *Art in America*, 81:12 (December), pp. 68–71.
Roberts, Martin (1998), '*Baraka*: World Cinema and the Global Culture Industry', *Cinema Journal*, 37:3, pp. 62–82.
Shohat, Ella and Robert Stam (1994), *Unthinking Eurocentrism: Multiculturalism and the Media*, London: Routledge.
Verne, Jules [1873] (1994), *Around the World in Eighty Days*, Ware: Wordsworth.

CHAPTER 2

Brief Encounters:
The Railway Station on Film

Lucy Mazdon

Writing in *The Guardian* in 2010 David Thomson questioned a recent poll which had named David Lean's *Brief Encounter* (1945) the best movie romance of all times:

> In how many other countries would a poll pick *Brief Encounter* as the best movie romance of all time? Even in Britain, I wonder how many people born since, say, 1975 would rate it so highly. But for a generation that remembers when the trains ran on time and station buffets were as tidy and inviting as the one in this movie, *Brief Encounter* is etched in nostalgia for an era when trapped middle-class lives contemplated adultery but set the disturbing thought aside. (Thomson 2010)

Thomson's invocation of nostalgia is revealing. As I shall suggest later in this chapter, Lean's film is very much of its time, its narrative of self-sacrifice and decency deeply rooted in the culture and mood of post-war Britain. As Thomson intimates, its charm and appeal for many spectators of the twenty-first century would to a large extent be connected to nostalgic fantasies of an earlier, less complicated society. *Brief Encounter* depicts a middle-class Britain on the cusp of change, a Britain irrevocably altered by the experience of the Second World War but still clinging to long-held 'British' values and behaviours, a deeply reassuring vision, it would seem, to both contemporary audiences and modern-day viewers.

Lean's film is of course famously set in and around a railway station. Lean had originally intended to film in London but due to the ongoing air raid risk relocated to Carnforth in north Lancashire, where the lights from filming were less of a danger. As I shall go on to discuss later in this chapter, the railway station is much more than a location or backdrop for the film's narrative of lost love. Rather it provides a crucial structuring framework for the binaries of arrival and departure, movement and stasis, intimacy and public appearance, adventure and everyday duty which lie at the heart of the film. Milford Junction, the railway station created from Carnforth in *Brief Encounter*, is itself a place of both movement and adventure and containment and sacrifice. While it brings the film's lovers together, it also contains and ultimately curtails their love affair, returning them to family, duty and respectability. As this chapter will reveal, the railway station, in particular the station of the age of steam, is itself a profoundly nostalgic space in the British cultural imagination. It thus offers a uniquely symbolic *mise en scène* as it embodies the very dynamics of the film's narrative and lasting appeal.

This chapter will make the cinematic representation of the railway station its focus. Via discussion of *Brief Encounter*, it will examine the different ways in which the space and iconography of the station is used in film. As a place of transit, the railway station is a privileged site for cultural encounters. The millions of travellers and workers whose paths cross on the trains, platforms, waiting rooms and shops of the world's stations are subject to forms of exchange and interaction which oppose different cultural identities. The station is a place of departure and homecoming, and these journeys can take many forms. In times of conflict the joyous anticipation of travel to pastures new may give way to exodus and deportation, while the return home becomes an anxious and confusing repatriation. The station thus produces another form of cultural encounter as it acquires new forms of memory and identity. Images from World War Two of the departure of evacuees from the London stations, of returning prisoners of war to the Gare d'Orsay in Paris and, of course, of the numerous cattle trains leaving stations across Nazi-controlled territories underline this on-going layering of history and iconography. The station is then both physical space and symbol or metaphor for cultural encounter of all kinds: encounter engendered by travel and tourism, conflict and displacement, memory and identity. One of the very earliest moving pictures, the Lumière brothers' *L'Arrivée d'un train en gare de La Ciotat/The Arrival of a Train at La Ciotat* (1896), puts a station at its heart, reminding us of the shared origins of both cinema and the modern station in the nineteenth century and presaging the countless filmic representations of the station which would ensue. This chapter will make this cinematic representation of the railway station its focus.

From the launch of the world's first steam-powered passenger service in 1825, the railway transformed social and economic life, becoming, paradoxically, a symbol of both machine-driven modernity and, later on as the steam train was retired and rail transport was largely replaced by road and air, the nostalgic past. The railway's relationship with and impact upon modernity cannot be overstated. Writing in 1902, H. G. Wells predicted that historians would posit 'a steam train running upon a railway' as the central symbol of the nineteenth century (Wells 1902: 4). If modernity, notoriously difficult to define, can be perceived as the reorganisation of capitalism and bureaucracy on ever wider scales, resulting in the reconstitution of social meanings and value systems, then the role of the railways becomes ever more apparent (Carter 2001: 8). As Karl Marx noted, the eradication of space by time enabled by the railways bolstered and accelerated the capitalist industrialisation which underpins this conception of modernity (Marx 1973: 539). As railways redefined and transformed the industrialised world, so they changed perceptions of space, time and geography, radically changing the way the world looked and felt (Schivelbusch 1986). In Britain the railways encouraged urbanisation, not least through the development of the so-called 'railway towns' built to house both those who constructed the railways and the future passengers. Conceptions of space and community were transformed as the railways enabled the rapid movement of goods and passengers, taking people away from the places and social structures which had previously confined them and opening up new forms of employment and leisure. And time itself was transformed as the imperatives of the railway timetable led to a unified 'railway time'. Where once time in Manchester marched at a different hour than time in Plymouth or London, the nation now moved at a single time. Through the creation of railway time, so potently symbolised by the station clock, the coming of the railways played a vastly significant role in the construction of nation and national identity in the nineteenth century. As Jeffrey Richards and John M. Mackenzie state:

> There is perhaps no more potent or dramatic symbol of the Industrial Revolution than the railways. Although the precise nature of the economic change the railways wrought is still debated, their impact cannot be gainsaid. They epitomized technological advance – a new method of transporting people and goods speedily and in bulk, of unifying nations and, in the words of the celebrated epigrammatist Sydney Smith, 'abolishing time, distance and delay'. (2010: 1)

Ian Carter remarks that 'the railway age laid tracks along which our world still runs'. Indeed, the modern world we recognise today developed after the coming of the railways (Carter 2001: 4). Given the radical transformations ushered in by rail, it is not surprising that cultural imaginings of the railway gathered apace during the nineteenth century. The railway companies themselves were at the vanguard of this process as they produced hundreds of beautifully illustrated railway posters, extolling the virtues of rail travel. As Andrew Martin suggests, the railway became a growing object of fascination for artists, writers, photographers and, later, filmmakers throughout the nineteenth and twentieth centuries (Martin 2013). From the horror at the pollution and danger of the train journey expressed by Dickens in *Dombey and Son* (1848) to Betjeman's nostalgic yet deeply impassioned writings and films about Britain's railways in the twentieth century, cultural artefacts of various kinds responded to and refracted the growing impact of the railways.

Carter describes J. M. W. Turner's *Rain, Steam and Speed: The Great Western Railway*, first exhibited at the Royal Academy in 1844, as the exemplary visual image of early railway years in Britain (Carter 2001: 51). The painting was much disparaged by contemporary critics and it confused and disturbed early viewers in equal measure. It seems to celebrate the power, the rush, the potential that the railway offered and yet to simultaneously reveal its danger. As such the painting, this early exemplar of 'railway art', encapsulates and makes visible that tension between modernity and nostalgia, fear and fascination, so central to future imaginings of the railway including, as we shall see, *Brief Encounter*. The cultural impact of the railways was vast. Alongside its representation in the visual art of painters such as Turner, Monet and Manet, canonical authors such as Tolstoy, Zola and Dickens explored the literary potential of the railways in their fiction. Dickens, whose works repeatedly explore the impacts of industrialisation and urbanisation, was one of the earliest British writers to realise the imaginative potential of the railways and 'from the 1840s, trains seep insistently through his published work' (Carter 2001: 73). Outside those works which now form the canon, the nineteenth century spawned an immense popular fascination with the railways. The emergence of 'Yellow Backs' or 'railway fiction', cheaply bound and often sensational popular novels designed to keep the reader's attention during a noisy and often disrupted journey and available for purchase at station bookshops, demonstrates how culture both articulated the impact of this new mode of transport and set out to service its needs.

More than any other medium, it was the cinema that played a major part in shaping the image of the railway in the popular imagination. In turn, the railway's associations with speed, danger and romance, along with its possibilities for travel, spectacle and cultural encounter, shaped cinema itself. Indeed, the two cultural forces developed in parallel as continually evolving nineteenth-century technologies, each a central, if often controversial, part of modern life. As Lynne Kirby has persuasively argued, rail travel was an important 'protocinematic phenomenon' (Kirby 1997). Kirby points out that film could be said to owe one of its hallmark techniques, the travelling shot, and, more broadly, the movement or 'journey' it can provide for its seated spectators, to the train. Moreover, images of train journeys, of peril on the railroads, of arrivals, departures and 'brief encounters' in railway stations, have provided an enduring cinematic motif. Kirby claims that the railway should be seen as a 'social, perceptual, and ideological paradigm providing early film spectators with a familiar experience [. . .] and an established mode of perception' and 'a highly charged cultural image, a potent legend that informed the development of narrative as well as nonnarrative film' (Kirby 1997: 2–3). From its earliest days, the cinema shared with the railway 'a mutual attraction based on similar ways of handling speed, visual perception, and the promise of a journey' (Kirby 1997: 3). Both cinema and railway reveal the technological and cultural instability which underpin modernity, and as such both were central to the shaping of the modern world and the perceptions of those who virtually or physically travelled through it.

Early cinema made much of the railway. From the aforementioned *L'Arrivée d'un train en gare de La Ciotat* (Lumière brothers, 1896) to *The Great Train Robbery* (Edwin S. Porter, 1903), the speed and exhilaration of the railways provided fruitful material for the pioneers of the new medium:

> Trains and stations already had an established visual image and impact, thanks to their regular appearances in paintings, engravings, and still photographs. But the cinema, first silent and then sound, enhanced their dramatic potential, with the deployment of the visual and aural imagery of fire-breathing engines, billowing smoke, bustling termini, chattering rails, and melancholy train-whistles. (Richards and Mackenzie 2010: 356)

With its connotations of speed, danger, excitement and progress, the railway was a rich source to both display the visual potential of the fledgling cinematic medium and, later, to develop the narratives which would thrill audiences. Films such as *Shanghai Express* (Josef von Sternberg, 1932), *Berlin Express* (Jacques Tourneur, 1948) and *Night Train to Munich* (Carol Reed, 1940) exploited the train's potential for the construction of an enclosed world, and for dramatic travel, in order to develop tales of crime, passion and espionage. In Renoir's masterful *La Bête humaine* (1938) the train becomes a symbol of both uncontrollable passion and of masculine working-class solidarity as, unlike its counterpart in Zola's source novel, it does not find itself driverless and hurtling to its doom but rather continues its journey while Lantier conversely falls to his death. In *The Railway Children* (Lionel Jeffries, 1970) and *The Titfield Thunderbolt* (Charles Crichton, 1953) the railway represents both disruption (the journey away from home, the closure of the branch line) and resolution and a return to the past (the train brings the children's father home, the residents reinstate the line). In other words, every aspect of the railway – its trains, its journeys, its places, its people – has been explored in cinema.

In so doing, cinema has extended the cultural impact of the railway while simultaneously using the images, tropes and motifs of rail travel to develop its own narratives and aesthetic. That early cultural symbiosis identified by Kirby can thus be seen to extend well beyond the days of early film. Writing in 1980 Wolfgang Schivelbusch bemoans the domestication of both travel and visual entertainment as the family car replaced rail travel and the television set replaced a visit to the cinema (Schivelbusch 1993: 62). Schivelbusch describes this shift in terms of decline or 'reduction':

> What comes after is a *reduction*. It is not merely in scale or dimension that the machines in question are reduced when they move from the public sphere into domestic use – cars are smaller than locomotives, television sets smaller than movie screens – but the essential character of things is also diminished: the heroic aspect is lost, so to speak. In comparison with their tiny successors the railroad and cinema are powerful instruments that excite the imagination, inviting near mythic associations. (1993: 62–3)

Central to these 'powerful instruments' is the railway station. Both as point of departure and arrival for the journeys undertaken by trains and their passengers, and as a frequent and powerful motif or location in cinematic imaginings of the railway, it is crucial to any understanding of the relationship between railways and cinema. As Richards and Mackenzie note:

> In the nineteenth century the train was more than just a means of transportation, it was a symbol of power, speed, progress, civilization, destiny. The station as the gateway to those sensations shared in this symbolism. Train and station were instantly dramatic, mysterious and exciting. (2010: 356)

The railway station was the physical embodiment of rail travel. In cities around the world vast buildings were erected to serve the needs of the railways. Yet these were not mere buildings. As Richards and Mackenzie remark, the railway station was arguably the nineteenth century's distinctive contribution to architectural forms (2010: 3). Huge technological skill went into the construction of the train sheds, while architects revived Classic, Gothic, Baroque and Renaissance styles to produce elaborate exteriors which would both vaunt the splendour of the railway and assuage anxieties about progress through this return to the past (again, that tension between modernity and nostalgia). The station was much more than functional. Akin to a secular cathedral, the imaginative splendour of London's St Pancras, New York's Grand Central and Paris's Gare de l'Est were testament to and celebration of a new religion and a new age, the era of the railway.

As the great age of the railways gave way to the dominance of road and air travel and the new spaces of travel became the motorway services and the airport, many of the great stations of the world fell into disrepair. The loss of a station was so much more than a simple change to urban geography. In the words of John Betjeman, that champion of the social importance of the railway, 'railway stations are most important in giving places an identity' (*Time with Betjeman*, BBC TV series, 1983). The station was a microcosm of the city, of wider society, a profoundly human place despite its grandiose architecture and technological brilliance. Writing in 1913, James Scott located the fascination of the railway station precisely in its human interest:

> A railway station speaks of epochs of decision in life, a parting of the ways, crossroads in conduct. Shall we embark upon this adventure; shall we definitely declare our hand; shall we make a break in habit; or a departure from principle? [. . .] When the train has borne us away and we settle into our corner, have we feelings of remorse or satisfaction? Where will the journey's end be? (1913: 89–90)

Marc Augé posits the places and spaces of travel and transport as 'non-place': 'If a place can be defined as relational, historical and concerned with identity, then a space which cannot be defined as relational, or historical, or concerned with identity will be non-place' (Augé 1995: 77–8). Non-place, according to Augé, designates two complementary but distinct realities: spaces which are formed in relation to certain ends (transport and transit for example) and the relations that individuals have with these spaces (1995: 94). While the two sets of relations may overlap to some extent, they cannot be confused with one another, 'for non-places mediate a whole mass of relations, with the self and with others, which are only indirectly connected with their purposes. As anthropological places create the organically social, so non-places create solitary contractuality (1995: 94). So does this make the railway station, clearly a place of transit, a non-place in Augé's terms? Interestingly, Augé draws a distinction between the contemporary journeys and spaces of the French TGV, which rushes the traveller past cities and towns at excessive speed, and those of earlier rail travel:

> The railway, which often passes behind the houses making up the town, catches provincials off guard in the privacy of their daily lives, behind the façade, on the garden side, the kitchen or bedroom side and, in the evening, the light side (while the street, if it were not for public street lighting, would be the domain of darkness and night). Trains used to go slowly enough for the curious traveller to be able to read their names on passing stations, but this is made impossible by the excessive speed of today's trains. (1995: 99)

In the France of thirty years ago, the railways, like the *routes départmentales*, would penetrate the intimacy of everyday life. Those who took the train were 'travellers' strolling along their route as Augé puts it (1995: 107) as opposed to the passengers of the TGV, entirely defined by their destination. So if we turn again to James Scott's account of the railway station as a place of decision making, of human interaction, then it would seem fair to say that despite its status as a place of transit and travel it is perhaps not a non-place in Augé's terms.

Perhaps more productively we can think of the station according to Doreen Massey's terms, rejecting the distinction between 'place (as meaningful, lived and everyday) and space (as what? the outside? the abstract? the meaningless?)' (Massey 2005: 6). Massey argues that space should be seen as the product of interrelations, as the sphere of the possibility of the existence of multiplicity, 'Without space, no multiplicity; without multiplicity, no space' (2005: 9). Massey goes on to suggest that space can be imagined as 'a simultaneity of stories-so-far [. . .] a product of interrelations' (2005: 9–10). Space, she argues, does not exist prior to identities/entities and their relations (2005: 10). Again, let us recall James Scott's description of the station, 'A railway station speaks of epochs of decision in life, a parting of the ways, cross-roads in conduct' (Scott 1913: 90). In other words, and as I suggested at the start of this chapter, the station is precisely a simultaneity of stories-so-far, a space whose meaning and significance arises from the interrelations, exchanges and crossings of its workers and passengers.

It is surely these 'stories-so-far' which make the station such a privileged and rich location for cinema. In many ways the station is in and of itself a deeply cinematic space. As a place of arrivals and departures, of sudden encounters, it has always possessed great dramatic potential. The hustle and bustle of the station platforms, the billowing smoke from waiting trains, the soaring architecture, enabled a visual spectacle ideally suited to cinema. From John Schlesinger's documentary account of a day in the life of London's Waterloo station, *Terminus* (1961), to the musical exuberance of Chhatrapati Shivaji Terminus in Danny Boyle's *Slumdog Millionaire* (2008) to the negotiation of railway and cinema's shared histories in Martin Scorsese's recreation of Paris's Gare Montparnasse in *Hugo* (2011) the station has provided the ideal setting for romance and danger; a starting point for human journeys of all kinds.

Arguably the seminal 'station' film, at least for British audiences, is David Lean's *Brief Encounter* (1945):

> Image after image of the station in films crowds into the memory. But it is perhaps David Lean's film of Noël Coward's *Brief Encounter* which lingers most forcefully

in the mind. In this film it was at Carnforth Station in Lancashire, amid the bustle of comings and goings and the steadily hardening rock-cakes of the buffet, that the entwined lives of that most English and most gentle pair of lovers Trevor Howard and Celia Johnson reached crisis point. (Richards and Mackenzie 2010: 16)

The film was based on Noël Coward's one-act play of 1936, *Still Life*. Set in England in the late 1930s, it centres around two main characters, Laura Jesson (Celia Johnson) and Alec Harvey (Trevor Howard). The film, narrated by Laura, recounts in flashback the passionate but ultimately doomed love affair she shares with Alec. Both married, they meet by chance at Milford Junction station and fall desperately in love. Every Thursday they journey into Milford, Laura to exchange her library books, have lunch at the Kardomah and visit the cinema, Alec to work at the hospital. Their love affair develops alongside these rather prosaic activities; for seven weeks they meet until, Alec having accepted a job in Johannesburg, they say their final goodbyes at the station. Duty and decency win the day and they both return, via train, to their families.

While Coward's play was set entirely in the refreshment room at Milford Junction, Lean's film adaptation moves out into the station's platforms and walkways as well as into the spaces of the town and countryside in which Laura and Alec play out their love affair. Nevertheless it is the station which is the film's central locale and, I would argue, lies squarely at the heart of its narrative and themes. The film opens in the station refreshment room. As we discover only later, we will witness Laura and Alec's final goodbyes and see the scene again towards the close of the film, this time in full realisation of its significance. So this is a crucial scene in terms of the film's narrative, its importance underscored by its (altered) repetition at the opening and closing of the film. Yet it is also crucial in the various ways in which it constructs the spaces of the station and situates both literally and metaphorically Laura and Alec's relationship within these spaces.

The film begins by showing the refreshment room staff at work. The camera then pans across to a well-dressed, clearly middle-class couple sitting at a table locked in unheard conversation. Rather than hear them we hear the talk of Albert, the ticket collector, who tells of a guilty passenger, and the sharp ripostes of Myrtle, the buffet proprietress. Thus the restrained middle-class intimacy of Alec and Laura is interrupted and overlaid by the working-class and very public repartee of Albert and Myrtle. Their tryst is then fully interrupted by the arrival of Laura's acquaintance Dolly. As we shall later learn, Dolly arrives just as Alec has said 'we've still got a few minutes'. Yet her appearance makes those last few moments of intimacy impossible. Richard Dyer suggests that the opening sequence reveals the film's recognition that all reality is perceived through emotions. Albert's talk of a guilty passenger suggests the guilt which we will later discover Laura is feeling about her relationship with Alec. Dolly's interruption, at precisely the moment Alec has stated they have just a few moments left, suggests the cruelty of this doomed love which Laura also feels so deeply (Dyer 1993: 22). However, the sequence also emphasises the particularities of the station setting and introduces the various ways in which this will permeate, indeed choreograph, Alec and Laura's relationship. The overlaying of Albert and Myrtle's voices as Laura and Alec sit in quiet, restrained conversation suggests the interactions of social class which typify the railway station. Dolly's sudden interruption and imposition of her company upon the couple who are desperate to have these last moments together, reminds us of the interruptions and curtailments, through meetings, departures and journeys, which again are so central to the social spaces of the station. The station, in other words, is a place of both intimacy and interruption, private and public. We can recall those familiar images of lovers kissing on station platforms, clutching hands as trains pull slowly away to understand its potential for the intimate. Yet it is also public, open to interruptions. Again, we can recall James Scott's account of the station as a place which 'speaks of epochs of decision in life, a parting of the ways, cross-roads in conduct. Shall we embark upon this adventure; shall we definitely declare our hand; shall we make a break in habit; or a departure from principle?' (Scott 1913: 89–90). If we accept this description it becomes abundantly clear just how appropriate the railway station is for the playing out of Laura and Alec's love affair, their choice between adventure and principle.

This contrast between public and private, between the everyday or the mundane and the possibility of excitement and adventure is of course central to *Brief Encounter*. Laura leads a life of cosy domesticity, a caring and dutiful wife to her husband Fred and mother to their two children. Her weekly trips to town for library, lunch and cinema are a change from her daily chores but remain entirely normal activities for a woman of her class of the 1930s and 1940s. But of course this changes when she meets Alec and suddenly the possibility of another life is glimpsed. Nevertheless, their relationship is understated, controlled, they do not in the end give way to the passion they both clearly feel. The restrained nature of their relationship, their decent and unselfish decision to return to their respective families, is emphasised by two moments of heightened passion in the film. As Laura and Alex attend the cinema they see a trailer for the 'stupendous – colossal – gigantic' *Flames of Passion*, a film which significantly they walk out of the following week. Later in the narrative, and as Laura returns home to Fred, we see her imagining the life she might have had with Alec. Strikingly, these images of travel and adventure unroll through the windows of the train. This recalls of course that early symbiosis between train travel and the cinematic described by Lynne Kirby. But it also reminds us of the centrality of the trains and of the station both to Laura's fantasies and ultimately her decision not to pursue them.

In *Brief Encounter* the station serves as a liminal space, a place of encounter certainly, but also a place on the threshold between duty and transgression. It is the grit in the eye from the passing Express train which causes Laura to meet Alec; as she struggles with the finality of their parting it is to the Express train she rushes in a brief, and ultimately abandoned, bid for suicide. In other words the station, a place whose representations and iconography have, as we have seen, long connoted danger and passion similarly engenders passion and danger for Laura and Alec. But of course it is also a place of familiarity and safety: the refreshment room with its idle chat and urns of tea; the train that takes Laura home to Fred. This duality or liminality which we have seen to be so crucial to cultural understandings and representations of the railway station, underpins and mirrors the relationship between Alec and Laura. The station enables their passion (it is there they meet). The comings and goings of the trains and their own journeys punctuate and choreograph their affair (the train nearly missed, the smoke which engulfs Laura as she returns to the station after the daring thrill of her first lunch with Alec, the sound of a train rushing past as they share their first kiss). The station and the trains which rush through it are far more than a mere backdrop to *Brief Encounter*'s narrative of restrained passion and doomed love. Instead they both orchestrate and reflect Laura and Alec's relationship and, I would argue, are as central to the film as the two lead characters themselves. It is no accident that David Lean urged those driving trains through Carnforth station to 'really rattle through', fully ensuring the diegetic presence of the noise and the steam of those rushing trains.

Brief Encounter is, perhaps more than many others, a film which is inextricably embedded in its time. Laura's guilt and sense of duty towards her husband and family may seem quite excessive, even problematic, to a twenty-first-century audience. Yet, as Richard Dyer argues, 'many of the emotions it mobilises are not in fact things of the past: betrayal and deception, divided loyalties, the pull between safety and excitement, cosiness and abandon' (Dyer 1993: 10). Nevertheless, the film's themes of doomed romance, duty, decency and parting must have been of particular resonance to contemporary audiences deeply marked by the experiences of the Second World War. This narrative of decency, of doing what is right even in the face of overwhelming passion, lies at the very heart of the film. As Laura wakes from her memories at the end of the film, Fred remarks 'Whatever your dream was it wasn't a very happy one, was it?' For a nation attempting to return to normality at the end of the war this sad but sensible conclusion was surely immensely soothing (Richards and Mackenzie 2010: 363).

This sense of 'rightness', of a return to order, was, just like the possibility of illicit passion, fully enabled by the spaces, places and iconography of the railway station. For the railway station, particularly the station represented in Lean's film with its refreshment room full of tea urns and iced buns, the platform plastered in advertising for tobacco, soap and tea, is indeed a place of familiarity, of 'cosy normality' (Dyer 1993: 67). It is also a place of order. As Richards and Mackenzie note:

> Even if British station arrangements lacked Continental rigour, the very fact of queuing for tickets, waiting on platforms, arriving punctually, presenting and re-presenting tickets, involved submission to the company's discipline and helped to promote obedience. The world of public transport is necessarily a world of discipline for staff and passengers alike and the station symbolizes it. (2010: 103)

This order is clearly marked in *Brief Encounter* by the emphasis on time. Writing just after the film's release in 1945, Dilys Powell remarked upon the extent to which the couple's relations are ruled by the train timetable, 'They never lose the consciousness by which Bradshaw for them appoints that joy has its inexorable end' (Perry 1989: 54, cited in Dyer 1993). Richard Dyer notes that 'Time, its pressure, its fleetingness, is endlessly referenced in the film' (Dyer 1993: 45). In the opening sequence alone we see Albert checking his watch and hear Myrtle assert that 'time and tide waits for no man'. As this sequence is repeated at the end of the film, the sense of time running out is forcefully invoked as Alec says, 'We've still got a few more minutes' only to be interrupted by Dolly meaning his private time with Laura will be ended for ever. This repeated referencing of time contains and orders Laura and Alec's relations. It brings in on time the trains which will carry them back to family and duty; it brings in Dolly, who will deny them their last moments of intimacy. And so once again the absolute integrity of the station to *Brief Encounter* becomes apparent. The station with its railway time, its station clock and its timetables contains and orders the turbulence of the journeys and interactions of its visitors, in just the same way Milford Junction, so wonderfully represented by Carnforth, contains and orders Laura and Alec's passion. And through the lovers' return to duty, a return enabled by and reflected in the railway station and its well-running trains, so contemporary British audiences would themselves have enjoyed a sense of a return to order and modern audiences a nostalgic longing for the fantasy of a much simpler, more ordered past.

Writing in *The Guardian* in November 2015, John Patterson asked, '*Brief Encounter*: is it still relevant at 70?' His response was unequivocal:

> Those trains will never stop being romantic: the lovers on the platform swathed in steam; the coal speck in her eye that introduces Laura to Howard's suave doctor; the train whistle, reminiscent of a key moment in their romance, which Laura can also hear in her living room. (2015)

With this statement Patterson reminds us forcefully of the iconography of the railway station and its extraordinary cinematic qualities. These images can be recalled in a whole host of other visual and particularly cinematic representations of the station. This was a cinematic iconography, a representation and mobilisation of the places and spaces of the railway station, which was solidified in *Brief Encounter*. While many people today may suggest Lean's film when asked to name a 'railway station film', I hope this chapter has shown this iconography has a much longer visual history. And the duration of this history, the wealth of films which draw on the aesthetic and dramatic potential of the railway stations, underscores the immense cultural significance and power of this extraordinarily evocative place. That the railway station is itself a profoundly cinematic space is rather wonderfully illustrated by Carnforth station, the location for Lean's film. While trains may no longer run along its tracks nor passengers alight at its platforms, over 60,000 visitors a year arrive to admire its *Brief Encounter* displays, including continuous screenings of the film in a tiny cinema with old-fashioned red plush seats, perhaps just like those sat on by Alex and Laura during their trysts at Milford's cinema. At Carnforth, film and station have become one, nostalgia for this great work of British cinema and for the days of steam rail travel have merged. It is a wonderful symbol of the complex and rich relationship between film and railway and their shared iconographies and imaginings.

Works Cited

Anonymous (2016), 'Nostalgia, *Brief Encounter*', <https://www.lancasterguardian.co.uk/lifestyle/nostalgia/nostalgia-brief-encounter-1-7932616> (last accessed 12 August 2017).

Augé, Marc (1995), *Non-Places: Introduction to an Anthropology of Supermodernity*, trans. John Howe, London: Verso.

Carter, Ian (2001), *Railways and Culture in Britain: The Epitome of Modernity*, Manchester: Manchester University Press.
Dickens, Charles [1848] (2002), *Dombey and Son*, London: Penguin.
Dyer, Richard (1993), *Brief Encounter*, London: BFI.
Kirby, Lynne (1997), *Parallel Tracks: The Railroad and Silent Cinema*, Durham, NC: Duke University Press.
Martin, Andrew (2013), 'On the Right Track', *The Guardian*, 17 November.
Marx, Karl [1857–8] (1973), *Grundrisse*, trans. Martin Nicolaus, New York: Random House.
Massey, Doreen (2005), *For Space*, London: Sage.
Patterson, John (2015), '*Brief Encounter*: is it still relevant at 70?', *The Guardian*, 2 November <https://www.theguardian.com/film/2015/nov/02/david-lean-brief-encounter-70th-anniversary> (last accessed January 2017).
Perry, George (ed.) (1989), *The Dilys Powell Reader*, London: Pavilion.
Richards, Jeffrey and John M. Mackenzie (2010), *The Railway Station: A Social History*, London: Faber and Faber.
Schivelbusch, Wolfgang (1986), *The Railway Journey: The Industrialization of Time and Space in the Nineteenth Century*, Oakland: University of California Press.
Schivelbusch, Wolfgang (1993), *Tastes of Paradise: A Social History of Spices, Stimulants and Intoxicants*, trans. David Jacobsen, New York: Vintage.
Scott, James (1913), *Railway Romance and Other Essays*, London: Hodder and Stoughton.
Thomson, David (2010), '*Brief Encounter*: the best romantic film of all time', *The Guardian*, 16 October <https://www.theguardian.com/film/2010/oct/16/brief-encounter-romance> (last accessed April 2018).
Wells, H. G. (1902), *Anticipations*, London: Methuen.

CHAPTER 3

Diasporic Dreams and Shattered Desires: Displacement, Identity and Tradition in *Heaven on Earth*

Clelia Clini

This chapter addresses the question of travel through the analysis of Deepa Mehta's 2008 film *Heaven on Earth*. Through the narration of the journey of a young Punjabi bride from India to Canada, the film provides a critical analysis of the concept of diaspora which on the one hand emphasises the difference between 'casual travels' and diasporic journeys (Brah 1996: 182), and on the other focuses on the political, economic and cultural conditions within which people move, as well as their positions in terms of gender, race and ethnicity.

'At the heart of the notion of diaspora,' observes Avtar Brah, 'is the image of a journey' (1996: 182). Indeed, as the literal meaning of the term diaspora points to the dispersal from an original homeland (Desai 2004: 18; Tölölyan 2007: 648), it would be impossible to imagine a *static* diaspora. Images of journeys abound in cinematic representations of the Indian diaspora, be they the ones offered by Indian popular films or by Western-based South Asian[1] filmmakers.[2] And yet, if all diasporas entail travelling, not all forms of travelling qualify as diasporas. Embedded in the notion of diaspora is 'a sense of uprootedness, disconnection, loss and estrangement' (Cohen 2008: 174), the problematic of identity and the related instability of questions of home and belonging (Brah 1996: 190–5; Mishra 2007: 2; Tsagarousianou 2004: 56–60; Williams 1999). Moreover, unlike 'casual travels', diasporas are thought of, analysed and narrated as communities[3] characterised by the specificity of the circumstances which prompted their movement away from their homeland.[4] However, even though diasporic communities share some internal characteristics, they are not monolithic, homogeneous social formations. On the contrary, as Brah observes, diasporas are 'contested spaces, even as they are implicated in the construction of a common "we"' (1996: 184). As a consequence, the scholar argues, in the analysis of diasporas we should remain 'attentive to the nature and type of processes in and through which the collective "we" is constituted. Who is empowered and who is disempowered in the specific construction of the "we"?' (1996: 184; see also Hall 1993: 235). This is a question openly addressed by Deepa Mehta in *Heaven on Earth*.

Inspired by Girish Karnad's 1998 play *Naga Mandala*,[5] *Heaven on Earth* tells the story of Chand, a young middle-class Punjabi woman who happily travels to Canada to marry Rocky, a man she has never met. Rocky lives with his parents and his sister's family in a two-bedroom house in the suburbs of Toronto and, as a limousine driver, he is the main provider in the family. Overwhelmed by his family's financial difficulties, soon after the marriage Rocky begins to unleash his frustrations on Chand, who becomes the target of his violence. With no one to help her within the family, Chand finds a friend in Rosa, a Jamaican-Canadian woman who works with her and who gives her a magical root to make Rocky fall in love with her – thus putting a stop to his violence. However, unable to go through with the plan, Chand gives it up at the last minute and pours the potion in the backyard, unknowingly hitting a cobra pit. It is the cobra that then falls in love with Chand, and he begins to appear to her at night in the form of a tender and loving Rocky.[6] Unaware of the real nature of her night lover, when Chand casually mentions having spent a day off work with her husband she is accused of cheating and is asked to prove her innocence by undertaking the 'snake ordeal': she will have to put her hand in the snake pit and retrieve the cobra – if she is telling truth the snake won't bite her, but if she is lying, the snake will kill her.

By focusing on Chand's difficult transition from Punjab to Canada, *Heaven on Earth* clearly addresses the dynamics of power (referred to by Brah) that structure Chand's new family in the diasporic space. In the analysis of the film, while addressing these dynamics, I will focus in particular on their intersection with questions of gender, race, class and cultural identity. Moreover, considering that the diaspora theme is a very popular trope in Bombay cinema,[7] I will also discuss *Heaven on Earth* in relation to this film culture. The analysis is divided into four parts: by applying Hamid Naficy's theoretical discussion of accented cinema to the film, I will first locate *Heaven on Earth* in relation to both Hollywood and Bombay cinema; I will then proceed with a discussion of the film's engagement with questions of gender, cultural identity and tradition and will conclude with a reflection on the film's engagement with the question of class in the diaspora.

Locating *Heaven on Earth*: Between India and Canada

While diasporas cannot simply be equated with travelling, the meaning of diaspora, or, to borrow Pnina Werbner's words, the meaning of 'the place which is diaspora' (2002: 119) is far from fixed. In films, the meaning of the diasporic journey changes according to the filmmaker's own perspective on diaspora and to the political, economic and cultural context of production: if representations, as Stuart Hall famously argued, are never neutral (1997) then it follows that 'who represents diaspora matters' (Tölölyan 2007: 654). A case in point is the portrayal of the Indian diaspora offered by Indian popular cinema and by the films directed by Western-based diasporic filmmakers such as Mehta, who is based in Canada. Her work, as Chaudhuri points out, 'attempts to confront aspects of Indian reality left out of the domestic popular cinema' (2009: 8) but, at the same time, she also engages in a dialogue with this film culture by referencing it, borrowing from it[8] (the most notable example being her 2002 film *Bollywood/Hollywood*) and often employing established Bollywood actors, as in the case of Preity Zinta in *Heaven on Earth*. The opening scene of *Heaven on Earth*, which sees the celebration of Chand's sangeet,[9] has been seen endless times in Indian popular films. And yet, starting from what could look like a classic Bollywood wedding scene, the film takes a completely different turn, as viewers are led into the nightmare of poverty and domestic abuse.

As a film which is 'in dialogue with the home and the host society' (Naficy 2001: 6) *Heaven on Earth* can be seen as an example of accented cinema, which, according to Naficy, is also characterised by an interstitial or artisanal mode of production (2001: 46). Films made in an interstitial mode of production, according to Naficy, should not be simply defined as marginal, because 'accented filmmakers are not so much marginal or subaltern as they are interstitial, partial, and multiple – not only in terms of their identity and subjectivity but also in terms of the various roles they play in every aspect of their films' (2001: 47). And so, interstitial films often see the filmmakers themselves financing their own project, often seeking additional financing 'from a range of public and private sources' (2001: 47), which is precisely the case in *Heaven on Earth*, where Mehta is the director, writer and producer (Hamilton Mehta production) and the film is co-produced with the Canadian Broadcasting Corporation.

Another characteristic element of accented cinema is its anti-hegemonic character, a stylistic response to the experience of migration, diaspora and exile that reflects the filmmaker's 'awareness of the vast histories of the prevailing cinematic modes' as well as their 'double consciousness' (2001: 22). Seeing Mehta's personal history of migration and her extensive professional knowledge of Indian, Canadian and Hollywood cinemas (Desai 2004: 49; Khorana 2009), this description serves her well and it also emphasises the fact that her portrayal of Indian migration comes from a point of enunciation very different to that of Bollywood filmmakers.[10]

The anti-hegemonic character of *Heaven on Earth* has to be read in fact in relation to both Hollywood and Bollywood films.

According to Naficy, accented films are anti-hegemonic because they challenge dominant modes of production in terms of both narrative and style. In particular, they challenge the realism of classical Hollywood's 'invisible' style that denies authorship to convey a sense of ideological neutrality (2001: 34). Counter to classical Hollywood films, in *Heaven on Earth*, which was 'shot handheld and in 16mm' (Mehta 2008: 12), the filmmaker uses the grainy look of the film and the movement of the camera to convey a sense of realism (2008: 12–13), thus 'making a virtue' of the 'low-tech, low-velocity, almost homemade quality' of the film (Naficy 2001: 21). In its quest for authenticity, the film is also shot in Punjabi, with occasional insertions in English when the action steps outside the household (mostly the laundry factory or a local shop). This linguistic choice reflects Mehta's desire to tell a story that would resonate with the reality of the setting: the film is located in the suburbs of Brampton, a place with a very high percentage of Punjabi immigrants and where 'signs are often both in Punjabi and English' (Mehta 2008: 7). This is an important element of the film also because the choice to shoot in 'accented languages' is, for Naficy, another way to counter the hegemony of the dominant mode of production: considering that 'characters' accents are often ethnically coded' (Naficy 2001: 24), their idiom is a way to signify their difference and the interstitial position they occupy (2001: 24–5). The film's style thus aims at authenticity by foregrounding the difference that characters embody in the Canadian context.

Mehta's linguistic choice is also interesting *vis à vis* Bollywood cinema, as it represents a challenge to its dominant representation of the Indian (Punjabi) diaspora. Since the mid-1990s, Bombay films have turned their attention to the wealthy Punjabi diaspora, increasingly portrayed as the paradigm of Indian success abroad (Panda and Prasad Mishra 2012: 54). In most Bollywood films set in the diasporic space, the distinctive characteristics of the dislocated Punjabi community are de-regionalised and portrayed as pan- Indian,[11] while characters generally speak Hindi rather than Punjabi. Furthermore, in most Bollywood films characters speak Hindi both at home and at work – as they usually work with other people of Indian origin – and, as a consequence, not only are the differences within the Indian diaspora flattened out, but also the difference of the environment within which people live and work is downplayed. In addition to that, the Indian diaspora represented by Indian popular films usually belongs to the upper middle class, so that even class differences disappear from the picture (Despande 2005: 193–6). *Heaven on Earth* rewrites this narrative of Indo-Punjabi success and, by focusing on a working-class, Punjabi-speaking family, it foregrounds the element of difference within the Indian diaspora erased by Bollywood, thus providing a counter- as well as a complementary narrative to the ones offered by Hindi films. Moreover, instead of implying a continuity between the homeland and the diaspora, *Heaven on Earth* emphasises the sense of displacement that comes with migration, as evident in the title chosen for the release of the film in India: *Videsh*. If, as Vijay Mishra observes, 'the homeland in Hindi is the *desh* against which all other lands are foreign, or *videsh*' (Mishra 2007: 2), the Hindi title given to the film strengthens the sense of dislocation of the characters. This sense of dislocation is highlighted by the coldness of the environment as well as by the isolation within which the family lives and it is rendered in the film by occasional turns to black and white.

Heaven on Earth is thus an accented film that challenges the hegemony of both Hollywood and Bollywood, operating 'both within and astride the cracks of the system, benefiting from its contradictions, anomalies, and heterogeneity' (Naficy 2001: 46). Intervening in the anomalies of Indian popular film narratives, the film also establishes a dialogue with this cinematic mode of production, filling up the gaps left by Bollywood films and providing, as we shall see, alternative perspectives on key Bollywood tropes such as the stability of the traditional family system, the reproduction of gender and sexual norms and the role of tradition in the diaspora.[12]

Travelling Brides and Displaced Traditions

As an accented film 'in dialogue with the home and the host society' (Naficy 2001: 6), *Heaven on Earth*, by translating Girish Karnad's play to the suburbs of Toronto, merges the question of the married woman and of the roles imposed by society on husband and wife –which are at the heart of the play (Dahiya 2013: 1; Kumar 2003: 141; Shradda 2016: 378) – with the question of migration. This way, the film introduces a reflection on the reconfiguration of gender norms in the diasporic family as the means to reproduce traditional values in a foreign land.

Talking about the task of cultural reproduction in the diasporic context, Arjun Appadurai argues that 'as families move to new locations [. . .] debts and obligations are recalibrated, and rumours and fantasies about the new settings are manoeuvred into existing repertoires of knowledge and practice' (1996: 43–4). This existing repertoire in *Heaven on Earth* is represented in terms of Punjabi clothes and food, but, most importantly, it is the (re)production of sexual and gender norms which is taken as the symbol of cultural authenticity. As soon as Chand arrives in Brampton, it becomes very clear what her role will be within the new family: despite the seemingly nice welcome she receives at the airport, where the whole family meets her, as soon as she steps into the house – but after having given the dowry to her in-laws – she is asked to serve the drinks. It soon turns out that Rocky has already arranged a job for her in a laundry factory, indifferent to the fact that she holds a bachelor degree, and her salary is sent directly to his bank account. When she is not at work, she is expected to cook and do the housework, under the severe gaze of Rocky and of her mother in-law. She is not supposed to question or challenge her husband, and she is completely subordinated to and, with no money, also dependent on him.

Chand's experience resonates with that of several other 'travelling brides' as reported by Nicola Mooney's research on the Jat Sikh communities of Toronto and Vancouver. As Mooney points out, in the diasporic context the vulnerability of women living in a strict patriarchal system is all the more heightened because, she explains:

> Cultural practices around Punjabi marriage are what most reflect the inferior social position of women in both Sikh and Hindu communities: dowry, hypergamous marriage and patrilocal residence constitute women as subordinate, disempower them from rights over property and remove them from the comparative security of their natal homes.[13] (Mooney 2006: 396)

Moreover, according to Mooney, women are seen as the embodiment of tradition and their responsibility for the reproduction of culture is predicated in moral terms, as 'a matter of honour and shame (*izzat* and *sharam*)' (2006: 396). In this context, men's surveillance over women, and their protection, is seen as an 'assurance of family honour' as well as a way to reinforce the masculinist identity of men (2006: 396). Similarly, in *Heaven on Earth*, the reproduction of strict gender norms and the identification of women's conduct with the preservation of cultural identity are very much emphasised.

The link between gender norms, sexuality and identity has been popularised, in India, since the emergence of anti-colonial nationalism, which emphasised the role of women as the 'repositories and transmitters of Indian culture' (Das 2012: 60). If woman is the symbol of national identity, the metaphor of the Motherland, then her purity needs to be preserved[14] (Chatterjee 1993: 120–1; Dwyer 2000: 130–1; Gopinath 1997: 467–8), all the more in a foreign environment. As a consequence, Desai argues, 'diasporas maintain and consolidate connections and imaginings of the homeland by performing national identities through gender and sexual normativities' (2004: 30). The association of gender and sexual norms with cultural identity is a popular theme in Bombay films, where, for decades, the preservation of cultural identity abroad has been linked to the sexual purity of the Indian woman, so that her chastity (or lack thereof) becomes the ultimate indicator of cultural authenticity (Desai 2004: 133–5; Gangoli 2005; Mankekar 1999: 738–42; Moodley 2003: 68). Instead, in *Heaven on Earth* the reproduction of gender and sexual norms as a way to preserve cultural identity is not accepted at face value but is problematised. As the adaptation of a play that criticises the rigidly gendered roles imposed by society (Dahiya 2013: 2), the film produces in fact a critique of patriarchy which is addressed both at the diaspora and the homeland.

It is especially through the representation of domestic violence that the film reinforces the perception of the inferior social position occupied by women in the Punjabi marriage mentioned by Mooney. Even if Rocky is the one who beats up Chand, the silence of his entire family normalises his actions, as if they were part of his prerogatives as a husband. The only two characters who mention Rocky's abusive behaviour are his sister and his mother, and they both dismiss it: Aman casually defends Rocky by saying that he, in reality, is a good man, and she also asks Chand to conceal her bruises with some make-up. His mother, on the other hand, is rather satisfied at her son's brutal treatment of Chand (she constantly winds him up against her) and, when Chand cries, she urges her not to because '[hitting spouses] is a common thing'. Strict gender norms also prevent Chand from calling the police: denouncing domestic abuse would mean dishonouring the family, as Aman reminds Chand when she points out to her that in their community they 'deal with problems in house'.

Exposing the isolation of the victim and the silence surrounding spousal abuse within South Asian immigrant households is a way for Mehta to give voice to the silenced bride. As Desai argues, filmmakers such as Mehta, by depicting 'these particular embodied experiences of violence rely on the cinematic apparatus and its significant role in the diaspora. The visuality of the film provides a site for intervention according to the filmmakers' (Desai 2004: 148). Indeed, the lack of appropriate intervention when it comes to domestic violence is a cause of concern for Mehta, who observed that 'an Asian woman will never call 911. There is a question of losing one's dignity. It's shameful, so the government has no clue how to deal with them'[15] (Khorana 2009). But Mehta breaks the silence around domestic abuse and also, as previously mentioned, questions the role of tradition in the perpetration of this violence. As she observes:

> The dynamics of immigration really turn the values that felt right at home and were working back home upside down. So the dynamics of the household change, and you

want to maintain them but you can't. The stress trying to maintain something that is non-existent and doesn't work for you shows on a woman first, but that does not mean that men aren't victims as well. (Khorana 2009)

Mehta's reflections are of particular importance because they pave the way for a critique of patriarchy which considers its detrimental effects on men as well as women. This is a point that she develops from Karnad's play, which provides 'a very sensitive take on men's circumscriptions by patriarchal codes' (Mohan 2009: 9; see also Dahiya 2013: 2). The fact that the husband in Karnad's play is named Apanna, which means 'any man' (Collelmir 2006: 3), seems to suggest that his situation is really a metaphor for the condition of men in general. In the film, both Baldev (Rocky's brother-in-law) and Rocky, even if for different reasons, feel the pressure of patriarchal norms. Baldev, who, unlike Rocky, is a caring husband and father, is unemployed and, despite the fact that he had been the one who sponsored them to get to Canada, is now dependent on his wife's family. As he (unwillingly) contravenes the gender norms of patriarchy he feels useless, as he clearly explains when he says that: 'a man who is dependent on his in-laws is worse than a dog'. Rocky too feels the burden of the expectations held upon him but, unlike Baldev, reacts violently. However, he is not portrayed as a straightforwardly violent character: the first time he meets Chand he shyly greets her, unable to look her in the eyes, and on their honeymoon night he seems on the verge of opening up to her when she asks him about his life. It is nevertheless on that very same night that he first hits Chand, after his mother interrupts their honeymoon. Frustrated at his mother, who interrupted what would have been their first sexual intercourse, but, at the same time, unable to tell her off because of his duties as a son, he lashes out at Chand when she suggests that, instead of going to sleep in the car with Baldev (and letting her sleep with his mother), they could rent another room. Rocky's mother's comment that that was the first time she had ever seen a hotel room reinforces the perception that Rocky is crushed under the burden of financial difficulties and familial obligations. His anxiety is especially heightened by his overbearing mother, who constantly asks him to earn enough money to sponsor his other brother to Canada and, simultaneously, winds him up against Chand. Just like Apanna, Rocky seems to be the 'slave' of patriarchal culture (Shradda 2016: 382) and his violence against Chand is the expression of his repressed anger. The film thus supports Appadurai's observation that in migratory contexts women 'become the pawns in the heritage politics of the household and are often subjected to the abuse and violence of men who are themselves torn about the relation between heritage and opportunity in shifting spatial and political formations' (Appadurai 1996: 44). It is important to note here that, in portraying Rocky as a victim of patriarchy, Mehta does not try to justify his violence, but to contextualise it.

The Subversive Power of Tradition

If, as suggested, within the diasporic household the maintenance of tradition is mostly concerned with the reproduction of sexual and gender norms and of men's surveillance over women, it is this practice which eventually liberates Chand. Extremely lonely and convinced that, if only she could make Rocky love her, her situation would improve, Chand accepts Rosa's help and decides to prepare a love potion for her husband. At this point the film unexpectedly shifts to magical realism with the introduction of a cobra living in the snowy Canadian landscape and which, hit by Chand's potion, falls in love with her.

The motif of the 'snake lover' is 'widespread in popular Indian narrative' (Kakar 1990: 52) and Karnad's play, upon which *Heaven on Earth* is based, is in fact inspired by two oral folktales from Karnataka (Mohan 2009: 2). As Kakar observes, snake myths abound in Hindu mythology and religion:

> In literature, folklore, myth, ritual, and art, the snake, and especially the cobra (*nag*) plays a prominent role in Hindu culture. Born of one of the daughters of Prajapati, the Lord of Creation, snakes are carried by Shiva, the Destroyer, around his neck and arms, while there is no more popular representation of Vishnu, the preserver of Hindu trinity, than of his reposing on the Sesha, the seven-headed cobra. Sculpted into the reliefs of Buddhist, Jain and Hindu temples, snakes, both single and entwined, are a ubiquitous presence in Indian sacred space. (Kakar 1990: 52)

The popularity of snakes resides in the fact that they are 'regarded as guardians of the life-giving powers of the waters in springs, pools and wells' (Sullivan 1997: 144) and have therefore been worshipped in India for centuries for 'fertility, prosperity and the healing of illness' (1997: 144). In Hindu mythology Lord Shiva, 'the most powerful Hindu god', according to Mehta (2008: 5) is traditionally represented with the king cobra Vasuki around his neck and he is known for granting 'anything to his devotees and worshippers' (Kumar 2003: 141).

As the film focuses on a Sikh and not a Hindu family, Mehta has made some changes to the narrative so as to maintain the centrality of the snake myth within the story. Not only has she translated Karnad's play into Punjabi,[16] but she has also adapted it to the new context by adding explicit references to Sikhism in the snake-centred tale that Chand's mother mentions on the morning of Chand's departure and that, it appears, she has told her numerous times since Chand was a child. As she associates it with her childhood and with her mother, Chand sees in the snake a reassuring figure and so, as a means to counter her loneliness, she invents a story for herself on her arrival in Canada in which she imagines being rescued by a king cobra. Every scene of violence is followed by a moment in which Chand tells herself a little bit of this story, which progresses until the cobra finally reunites her with her mother.

And the snake does indeed come to Chand's rescue when he falls in love with her. Assuming Rocky's form – 'I am a serpent but not just a serpent', a voiceover says as the snake enters Chand's room – the serpent begins to visit Chand at night, and really anytime Rocky is not around, and he grants her all the love she has been craving. As the boundary between reality and fantasy blurs, it is not clear – not to the viewer, nor to Chand – whether her loving husband is a figment of her imagination or whether he really is Rocky. The cobra functions here as Rocky's double, as he is exactly what Rocky is not, or cannot be, given the 'rigid system of masculinity' he seems to be entrapped in (Mohan 2009: 9). If the real Rocky brutalises and imprisons Chand in a life she did not want, it is the cobra that allows Chand to break free. Following an attack from Rocky, one morning Chand is too battered to go to work and calls in sick. Once she is left alone in the house the cobra turns up in her bedroom and tenderly consoles her, but they are not alone in the house: during the day Rocky's family rents out the house to two (unseen) tenants and Chand informs them that she will stay in her room for the day and that her husband is looking after her. However, later on Rocky is livid at hearing that she 'pretended' to be with him in their bedroom. He thus furiously beats her up and accuses her of cheating. With the whole family against her, Chand is challenged by her mother-in-law to swear on a burning iron, as 'their traditions prescribe' (she says), to prove her innocence. Tradition, once again, is invoked to police the sexual conduct of women, as this scene is a clear reference to Sita's trial in the *Ramayana*, when she undergoes the fire trial to prove her purity.[17] But it is precisely the reproduction of tradition which, this time, liberates Chand.

After she unsuccessfully pleads with Rocky that she is innocent, once again Chand is visited by the cobra/Rocky, and it is he who suggests to her that she take the snake ordeal instead. She is then led to the garden where, in front of the whole family, she puts her hand in the anthill to retrieve the cobra. As she successfully holds the cobra in her hands and wraps it around her neck, an aura of light surrounds her head, making her look like a female version of Lord Shiva, and the family watches in awe while she swears on the snake that she 'has only touched her husband and that cobra with her hands'. Just like Sita, through the trial Chand acquires a new goddess-like status, and it is at this point that, finally empowered, she takes her passport and leaves. Following *Naga Mandala* then, in *Heaven on Earth* tradition is invoked to produce a 'demystification of dominant beliefs and practices' (Collellmir 2006: 1), for, instead of subjugating Chand, tradition is the instrument of her empowerment. The irony of Chand's success lies in the fact that the very ritual that was conjured to ostracise her, leads to her 'mystic elevation':

> As a test of her chastity, the trial defeats the purpose for which it was devised in the first place. The snake ordeal mocks the classic Hindu mythic chastity test, the test of truth. In the *Ramayana*, Sita comes through the ordeal of fire because she *is* truly chaste and faithful. In Karnad's play, the woman comes through the ordeal of handling a venomous snake only because the snake is her lover. (Mohan 2009: 9)

The reproduction of the snake ordeal in the film remains true to Girish Karnad's take on folk theatre, which, he argued in his introduction to *Three Plays*: 'although it seems to uphold traditional values, it also has the meaning of questioning those values, of making them literally stand on their head' (Karnad 1999: 14, quoted in Collellmir 2006: 2). Furthermore, the snake myth reference in the story serves the purpose of challenging sexual and gender normativities, because, even if unwittingly, Chand has indeed been unfaithful to Rocky and it is her lover, the cobra, which gives Chand 'the chance to choose and achieve liberation' (Collellmir 2006: 7).

If *Heaven on Earth* faithfully reproduces the subverting character of Karnad's play, it also takes a step further by having Chand leave Rocky. In *Naga Mandala* in fact, Rani, after the trial, remains with Appana. Moreover, if in Mehta's film Chand's infidelity is exposed by their tenants, in Karnad's play it is Rani's pregnancy that makes Appana realise that she must have slept with someone else. These are two important differences because, as Mohan observes, as much as Karnad's play 'makes a mockery of the misogyny and male-centredness of the patriarchal system, as also the exaggerated male claims and ambitions to control female sexuality [. . .] it is not disruptive of entrenched oppressive structures' (Mohan 2009: 13). The fact that the play closes with the restoration of the heteronormative order and the birth of a son somehow downplays the subversive nature of the story, as it is not only Rani's successful trial, but also her pregnancy, that saves her from the abuses of her husband. As Sudhir Kakar observed, in fact: 'the status of motherhood [. . .] for an Indian girl consolidates her identity as a woman and can mean a significant improvement in the politics of a joint family' (Kakar 1990: 58).

In Mehta's film instead, the entire status quo is challenged: by the end of the film Chand has developed her own agency and breaks with Rocky and his family, thus breaking with the strict patriarchal norms they uphold. What is most subversive about her story is the fact that it is tradition, in the form of the trial, that is the instrument through which Chand recovers her own agency. Following Naficy, we can say that Chand, by the end of the film, has undergone two kinds of journey: the first one is the diasporic journey to Brampton, while the second is a 'journey of identity', a metaphorical journey that has brought about significant changes within the character of Chand (Naficy 2001: 21), allowing her to grow and develop her own agency. Through the story of Chand Mehta thus simultaneously questions the patriarchal character of the Indian family and its reproduction in the diasporic setting. In the process, she also provides a contribution to the debate over the notion of diaspora and the diasporic journey.

Diaspora, Travels and Transnational Mobility: The Working-class Experience

A final aspect of the film that is worth focusing upon – and which is a key component of Chand's journey – is the socio-economic context within which her joint family lives. As Mehta explained, one of the aims of the film was to explore 'the reality of dislocation; the effect that immigration has on people who leave their native land to come to Canada in search of monetary security and instead find themselves living on the fringes, trying desperately to simulate elements of their homeland in isolation from the mainstream' (2008: 12). The low socio-economic condition of the family is strongly connected to the politics of the household.

Despite the fact that Rocky and his family have been living in Canada for years, they appear isolated from the broader context within which they live: apart from a few friends of Rocky seen only the night before Chand's arrival, no one seems to have any meaningful relationship outside the family. The film suggests that their isolation is a consequence of their precarious financial conditions as in fact, busy as they are in trying to make ends meet, they do not have time for a social life, nor could they afford it. If, as Brah posits, 'the question of home is intrinsically linked with the way in which processes of inclusion and exclusion operate and are subjectively experienced under given circumstances' (1996: 192), the isolation of the family makes it hard for them to develop a sense of belonging, which explains why they hold on to their homeland by recreating its traditions in the diasporic space. The emphasis on their working-class background is of particular relevance because it not only, as previously mentioned, provides a counter-representation to the ones offered by Bollywood films, it also promotes a reflection on diaspora which foregrounds the need to focus on the material reality of displacement, as mentioned by Mehta. This way, the film explores the tension between the literal and the metaphorical understanding of the notion of diaspora.

Besides indicating the lived experiences of people in motion, the literal experience of displacement, the notion of diaspora is also used metaphorically as a critical tool to challenge the alleged boundedness of culture and identity through its emphasis on processes of adaptation, translation and hybridisation (Hall 1993, Gilroy 1993, Bhabha 1994). With globalisation and the growing mobility of the twenty-first century, the metaphorical understanding of the term has gained prominence especially in discourses on globalisation and mobility, so that, as Tölölyan argues, diasporas have come to be 'celebrated as exemplars or advocates of penetrated and porous borders, heterogeneity, hybridity, and, importantly, mobility' (Tölölyan 2007: 653). Vijay Mishra too observes that diasporas are often celebrated as 'the exemplary condition of late modernity [. . .] fluid, ideal, social formations happy to live wherever there is an international airport and stand for a longer, much admired, historical process' (Mishra 2007: 1). Diasporic subjects have thus become 'travellers on the move' (2007: 4), the symbol of transnational mobility. The problematic attachment of assumptions of 'easy mobility for all' with discussion of diasporas (Tölölyan 2007: 654) fully emerges once we focus on the specific social, economic and political conditions of mobility.

Heaven on Earth clearly shows how not all diasporic subjects are hyper-mobile and cosmopolitan. Despite its journey across continents to reach Canada, Rocky's family is excluded from the hypermobility of the transnational, postmodern subject, and no pleasure is involved in their diasporic journey. This is a point clearly expressed by Rocky during his two-day honeymoon to Niagara Falls: enchanted by the view, Chand asks him to take a photograph, to which he replies, coldly, that 'photos are for tourists'. If tourism is commonly understood as a celebration of choice (Kaplan 1996: 27) this brief exchange between the couple expresses vividly Rocky's perception that life, for him and Chand, is not a matter of choice. Rocky and Chand's journey has nothing to do with the culture of leisure and consumption usually associated with tourism (1996: 5), nor with the 'safety' of the tourist, who has the chance to immerse himself in a 'strange and bizarre element' aware of the fact that it will only be a temporary experience (Bauman 1996: 29). More, Rocky and Chand's journey has nothing to do with the celebrated fluidity of the border zone they occupy. This is quite an important point because it is connected to Brah's warning that we should always be aware of the social, economic and political conditions of the people who travel (Brah 1996: 182). Against utopian celebrations of diaspora that, in Mark Shackleton's words, too often 'forget the sufferings of the underprivileged and do not pay sufficient attention to the historical, geographical and political contexts' within which the movement of people takes place (2008: ix), *Heaven on Earth* highlights the material realities of displacement and shows how they influence the way in which diasporic subjects structure their lives in the diaspora. In so doing, the film draws attention to the unequal dynamics of power, of inclusion and exclusion that characterise the diasporic space, and emphasises the connection between questions of class, gender and ethnicity.

Excluded from dreams of upward mobility paradigmatic of the transnational postmodern, Rocky's family, rather than embodying hyper-mobile cosmopolitan subjects, resembles the proletarian diaspora, 'the disadvantaged product of modernized polities' mentioned by Armstrong (1976: 393), as it is clear that the low socio-economic status of the family determines its exclusion from the celebrated 'liberatory effects of dispersion' (Parry 2004: 100). Moreover, by addressing the material conditions of the displaced diasporic family the film also emphasises that, as Mishra observes, 'contrary to idealist formulations about diasporas', they are also 'bastions of reactionary thinking' (2007: 17, see also Werbner 2002: 120), as seen in the way in which the family reproduces tradition in the diasporic space.

Conclusion

To conclude, *Heaven on Earth* offers a representation of the diasporic experience that counters popular celebrations of 'the massive immigration of the twentieth century as a hybridising phenomenon that eradicates monolithic notions of identity' (Behdad 2005: 402) emphasising how, as Behdad points out, many 'underclass migrants' are caught 'in the tail-spin of a globalization that has taken them away from their hopes for upward mobility into a state of economic and political disenfranchisement' (2005: 403).

An intersectional approach that jointly considers questions of race, class and gender is imperative here, as the film tackles questions of inclusion and exclusion in the diasporic space which cut across these signifiers. Similarly to the representation of the diasporic family that is common in contemporary European cinema, in *Heaven on Earth* 'the domestic space' becomes 'a symbolic [. . .] battleground onto which social conflicts are displaced' (Berghahn 2013: 11), as violence is in fact located in the context of the dislocation, isolation and emotional stress of a life at the margins (Mehta 2008: 13). Chand's exclusion both from society and her new family is portrayed as the consequence on the one hand of the low socio-economic status of the family, and on the other of the strict patriarchal norms which govern the household, where violence is justified as an expression of tradition. The film explores the problematic notion of tradition as it turns it from a constraining into a liberating force. Chand's journey to Brampton is, as already mentioned, also a journey towards self-awareness and empowerment, which will lead her to question, and finally challenge, the patriarchal traditions upheld by Rocky and his family.

Heaven on Earth emphasises the complex character of the diasporic journey because it simultaneously addresses the trauma of displacement and it shows how diasporas 'are also potentially the sites of hope and new beginnings' (Brah 1996: 193). The film thus serves as a reminder that diasporas 'are contested cultural and political terrains where individual and collective memories collide, reassemble and reconfigure' (1996: 193).

Notes

1 The term 'South Asian' is used here to refer to those filmmakers whose families left India prior to Partition, the division of British India into the two independent states of India and Pakistan (as in the case of Gurinder Chadha). See Desai 2004: 6.
2 See for example Mira Nair's *Mississippi Masala* (1991) and *The Namesake* (2006), Gurinder Chadha's *Bhaji on The Beach* (1993) and *Bend it Like Beckham* (2002), Srinivas Krishna's *Masala* (1991) and Aditya Chopra's *Dilwale Dulhania Le Jayenge* (1995), Karan Johar's *Kabhi Khushi Kabhie Gham* (2001) and *Happy Ending* (Raj Nidimoru and Krishna D. K., 2014), for Bollywood films.
3 Both Tsagarousianou and Naficy insist on the horizontal character of the diasporic consciousness: a collective sense of identity which involves not only the original homeland but also other 'compatriot communities elsewhere' (Naficy 2001: 14; Tsagarousianou 2004: 59–60). For a detailed analysis of the notion of diaspora see Cohen 2008, Brah 1996, Clifford 1992, Gilroy 1993, Hall 1993, Safran 1991.
4 In this respect Appadurai talks of 'diasporas of hope, diasporas of terror and diasporas of despair' (1996: 6).
5 Girish Karnad is a famous Indian playwright and writer (predominantly in the Kannada language) and also an actor and director in both the Hindi and the Kannada film industry.
6 Andrews explains how 'in the myths of India and southeast Asia, nagas were serpents who inhabited rivers and pools and the waters believed to exist beneath the earth. The Nagas of Indian myth appeared either as cobras or

as half cobras, and they had the ability to change forms at will' (1998: 135). See also Sullivan 1997: 144.

7 Bombay cinema and Bollywood are two overlapping but not identical terms. They both reference the Indian popular film industry, are in Hindi and based in Mumbai (former Bombay), but there are important different nuances to the terms. While Bombay cinema refers to the output of the Indian popular film industry since its early days, the term Bollywood is most commonly used to refer to the films produced since the mid-1990s, when the Bombay film industry began to acquire a quite strong transnational character (in terms of production, distribution, funding and narratives). The term also refers to the transnational culture industry that has emerged, in those very same years, around films (see Prasad 2008: 43–4; Rajadhyaksha 2003: 30; Punathambekar 2013: 1–2). In this context, Bollywood will be used strictly in reference to films produced since the second half of the 1990s. For a more detailed discussion of the debate over the term Bollywood see also Mishra 2006, Dudrah 2012, Thomas 2013, Vasudevan 2008.

8 See Jigna Desai, 'Homo on the Range', in *Beyond Bollywood*, 2004, pp. 159–91.

9 The sangeet is a pre-wedding celebration which involves only women. Mehta compares it to a bachelorette party (2008: 2).

10 While Mehta fits in with Naficy's profile of the accented filmmaker, she does not only make accented films. If her personal experience locates her in a specific position of enunciation when it comes to diaspora, this position does not 'contain her', to borrow a felicitous expression from Stuart Hall (Hall 1996: 169).

11 Mishra for example draws the attention to the popularisation of the Karva Chauth fast (Mishra 2002: 256).

12 On the centrality of the Indian diaspora in Bollywood see Prasad 2008, Rajadhyaksha 2003. On the centrality of sexual and gender norms in Bollywood diaspora films see Brosius and Yazgi 2007, Mankekar 1999, Mehta 2005, Sharpe 2005.

13 On Indian immigrant women perceived as the repositories of an essential 'Indianness' see also Bhattacharjee 1992.

14 See also Rachel Dwyer's genealogy of the most prominent theories on love in the West and in India, where she traces the roots of the idea of the Indian family as based on the control over women in Indian religious and mythological literature (2000, 8–57).

15 On the problematic silence which surrounds domestic abuse among diasporic communities and the difficulty of state politics in dealing with it, see also Desai 2004: 147–9.

16 In her notes to the making of the film, Mehta explains that the idea to use the play Naga-Mandala to tackle migration and the condition of the woman within marriage came after she saw the Punjabi version of the play, directed by Neelam Mansingh Chowdhry (2008: 8).

17 Referenced by Mehta also in *Fire*. See Desai 2004: 239.

Works Cited

Andrews, Tamra (1998), *Dictionary of Nature Myths: Legends of the Earth, Sea, and Sky*, Oxford: Oxford University Press.

Appadurai, Arjun (1996), *Modernity al Large: Cultural Dimensions of Globalization*, Minneapolis and London: University of Minnesota Press.

Armstrong, John A. (1976), 'Mobilized and Proletarian Diasporas', *The American Political Science Review*, 70:2, pp. 393–408.

Bauman, Zygmunt (1996), 'From Pilgrim to Tourist – or a Short History of Identity', in S. Hall and P. du Gay (eds), *Questions of Cultural Identity*, London: Sage, pp. 18–36.

Behdad, Ali [2000] (2005), 'Global Disjunctives, Diasporic Differences, and the Global (Dis-)Order', in H. Schwarz and S. Ray (eds), *A Companion to Postcolonial Studies*, Oxford: Blackwell, pp. 396–409.

Berghahn, Daniela (2013), *Far-Flung Families in Film: The Diasporic Family in Contemporary European Cinema*, Edinburgh: Edinburgh University Press.

Bhabha, Homi K. (1994), *The Location of Culture*, London and New York: Routledge.

Bhattacharjee, Anannya (1992), 'The habit of ex-nomination: Nation, Woman, and the Indian Immigrant Bourgeoisie', *Public Culture*, 5, pp. 34–5.

Brah, Avtar (1996), *Cartographies of Diaspora: Contesting Identities*, London: Routledge.

Brosius, Christiane and Yazgi, Nicolas (2007), 'Is there no place like home? Contesting cinematographic constructions of Indian diasporic experiences', *Contributions to Indian Sociology*, 41:3, pp. 355–86.

Chatterjee, Partha (1993), *The Nation and its Fragments: Colonial and Postcolonial History*, Delhi: Oxford University Press.

Chaudhuri, Shohini (2009), 'Snake charmers and child brides: Deepa Mehta's *Water*, "exotic" representation, and the cross-cultural spectatorship of South Asian migrant cinema', *South Asian Popular Culture*, 7:1, pp. 7–20.

Clifford, James (1992), 'Travelling Cultures', in L. Grossberg, C. Nelson and P. Treichler (eds), *Cultural Studies*, New York: Routledge, pp. 96–116.

Cohen, Robin (2008), *Global Diasporas: An Introduction*, 2nd edn, London: Routledge.

Collellmir, Dolors (2006), 'Mythical Structure in Girish Karnad's Play *Naga-Mandala*', *BELLS: Barcelona English Language and Literature Studies*, vol. 15 <http://www.raco.cat/index.php/Bells/article/view/82962> (last accessed 25 June 2016).

Dahiya, Jyoti (2013), 'Naga-Mandala: A Story of Marriage and Love', *Galaxy: International Multidisciplinary Research Journal*, II:V, pp. 1–4.

Das, Ashidhara (2012), *Desi Dreams: Indian Immigrant Women Build Lives Across Two Worlds*, Delhi: Primus Books.

Desai, Jigna (2004), *Beyond Bollywood: The Cultural Politics of South Asian Diasporic Film*, London: Routledge.

Despande, Sudhanva (2005), 'The Consumable Hero of Globalized India', in R. Kaur and A. Sinha (eds), *Bollyworld: Popular Indian Cinema Through a Transnational Lens*, New Delhi: Sage, pp. 186–20.

Dudrah, Rajinder (2012), *Bollywood Travels: Culture, Diaspora and Border Crossings in Popular Hindi Cinema*, New York: Routledge.

Dwyer, Rachel (2000), *All You Want is Money, All You Need is Love: Sexuality and Romance in Modern India*, London: Cassell.

Gangoli, Geetanjali (2005), 'Sexuality, Sensuality and Belonging: Representation of the "Anglo-Indian" and the "Western" Woman in Hindi Cinema', in R. Kaur and A. Sinha (eds), *Bollyworld: Popular Indian Cinema Through a Transnational Lens*, New Delhi: Sage, pp. 143–62.

Gilroy, Paul (1993), *The Black Atlantic: Identity and Double Consciousness*, London: Verso.

Gopinath, Gayatri (1997), 'Nostalgia, Desire, Diaspora: South Asian Sexualities in Motion', *Positions: East Asia Cultures Critique*, 5:2, pp. 467–90.

Hall, Stuart (1993), 'Cultural Identity and Diaspora', in J. Rutherford (ed.), *Identity: Community, Culture, Difference*, London: Lawrence & Wishart, pp. 222–37.

Hall, Stuart (1996), 'New Ethnicities', in H. A. Baker, M. Diawara and R. H. Lindeborg (eds), *Black British Cultural Studies: A Reader*, Chicago: University of Chicago Press, pp. 163–72.

Hall, Stuart (1997), 'The Work of Representation', in S. Hall (ed.), *Representations: Cultural Representations and Signifying Practices*, London: Sage, pp. 1–74.

Kakar, Sudhir (1990), *Intimate Relations: Exploring Indian Sexuality*, Chicago: University of Chicago Press.

Kaplan, Caren (1996), *Questions of Travel: Postmodern Discourses of Displacement*, Durham, NC: Duke University Press.

Karnad, Girish (1999), *Three Plays: Naga-Mandala, Hayavadana, Tughlaq*, New Delhi: Oxford University Press.

Khorana, Sukhmani (2009), 'Maps and movies: talking with Deepa Mehta', *Bright Lights Film Journal*, 63, <http://ro.uow.edu.au/cgi/viewcontent.cgi?article=1397&context=asdpapers> (last accessed 12 June 2016).

Kumar, Nand (2003), *Indian English Drama: A Study in Myths*, New Delhi: Sarup & Sons.

Mankekar, Purnima (1999), 'Brides Who Travel: Gender, Transnationalism, and Nationalism in Hindi Film', *Positions*, 7:3, Winter 1999, pp. 731–61.

Mehta, Deepa (2008), 'Heaven on Earth: Director's Notes', *Mongrel Media*, pp. 1–35, <https://s3.amazonaws.com/cdn.filmtrackonline.com/mongrelmedia/starcm_vault_root/images%2Ffiles%2F40%2F400f86c9-eac5-44ab-92fe-f4fb780eca49.pdf> (last accessed 10 May 2018).

Mehta, Monika (2005), 'Globalizing Bombay Cinema: Reproducing the Indian State and Family', *Cultural Dynamics*, 17:2, pp. 135–54.

Mishra, Vijay (2002), *Bollywood Cinema: Temples of Desire*, New York: Routledge.

Mishra, Vijay (2006), 'Bollywood Cinema: A Critical Genealogy', *Working Paper 20*, Asian Studies Institute, Victoria University of Wellington,

<http://researcharchive.vuw.ac.nz/bitstream/handle/10063/4254/paper.pdf?sequence=2> (last accessed 10 July 2016).

Mishra, Vijay (2007), *The Literature of the Indian Diaspora: Theorizing the Diasporic Imaginary*, London and New York: Routledge.

Mohan, Anupama (2009), 'Girish Karnad's Naga-mandala: Problematising Feminism', *Intersections: Gender and Sexuality in Asia and the Pacific*, 22, <http://intersections.anu.edu.au/issue22/mohan.htm> (last accessed 2 June 2016).

Moodley, Subeshini (2003), 'Postcolonial Feminisms Speaking Through an "Accented" Cinema: The Construction of Indian Women in the Films of Mira Nair and Deepa Mehta', *Agenda: Empowering Women for Gender Equity*, 58, pp. 66–75.

Mooney, Nicola (2006), 'Aspiration, reunification and gender transformation in Jat Sikh marriages from India to Canada', *Global Networks*, 6:4, pp. 389–403.

Naficy, Hamid (2001), *An Accented Cinema: Exilic and Diasporic Filmmaking*, Princeton: Princeton University Press.

Panda, Punyashree and Prasad Mishra, Minakshi (2012), 'The Punjab of Bollywood versus the Punjab of Newspapers: Taking Stock of the Contemporary Image of Punjab in Different Media', *SEARCH: A Journal of Arts, Humanities & Management*, II, pp. 52–9.

Parry, Benita (2004), *Postcolonial Studies: A Materialist Critique*, London and New York: Routledge.

Prasad, Madhava (2008), 'Surviving Bollywood', in A. Kavoori and A. Punathambekar (eds), *Global Bollywood*, New York: New York University Press, pp. 41–51.

Punathambekar, Aswin (2013), *From Bombay to Bollywood: The Making of a Global Media Industry*, New York: New York University Press.

Rajadhyaksha, Ashish (2003), 'The "Bollywoodization" of the Indian Cinema: Cultural Nationalism in a Global Arena', *InterAsia Cultural Studies*, 28, pp. 25–39.

Safran, William (1991), 'Diaspora in Modern Societies: Myths of Homelands and Return', *Diaspora*, 1:1, pp. 83–99.

Shackleton, Mark (2008), 'Introduction', in M. Shackleton (ed.), *Diasporic Literature and Theory – Where Now?*, Newcastle Upon Tyne: Cambridge Scholars, pp. ix–xiv.

Sharpe, Jenny (2005), 'Gender, Nation and Globalization in Monsoon Wedding and Dilwale Dulhania Le Jayenge', *Meridians: Feminism, Race, Transnationalism*, 6:1, pp. 58–81.

Shradda (2016), 'A Feminist Critique of Girish Karnad's Naga-Mandala', *International Journal of English Language, Literature and Humanities*, IV:II, pp. 377–85.

Sullivan, Bruce M. (1997), *Historical Dictionary of Hinduism*, Lanham: Scarecrow Press.

Thomas, Rosie (2013), *Bombay Before Bollywood: Film City Fantasies*, Albany: SUNY Press.

Tölölyan, Khachig (2007), 'The Contemporary Discourse of Diaspora Studies', *Comparative Studies of South Asia, Africa and the Middle East*, 27:3, pp. 647–55.

Tsagarousianou, Roza (2004), 'Rethinking the concept of diaspora: mobility, connectivity and communication in a globalised world', *Westminster Papers in Communication and Culture*, 1:1, pp. 52–65.

Vasudevan, Ravi (2008), 'The Meanings of "Bollywood"', *Journal of the Moving Image*, 7 <http://jmionline.org/articles/2008/the_meanings_of_bollywood.pdf> (last accessed 12 February 2011).

Werbner, Pnina (2002), 'The Place which is Diaspora: Citizenship, Religion and Gender in the Making of Chaordic Transnationalism', *Journal of Ethnic and Migration Studies*, 28:1, pp. 119–34.

Williams, Brownyn T. (1999), '"A State of Perpetual Wandering": Diaspora and Black British Writers', *JOUVERT: A Journal of Postcolonial Studies*, <http://english.chass.ncsu.edu/jouvert/v3i3/willia.htm> (last accessed 10 May 2015).

CHAPTER 4

Chronotopic Ghosts and Quiet Men: José Luis Guerín's *Innisfree*

Michael Pigott

In 1988 José Luis Guerín took a film crew from Spain to the western coast of Ireland, in search of the filming locations of John Ford's *The Quiet Man* (1952). The resultant film, *Innisfree* (1990), blends documentary with fiction, and the present with the past, to seemingly uncover the physical, cultural and spectral remnants of the Hollywood production in this small rural locality. *Innisfree* is both the product of a journey (the Spanish filmmaker's fannish field trip) and the representation of several journeys and returns. This essay will examine Guerín's depiction of the ghostly persistence of *The Quiet Man* in the landscape, by using Mikhail Bakhtin's concept of the chronotope to identify the lasting significance of real and imagined time-spaces in the cinematic landscape. Just as immigrant Irishman Sean Thornton (John Wayne) returns to his spiritual homeland from Pittsburgh, USA to reclaim his family land, Ford himself returns to the land of his parents' birth. In *Innisfree* Thornton's, Ford's and Guerín's imagined Irelands all mingle and intertwine in a confusing crossroads of time, fiction, memory and landscape.

Fragments

The narrative and temporal structure of *Innisfree* is complex. Its form defeats conventional, linear, coherent approaches to critical analysis. Therefore, this essay will adopt something of the lane-hopping, time-travelling, fragmentary structure of the film. It calls for a mixture of rudimentary, pragmatic analysis and impressionistic theory. Perhaps we should begin with the former. We might identify the main timelines and storylines as follows:

a. 1988, the present day of the production, when the Spanish film crew document the people, places and customs of Cong, Co. Galway, Ireland.

b. 1951, the shooting of *The Quiet Man* in Cong and other locations around the west of Ireland, encountered through behind-the-scenes and personal photographs, and the recounted tales and memories of the Cong residents.
c. 1927, the Inisfree of *The Quiet Man*, a forged geography constructed of a variety of locations around Cong. Sean Thornton (John Wayne), an Irish immigrant, returns from Pittsburgh after killing a man in the boxing ring. He seeks a peaceful life in the family home his mother spoke of. He falls in love with local woman Mary-Kate Danaher (Maureen O'Hara) but her brother 'Red' Will proves to be an obstacle to their happiness.
d. The tale of Captain Webb, a highwayman who murdered his wives by throwing them into a deep hole in the forest, a landmark now known as Captain Webb's Hole.
e. The tale of MacNamara, a highwayman who stole from the rich and gave to the poor, or, as a second voiceover interjects over the first teller's tale, who stole from the English and gave to the Irish.
f. The story of the red-headed Irish hitchhiker, who has returned to Cong after a time in Pittsburgh, having immigrated in order to find work. In a triumph of convolution, she ultimately finds herself inhabiting the role of Mary-Kate Danaher in a roadside tourist-trap cottage.
g. The unnamed young man and woman who conduct a clandestine courtship under the nose of the woman's bar-owner father. They follow the routines of courtship laid out by Sean and Mary-Kate in *The Quiet Man*.
h. The younger boy and girl who conduct a similar courtship under the chaperone eyes of his dejected friend.

Chronotope

Mikhail Bakhtin's concept of the 'chronotope' is at once brilliantly simple and brilliantly opaque. Because of this, as Michael Holquist says, it suffers from its own form of 'heteroglossia' (2010: 19). It is a popular concept precisely because it seems to offer itself to multiple interpretations and uses. In the midst of an ambiguity that was generated by Bakhtin himself, through multiple contradictory attempts to more precisely define this slippery concept, it fundamentally identifies a conjunction of time and space in the novel. The chronotope, or timespace, is both a thing in between time and space (a third substance that is a hybrid of the two) and an encompassing substance that contains the two. The concept emphasises the cultural specificity encoded into the representation of a particular timespace, and stresses the importance of privileging neither the temporal nor the spatial dimension during the analysis of narratives. Both should be treated equally, and the inseparability of the two should be recognised.

Chronos – time, *topos* – place. 'Time, as it were, thickens, takes on flesh, becomes artistically visible; likewise, space becomes charged and responsive to the movements of time, plot and history' (Bakhtin 1981: 84). To think the chronotope in the novel is to see the confluence of character, belief, action and experience enduring, for a time, in association with space. It is to identify the atmosphere or ambiance of a certain time in a certain place, the vital specificity of a period, the fecund peculiarity of an era, which can leave a residue. It is also to encounter the text as an 'x-ray' of 'the forces at work at a given time in the culture system from which they spring' (1981: 425–6). The chronotope offers a way of looking at any text as a socio-culturally determined understanding of how space and time fit together, and may be navigated.

While Bakhtin primarily intended the chronotope to be used within literary criticism, as a means to analyse the way that narrative and genre use language to compose time and space, it also offers something peculiarly appropriate to the study of film, a medium that has provided an enduringly intractable fusion of time and space. The chronotope captures and directly addresses the sense of entanglement of time and space in the moving image. The shot and the scene are blocks of duration of different scales, which are used to construct the narrative timeframe of the whole film. They simultaneously show and represent time passing in space, and a space enduring and changing over time.

The concept also offers a way to account for the specificity of certain cinematic representations of time and place. The cinematic chronotope names the texture of a certain place at a certain time, which emerges from a confluence of historical event, cultural condition, people, music, architecture, weather and light (amongst many other more or less ephemeral factors). It is a world and a way of knowing that world, both of which are contingent properties. Time does not always (if ever) flow in the same way. Just as space is topographically diverse, differing from point to point, so is timespace. The film abstracts an era from the incessant, regular onward flow of time. In fact, cinematic time has always flowed at different rates, in different ways, bearing different qualities and valences. It is the antithesis of clock-time because it represents the aestheticisation of time. The concept of the chronotope offers a means for recognising and analysing this aspect and process of cinema.

This is a particularly useful way of approaching the films of José Luis Guerín, several of which could be said to adopt a mode of chronotopic collage. They are directly concerned with the link between time and place, the heterogeneity of timespaces, and the possibility of interaction between different timespaces. They portray or create multiple distinctive chronotopes within a single film and permit a kind of audiovisual seepage between them.

Language

Innisfree begins in a foreign tongue. Not Spanish, which is the language of Guerín, the production crew, and the majority of the film's funders, nor English, which is the language spoken by most of the residents of contemporary Cong, and the language of John Ford and *The Quiet Man*, but rather Gaelic, a native language that is in many ways foreign to its own native land. Two men examine the remains of a ruined stone cottage, which has no roof and less than half its walls. Though we may well not guess it, they are Bartley and Padraig O'Feeney, descendants of the O'Feeney clan to which Ford rightfully claimed ancestry. In Gaelic they identify the place where the back door was, where the bed was, gesturing broadly to visually place these missing fixtures. All the while a fire burns incongruously in the hearth, and a painted wooden chair stands in the corner with a pile of books on it, as if temporarily set down while the reader is away, along with a harmonica. This archaeological return incorporates an impossible visual combination of temporalities. Even as the pair decipher the past usage of this ruin, its past is also visibly present in the enduring pleasure of the dancing flames, and the quiet pastime of reading by the fire. Importantly, neither of these elements are registered or recognised by the brothers.

Another chair without a sitter will appear at several other points during the film; a director's chair, with Ford's name on it, is first seen outside this same ruined cottage, and later placed amidst the thick grasses near the parish church of Cong. The empty seat is a quiet observer, an absence that registers a past sitter, a point of perspective, a mute and inanimate witness. It transposes a sightline from one time into another. Through its first appearance it registers Ford's return to his ancestral home, but in the later one it extends this trans-temporal surveying to the wider landscape of Cong, more emphatically a dislocated (absent) viewer, a floating ghost, unmoored in time or logic.

The Time is Out of Joint: Hauntology and Landscape

Hauntology is the study of ghosts. For Jacques Derrida, the ghost is the thing that haunts a text, the unspoken secret that drives it, the trauma or rift, or memory, or presence, or absence, that sets fictional life in motion. Almost any text will maintain some spectral presence that lingers just on the edge of perception, which more or less quietly and clandestinely opens up the texts potential, and introduces ambiguities, uncertainties. The dawning awareness of the ghostly presence is the dawning awareness not of the secret truth underlying the text, all texts, but rather the more accurate, more powerful awareness of not-knowing, a recognition that there is something behind or below, certainly, but a something that is beyond comprehensive knowing – not because of some obscure, mercurial, even spiritual difficulty, but because it doesn't properly exist. For Derrida it is less about finding something out, than about the productive act of realising that there is something else, something other, there. The shape of the ghost may even be intuited, traced, sketched, its roots followed, and its ramifications identified, though it will remain just beyond our grasp.

Hauntology is a pun on 'ontology'. The spectre or ghost is in a limbo state of both being and non-being, it is there and it is not there at the same time. What this means to the spectre, it is difficult to say, but to the reader, it means that the spectre is present to them, while also being absent to them, both there and not there. Any potential communion with the spectre must be undertaken as a venture into understanding rather than knowledge. As Colin Davis writes: 'Conversing with spectres is not undertaken in the expectation that they will reveal some secret, shameful or otherwise. Rather it may open us up to the experience of secrecy as such: an essential unknowing which underlies and may undermine what we think we know' (2007: 11).

Recently, Mark Fisher and others have used the concept to identify the persistence of certain antiquated sounds and styles in the music and broader popular culture of today (2014: 98). However, these presences often take the form of explicit references to a past that is more or less fictional: a seventies synth-driven occult-socialist enterprise that never really existed, the renovated regional culture of a midlands UK town that never existed, a utopian rave culture that never quite existed either. Transmitted through multiple forms in multiple texts, these ghostly presences triangulate a past that never was, that somehow still haunts the present as a kind of unfinished business, a path not taken that we nevertheless remember, perhaps as a lost possibility, confused with a real memory.

I would like to suggest that the idea of haunting is implicit in the concept of the chronotope. Bakhtin's insistence on the inseparability of time and space necessitates that we recognise the passing of timespaces, the death and replacement of one timespace with another. Every chronotope has its own passing inscribed into it. Every timespace bears the latent image of the timespaces that preceded it. Guerín's *Innisfree* works towards the recognition of the chronotopic ghosts that permeate the spaces we inhabit. Indeed, Guerín's body of work consistently seeks to demonstrate that each present is relative, each expired chronotope is embedded in its replacement.

In(n)isfree

Guerín's film begins with the title 'Things seen and heard in and around Innisfree between 5th Sept. and 10th Oct. 1988'. This description is straightforward and suggests a straightforward observational documentary approach will follow. In one way it is an entirely fitting description – the film is a compilation, a collage of images and sounds hinging around a single location, which is the Inisfree of *The Quiet Man*, a film shot more than thirty years prior to the aforementioned date. The specificity of the narrow timeframe identified here offers a sense of precision and fidelity in the relationship between the location filming and the document that the audience is about to witness. Additionally, it suggests a journey, and an audio-visual diary inscribed during the trip.

However, the plain and specific opening title is also a misdirection. First of all, there is not really any such place as the putative 'Innisfree'. The majority of locations that we see in *Innisfree* are in the environs of the small village of Cong, Co. Galway, where much of *The Quiet Man* was indeed shot. The Inisfree of *The Quiet Man* is, like many film-places, a forgery, a fiction, a composite and a conjuring. *Innisfree*, therefore, is not a documentary about a real place, but rather a documentary about the idea of a place, about a forgery that has become a reality, or perhaps more correctly (though no less confusingly), about the effect that the forgery has had on a real place that somehow remembers when it was the forgery.

Secondly, it is a misspelling that further confuses the origin of the myth. Guerín's Innisfree has two n's, like the island in the poem by W. B. Yeats, but unlike the Inisfree of *The Quiet Man*. If the fiction holding the geography together is the source of the title, then why this distinction (or error)? Perhaps to suggest that Innisfree is a third place, a fiction cut loose from its moorings, and to consolidate the mythical connection with the utopian fantasy of rest and a quiet life.

Additionally, the opening title tells us nothing of the fluidity with which the image track and soundtrack of the ensuing film will draw from the distinct timespaces of *Innisfree*, nor the way in which it will blend fiction with reality, allowing the sounds, characters and images of *The Quiet Man* to merge with and reinhabit the landscape. The simple audio-visual diary proposed by the title will be afflicted by a kind of audio-visual seepage, of the images and sounds of *The Quiet Man* seeping into the landscape of Cong. The film will also add its own series of fictional conceits, such as the character of the red-headed girl whom the film sporadically follows, offering a more concrete representation of the tourist and the alienated traveller within the text itself, yet further troubling the 'straight' understanding of this film as a documentary.

On the one hand, the film is this search for the lingering, disembodied presence of the other film in the locations in which it was originally shot. On the other hand it is a documentary about the culture and customs of the contemporary community of Cong, though this latter project seems to be constantly confounded by the entanglement of one time with the other, of the reality with the fiction, of one chronotope with another. Cong, it seems, can't forget that it is also Inisfree. Or, at least, it can't seem to forget that it was once Inisfree, and in this remembering is a melancholy, a nostalgia for a chronotope that never really was, though evidence of it can still be seen on screen. Hollywood never quite left the townland, and Cong never quite gave up on being Inisfree. The ghost of this forged identity still haunts the fields, houses, roads and bars of the area.

Real Ghosts

In the local pub, the residents share stories, for the camera, of the IRA and the Black and Tans. The scene tells us little in the way of fact, but much about the shared sense of a violent past for this older generation, many of whom can remember the days of the revolution and civil war. Later, in a curious coda to this strand, the ethereal strains of a tune echoing across the valleys is broken by a cow standing on an unexploded landmine – a sudden and surreal intrusion onto the pastoral and peaceful landscape. It indicates the remnants of a violent history that remain in the present, buried so shallow that they are prone to reveal themselves again, suddenly and shockingly. Perhaps it also echoes the surreal intrusion of a Hollywood production onto the continuity of the landscape and culture of Cong.

Arrivals

After the opening scene in which the O'Feeney brothers recall the layout of the ancestral cottage, we move to the home of Lord Killanin, producer of *The Quiet Man*. A link is made between the incongruously burning fireplace in the rough stone hearth and the fireplace of a more aristocratic home, being tended to by an elderly woman, while Lord Killanin sits at his table picking through an archive of correspondence with John Ford. Ford's letters speak of trips to Ireland, journeys of exploration and reconnaissance for films to be shot, projects to be cooked up at least partly for the fun of travel in ancestral lands. While Killanin reads, we cut to a travelling shot of railway tracks, as if from the point-of-view of the engine of a train, looking down at the rapidly disappearing sleepers. The soundtrack, which has already introduced elements of the orchestral score of *The Quiet Man*, now begins to overlay the sounds of train whistles and steam engines from the soundtrack of the earlier film. The motion of the shot slows, and the invisible train comes to a halt.

The next shot is a static establishing shot of the derelict and decaying Ballyglunin station, which played 'Castletown' station in *The Quiet Man*. The platform is on the left with six thin, vertical metal pillars holding up an awning, and the track on the right extending off towards the horizon (Figure 4.1). It employs the same framing and composition as the first shot of *The Quiet Man* following the credits (Figure 4.2), except that in the original a workman walks along the platform, there are crates on a cart, and as the train pulls in a woman rushes into frame to meet it. The next shot in *The Quiet Man* is a mid-shot of the side of the train, as Sean Thornton excitedly rolls down the window. The next shot in the *Innisfree* sequence puts the camera in the same position, but without a train we find ourselves looking at the decrepit shelter on the other side of the tracks. In both films Father Lonergan (Ward Bond), in voiceover, has already begun to tell the tale of the film: 'Well then, now, I'll begin at the beginning . . .' On the word 'now' both sequences cut to the next shot. In *The Quiet Man* we see the workman and the train conductor at the far end of the train, while the equivalent shot in *Innisfree* shows us a washing line blowing in the wind, over the ditch on the other side of the tracks: '. . .the train pulled into Castletown, three hours late as usual . . .' Both sequences cut to a shot of the station building with the green and white sign for 'Castletown' standing in the flowerbed. However, this is a moment of divergence from the established pattern, because the sign in *Innisfree* must be an interference. It is a remnant of the fictional role that Ballyglunin station once played, an improbable, lingering trace that confirms the identity of these two places, and draws them closer together. Apart from this manipulation, the *Innisfree* sequence goes on in the same way, mimicking the framing and editing pattern of *The Quiet Man* while Lonergan's voiceover continues.

By following so precisely the patterns of the original it makes the absence of life exceedingly clear. The insistence on precisely mimicking the shots and sequence of the original enforces the idea that these shots *should* have life in them, and in a way they *do* have life in them, though it remains on

Figure 4.1 Ballyglunin station, *Innisfree*.

Figure 4.2 Ballyglunin station as 'Castletown' station in *The Quiet Man*.

the edge of realisation, somewhere between being and not-being. It also constructs the film sequence itself as a space that should be inhabited. An emptied chronotope; this station is the station of a ghost town.

This scene combines visual and aural traces of three different arrivals. Killanin's voiceover references Ford's planned trip to Ireland to scope out locations, the underlying shot of train tracks visually marking the rush of the journey. The train, however, pulls into the same station where Sean Thornton disembarks in *The Quiet Man* – indicated through the direct appropriation of the audio from the original scene, and through the precise mimicking of shots from the original. Finally, it is also the arrival of Guerín and crew at the site of his pilgrimage, the first stop (if we exclude the prologue at the O'Feeney cottage) on his tour of *Quiet Man* locations. Unlike Thornton, who arrives to an overly friendly gaggle of locals intent on helping him, exploiting him and even integrating him in various ways (one woman essentially offers her niece), Guerín arrives on a ghost train, into an empty, abandoned station, where weeds grow, the wind blows and the voices of ghosts now echo.

As an opening shot this sets up the main theme of the film: the spectral intrusion of one chronotope into another, or, to put it another way, the spectral remains of the past in the present. This coalescence also suggests the inherent ephemerality of any timespace. The time of the film, the time of the production, and the time of the documentary all seem to have equal valency, in that each is as ethereal as the others. None, not even the present day, is afforded the feeling of concreteness, of constancy, of immutability. The film sets out precisely to erode that impression. Here, too, we have the first instance of tourism as a form of ghostly presence, and of the tourist as ghost – present in, but not belonging to, the places that they temporarily inhabit.

A Visual Manual

Fragmentation, dispersal and superimposition are recurring features of the organisation of the multiple threads of both narrative and soundtrack. Overlapping voices tell us tales of John Ford, offering competing memories, suggesting a dense web of memory that holds the community together, but equally it is a dense web that prevents entry. At a midpoint in the film, this is made explicit. A local resident tells us that he was born just after the filming of *The Quiet Man*, but that it persisted in the local culture, often in the form of lines from the film, such as 'the horse has more sense than I do', which have become part of the local vernacular. The root lies in the film, but the words now lead a life of their own. He goes on to say that the stories were handed down to him, and he presumes he will hand them down to his children.

The Quiet Man makes much of the local traditions of courtship; as a source of culture-clash for Sean, an obstacle to create narrative tension, and a set of exotically quaint cultural practices to extract fun from. However, in the Cong of 1988 the courting residents, such as the bar-owner's daughter and her suitor, and the two children who walk by the river, followed by the glumly excluded friend who has become a default chaperone, seem to understand courtship through the lens of *The Quiet Man*. As staged as these courtships clearly are, they tell us that *The Quiet Man* might still operate as a lynchpin of local oral history, a strange foreign interpreter of their traditional cultural practices, a visual manual of how their land is to be lived.

The Pilgrimage, or, Other Ghosts

John Ford is reputedly Guerín's favourite filmmaker, so the production of *Innisfree* is positioned extra-textually as the journey of a fan, as a pilgrimage to the sanctified locations of a beloved text, to indulge in its aura, but also to seek some traces of its reality in the landscape.

Several of Guerín's films take the form of a journey of some sort. His own personal involvement usually sits just behind the text itself, filling out the backstory, lore and press releases of the films, or in some cases it sits right at the surface, as is the case in *Guest* (2010), which records the filmmaker's alienated experiences at film festivals around the world, or *Unas fotos en la ciudad de Sylvia* (2007), which portrays a film director's return to the city of Strasbourg to make a film about a philosophical and physical search for a woman he met there twenty-two years earlier. The film is composed entirely of still photographs and intertitles, as if a collage of the preparatory notes and research for the film he is making. *Unas fotos* is itself a sort of enriching mythologisation of one of Guerín's most successful films, *In the City of Sylvia* (2007), which itself depicts a journey that is a return, and an attempt to trace, and perhaps confront, a ghost. In this film a young man returns to Strasbourg, spots a woman on the tram whom he believes he recognises from an earlier period lived in the city, and through the mostly dialogue-free remainder of the film he follows her elusive, constantly escaping figure through the narrow pedestrianised streets of the city. The return journey, and the pursuit of the escaping figure, is also simply a device to encounter the city in a certain way, to have a reason to walk the streets. As the companion piece *Unas Fotos* makes clear, the young man can be read as a veiled embodiment of the director himself, and the elusive figure of the woman, who may or may not be the one from his past, sublimates his inability to reconnect with this place that he once might have called home. The first part of the film quietly conveys the sense of amplified alienation that comes with a return. Nothing is quite so alien as a place, once familiar, that has now become strange, that has moved on with its own history in one's absence, through which new faces have passed and new lives taken root. It is the curse of the traveller that time continues to pass in the home one has left. After several failures to recover an emotional grip on the town he apparently once knew, the woman emerges from the crowd of strangers as a figment of his desire to re-possess this place. Time may have dimmed his memory of this woman, but it is precisely this uncertainty that permits the subsequent pursuit. To him, she represents a spectre from his past life flitting through the present, a physical manifestation of the town and life he once knew and the struggle to regain a sense of familiarity.

In this case the tenor of the journey is affected by its nature as a return. For John Ford, too, the making of *The Quiet Man* was an opportunity for a return. Ford had travelled to Ireland several times, the first a fabled voyage on the *Cambria* across the Irish Sea in 1921, when he claimed he sailed on the same ship as Irish rebel leader Michael Collins returning from treaty negotiations in London with the draft of an agreement for consideration by the fledgling Republican government. Ford journeyed on to the west of Ireland in search of the O'Feeney family home (the same ruined cottage from the prologue) and supposedly arrived just as it was being burned down by the Black and Tans.

To return to the main pilgrim, Guerín, I would suggest that he and his film crew also serve as ghosts. *Innisfree* references the unseen film crew in a number of ways. There is the invisible, impossible train in the 'Castletown Station' scene, and later a very similar point-of-view shot from a car hurtling around the winding, narrow roads of the west of Ireland. If we had believed that this was only a disembodied travelling shot of the roads around Cong, then the film makes sure that we know that it is a real car, grinding to a halt and reversing to pick up a red-headed hitchhiker. Next we see her sitting on a wall, apparently being questioned about where she is going, and what she knows of *The Quiet Man*. It seems as if she has accidentally provided the documentary makers with an interesting subject for interview, except that the voice of the interviewer is noticeably absent. Her answers are interspersed with silences where the questions should be. The film crew, as tourists, are a certain kind of ghost – one that passes through, observes, but has little chance of meaningfully interacting with the place that they temporarily haunt.

The Wild Colonial Boy

Sound is a privileged medium for hauntings. Many of the snippets of *The Quiet Man* that we hear in *Innisfree* give the impression of auditory hallucinations – the kind of thing one means when one says that someone is 'hearing things', that is, voices and sounds from elsewhere, which give the impression of presence, but that we know are not really there.

Sound is also invisible, and can fill a space without being seen. Sound waves can cover great distances and physically link distant points and distant people. In one scene, the elderly woman, whom we saw sharing stories in the pub, takes up the harmonica that we might have noticed on the chair in the ruined cottage in the prologue. She tentatively sounds the first few notes of *The Wild Colonial Boy*,[1] then repeats with gradually more confidence, a call waiting for a response. Elsewhere in the valley another local resident, sitting outside his home holding an accordion, listens to the faint wisps of tune coming down the wind. He finds the rhythm, waits for the right moment to enter and begins to play along. The tune, which features prominently in *The Quiet Man*, affords a mode of communication and a medium through which to assert shared identity. The performance is spread out, like the disparate farmhouses of rural Ireland, yet it also consolidates a sense of the sound as substance. The tune hangs in the air and descends on the valley like a mist.

The Film Itself

We watch as the film itself arrives back in the village, echoing Sean Thornton's arrival to a horde of gawping onlookers in the village centre of Inisfree. A bus arrives bringing old friends for a special screening of *The Quiet Man*, met by the jubilant current residents. At the same time, an orange van enters from the other side of the frame. On it is written 'Brodella Youth Association' and from its boot a set of four film cans proudly emblazoned with 'The Quiet Man' are taken, along with a 16mm projector. The film itself returns home, like a prodigal son back from America.

The scene is reminiscent of one in which a print of *Frankenstein* (1931) arrives at the village in Victor Erice's *Spirit of the Beehive* (1973), another Spanish film about a Hollywood film that intrudes on a rural peace, although in this case the peace is painfully precarious and brutally imposed, the violence not even below the surface yet. The film in question features a central character who, like Sean Thornton, yearns only for friendship and rest, but who harbours the potential for great violence.

Frankenstein haunts the Spanish village, a ghostly figment for the young protagonist Ana (Ana Torrent). For her, the monster comes to embody a threat that is also a kind of protective familial love. In addition to the visual and sonic apparitions of In(n)isfree, which attain a sense of the uncanny, 'a feeling of something not simply weird or mysterious but, more specifically [. . .] something strangely familiar' (Royle 2003: vii), the film itself is registered as an apparition, ceremonially returning in physical form, strangely familiar, as if it never really left.

Conclusion: Rear Projection, or, Moving While Standing Still

In the latter half of the film, once a chronotopic fluidity has been established, there are several striking shots made using the antiquated rear-projection technique to suggest motion: of a young man on a galloping horse, and the Irish *cailín* on a bicycle. These brief shots are interpolated into otherwise naturalistic sequences. The young man is taking part in the 'Innisfree Race Meet', a spectacle that may or may not be staged for the film. In either case, it is a real race with real horses, and yet the sequence is interspersed with three strikingly non-naturalistic shots that mimic the peculiar visual style of the rear-projected travelling shots used to depict Sean Thornton's furious race against Red Will, the young man clearly bestride a saddle but no horse. The red-headed young woman has just closed up the *Quiet Man* tourist cottage that she is now responsible for, and, still in full 'Mary-Kate' costume, she begins her bicycle journey home through woods, over bridges and past now very familiar locations. In the middle of this sequence is a rear-projection shot of the local landscape floating by as she cycles (Figure 4.3). Her subsumption into the complex tangle of fiction and reality in this strange place is momentarily complete, as *The Quiet Man* becomes a way of sensing the landscape, an optic through which it is seen and understood. These shots are clearly artificial, proudly confessing their debt to the original, and to the dream machine of Hollywood. They also succinctly assert the notion that the residents of Cong understand themselves as residents of In(n)isfree, and experience their everyday lives in a sort of magical amplification: half nostalgia and half Hollywood.

Of course, this is also a fiction for us, and for Guerín – a reassuring fantasy that the people of Cong live their lives through the lens of *The Quiet Man*, that the landscape is haunted by the sounds of Ward Bond's deep voice and wisps of Victor Young's score, that the traits of the film keep reasserting themselves through the landscape and people of this place.

Figure 4.3 Rear projection of In(n)nisfree.

Why wouldn't we hope that this were so? In the convolutions of past and present, fiction and reality, and in the over-egged conceits of the red-headed *cailín*, the tune played across the valleys, and the use of rear projection, we feel the force of Guerín's desire for this to be the case. And perhaps this is our desire also.

Note

1 A traditional Irish-Australian ballad of unknown authorship, which is used prominently in *The Quiet Man*, both diegetically, as a song that is sung in the pub to welcome Sean Thornton into the community, and as a theme within the non-diegetic score.

Works Cited

Bakhtin, Mikhail (1981), *The Dialogic Imagination*, Austin: University of Texas Press.

Davis, Colin (2007), *Haunted Subjects: Deconstruction, Psychoanalysis and the Return of the Dead*, London: Continuum.

Derrida, Jacques (1994), *Spectres of Marx: The State of the Debt, the Work of Mourning and the New International*, London: Routledge.

Fisher, Mark (2014), *Ghosts of My Life: Writings on Depression, Hauntology and Lost Futures*, London: Zero Books.
Holquist, Michael (2010), 'The fugue of chronotope', in N. Bemong, Pieter Borghart, Michel De Dobbeleer, Kristoffel Demoen, Koen De Temmerman and Bart Keunen (eds), *Bakhtin's Theory of the Literary Chronotope: Reflections, Applications, Perspectives*, Ghent: Academia Press, pp. 19–34.
Royle, Nicolas (2003), *The Uncanny*, Manchester: Manchester University Press.

CHAPTER 5

Memories, Notebooks, Roads: The Essayistic Journey in Time and Space

Adam Ludford Freeman

> And might it not be, continued Austerlitz, that we also have appointments to keep in the past, in what has gone before and is for the most part extinguished, and must go there in search of places and people who have some connection with us on the far side of time? (Sebald 2001: 359–60)

Twenty years before he directed *Sans Soleil* (1983), one of the most widely discussed and celebrated essay films, Chris Marker made the experimental sci-fi film *La Jetée* (1962), in which a time traveller journeys from a post-apocalyptic Paris back to his childhood aided by a vivid memory. As the traveller realises that the incident he witnessed as a child and which has haunted his life was, paradoxically, his own death, the voice-over narration explains:

> When he recognised the man who had trailed him since the underground camp, he understood there was no way to escape time, and that this moment he had been granted to watch as a child, which had never ceased to obsess him, was the moment of his own death.

La Jetée articulates a temporal journey, where the traveller revisits the past, like cameraman Sandor Krasna in *Sans Soleil*, whose epic journey through global spaces is also one through time and memory. This engagement with time, place and memory within the act of journeying characterises a fundamental interplay in the essay film and will be discussed in this chapter in relation to *Reminiscences of a Journey to Lithuania* (Jonas Mekas, 1972), *Which Way Is East: Notebooks from Vietnam* (Lynne Sachs, 1994) and *Content* (Chris Petit, 2010). Lithuania, Vietnam and the drifting locations of Petit's film are the landscapes of three films diverse in scope and aesthetics but linked thematically by the reverberation of war and conflict. The films are further united by the understanding, reminiscent of *Sans Soleil* and *La Jetée*, that there is no way to escape time and that a journey in space is necessarily also a journey in time.

Film essayists have sought to explore the world through spatial movement, where travelling becomes a tool to explore place and the subjective self across a multitude of spaces. Their representations of the spaces of the world through travel are thus fundamental to the spatio-temporal mechanisms of cinema inasmuch as, according to Jeffrey Ruoff, 'the cinema is a machine for constructing relations of space and time: the exploration of the world through images and sounds of travel has always been one of its principle features' (Ruoff 2006: 1). This relationship is firmly cemented within the realm of the essay film, a cinematic form that, according to Timothy Corrigan, emphasises 'travel and space as a central motif around which complex ideas and reflections have been put into play' (Corrigan 2011: 105). Following this train of thought, Catherine Russell considers how a spatial journey can also be a journey in time, noting how the auto-ethnographic diary film (which she describes as an essayistic form) can be read as a journey in time 'between the times of shooting and editing' (Russell 1999: 279). The geographic journey is experienced and recorded in the past, at the time of shooting. A temporal journey is enacted back in time from the present moment of editing, where the images and experience are returned to and revisited as memories. Russell's argument places an emphasis on the temporality of the filmmaker in the act of production and on the status of past-recorded images revisited in the present. This chapter builds upon this scholarship on the essay film and space, but with a shift in focus to consider how a movement in time is performed not only through a return to recorded images as memory, but through the spatial journey itself, which allows for an engagement with the temporal depth of places, their pasts and histories. Further, individual recollections and the personal memory of the filmmaker are situated or spatialised within landscapes and revisited through the act of travel.

To consider how time and place are represented in the essay film has a lot to do with how places and spaces are thought about and conceptualised with regard to temporality. Geographer Doreen Massey sees places as accumulations of layers of time within locations, converging historical trajectories and the sum of 'stories so far' which meet in the present of place (Massey 2005: 130). Similarly, Matthew Potteiger and Jamie Purinton consider how narratives are present within landscapes as temporal layers, where they 'intersect with sites, accumulate as layers of history, organise sequences, and inhere in the very materials and processes of the landscape. In various ways, stories take place' (Potteiger and Purinton 1998: 100). Considering the relationship between place and time specifically within the essay film, André Bazin has argued that Marker's *Letter from Siberia* (1957) positions the journey through a foreign land as essential in the construction of 'an essay on the reality of Siberia past and present', suggesting that the temporal strata of place can be activated and explored through geographic movement and essayistic representation (Bazin 2003: 44–5). Nora Alter (2006: 24) makes a similar claim in relation to the 'blurring of past, present and future' in Marker's *Dimanche à Pekin* (1956) implying that to represent the reality of a place is to enmesh multiple layers of time.

Through a focus on time and place in the essayistic journey film, this chapter will establish how present-day spaces can be seen as historical palimpsests, formed of compacted time in location, both visible, concrete and material, but also conjured through resonance, narrative and the reverberation of memory, with its fundamental function in lending form to the temporal layers and narratives of place. Accordingly, historian Simon Schama suggests that landscape 'is a work of the mind' whose 'scenery is built up as much from strata of memory as from layers of rock' (1995: 7). Such landscapes have both a physical form and one constructed through human relationships to and within them, forging a synchronous landscape of memory within a physical space that, as anthropologist Tim Ingold suggests, defines the perception of a landscape as 'an act of remembrance, and remembering is not so much a matter of calling up an internal image stored in the mind as of engaging perceptually with an environment that is itself pregnant with the past' (Ingold 1993: 153). These considerations will guide the following study in the ways in which, anchored to specific sites and locations that act as memory containers and historical markers, essay films have traced such itineraries from the present of place, back into memory and the past, aided by spatial movement.

New York (Lithuania)

In Jonas Mekas' *Reminiscences of a Journey to Lithuania*, personal memory articulates a return journey in time and space to Semeniškiai, Lithuania, the birthplace of Mekas and his brother Adolfas, who go back to the village of their childhood after a twenty-seven-year absence which followed their escape as refugees during the Second World War. The film is composed of four distinct locations: New York City and its surroundings; Lithuania, consisting of '100 glimpses', as an intertitle in the film states, largely shot on the family farm and the surrounding landscapes in and around Semeniškiai; Elmshorn, a suburb of Hamburg, where the brothers revisit the site of their imprisonment in a German forced labour camp; and lastly Vienna, the intended destination for the brothers when they first escaped Lithuania in 1944. The filmic travel encounter with these four distinct spaces provokes, aids and performs a journey in time where autobiographical detail and memories are spatialised. 'Place serves to situate one's memorial life', suggests philosopher Edward S. Casey (Casey 2000: 184), and through travelling to the spaces of his past Mekas passes into these chambers of memory, within which the past echoes on film.

The journey begins in New York, which is geographically situated as a present-day *home* for Mekas. However, the footage of New York in the opening section of the film is over twenty years old, and depicts the Mekas brothers' early life in America, or in the memory spaces of New York. As Russell states, this return to footage recorded in the past can denote one potential way that film essayists may journey through time. This footage is mostly black and white and is dated using various intertitles, including a scene at a pier in 1950 and a gathering of the Lithuanian community in 1951, accompanied by the filmmaker's reminiscing thoughts and feelings on those 'miserable post-war years' in America. Through this narration, spoken at a temporal remove from the past experience and with the aid of recorded images, Mekas travels back in time, back to the memorialised spaces of the city. In one sequence, we see a montage of scenes of Williamsburg, children playing on the street, men smoking, sitting in doorways, bustling streets, clothes drying on washing lines, while Mekas places himself within this archival space with the sentence 'I walked the streets of Brooklyn'. The filmmaker continues: 'the memories, the smells, the sounds that I was remembering, were not from Brooklyn' and alludes to the memories of Lithuania, thereby emphasising a geographical displacement expressed by the remembrance of one place through the prism of another. There is a temporal layering here expressed through the narration of multiple memories encased within each other and spoken over images which themselves belong to the past. Mekas, as an immigrant in America unable to make a physical return to Lithuania, uses memory as a device to travel across space. In this way he is simultaneously present within, and absent from, the spaces he remembers. As Casey explains, 'in remembering we can be thrust back, transported, into the place we recall' and 'into the time in which the remembered event occurred' (Casey 2000: 201). Thus, through these memories from New York back to the past in Lithuania, an inner journey into the spaces of the past conjured up through memory is already beginning before Mekas even embarks on his physical journey to Eastern Europe, a physical journey that can only be taken many years later as post-war political obstacles subside.

Rebecca Solnit has discussed the idea of space as a memorial device experienced and articulated by means of physical explorations provoking 'unsought memories of events to return as one encounters the sites of those events' and tracing 'the spirit of thought of what passed there before' (Solnit 2000: 76). Whilst the images of New York in *Reminiscences of a Journey to Lithuania* are situated in the 1950s, scenes of the journey back to Lithuania in 1971 are temporally situated in the present of the film to trace the type of itinerary of memory evoked by Solnit. And yet, for Mekas, Lithuania is associated with and attached to the past as a personal place of memory, geographically and temporally located at a distance bridged by the act of journeying. The first few glimpses of Lithuania in the film are brightly coloured shots of people, Mekas's family and landscape accompanied by ecstatic music, followed by a number of brief moving shots where the viewer is positioned as traveller, passing through landscapes, travelling with Mekas through Lithuania. After the compact architectural spaces of New York and the narration of memories of Semeniškiai, these open landscapes are a revelation, a nostalgic reverie, literally moving into the geography of those spoken histories and spaces of memory. As the film moves in space, so too the voice-over reflections flow with the spatial movement of the camera and work to enact the temporal movement of the film to a place that conjures past and present simultaneously. David Lowenthal makes a claim for the necessity of accessing the past from the present and states: 'We know the future is inaccessible, but is the past irrevocably lost? Is there no way to re-capture, re-experience, relive it? We crave evidence that the past endures in recoverable form.' (Lowenthal 1985: 14) Mekas's return journey is also one in which the filmmaker seeks to reconcile his memories with spaces, in an attempt to recover the past, to redeem it through a spatial encounter and to recapture it through filming. Accordingly, the '100 glimpses' of Lithuania serve to reassemble these spatial memories fragment by fragment.

A short sequence of *Reminiscences of a Journey to Lithuania* composed by a tracking shot of a house in Semeniškiai, which is followed by a medium shot of Mekas's mother and a close-up of an open attic window, is accompanied by Mekas's narration: 'the house, the attic in which I lived during my studies, and I had a rope dangling to slide down in case the Germans banged at the door'. As it triggers a temporal movement into the past of the place, the spatial encounter with this location allows Mekas to narrate stories and articulate memories attached to a type of landscape that, Potteiger and Purinton suggest, 'becomes a vast and mnemonic device' (1998: 20). Similarly, Mekas's visit to the old school building triggers memories of childhood: 'Where are you now my old childhood friends, how many of you are alive? Where are you scattered through the graveyards, through the torture rooms, through the prisons, through the labour camps of western civilisation?' Here personal recollection gives way to musings on the experience of Nazi and Soviet occupation, on a war Mekas escaped and a place that did not. These sites thus become the voice of a shared experience and conjure an image of the past within the localised spaces of Lithuania and across a broader sweep of time and space. Mekas continues his journey to Hamburg and Vienna, where he meets friends from New York in the location he failed to reach during the war and thus the journey into memory and place brings the filmmaker back into the present and closes a spatial and temporal loop.

Vietnam (1955 – 1975 – 1994)

Where *Reminiscences of a Journey to Lithuania* traces an autobiographical route across the spaces of personal memory and history, Lynne Sachs's *Which Way is East* is the exploration of a foreign land, its memory, history, people and places. The opening line of dialogue spoken by Sachs states: 'When I was six years old, I would lie on the living room couch, hang my head over the edge, let my hair swing against the floor, and watch the evening news upside down.' This brief memory situates the viewer within the home geography of the filmmaker in America and reveals a personal experience of the Vietnam War, which stretched from 1955 to 1975, viewed through the screen of a television set. The memory of a televised war ignites a physical journey to Vietnam, from Ho Chi Minh City to Hanoi, where Lynne and her sister Dana assemble everyday images of streets, people, landscapes, historical sites, shops, domestic and interior spaces, accompanied by voice-over narration of the discovery of the debris of war and the marks of the conflict impressed upon the present-day spaces of Vietnam. However, where *Reminiscences of a Journey to Lithuania* tends towards a singular expressive voice and the spaces of Mekas's individual memory, there is a plurality of voices and spatial stories in *Which Way Is East*, emerging through encounters with Vietnamese people who narrate histories through personal memory and testimony, reminiscences and traditional Vietnamese proverbs.

David Lowenthal suggests that 'many remember historical trauma as though past and present were contemporaneous' (1985: 28). This idea resounds clearly in Lynne's account of a heavy storm followed by a Vietnamese voice stating: 'It is raining so heavy. It reminds me of the war we fought against the American B52s. Back then, those war planes kept flying over Hanoi every day. They dropped so many bombs. The explosions sounded like this.' This testimony accompanies images of shops, people on the street and lights on the city streets at night, as the hand-held camera passes through the busy thoroughfares of Hanoi. In this sequence a memory is triggered by the present occurrence of a storm and this has the effect of invoking or reverberating histories and memories in the present of place and of conjuring the past within the spaces in which the memories are situated. The encounter with a space that engages the travellers with past memories creates a movement into the past, to a memory that serves to unify layers of time through the pairing of present images of place and the past events of war and violence.

As well as aural testimonies of people met through travelling, encounters with places and sites through the journey provide the conditions through which the abovementioned temporal movement into the past unfolds. As I have argued in relation to *Reminiscences of a Journey to Lithuania*, places themselves contain historical narratives and traces of memories, markers and material forms of the ancient or recent past. Sachs engages with these sites and conveys their histories through narration, thus creating a material archive, unfolding like the growth rings of a tree. Accordingly, Les Roberts has suggested that places constitute their own archive and, speaking specifically of urban spaces, states that 'landscapes bear the archaeological traces of the recent past in any number of ways' and 'can be "read" for signs and narratives that convey aspects of a city's past and of those who have inhabited its spectral but otherwise coeval urban spaces' (2014: 102). The idea of the archival structure of places resonates as an effective tool in deciphering meaning in the layering of time embodied in a location. Lowenthal has stated that '[l]ike archives, tangible relics make the past present' (1975: 11), and accordingly *Which Way Is East* articulates a multitude of histories through the portrayal of architecture and landscape. This congealing of time materially in place can be observed in the sequence of a visit to the ancient ruins of the Hindu temples of Mỹ Sơn. A stationary shot of a barely legible image of ruins in the jungle, in over-saturated colours, is distorted through overlays of fragments of contemporary Vietnam which move across the image, fade in and out, including abstract street scenes and glimpses of bodies moving, thus creating rich filmic textures and abstracting the space. The narration, spoken by Lynne, states that this was 'once the intellectual centre of Vietnam' and that it remained mostly intact and 'survived centuries of monsoons and war' before a US bomb scattered most of the ancient stonework across the hillside. We hear birdsong on the audio. Here, then, architectural remains reveal multiple histories, from the ancient time of the buildings themselves, to the events that befell them over time, encompassing World War Two and the first Indo-China War, and finally to the destruction of the temples by bombs in the Vietnam War. The treatment of the film footage through distortion, layering and fragmentation mirrors the story of obliteration and of the strata of time compacted and overlaid within a location that is given a temporal depth as the visual ruins and spoken voice conjure spatial histories and capture the flow of time made material in place.

In *Which Way Is East*, memory, testimony and the narrative of specific sites are often woven together through the travel encounter. In this way the film becomes a multi-layered accumulation of sites, perspectives and experience, where a cacophony of voices and narratives form a complex portrait of place, memory and history. In one sequence, wooden buildings, the jungle and hills are shot from a moving vehicle while Sachs states that 'Driving through the Mekong Delta, a name that carries so much weight, my mind is full of war and my eyes are on a scavenger hunt for leftovers.' This is followed by images of rice crops floating on water in ponds which are claimed to be craters from American bombs, giving a material dimension to a history inscribed into the landscape itself. As Fred Inglis states, landscape 'is the most solid appearance in which a history can declare itself' (1977: 489), thus this cratered Vietnamese landscape bears the physical markings of the past, it is an 'archival' space. Sachs's own memories filter into the present-day narrative when she visits an underground complex of tunnels that were used by the Việt Cộng during the war and, upon entering them, she remembers old war movies she watched with her father. Her detachment from the historical dimensions of Vietnam and her outsider status are emphasised through this reference to movies, a gap that the foreign filmmaker's spatial encounters and movements in time can only fractionally fill. The tunnels and craters, as physical remnants of history, act as memory markers or historical indicators. A local woman reveals she had spent years in the tunnel, where her husband died, and even gave birth to her daughter there. Here, history is given a voice by those who witnessed the events, and the physical place is imbued with historical narrative while the landscape acts as mnemonic device, or as what Pierre Nora defines as a site of memory, whose function is 'to stop time, to block the work of forgetting [. . .] to immortalize death' (1989: 19). Through the spatial journey, encountering and experiencing these sites, histories are unlocked and their narratives are woven into the essay. Thus, material places and locations, the subjective experience of the filmmaker travelling to and encountering these spaces, the socio-political history of the place told through personal narrative and memory of the Vietnamese people all collide, and the sites of the journey and the people encountered become departure points for an investigation into the past, which resurfaces in the present.

Drifting Spaces

Whereas *Reminiscences of a Journey to Lithuania* and *Which Way Is East* follow coherent geographical itineraries to the country of the filmmaker's childhood and to a foreign land associated with distant memories of a televised war, Chris Petit's film *Content* (2010) drifts through space without a concrete route or intended destination. *Content* is a complex multi-textual essay film structured as a fragmentary road trip through physical space combined with a mirrored journey through cyberspace and the digital realm. Through this dual movement, a third journey is enacted in the shape of a drift through time, through a non-linear, fragmentary history of the twentieth century, told through the convergence of personal memory, spatial narratives and archival imagery. The film is not concerned with one specific place or a single journey, but with multiple journeys taken and disparate spaces encountered, evoked through fleeting glimpses from a car window of numerous landscapes in England, Europe and America, and through the accumulation of many different forms of image from these multiple spaces, such as postcards, maps and photographs. The movement in *Content* then, the idea of 'drift' rather than a journey per se, both due to its physical spatial movement and to the complex thought process that emanates from this spatial drift, may be thought of in terms of a psychogeographical *dérive*, a technique defined by Guy Debord (1956) as a 'rapid passage through varied ambiances' by means of a spatial movement carried out with an 'awareness of psychogeographical effects'. Whilst a *dérive* may typically constitute a practice carried out on foot, *Content*'s endless car journeys along roads mirrored by an equally endless movement through a digital stream of images resonate with the definition provided by Debord. The film accumulates various motorcar *dérives* as film footage, which are recalled from a digital image bank alongside a vast array of other imagery. The montage of these fragmented journeys and geographical drifts constructs an endless accumulation of multi-directional movements across varied terrain and thus intensifies the nature of the *dérive*. Petit outlines the effect of driving in the film on the voice track, explaining that the journey is 'carried along not by the constant motion and linear unfolding of the road, but by driving's dreamlike state of mind, which takes me back to haunt old haunts'. These words are spoken over images, shot from the car window, of the Westway in London, the elevated dual carriageway section of the A40 trunk road running from Paddington to North Kensington. As the voiceover refers to 'old haunts' taking the shape of both past memories and places revisited, the movement along the Westway is a form of drift or *dérive*, resulting in reverie experienced as a dreamlike flow through space and time which triggers personal memories and spatial narratives where the road leads into the past. This establishes a key device in the film which returns in a sequence filmed along a highway with a camera mounted on the windscreen; as the road unfolds, Petit's narration takes us back to his childhood and recalls 'grown up silences' or 'what wasn't talked about in front of the children'. The road literally becomes a road into the past, into personal memory expressed through the essay voice, which unfolds through drifting movements where personal memory and historical events become entangled throughout the spaces and archival fabric of the film.

Reminiscences of a Journey to Lithuania and *Which Way Is East* largely eschew the use of found archival imagery in the recall of the past in favour of filmed images of the travel encounter, whereas *Content* exhibits a complex relationship to archival images, including maps, old postcards, paintings, film clips and photographs. What complicates the status of these archival images and objects is that they all appear, despite original context, to be emanating from the same digital archive, from one endless digital repository, accessed though a scrolling digital interface, or from the internet. Jaimie Baron has argued that filmmakers are drawn to the 'endless storehouses of digital documents that can easily be accessed and reused in infinite ways' (2014: 142); accordingly, *Content* engages with this proliferation of images: it opens up this endless store, which contains a seemingly infinite mass of images, placing them into orbit with one another, collating them into the fabric of the film and making sense of this wealth of images by thinking through them as they emerge from the digital archive into the film along lines of thought, themes and spatial coordinates. This multi-textual collage expands the parameters of the film, creating a wider web of connections, thus broadening the spatial and temporal fields where meaning can be created and history and memory recalled.

Isabelle McNeill has argued that,

> [T]he vast interconnected space of contemporary media, film multimedia and the internet doesn't flatten time and space but creates inter-textual mnemonic spaces through which to think and view by surfing and navigating. Like the city flâneur moving through spaces, the subject navigates media. (2010: 137)

Here the spatial and the digital are positioned in parallel to one another and McNeill considers the possibilities for engaging with this dual navigation of archive and space as a process with a potentially expansive effect on representation through interconnection. This statement resonates well with *Content*, in which navigating the digital archive mirrors movement through physical space and where the drift through an excess of global spaces is related to endless browsing and surfing through a cyberspace of objects and sites embodying a mnemonic quality. Through this dual digital and spatial navigation, *Content* pauses within the drift, arrives at particular images and places, sites and objects in which history and memory are anchored, and through the collision and alignment of these multiple elements conjures up these places and creates meaning.

One specific sequence can show how *Content* both navigates an extensive wealth of media and moves through multiple spaces to construct a complex multi-textual web of place and time, thus outlining how the physical drift through space and the digital archive performs a movement in time. This sequence begins with a YouTube video of the Auguste and Louis Lumière film *La Sortie de l'Usine Lumière à Lyon/Workers Leaving the Lumière Factory in Lyon* (1895), and this is followed by a scroll through the digital image bank, a repeated motif throughout the sequence. Next, street scenes and images of present-day distribution warehouses are juxtaposed with *La Sortie de l'Usine Lumière à Lyon* and illustrate a shift from the bustling factory of a nineteenth-century industrial economy to the hidden operations of a service and consumer economy in the present. Like *Reminiscences of a Journey to Lithuania* and *Which Way Is East*, war frequently appears as a central preoccupation in *Content*. In this sequence personal and historical narratives of war intertwine, invoked through spaces and archival objects. The narration establishes a link between the commercial landscapes of distribution warehouses seen in the images and the Cold War landscapes of the defunct military facilities at Orford Ness in Suffolk, where the filmmaker digresses along a personal recollection of growing up in the spaces of military habitation as a child of an army officer. The scenery changes to Poland, where the film recounts the story of Hans Stosberg, who was employed to design plans to modernise the town of Auschwitz in 1941 after the Nazi invasion. The plans and maps of this project are then juxtaposed with film images of landscapes around present-day Auschwitz, layering the past over the present of place through archival images and narrated histories. A link between the Second World War and the filmmaker's biography is further established through images of the Barbican Estate in London, where the filmmaker lives, and where rubble from bomb damage was shipped to East Anglia to build runways for bomber fleets to take off to bomb German cities, including the city of Hanover, where Stosberg was born and which is evoked in the film by means of an old postcard. This is followed by archival images narrating the story of the destruction of German cities during the Second World War. As it is revealed that Stosberg was also employed to rebuild Hanover after the war, another pre-war postcard of Hanover is juxtaposed with a present-day image on location of the runway in East Anglia built from the bomb damage debris. This sequence illustrates a complex web of associations which links places, moments in history and personal memory through disparate trails of thoughts using archival images and the internet to shape the film fabric, as well as locations and physical spaces to weave an intertwining network of place, memory and representation. The appropriation of diverse film fragments and images along with digital film footage of locations encountered through journeys in the present creates an interplay between the past and contemporary place, between varying subjects, across multiple places and between many layers of time.

The archival function of place and landscape is to act as evidence of history, as seen in footage of the Barbican estate, the runway in East Anglia and the area surrounding the Auschwitz concentration camp, whose narratives are told through voiceover. *Content* thus enacts a movement in time similar to the journey through spaces in which memory and history are anchored in *Which Way Is East*, or the autobiographical and historical spaces of Lithuania for Mekas in *Reminiscences of a Journey to Lithuania*. Through visiting physical sites, reached through global spatial drift, Petit accesses the past through the specificity of places and memorial spaces. Further, a drift through digital space is used to evoke and illustrate these spatial pasts, to give them visual and concrete form and to make the past present through the material remnants of history. The spatial, archival and digital drift provides the conditions through which to navigate a multitude of coordinates and interconnections across global spaces and times, between historical events and autobiographical past. The film bridges the gap between diverse subjects, disparate places and different times, between diverse archival images, and collates the global spatial drift through travelling to and pausing at sites, whilst also pausing in the flow of archival images, generating meaning and recalling history and personal memory through constellations of images, temporal layers and spatial narratives.

The three essay films explored here all engage with a geographical and temporal journey, a spatial movement that opens up the possibility for another parallel and intertwining movement of journeys through time, into the pasts of place and into memory. The essay film form, through its subjectivity, reflexivity and first person mode of address, lends itself to the inscription and exploration of memory through a personal encounter with space. Through specific sites in which history and memory are anchored, the journey becomes a flight into the past told through the narrated histories of these spaces, at times using archival material to place the film materially in the past. War and atrocity are central threads running through the three films and reverberate through memories, sites and narratives. The devastation of war and its aftermath is heavily inscribed in psyche and space and is revived and revisited through memory, testimony and site. The actual experiential conditions of travelling lead the filmmakers into a labyrinth of personal memory, historical narratives and spatial coordinates and shapes a web of space and time woven from these converging points. Paul Arthur notes that since 'film operates simultaneously on multiple discursive levels – image, speech, titles, music – the literary essay's single determining voice is dispersed into cinema's multi-channel stew' (2003: 59). The essay film form then is an expansive form of representation, which through its multi-textuality, multi-layeredness and potential for multivocality, provides the filmic conditions for these many layers of time and space and manifold narratives collated through the journey, to be intertwined.

What the essayistic journey allows for, then, is a movement not only across and between spaces through travel, but also a vertical movement, down into the layers of place, into its temporal depths. Massey sees places not as 'points on a map' but as 'integrations of space and time; as *spatio-temporal events*' (2005: 130–1) which are 'woven together out of ongoing stories'. These films embody this idea of accumulating temporal layers, creating a dense filmic rendering of place across topographical spaces and along temporal avenues, a spatial representation built up from the many pasts of place, as well as the present. The journey becomes an essayistic tool, a mode of excavating these layers, creating a filmic rendering of places that accounts for their many temporalities and multiplicities in the present. Like *La Jetée*'s emissaries sent back in time or Sandor Krasna's dispatches from global time and place in *Sans Soleil*, these filmmakers embarked on journeys where time rolls back and returns as it builds itself around them in the form of spatial memories, through which the past is relived.

Works Cited

Alter, Nora (2006), *Contemporary Film Directors: Chris Marker*, Urbana and Chicago: University of Illinois Press.

Arthur, Paul (2003), 'Essay Questions', *Film Comment*, January/February, pp. 58–63.

Baron, Jaimie (2014), *The Archive Effect*, London: Routledge.

Bazin, André [1958] (2003), 'Bazin on Marker', trans. David Kehr, in *Film Comment*, July/August, pp. 44–5.

Casey, Edward S. (2000), *Remembering: A Phenomenological Study*, Bloomington: Indiana University Press.

Corrigan, Timothy (2011), *The Essay Film: From Montaigne, After Marker*, Oxford: Oxford University Press.
Debord, Guy (1956), 'Les Lèvres Nues #9', reprinted in *Internationale Situationniste #2* (December 1958), trans. Ken Knabb <http://www.cddc.vt.edu/sionline/si/theory.html> (last accessed 19 January 2016).
Inglis, Fred (1977), 'Nation and Community: A Landscape and its Morality', *The Sociological Review*, 25:3, pp. 489–514.
Ingold, Tim (1993), 'The Temporality of the Landscape', *World Archaeology*, 25:2, pp. 152–74.
Lowenthal, David (1975), 'Past Time Present Place: Landscape and Memory', *Geographical Review*, 65:1, pp. 1–36.
Lowenthal, David (1985), *The Past Is a Foreign Country*, Cambridge: Cambridge University Press.
Massey, Doreen (2005), *For Space,* London: Sage.
McNeill, Isabelle (2010), *Memory and the Moving Image: French Film in the Digital Era,* Edinburgh: Edinburgh University Press.
Nora, Pierre (1989), 'Between Memory and History: *Les Lieux de Mémoire*', trans. Marc Roudebush, *Representations,* 26, Special Issue: Memory and Counter-Memory, Spring, pp. 7–24.
Potteiger, Matthew and Jamie Purinton (1998), *Landscape Narratives: Design Practices for Telling Stories,* New York: John Wiley and Sons.
Roberts, Les (2014), 'Navigating the "Archive City": Digital Spatial Humanities and Archival Film Practice', *Convergence: The International Journal of Research into New Media Technologies*, 21:1, 9 December, pp. 100–15
Ruoff, Jeffrey (2006), *Virtual Voyages: Cinema and Travel,* Durham, NC: Duke University Press.
Russell, Catherine (1999), *Experimental Ethnography: The Work of Film in the Age of Video*, Durham, NC: Duke University Press.
Schama, Simon (1995), *Landscape and Memory*, London: HarperCollins.
Sebald, W. G. (2001), *Austerlitz,* trans. Anthea Bell, London: Penguin.
Solnit, Rebecca (2000), *Wanderlust: A History of Walking,* London: Verso.

Part 1b

Expanding Europe: Interstitial Production and Border-crossing in Eastern European Cinema

CHAPTER 6

Shadows of Unforgotten Ancestors: Representations of Estonian Mass Deportations of the 1940s in *In the Crosswind* and *Body Memory*

Eva Näripea

Introduction

From time immemorial, wars have been a major engine inducing massive waves of dislocation. While Europe, including Estonia, currently stands at the receiving end of one such tide, the most recent armed conflict that propelled extensive emigration from Estonia was World War Two. This chapter examines two cinematic representations of one of the most dramatic collective journeys of Estonian history – the massive Soviet deportations of Estonians in June 1941 and in March 1949. Belonging to an emerging wave of Baltic films inspired by the tragic events that uprooted tens of thousands of natives in these countries, both Martti Helde's feature-length debut *Risttuules/In the Crosswind* (2014) and Ülo Pikkov's animated short *Kehamälu/Body Memory* (2011)[1] stand out for their inventive audiovisual design. *In the Crosswind* mesmerises its audiences with a stunning image track. It is composed of a series of *tableaux vivants*, with the camera roaming the three-dimensional spaces around human figures frozen in moments of despair. *Body Memory* is equally penetrating in its minimalist visual form, which is employed to present an experimental and abstract narration of the memories related to this traumatic journey, inscribed into the collective body and mind of the nation. While Pikkov's *Body Memory* is an allegorical tale of the collective bodily memories of past sorrow and pain, Helde's *In the Crosswind* concentrates on the story of a fictional twenty-seven-year-old Estonian woman named Erna Tamm who was deported to Siberia in June 1941. Helde draws on the letters of his relatives, but also on other memoirs and archival material documenting the deportations (Bencze 2014). Based on these, he offers a powerful account of the nightmarish journey that lasted for Erna until 1954, when she was finally allowed to return to Estonia, only to discover that her husband Heldur had died in a Siberian prison camp shortly after their separation.

This chapter investigates how *Body Memory* and *In the Crosswinds* engage with the Stalinist deportations and (collective) memories of them, concentrating in particular on the ideological aspects of narrating national history and identity. For this purpose, I employ David Martin-Jones's (2006) account of cinematic representations of national history and identity, which theorises these concepts in the light of Gilles Deleuze's (1989) and Homi K. Bhabha's (1990) works.

Narrative Time and National Identity: Theoretical Framework

Portraying these involuntary journeys, *In the Crosswind* and *Body Memory* address the complex questions of collective (national) memory and identity. Doing so by means of experimental audiovisual form, and by complicating the mode of spatiotemporal representation, Pikkov's and Helde's films appear to suggest that the Deleuzian notion of the 'time-image' (Deleuze 1989) might be a productive frame of reference for understanding how these representations relate to narrating national identity and to a collective sense of national history. In his *Deleuze, Cinema and National Identity: Narrative Time in National Contexts* (2006), David Martin-Jones proposes that Gilles Deleuze's dyadic typology of cinematic representations of time – on one hand, the movement-image (or more precisely, the action-image) of 'linear narrative, based upon the continuity editing rules', and on the other hand, the time-image that 'experimented with discontinuous narrative time' – can be effectively applied for explaining 'the way national identity is constructed in cinema' (Martin-Jones 2006: 1–2). Specifically, in addition to Deleuze, Martin-Jones relies on Homi K. Bhabha's argument (Bhabha 1990) that nation is narrated using two parallel 'tracks' of time – a suggestion offered by Bhabha as part of his revision of Benedict Anderson's famous statement that a nation is 'an imagined political community' (Anderson 1983: 6). As Martin-Jones explains, in Bhabha's model the narration of a nation is, on one hand, 'defined by a progressive, teleological view of the present that problematically established its origins in an ancient or almost timeless past' and, on the other hand, it is 'performed in the present in such a way as to both erase and then recuperate this past' (Martin-Jones 2006: 33). According to Bhabha, then, in any national narrative an ambivalence arises from the interplay of two forces – on one hand 'the continuist, accumulative temporality of the pedagogical', and on the other hand 'the repetitious, recursive strategy of the performative' (Bhabha 1990: 297). Martin-Jones connects Bhabha's ideas with the Deleuzian dyad and argues that movement-images, seeking temporal linearity, correspond to the 'pedagogical' view of national identity and history, establishing and supporting a 'correct', widely accepted understanding of the national past; while time-images, essentially labyrinthine by nature, tend to offer several viewpoints on history, 'without any one being specifically given as "correct"' (Martin-Jones 2006: 28). Furthermore, the performative rethinking of the national past constitutes a deterritorialising force that seeks to undermine the pedagogical, singular and linear approach to national history that in its turn attempts to reterritorialise, stabilising the rhizomatically expanding pathways of the labyrinth. Martin-Jones also suggests that in many films the elements of movement-image and time-image co-exist, interact and intertwine, even though one or the other ultimately defines the overall 'ideology' of narrating time and space, nation and history, giving a clue as to what kind of national narrative – either linear-pedagogical (that is, dominant) or disrupted (that is, subversive) – a particular film eventually tends to support (Martin-Jones 2006: 2). Drawing on these theoretical premises, the following discussion of *Body Memory* and *In the Crosswind* attempts to determine which of these two versions of national narrative dominates in each film's account on a particular moment of twentieth-century Estonian history.

The massive Soviet deportations of Estonians in June 1941 and in March 1949 cast a long and enduring shadow on Estonian history and national identity. Starting in the early hours of 14 June 1941, merely days before Hitler launched his surprise attack against the USSR, more than 9,000 Estonians, about two thirds of them women and children from urban areas, were exiled to Siberia (Rahi-Tamm 2004: 25; Hiio *et al.* 2006: 377); during the night of 24–5 March 1949, over 20,000 people, condemned as 'kulaks', 'bandits' and 'the people's enemies' by the Soviet authorities, met the same fate,[2] crammed into unheated freight cars, men separated from their wives, children and parents. The men were typically sent to prison camps, while the rest of the families were scattered to Siberian villages where they were forced to do hard labour in order to provide a living for themselves and the members of their families who were unable to work due to their age or health. These journeys lasted several weeks and many of the weaker 'travellers' died before reaching their final destination. Many more did not survive the starvation and fatigue experienced during the prolonged exile, and only a minority of the deportees returned to Estonia after Stalin's death.

The brutality of the deportations is of course unquestionable. And so is the radical impact of the change of political regime on Estonian society. Yet the dominant narrative of the national past has a tendency to gloss over the numerous finer nuances, distinctions and ambivalences of day-to-day life in favour of constructing neat oppositions, coherent stories and teleologies. My account of *In the Crosswind* and *Body Memory* will investigate how the films navigate these troubled waters and to what extent they manage to escape the stumbling blocks of given 'truths' and sweeping generalisations. Before that, however, it is necessary to provide some context to the two films, both in terms of cinematic works dealing with the same topic and the wider background against which these films have emerged.

Deportations On-screen

Throughout most of the Soviet period, the ghastly events of 'ethnic cleansing' were obviously off-limits to any cinematic representation; in fact, they were altogether banished from public discourse. The first fiction films to approach the trauma of forced exile were *Äratus/Awakening* (1989) by Jüri Sillart and, to a somewhat lesser extent, *Inimene, keda polnud/A Man Who Never Was* (1989) by Peeter Simm, both made on the brink of the Singing Revolution and after the abolition of censorship in the Soviet Union. However, neither film ventured, narratively speaking, beyond Estonian borders and it took over two more decades before the fictionalised imagery[3] of journeys to Siberia reached the silver screen. A similar pattern can be observed in other Baltic states. In Latvia, the first portrayal of deportations in narrative mode, *Chronicles of Melanie (Melānijas hronika)*, by Viestur Kairish, premiered in November 2016. In Lithuania, the most outstanding fictional representations of these coerced journeys to (and in) Siberia include *Ekskursantė/The Excursionist* (2013) by Audrius Juzėnas and *Gyveno senelis ir bobutė/Grandpa and Grandma* (2007), an animated (semi-)documentary by Giedrė Beinoriūtė. The newest Lithuanian production inspired by the harrowing events is *Ashes in the Snow* (2017), made in collaboration with the US Sorrento Productions, directed by Marius A. Markevicius, an American of Lithuanian descent, and starring, among others, Martin Wallström and Bel Powley (see McNary 2016). As in Estonia, Latvian and Lithuanian fiction films about deportations were complemented by documentary treatments of the subject. All in all, they form a clearly discernible 'wave' of deportation films, symptomatic of a much wider, and largely non-cinematic, process described below.

* * *

After the collapse of the Soviet Union, Estonia, similarly to other newly independent Eastern European nation-states, began to seek recognition of these and other Soviet atrocities by their new Western allies. However, these allies have been reluctant to provide it, partly because of their responsibility for what happened as a result of their involvement in the decisions made at the Yalta Conference in February 1945. Additionally, as Jakob Ladegaard has aptly pointed out, this blindness of the West might be linked to the fact that,

> the Holocaust dominates western cultural memories of World War II. While some argue that the Holocaust therefore serves as a foundation for a 'common European cultural memory' (Levy and Sznaider 2002: 102), Duncan Bell points out that such claims privilege western perspectives and overlook the conflicting memories of World War II in the new Europe (Bell 2006: 17–18). Estonia is a case in point: the murder of about 1000 of the country's Jews (the remaining 2000 escaped to Russia) has not commanded the same attention in public debates as the prolonged Soviet repression. This fact is criticized by the historian Anton Weiss-Wendt, who sees Estonian insistence on international recognition of the Soviet crimes as an 'unproductive comparative victimization contest' (Weiss-Wendt 2008: 484). (Ladegaard 2014: 158)

Both *Body Memory* and *In the Crosswind*, as well as other recent fiction and documentary films representing Soviet deportations and other repressions of Estonians, but equally the natives of the other two Baltic countries during and after World War Two, form a part of the process of seeking Western acknowledgement of the suffering of the Baltic nations under the Soviet occupation. This is made especially clear in the dedication of *In the Crosswind* 'to the victims of the Soviet Holocaust', a title that appears at the end of the film and that has, according to Helde, created much controversy among its foreign audiences. Yet the formal and narrative choices made by authors of both films strongly suggest that these cinematic works were primarily intended to address spectators abroad,[4] even if *In the Crosswind* also resonated extremely well with domestic audiences. Indeed, the boldly innovative, one might even say experimental, audiovisual form of the films under discussion encourages consideration of them as transnational, rather than national, productions – something that has not gone unnoticed by commentators of both *Body Memory* (Ladegaard 2014; Dima 2014; Richter 2014; Vestergaard Kau 2014) and *In the Crosswind* (Gray 2015). This is further supported by their use of tried and tested Holocaust iconography (crowded freight cars, piles of boots in a concentration camp, and so on), as well as of images that transcend the concept of the national as pertaining to a specific ethnic group – for instance, the train (see Barton 2014) and the archetypal homestead, but also the centrality of specifically *female* experience and suffering standing for the collective 'body' of the nation, in both films; clearly biblical references (the apple tree and the snake) in *Body Memory* and the stark opposition between 'golden' and 'dark' times in *In the Crosswind*. As audiovisual form is perhaps the first feature of both films catching the viewer's attention, I will begin my discussion with that.

Playing with Form

The most striking formal feature of *In the Crosswind* is without any doubt its cinematography – or, more precisely, its unusual combination and interplay of complex patterns of camerawork and *mise en scène*, captured on a black-and-white (digital) image track. While the camera slowly pans, tracks and dollies along curvilinear trajectories, gradually unfolding the narrative of each scene, the objects and characters within the scene remain completely still, as if frozen in space in the middle of a moment, forming a sequence of *tableaux vivants*. Furthermore, the film is based on a twofold visual design. The brief episodes depicting life before the deportation and after Erna's return to her homeland consist of shorter takes representing the characters moving freely in the space of the frame. At the same time, the plight of the deportees, both during their journey to Siberia and throughout their years of exile, is composed of thirteen sequence shots, the longest of them running over seven minutes. These audio-visual patterns position Martti Helde's directorial debut in the venerable company of cinematic masterworks by Béla Tarr, Theo Angelopoulos and many other proponents of the so-called 'slow cinema' (see, for example, Flanagan 2012). Nevertheless, Helde's film stands out for its consistent use of stop-action throughout almost the entire film.

The impact of these eerily beautiful images is reinforced by the film's equally remarkable soundtrack, painstakingly designed by Janne Laine. Devoid of dialogues, it conveys the main narrative information by means of Erna's strangely 'disembodied' voiceover that recites her (mostly real, but never sent) letters to Heldur, as well as Heldur's (fictional) 'response' at the end of the film. This unusual rendition of a 'dialogue', transcending time rather than space (Tomberg 2014: 96), is complemented by various 'diegetic' sound effects. Especially in comparison with the highly abstract black-and-white imagery, these come across as uncannily 'realistic' – the whistling of the wind, the chirping of birds, the barking of a dog, an ominous knock on the door, the threatening footsteps of marching soldiers, the anxious clatter of train wheels on the tracks, indistinct chatter, Russian news on the radio, and so on. The moments of heightened drama are accompanied by 'swooning, sensual, sagacious' melodies of the score (composed by Pärt Uusberg), that tie the soundscapes and the photography 'with a silky knot' (Grozdanovic 2014).

According to Helde, the initial impulse for the idea of *tableaux vivants* came from a letter by a deportee that the young director read in the archives when he started preparations for the film. The deportee wrote that she felt as if time had frozen on the night of the deportation (Tuumalu 2014) – 'that my body is in Siberia, but my soul is still in my homeland' (Bencze 2014). Indeed, the entire audiovisual design of *In the Crosswind* highlights the significance of time and its (perceived) duration, both for the experience of the deportees and for the director in representing it. As Donald Tomberg observes, time unrolls in extended moments that are clearly distanced from the everyday perception of time:

> presented as such, it all becomes a place of memories, reminiscing. The time before the deportations slides by, as an archetype of domestic time, the Siberian time emphasises monumentally the sense of being present in the moment (unmoving images). Time is perceived differently – the way we could find an image of time in our memory. (2014: 94)

Body Memory approaches the topic of deportations by a combination of sepia-toned puppet animation and black-and-white live-action footage. The film opens and closes with shots of an easel with a blank canvas and a box of oil paints, standing in an apple orchard next to train tracks, under a sombrely darkened sky and surrounded by barren, November-like landscape. In the closing sequence an old freight train with a long row of freight cars running on them morphs into a serpentine beast and ultimately both the beast and the tracks slowly disappear into nothingness. The inside of what is presumably one of these slatted cattle cars is presented as puppet animation, filled with the female figures made up of wool string that start to unravel, as if tied to the apple tree, once the car takes off. As Ruth Barton has suggested, the film's

> *mise en scène* evokes the landscapes of peasant middle Europe. In the same vein, his wool figures are suggestive of pastness, of an era of craft skills and domestic labour, a world that will, literally, unravel, as its representatives are uprooted and deported in the slatted cattle truck. Even the animation technique, stop motion, is, in the era of computer-generated imagery, a throwback. (2014: 154)

I would add, however, that in the context of the abundance of digitally generated images Pikkov's choice of the 'archaic' technique also comes across as strikingly fresh. Moreover, the carefully choreographed (see Wong 2014), highly abstract, yet deeply touching representation of the terror and desperation of female deportees experienced over several weeks of their journey into the frightening unknown and compressed into merely six minutes of screen time, appears to evoke a spatiotemporal order that differs radically from both everyday perceptions of time and mainstream modes of spatiotemporal expression, not unlike in *In the Crosswind*. The two films also share a structural similarity, in that they are divided into two clearly recognisable formal regimes – the live-action of the opening and closing sequences versus the puppet animation of the deportation journey in *Body Memory*, and the stop-action of the thirteen long takes framed with the shorter shots of 'traditional' cinematic representation in *In the Crosswind*.

Significantly, both *In the Crosswind* and *Body Memory* are conceived (see Raskin 2014) – as well as perceived by commentators (see Ruus 2014) – as portrayals of *collective* memories and, by extension, reflections of/on national identity. Importantly, they are presented by a generation whose understanding of the deportations is based on mediated information and recollections rather than immediate experience. This invites us to pose a question as to what type of 'national narrative' they are inclined – to the 'linear-pedagogic' or to the 'disrupted-subversive'?

Labyrinth and Linearity in *In the Crosswind* and *Body Memory*

The major portion of *In the Crosswind*, presented in frozen images of *tableaux vivants*, appears to offer a representation of time that could be conceptualised as the Deleuzian time-image. In opposition to the movement-image that provides an edited version of time (Martin-Jones 2006: 22), these *tableaux vivants* allow the audience quite literally to 'see the passing of time in itself' (2006: 24). Moreover, as the deportees are completely under the sway of the perpetrators (the soldiers and the Siberian kolkhoz chairman in particular and the Stalinist regime in general), having lost all control over their life, the 'individualist ethos' of the movement-image is replaced by the time of dislocation, with characters 'unable to . . . react in order to influence his or her physical context' (2006: 24).

The same can be argued in relation to *Body Memory*. As a number of commentators have observed, the yarn puppets that gradually disintegrate as the train embarks on its dreadful journey and takes them further and further away from their homeland, 'are turned into marionettes controlled by some outside force' (Ladegaard 2014: 159). They are without any 'source of power available to them to survive this violent encounter and to resist the unknown source of terror controlling them from outside' (Richter 2014: 168–9). Furthermore, the string figures, while clearly representatives of the female gender, have little individual agency to begin with. In fact, they lose any trace of it as they form a single ball of thread in the final part of their journey, before all the yarn runs out of the slatted walls of the car, pulled by an invisible, overwhelmingly strong force that ultimately dismembers the travellers completely.

Significantly, Martin-Jones argues that the time-image is labyrinthine – 'without a centre, whose pathways expand outwards infinitely, [. . .] "rhizomatically"', forming parallel universes that exist 'in a virtual state, and become actual in the present along a series of infinitely bifurcating pathways' (Martin-Jones 2006: 23). This labyrinth of time emerges in *In the Crosswind* most powerfully on one occasion. About midway through the film Erna's voiceover describes her dream and, in parallel, the film's image-track reveals Heldur's fate – his execution without a proper trial at a Russian prison camp. Erna's dream, meanwhile, is about Heldur – how the two of them are in their garden at home, Heldur pruning apple tree branches. The seasons keep changing throughout the dream, from spring to autumn, the blossoming apple tree bears fruit, and Heldur appears and disappears intermittently, finally leaving Erna behind for good. For a moment, the images and soundtrack form a centreless labyrinth, merging dreams with reality. Yet by the end of the scene, this deterritorialised labyrinth is firmly reterritorialised, as Heldur's execution confirms the 'linear' understanding of history, with its sense of a radiant, untroubled past – now gone forever in the face of the horrors induced by the war – signified by the nostalgic figure of the apple tree in Erna's dream.

In *Body Memory*, the labyrinth emerges briefly at the very end of the film, as the disappearance of the serpentine beast and the train tracks opens an empty space of ambivalence, suggesting the possibility of a future without the dark shadows of this particular ancestral trauma. At the same time, while the tracks and the beast vanish, the grey sky still hangs low over the equally bleak, snow-spattered and barren landscape that could be read as a pessimistic assessment of the country's (and perhaps even the world's) current state of existence.

Yet, *In the Crosswind* and *Body Memory* also feature a number of traits clearly characteristic of the movement-image. For instance, the overall narrative flow of both films is fairly linear. The rather abstract story told in *Body Memory* literally follows the linear trajectory of the train tracks; the narrative of *In the Crosswind* does not reject a clearly established chain of causality, moving chronologically from the literally and metaphorically bright pre-war era to the traumatic events of a particular June morning in 1941, to the extended plight of the deportees on their way to and in Siberia and, finally, to Erna's return to Estonia many years later. Even the circular structure of the narration, beginning and ending with shots of Erna after her arrival in Stalinist Estonia, suggesting that the entire film can be read as an extended flashback, complemented by a couple more recollections of the past in her independent homeland, does not seriously violate the 'norms' of narrative form perpetuated in mainstream, 'classical' cinema. In fact, according to Martin-Jones, the 'pedagogical' recovery of the past 'is often achieved through the use of a flashback structure that begins with the end of the story and flashes back to the "beginning", thereby establishing a teleological progression' (Martin-Jones 2006: 28).

Perhaps even more important is the way *In the Crosswind* starkly contrasts the blissful existence of Erna's family in pre-war Estonia with their misery during World War Two and beyond. In particular, the brightly lit scenes of the family, drenched in the light of early-morning or late-afternoon sun, having breakfast, playing in the spacious garden of their country estate with their daughter, riding a boat on the waters of the calmly flowing river – all these overtly nostalgic, 'syrupy' (Ruus 2014) images signal the discourse of 'the good old times', ignoring quite uncritically the bleak political realities of Konstantin Päts's authoritarianism of the late 1930s and the equally dreary times of World War Two that had commenced well before the cataclysmic events in June 1941. In the early 1990s, the discourse of Päts's 'Golden Era' was 'normalised' and popularised, as well as politicised, by historians whose formative years coincided with the Singing Revolution of the late 1980s and who subsequently became a defining part of the political elite in post-socialist Estonia. *In the Crosswind* does apparently little to shake the foundations of this significant aspect of the 'dominant view of national history', which, according to Martin-Jones, is something movement-images tend to support. As described above, borrowing from Homi K. Bhabha (Bhabha 1990), Martin-Jones argues that the tendency of movement-image to present a linear version of 'national time' results in a 'pedagogical' approach to national history and identity, one that relies on the present (political) needs in order to 'decide which "rhetorical figures" [. . .] constitute the nation's origins' (Martin-Jones 2006: 33).

This 'pedagogical' understanding of the national past can be further theorised in relation to Mikhail Bakhtin's chronotopic model, in particular Bakhtin's idyllic chronotope that,

> finds expression predominantly in the special relationship that time has to space [. . .] an organic fastening-down, a grafting of life and its events to a place, to a familiar territory with all its nooks, crannies, its familiar mountains, valleys, fields, rivers and forests, and one's own home. Idyllic life and its events are inseparable from this concrete, spatial corner of the world, where the fathers and grandfathers lived and where one's children and their children will live. This little spatial world is limited

and sufficient unto itself, not linked in any intrinsic way with other places, with the rest of the world. But in this little spatially limited world a sequence of generations is localized that is potentially without limit. [. . .] This unity of place in the life of generations weakens and renders less distinct all the temporal boundaries between individual lives and between various phases of one and the same life. (Bakhtin 2004: 225)

The archetypal homestead of Erna's family, with a blossoming wild apple tree in its centre, is one of the most memorable images of the film's representation of the pre-war period. It is the very equivalent of nostalgic 'nationscape', a historically specific version of Bakhtin's idyllic chronotope, which I have analysed elsewhere in relation to Soviet Estonian cinema (Näripea 2011). The 'nationscape' is a notion that once bore connotations of political resistance to Sovietisation but that has in the post-Soviet period, and perhaps especially now that nationalism is once again raising its ugly head all over the world, come to signify adherence to undesirable isolationist sentiments. Although a particular narrative detail – the fact that Heldur is a member of the Defence League, a military organisation whose representatives were indeed one of the prime targets of Soviet repressions – might point to the possibility that Erna's family as part of the military elite does not stand for the *entire* Estonian society of the era, the film on the whole makes it very clear that it addresses *collective* rather than *individual* concerns and fates. In doing this, *In the Crosswind* virtually erases the aspect of class distinctions – another omission that makes the film vulnerable to criticism in terms of too-sweeping generalisations that silence any alternative voices and give preference to the 'pedagogic' narration of the nation.

The almost boundless series of miseries endured by Erna and her sisters in exile further support the 'pedagogic' rendition of history, in this case the Russian repressions of Estonians exiled to Siberia – that the majority of deportees were female; that the Russian functionaries abused and raped these women; that many children died of starvation (including Erna's daughter, Eliide); that most Estonian officers were ruthlessly and without a proper trial executed in prison camps (as Heldur was), and so on. Furthermore, the film reaffirms a number of long-held perceptions Estonians have had of Russia and the Russians, for instance that Russian villages were shabby and 'primitive' or that the ordinary Russians respected Stalin deeply, sincerely and without exception believed in the Communist 'utopia' and were all shocked to tears by the dictator's death. Without any intention to belittle the plight and trauma of those who suffered the Russian atrocities, or to question instances backed by factual support, the purpose of this discussion is to suggest that *In the Crosswind* demonstrates quite clearly an inclination towards a certain narrative of the nation, established at a particular point in the process of nation-building and subscribing to a specific set of 'truths'.

On one hand, *Body Memory* offers some subtle critiques of the dominant perceptions of national history. For example, the consistently sombre atmosphere of its opening and closing scenes seems to imply that the era before the deportations, as well as the condition of the contemporary world at large, and that of Estonia in particular, might not be completely cloudless. The film also appears to hint that the relationship of the women packed into the cattle cars was not always one of mutual support (as openly stated in *In the Crosswind*) and included darker acts of self-preservation, exemplified in the film's scene with a pregnant woman: when the thread of which the pregnant figure is made is completely unravelled and the egg representing her baby falls to the floor of the cattle car, another figure kicks it, instead of trying to save it. On the other hand, however, similarly to *In the Crosswind*, or more precisely even more radically than in Helde's film, *Body Memory* eradicates the question of class difference altogether, which is, as indicated above, highly problematic in terms of *whose* collective memories are voiced and whose are muted. Furthermore, as Jakob Ladegaard has pointed out, Pikkov's film relies rather uncritically on 'a Romantic national mythology' (Ladegaard 2014: 158–60) that becomes especially clear in the opening scene with the shots of a painter's easel mounted under an apple tree. Ladegaard emphasises that the Romantic painters played an important part in constructing national identities in the nineteenth century – an era that also gave birth to the Estonian national awakening movement. By positioning himself as a direct heir of Romanticism, as suggested by Ladegaard, Pikkov also becomes an obvious subscriber to the pedagogical discourse of the national narrative as proposed by Bhabha and Martin-Jones, in which the deterritorialising currents of labyrinthine time are firmly reterritorialised in a linear form, established by the dominant, pedagogical understanding of national history and identity.

Conclusion

The discussion of *In the Crosswind* and *Body Memory* suggests that both films tend to support and sustain the pedagogical narrative of the nation, as theorised by David Martin-Jones's mobilising of Homi K. Bhabha's and Gilles Deleuze's concepts. The pedagogical rendition of national history is especially striking from the domestic, Estonian point of view, as both films rely heavily on an understanding of national history and identity that was established during the transformative years of the Singing

Revolution and the following era of intensive nation-building; and the perceptions and 'truths' offered on-screen are easily recognisable and relatable to local audiences who are familiar with this discourse. While it can be argued that their representation of the gendered, specifically female, experience of deportations is an attempt to provide an alternative perspective on these journeys, the films tend to undermine other paths of socio-political divisions, such as class, and eventually reduce historical complexities into rather black-and-white summaries. However, combining impressive, even flamboyant, audiovisual design that transcends the narrow limits of the 'national' with equally transnational, yet clichéd, iconography of the Holocaust, tear-jerking characters, melodramatic storylines and sentimental metaphors, these representations of displacement have undoubtedly contributed to the better understanding and awareness of these tragic, but still obscure, historical episodes among the global audiences for whom such narrative devices are well-known from countless other war films. Finally, as the films discussed above form part of a wider Baltic 'wave' of deportation films featuring female protagonists, this initial analysis will hopefully function as a call for further investigations of these cinematic shadows of unforgotten ancestors.

The research for this article was funded by Eesti Teadusagentuur, grant no. IUT32-1.

Notes

1 Available at <https://vimeo.com/62741577> (last accessed 1 October 2016).
2 7,500 families, over 2.5 per cent of the Estonian population, about 70 per cent of them women, children and the elderly (Rahi-Tamm 2004: 29; see also Strods and Kott 2002: 20; Kasekamp 2010: 145–6).
3 Documentary portrayals of the deportations started to appear in parallel from the late 1980s, and are much more numerous, including perhaps most notably Imbi Paju's *Tõrjutud mälestused/Memories Denied* (2005) and Andres Sööt's *Ajapikku unustatakse meie nimi/Our Name Will Gradually Be Forgotten* (2008). Other recent Estonian feature films depicting Soviet atrocities, including deportations, during and in the aftermath of World War Two are *Vehkleja/Miekkailija/ENDEL – Der Fechter/The Fencer* (directed by Klaus Härö and co-produced with Finland and Germany, 2015), *Elavad pildid/Living Images* (directed by Hardi Volmer, 2013) and *Puhastus/Puhdistus/Purge* (an adaptation of Sofi Oksanen's immensely successful novel of the same title; directed by Antti J. Jokinen and co-produced with Finland, 2012). These are omitted from this analysis because the *journeys* of deportation are not central to their narratives.

4 The fact that the list of festivals where *Body Memory* was screened expands over four pages in the 2014 special issue of *Short Film Studies*, and includes twenty-seven awards, testifies to the film's undoubted success worldwide. *In the Crosswind* has also been quite popular on the festival circuit, scoring a number of awards (see <http://www.plutofilm.de/films/in-the-cross wind/0007> (last accessed 30 September 2016).

Works Cited

Anderson, Benedict (1983), *Imagined Communities: Reflections on the Origin and Spread of Nationalism*, London: Verso.

Bakhtin, Mikhail (2004), 'Forms of time and of the chronotope in the novel', in Mikhail Bakhtin (ed.), trans. Caryl Emerson and Michael Holquist, *The Dialogic Imagination: Four Essays by M. M. Bakhtin*, Austin: University of Texas Press, pp. 84–258.

Barton, Ruth (2014), 'Into what future?', *Short Film Studies*, 4:2, pp. 153–6.

Bell, Duncan (2006), 'Introduction: Memory, trauma and world politics', in Duncan Bell (ed.), *Memory, Trauma and World Politics – Reflections on the Relationship Between Past and Present*, Basingstoke: Palgrave Macmillan, pp. 1–29.

Bencze, Anja (2014), 'Martti Helde's "In The Crosswind": A bold film with a dramatic impact', *Euronews*, 21 November, <http://www.euronews.com/2014/11/21/martti-heldes-in-the-crosswind-a-bold-film-with-a-dramatic-im pact> (last accessed 1 October 2016).

Bhabha, Homi K. (1990), 'DissemiNation: Time, Narrative, and the Margins of the Modern Nation', in Homi K. Bhabha (ed.), *Nation and Narration*, London and New York: Routledge, pp. 291–322.

Deleuze, Gilles (1989), *Cinema II: The Time-Image*, trans. Hugh Tomlinson and Robert Galeta, Minneapolis: University of Minnesota Press.

Dima, Vlad (2014), 'The return of the animated dead in *Body Memory*', *Short Film Studies*, 4:2, pp. 163–6.

Flanagan, Matthew (2012), '"Slow Cinema": Temporality and Style in Contemporary Art and Experimental Film', PhD thesis, Exeter: University of Exeter.

Gray, Carmen (2015), 'Remembering 1941: How the Baltic states are confronting their deportation trauma on film', *The Calvert Journal*, 27 May, <http://cal vertjournal.com/articles/show/4159/deportation-films-soviet-baltic-states> (last accessed 1 October 2016).

Grozdanovic, Nikola (2014), 'TIFF review: Audacious "In The Crosswind" will leave you awestruck', *IndieWire*, 16 September, <http://www.indiewire.com/2014/09/tiff-review-audacious-in-the-crosswind-will-leave-you-awestr uck-272260/> (last accessed 1 October 2016).

Hiio, Toomas, Meelis Maripuu and Indrek Paavle (eds) (2006), *Estonia 1940–1945: Reports of the Estonian International Commission for the Investigation of Crimes Against Humanity*, Tallinn: Estonian International Commission for the Investigation of Crimes Against Humanity.

Kasekamp, Andres (2010), *A History of the Baltic States*, Basingstoke and New York: Palgrave Macmillan.

Ladegaard, Jakob (2014), 'Apple trees and barbed wire: Estonian memories of Soviet occupation in *Body Memory*', *Short Film Studies*, 4:2, pp. 157–61.

Levy, Daniel and Natan Sznaider (2002), 'Memory Unbound – the Holocaust and the Formation of Cosmopolitan Memory', *European Journal of Social Theory*, 5:1, pp. 87–106.

Martin-Jones, David (2006), *Deleuze, Cinema and National Identity: Narrative Time in National Contexts*, Edinburgh: Edinburgh University Press.

McNary, Dave (2016), 'Lisa Loven Kongsli, Sophie Cookson join Bel Powley's "Ashes in the Snow"', *Variety*, 12 May, <http://variety.com/2016/film/festivals/bel-powley-ashes-in-the-snow-lisa-loven-kongsli-sophie-cookson-1201772676/> (last accessed 2 October 2016).

Näripea, Eva (2011), *Estonian Cinescapes: Spaces, Places and Sites in Soviet Estonian Cinema (and Beyond)*. Dissertationes Academiae Artium Estoniae, vol. 6, Tallinn: Estonian Academy of Arts.

Rahi-Tamm, Aigi (2004), 'Inimkaotused', in Ülo Ennuste, Erast Parmasto, Enn Tarvel and Peep Varju (eds), *Valge raamat. Eesti rahva kaotustest okupatsioonide läbi 1940–1991*, Tallinn: Eesti Entsüklopeediakirjastus, pp. 23–42.

Raskin, Richard (2014), 'An interview with Ülo Pikkov on *Body Memory*', *Short Film Studies*, 4:2, pp. 138–40.

Richter, Nicole (2014), 'Unravelling the body without organs in *Body Memory*', *Short Film Studies*, 4:2, pp. 167–70.

Ruus, Jaan (2014), 'Tardunud mälestused', *Eesti Ekspress*, 3 April, <http://ekspress.delfi.ee/areen/tardunud-malestused?id=68366859> (last accessed May 2018 (NB paywall)).

Strods, Heinrihs and Matthew Kott (2002), 'The file on operation "Priboi": A re-assessment of the mass deportations of 1949', *Journal of Baltic Studies*, 33:1, Spring, pp. 1–36.

Tomberg, Donald (2014), 'Ajaga risti', *Teater. Muusika. Kino*, 5, pp. 90–7.

Tuumalu, Tiit (2014), 'Helde(ne) aeg – küüditamine!', *Postimees*, 24 March, <https://kultuur.postimees.ee/2737580/helde-ne-aeg-kuuditamine> (last accessed May 2018).

Vestergaard Kau, Edvin (2014), 'From concrete horror to symbolic significance in *Body Memory*', *Short Film Studies*, 4:2, pp. 145–8.

Weiss-Wendt, Anton (2008), 'Why the Holocaust does not matter to Estonians', *Journal of Baltic Studies*, 39:4, pp. 475–97.

Wong, Yutian (2014), 'Choreography of confinement in *Body Memory*', *Short Film Studies*, 4:2, pp. 141–4.

CHAPTER 7

The Holocaust and the Cinematic Landscapes of Postmemory in Lithuania, Hungary and Ukraine

Maurizio Cinquegrani

In recent years Holocaust documentaries have focused with consistency on the complex network of connections between personal and collective histories inherent to postgenerational journeys to ancestral homes or to the sites of the destruction of the Jews of Eastern Europe. This chapter follows three of these journeys and the documentary accounts of the itineraries of three travellers: a news reporter who is searching for her grandfather's house in Lithuania, an estranged Hassidic woman who is looking for an old couch in Hungary and a Roman Catholic priest who is following the footsteps of his grandfather to Ukraine. By means of familial connections with the past, these travellers explore landscapes characterised by profound absences and their journeys to Eastern Europe aim at exhuming and unlocking memories of the annihilated Jewish communities of these three countries. As Brad Prager has argued, Holocaust documentaries have used testimonies situated in present-day landscapes to 'awaken memories of other, older landscapes and testimonial performances' (2015: 25). Documentaries such as those investigated in this chapter have also engaged with these landscapes in order to retrieve distant histories of life and destruction, of loss, nostalgia, longing and mourning. These films have also contributed to addressing the Holocaust as a spatially complex event beyond its canonical localisation in Auschwitz. As Naomi Mandel suggests, the specific identification of the Holocaust with one location can give the false impression that 'the Holocaust is (merely) what occurred at the camps' whereas in fact it is the 'dissolution of an entire network of human relations, not just the killing, that constitutes the Holocaust' (2001: 219). With the same preoccupation for the ways in which Holocaust testimonies can maintain a limited topographical engagement with the complexity of the genocide, Hannah Pollin-Galay has argued that 'selected sites of mourning are elevated to a mythical register, while the surrounding space, which might reveal signs of contemporary culture and events, is largely left out of the tour' (2013: 29). As they articulate a reflection on the destruction of a network of human relations based on a focus on the places of extermination as well as the surrounding spaces, cinematic journeys to the sites of the Holocaust can contribute to tracing the topography of these landscapes by means of an investigation of individual histories and familial itineraries.

Claude Lanzmann's landmark Holocaust documentary *Shoah* (1985) has been discussed by Stella Bruzzi as a cinematic journey more preoccupied with addressing 'moments of encounter and examining the act of journeying than of reaching a fixed destination' (2006: 83). Similarly, Ron Steinman's *My Grandfather's House: The Journey Home* (2004), Pearl Gluck's *Divan* (2003) and Romain Icard's *Shoah par balles: L'histoire oubliée* ('Holocaust by Bullets: the Forgotten History', 2008), the three case studies addressed in this chapter, are primarily concerned with charting itineraries and with mapping the sites of memory, or the *lieux de mémoire*, of the Holocaust in Eastern Europe. *Lieux de mémoire* are defined by Pierre Nora as places where memory is seized by history and by the consequent requirement for every group to redefine its identity through the re-elaboration of its own past (1984: 7). In the context of the aftermath of the Holocaust, this re-elaboration has a distinctive international character which is reflected in the transnational journeys recorded in the three documentaries discussed here and in their exploration of the territories where the Final Solution unfolded. Documentaries such as *My Grandfather's House*, *Divan* and *Shoah par balles* are based on site-specific investigations of spaces associated both with collective histories of the destruction of the Jews at the hands of the Nazis and their collaborators and with the familial connections to the places where the Jews lived before the Holocaust. The protagonists of these documentaries experience the journey as a response to events which took place before their birth and which affected in different ways their families and communities; they have no memories of the events by recall but they share memories by imagination, which resulted from the exposure to family histories, photographs and reticent silences during childhood and later in life. This type of connection with the past has been discussed by Marianne Hirsch in terms of postmemory, a concept theorised as the process of transmission of trauma from those who witnessed the events to that postgeneration for which the traumatic occurrences that preceded their births appear to have become memories in their own right (2008). As we shall see, the destinations of the journeys followed in the documentaries addressed in this chapter can thus be thought of as *sites of postmemory*, where events that had belonged to the past and to myth are anchored in the present and in reality by means of personal environment-based explorations.

A House

Ron Steinman's *My Grandfather's House: The Journey Home* follows news reporter Eileen Douglas's journey to Lithuania and her attempt to locate her grandfather's house in Kaunas, the city where Sam Nadel had lived until he fled to America in 1911 to escape from conscription in the Tsar's army. The woman's journey of discovery to the place where, as she puts it, 'it all began', takes Douglas from New York City to the United States Holocaust Memorial Museum in Washington, and from her mother's attic in Syracuse to the streets and archives of Kaunas. In this film, archival footage and records, old family photographs and letters, personal reminiscences and interviews are used by Steinman to evoke the lost world of Lithuanian Jewry. As it provides an account of Douglas's journey to Kaunas in the footsteps of her grandfather, *My Grandfather's House* also aims at exhuming information on the family members who remained in Lithuania and were killed during the Holocaust, and charts an encounter with the fading remains of a long-gone life based on the act of travelling to familial *sites of postmemory* in an attempt to integrate the information provided by photographic remnants. The profound changes that have affected the physical environment of Kaunas, however, result in an expedition where proximity with the past by means of journeying is only partly achieved: Douglas discovers that her grandfather's house was demolished well before the time of filming.

My Grandfather's House begins with archival photographs of a snowy landscape in Eastern Europe and with footage of the Tsar's army on the march in the early 1900s. The opening sequences of the film use both photographs from Douglas's childhood and photographs of family members who were murdered by the Nazis and their collaborators.[1] Marianne Hirsch has argued that family photographs of a world annihilated by force can diminish distance between past and present and contribute to establishing an 'intimate material and affective connection' (2008: 116). Photographs taken before the war thus captured what no longer exists and provide the process of mourning with a visual referent. *My Grandfather's House* integrates these archival images with present-day footage and oral testimonies in order to bridge separation between past and present; in this context, family photographs become what Hirsch has described as 'leftovers, debris, single items that are left to be collected and assembled in many ways', which allow past events to be seen in the present 'in the form of a ghostly revenant, emphasizing, at the same time, its immutable and irreversible pastness and irretrievability' (1997: 13, 20). Pervaded by this sense of pastness, photographs taken in Kaunas at the beginning of the twentieth century illustrate the testimonies of several Lithuanian expats living in Syracuse and initiate the postmemory journey in time before the actual journey in space.

The photographs used in the film also provide the information that is used by Douglas to create an itinerary for her journey to Lithuania and into the past. Words written in Yiddish on the back of old photographs and a number of family letters reveal information on Douglas's ancestors in Lithuania while an online search leads to the discovery that Sam Nadel's sister, Ethel, died in Mesininku Street, in the Kaunas ghetto, at the age of forty-seven on 15 January 1943. Letters and photographs also explain that, while other relatives were murdered by Lithuanians even before the Germans arrived in Kaunas, several members of the family were deported to Siberia during the Soviet occupation and were thus saved from extermination by deportation; Sam's brother David was instead sent to a concentration camp in Estonia, while his family perished in the ghetto. These records are the first empirical evidence of the association between Douglas's own family and the Holocaust, and shed light on those doubts, silences, questions and reticent explanations that characterised her childhood experience and that of many members of the postgeneration. As Eva Hoffman has argued, several layers of mediation are required by those who did not live through the Holocaust in order to receive its knowledge and, as she reflected in writing on her own second-generation identity, has suggested that 'the memories – not memories but emanations – of wartime experiences kept erupting in flashes of imagery; in abrupt but broken refrains' (2004: 9). By means of her research, Douglas uses the archive as a medium that can facilitate her acquisition of knowledge of the Holocaust during a journey where the visual referents and the sites collide in those flashes of imagery evoked by Hoffman.

My Grandfather's House conveys the theme of travelling with two brief scenes filmed on board the car taking Douglas to the airport and on the plane flying to Vilnius. Douglas and her cousin arrive in Kaunas during a solar eclipse, walk the streets of the city and identify the site of the Hebrew school which was attended by their relatives. A visit to the Kaunas public archives reveals that Sam Nadel's family moved from a small *shtetl* to Kaunas in the second half of the nineteenth century and includes information on the house inhabited by the family in 1910. Local maps contribute to the identification of the exact location of the building and also reveal that it was demolished in 1986. Douglas visits the car park where the house used to stand; here, a few old houses, a cobbled pavement and the original market square survive and help Douglas to establish a connection with the past by means of the experience of the streets where her grandfather and the relatives who died in the Holocaust lived, shopped, walked and worked. The visit continues to the wooden houses and the unpaved road of Vežėjų Street in the former village of Vilijampolė (Slabodka in Yiddish), now a district of the city; this is the area where the ghetto was located and where the family was deported by the Nazis.[2] In the absence of survivors whose testimonies can contribute to bridge the gap between past and present, documents and photographs are again used by Douglas to make sense of this location and to establish a connection with the events that took place here during the war. As David Lowenthal suggests, each object 'is invested with a history of real or imagined involvements; their perceived identities stem from past acts and expectations' (1975: 5–6). Physical remnants in Vilijampolė, including houses and pavements, and photographic relicts fulfil this function in Douglas's journey in time and space; in the second documentary explored in this chapter, a very specific object, its real and imagined involvement and identity, is at the core of the act of journeying.

A Couch

In Pearl Gluck's *Divan*, the filmmaker travels from Brooklyn to Budapest, Hungary, in order to investigate her family's history and to reclaim an ancestral couch that belonged to her great-grandfather and upon which several esteemed Hasidic *rebbes* allegedly slept. The legend of the couch began in Rohod, a village in the Szabolcs-Szatmár-Bereg region of Hungary. In the opening sequences of the film, Gluck uses present-day black and white footage of the area to introduce the story with her own voiceover narration: during a Shabbat in 1879, her great-great-grandfather offered overnight hospitality to a traveller who was later identified as a famous Hasidic *rebbe*. The man left behind a vast sum of money hidden in the couch and this treasure was eventually used to build the local synagogue. The story ignites a personal account of Gluck's Hassidic background in New York, her parents' divorce and her estrangement from her father and her community, and this documentary thus becomes a personal reflection where the search for the ancestral couch can be read as a journey in time and space informed by the filmmaker's conflicting feelings towards her Hassidic background.

Like *My Grandfather's House*, Gluck's documentary exemplifies the necessity felt and experienced by a member of the postgeneration to bridge the gap between past and present by means of journeying. Both films use recurring tropes of travel narratives but, whereas *My Grandfather's House* primarily uses archival material to outline its journey in time, *Divan* includes contemporary maps that anchor its itinerary to a present landscape informed by past experiences and shared memories. Stella Bruzzi has described travel documentaries as chaotic narratives that 'can seem to have marginalized purposefulness, although their coherence tends to be cerebral, political or emotional rather than formal, as they frequently conclude ambiguously or their journeys left unresolved' (2006: 119). Accordingly, *My Grandfather's House* and *Divan* sketch unresolved narratives where both the search for the house and the couch are used to justify two explorations in space and time in the attempt to establish a link between memory, postmemory and identity. In *My Grandfather's House*, the attempt to locate Sam Nadel's home in Kaunas fails because the building had already been torn down at the time of filming; in *Divan*, the couch is located in Hungary but the plan to take the familial relict to New York fails on account of local resistance from the Jewish community.

The journey at the core of *Divan* is structured in relation to two main topographical oppositions. On the one hand there is the distance between Europe, its history and heritage and present-day life in the United States; on the other, there is a material and cultural gap between the traditional Hassidic area in Borough Park, the neighbourhood in the south-western part of Brooklyn where Gluck comes from, and, on the other side of the East River, Manhattan, where the filmmaker now lives. In the opening scenes of the film, footage of Hasidic Jews in Borough Park is accompanied by Gluck's voiceover explanation that the area is 'a whole Yiddish country nestled in Brooklyn'. These present-day images of the area are juxtaposed with amateur footage from the 1970s showing Gluck, who was born in 1972, as she was growing up in this Yiddish world where she dreamt of marrying a Torah scholar and having ten children. Borough Park is presented as an enclosed local community with many residents who have at times proudly claimed that they have never crossed the bridge to Manhattan. Gluck, on the other hand, became a rebel when she was thirteen, inspired by Barbra Streisand's character in *The Way We Were* (Sydney Pollack, 1973); at fifteen and after her parents' divorce, she followed her mother to Manhattan and became estranged from her father. Recurring shots of the bridges on the East River between Manhattan and Brooklyn, and scenes filmed aboard a train carriage of the B Sixth Avenue Express line as it crosses the river, as well as the close-up shot of the transport map of New York, convey the physical proximity of the enclosed community in Borough Park with Manhattan's cosmopolitanism, while Gluck's voiceover narration articulates a reflection on their cultural distance. The final sequence of the film shows the filmmaker's father visiting his daughter in Manhattan for the first time and thus bringing the two worlds a little closer.

In *Divan*, the idea of journeying is conveyed by a world map including an animation showing a plane heading from New York to Budapest and thus providing a visual referent to the other topographical opposition implied in its narrative. Once in Hungary, Gluck gives an account of her family's history, including her grandparents' survival and her father's birth in 1948, which accompanies various shots of the iconic Széchenyi Chain Bridge and Dohány Street Synagogue in part taken from a moving car driving the filmmaker from the airport to the King's Hotel in the Jewish neighbourhood of the city. Here, Gluck collects stories from members of the Jewish community of the city, including the kosher butcher, the baker and other shopkeepers, as well as the only relative who still lives in Budapest, Jolán Kuruc, who is the first cousin of Gluck's grandfather. As it establishes a spatial and temporal shift, the employment of oral histories recorded on location conforms to that attempt to use site-specific testimonies articulated by Andreas Huyssen as 'a potential antidote to the freezing of memory into the one traumatic image' (1993: 258).

A regional map illustrates the journey to Debrecen, the second-largest city of Hungary located about 140 miles east of Budapest. Gluck visits Baruch Rose, her grandfather's first cousin, the man who holds the key to the building where the couch is stored. As they drive to Rohod, about fifty miles north of Debrecen, another regional map and the road signs are used to detail the itinerary. Gluck and Baruch arrive in the rural village of Rohod and visit what is left of the family estate, a group of derelict barns. The filmmaker is also taken to what used to be the local synagogue, now a rundown and crumbling building, in which she sees the place where the Torah was kept as well as the former women's section. The *mezuzah* can be seen on the doorpost but the community has disappeared, with 95% of the Jews who lived in this part of the country having been killed by the Nazis. During the visit to the building where the divan is located, a former section of the synagogue which was turned into a stable during the war, it is revealed that Baruch Rose cannot let go of the divan because he sees it as a witness to the destruction of the Jews of Rohod. This couch is used in the film as a point of contention and ultimately as a narrative device that initiates the postmemory journey and embodies the roots of the Jews of Borough Park in Hungary, thus revealing a transnational connection between past and present.

The journey continues to the borderlands of Hungary and Ukraine, to the towns of Nagykálló, Hodász, Beregszász and Mezőkaszony. Here, Gluck visits local Jewish cemeteries and identifies the memorial built for the third and last rabbi who slept on the couch, Yisroel Tzvi Halevi Rottenberg, who died in Auschwitz in 1944. Footage of this journey is intercut with interviews with Gluck's siblings recorded in New York while they sit on an old couch bought by the filmmaker at a flea market in Hungary after she failed to obtain the original item. This juxtaposition is both geographical and temporal, with present-day life in America on the one hand and the experience of history in Europe on the other. Editing merges these two layers in one narrative that echoes what Huyssen has described as the simultaneity of past and present: 'A sense of historical continuity or, for that matter, discontinuity, both of which depend on a before and an after, gives way to the simultaneity of all times and spaces readily accessible in the present' (1993: 253–4). As this simultaneity ignites their reflection upon identity and survival, Gluck and her siblings articulate a postgenerational connection with the past that travels across three generations and integrates the information they acquired while growing up in a transatlantic Yiddish neighbourhood existing in the shadow of the world that was destroyed during the Holocaust. Like in *My Grandfather's House*, postmemory is conventionally presented as a negotiation between survivors and the postgeneration. An aspect of postmemory excluded in these contexts is the transmission of knowledge from the Holocaust bystanders to their own postgeneration; attached to another journey to Eastern Europe, this is the type of postmemory articulated in the journey recorded in the third documentary investigated in this chapter.

Bullets

In Romain Icard's *Shoah par balles: L'histoire oubliée*, Father Patrick Desbois travels to the mass graves of the Jews killed in Ukraine by the *Einsatzgruppen*, the Nazi mobile units responsible for the extermination of one and a half million Jews in Eastern Europe. Released shortly after the publication of Desbois' written account of the journey, this documentary follows the Roman Catholic priest to the killing fields, the forests, the farms and the small hamlets of the Ukrainian regions of Lviv, Nikolayev, Zaporozhye, Novozlatopol, Volhynia and Ivano-Frankivsk, on the trail of the so-called Holocaust by bullets. The priest's familial postmemory connection with these sites is provided by the experience of his own grandfather, who was deported by the Gestapo from Paris to Labour Camp 325 near the city of Rava-Ruska, in the Zhovkva region of western Ukraine, and who witnessed the destruction of the Jews of these lands.[3] The reticent accounts about French POWs heard by Desbois during his childhood alluded to the fact that the harsh reality of Labour Camp 325 was even more horrific for another group of prisoners; only later in life did Desbois understand that his grandfather was referring to the Jews of Lviv, who were brought to the camp for work and were eventually executed on-site or at the extermination camp in Bełżec, twenty miles north of Rava-Ruska.

Like *Divan* and *My Grandfather's House*, *Shoah par balles* is an account of a journey in time and space to a place where a member of the postgeneration can anchor familial stories to the landscape where they took place. The film opens with a close-up shot of barbed wire, the type of shot often associated with Auschwitz documentaries, filmed on the site of the labour camp near Rava-Ruska, today a border town between Poland and Ukraine and then part of the territories of what, in the interwar period, used to be the Second Commonwealth of Poland. *Shoah par balles* thus rejects the recurring identification of the Holocaust with what happened in Auschwitz and, by means of journeying, contributes to illustrate the spatial complexity of the event. Rob van der Laarse has suggested a useful reading of the focus on Auschwitz in the historiography of the extermination of the Jews and one that can also be applied to the narrative focus of many Holocaust films:

> If Auschwitz has become our common heritage, it is because it was the place where 'our' Jews from Western European cities went to, and from which we know so much because of its many survivors. But what do we know about the experiences of Eastern European Jews and non-Jewish populations? Many of them were already dead before the building of Birkenau in 1942, and almost none of the survivors were able to publish war memories. (2013: 214)

As a series of establishing shots of derelict spaces with crumbling buildings introduce the location on a frosty winter morning, *Shoah par balles* provides a shift in focus from the Jews killed in Auschwitz to those victims evoked by van der Laarse who were already dead when the infamous camp was being built. Information on the circumstances of the killings in the East is provided by a female voiceover that contextualises the sporadic narration given by Desbois. The journey from France to Ukraine is not accounted for and the film focuses on the local itinerary, which includes several villages in western Ukraine. As the narrator refers to an inmate who told his experiences to his grandchild, a long shot shows Desbois walking in the snowy landscape of the town of Rava-Ruska in the direction of the camera and, as his own voice replaces that of the narrator, explaining that he has been travelling to Ukraine with a team of forensic scientists in order to try to understand the Holocaust beyond the familiar context of Auschwitz and other camps in occupied Europe.

Linda Williams argues that Lanzmann's *Shoah* has shown that the truth of the Holocaust exists only as a collection of fragments and not as a totalising narrative (1993: 18). Similarly, *Shoah par balles* addresses the relationship between past and present, memory and testimony in a site-specific cinematic inquiry and thus contributes to unveiling fragments of the events which took place in the Eastern killing fields during the war. This aim is achieved by means of the physical exploration of the sites, a series of interviews with men and women who witnessed the destruction of the local Jewish communities and the use of archival images such as the footage filmed during the *Einsatzgruppen* executions in Liepāja, Latvia, 1941. A parallel between the journey of the Wehrmacht and the POWs from Western to Eastern Europe and the present-day exploration of the sites is established when footage taken from the car taking Desbois to Rava-Ruska is juxtaposed with archival images of Operation Barbarossa, Germany's invasion of the Soviet Union in summer 1941. Archival film of the German military campaign in the East includes a view taken from a moving train with a camera filming the railway tracks, and thus emphasises the theme of travelling and movement. This theme is also implied in the sequence showing Desbois preparing the journey with a local map of the Rivne area populated with red dots highlighting sites of mass graves near Kostopil, Oleksandriya, Sarny and Tuchyn.[4] Here, the remains of hundreds of victims buried in a mass grave near a Jewish cemetery are uncovered by the team, along with countless bullets used by the *Einsatzgruppen* to carry out the killings.

Ilan Avisar has argued that Alain Resnais's *Nuit et brouillard/Night and Fog* (1955), which was filmed in Auschwitz, presents an incongruous association between the peaceful rural landscape and the knowledge of the horrors which took place there. Similarly, the landscapes of Ukraine investigated by Desbois are also characterised by a contrast between harrowing memories of the extermination camps and the quiet beauty of the present-day landscape. For example, bystander Leonid Kvil takes Desbois and his team to a site near Busk, where two large vans took Jewish children to the pits where they were executed; this sequence includes scenes filmed in a nearby village where locals share accounts of the Nazi occupation as they sit outside their homes. These images of a rural landscape and community are difficult to reconcile with the devastating violence evoked by these stories and by the human remains emerging from the fields all around them; ultimately, the priest's attempt to retrieve past events from these present-day landscapes does not provide an all-encompassing picture of the Holocaust by bullets but, like Lanzmann in *Shoah*, Desbois and Icard succeed in gathering fragments of a past too complex and harrowing to be grasped in its entirety.

Conclusion

The travellers encountered in these documentaries share a familial connection with the Holocaust, which has taken them to explore sites of postmemory beyond the traditional association between the persecution of the Jews and the territories of the Third Reich, and beyond the identification of the Final Solution with the concentration and death camps in Auschwitz. Their journeys in time and space have embraced David Lowenthal's idea that 'physical residues of all events may yield potentially unlimited access to the past' and that, given the right methodology, no historical record can elude retrieval (1985: 19). Unlike *Divan* and *My Grandfather's House*, however, *Shoah par balles* does not seek an individual or familial story associated with a house once inhabited by Jews or a couch once used by a particular Hassidic *rebbe*; Icard's film is concerned with a collective memory of annihilation whose persistence in the presence is provided by a mosaic of testimonies and by the bullets that can still be seen on the killing grounds of Ukraine. As it originates from the earlier journey westwards undertaken by a survivor, each film provides an account of travelling from West to East and, as highlighted in this chapter, uses different combinations of voiceover narration, location shooting and archival material. The actual journey bridging the gap between past and present is at the core of their narratives and it allows these films to gather a series of fragments of a historical event whose totality is beyond reach, in an attempt to overcome the temporal chasm between the present of the filmmakers and an irreversible and irretrievable past. And yet, rather than looking back at the Holocaust and becoming frozen in the process, these documentaries aim at identifying the ways in which the past is still inscribed in a present made of remnants and absences and informed by processes of persistence and disfigurement inherent to the sites visited by members of the postgeneration.

Notes

1 In 1983 Douglas found a number of family photographs inside a drawer in the suburban house where she grew up.
2 The journey to Lithuania also reveals a failed attempt to identify her great-grandmother's grave at one of the Jewish cemeteries and provides an account of the encounter with an elderly woman in Vilnius who was deported to Siberia with Douglas's family. After a short sequence filmed in Israel during a family reunion, the film ends with a scene filmed at Sam Nadel's grave in the state of New York.
3 The film explains that between April and June 1942 the Nazis deported to Rava-Ruska about 10,000 French POWs from Germany; the number

eventually grew to 25,000. An even larger number of Jews and Soviet POWs were also taken to the camp and many died as a result of abuse, starvation and executions.

4 During the visit to these villages, Yossip Revonuk, Temofis Ryzvanuk, Olga Havrylivna, Stephen Unchik, Nadia and Misha Stepanova and Adolf Vislovski are among several witnesses recalling the executions and leading Desbois and his team to the locations.

Works Cited

Avisar, Ilan (1988), *Screening the Holocaust: Cinema's Images of the Unimaginable*, Bloomington: Indiana University Press.

Bruzzi, Stella [1997] (2006), *New Documentary: A Critical Introduction*, London and New York: Routledge.

Desbois, Patrick (2008), *The Holocaust by Bullets: A Priest's Journey to Uncover the Truth Behind the Murder of 1.5 Million Jews*, London and New York: Palgrave Macmillan (originally published in French by Michel Lafon in 2007).

Hirsch, Marianne (1997), *Family Frames: Photography, Narrative, and Postmemory*, Cambridge, MA: Harvard University Press.

Hirsch, Marianne (2008), 'The Generation of Postmemory', *Poetics Today*, 29:1, pp. 103–28.

Hoffman, Eva (2004), *After Such Knowledge: Memory, History and the Legacy of the Holocaust*, New York: Public Affairs.

Huyssen, Andreas (1993), 'Monument and Memory in a Postmodern Age', *The Yale Journal of Criticism*, 6:2, pp. 24–261.

Laarse, Rob van der (2013), 'Archaeology of Memory: Europe's Holocaust Dissonances in East and West', in *Heritage Reinvents Europe*, Dirk Callebaut, Jan Mařik and Jana Mařiková (eds), European Archaeological Council Occasional Paper No.7, Budapest: Archaeolingua, pp. 121–30.

Lowenthal, David (1975), 'Past Time, Present Place: Landscape and Memory', *Geographical Review*, 65:1, pp. 1–36.

Lowenthal, David (1985), *The Past Is a Foreign Country*, Cambridge: Cambridge University Press.

Mandel, Naomi (2001), 'Rethinking "After Auschwitz": Against a Rhetoric of the Unspeakable in Holocaust Writing', *Boundary 2*, 28:2, pp. 203–28.

Nora, Pierre (ed.) (1984), *Les Lieux de Mémoire: La République*, Paris: Gallimard (Bibliothèque illustrée des histoires).

Pollin-Galay, Hannah (2013), 'The Holocaust is a Foreign Country: Comparing Representations of Place in Lithuanian Jewish Testimony', *Dapim: Studies on the Holocaust*, 27:1, pp. 26–39.

Prager, Brad (2015), *After the Fact: The Holocaust in Twenty-First Century Documentary Film*, London and New York: Bloomsbury Academic.

Williams, Linda (1993), 'Mirrors Without Memories: Truth, History, and the New Documentary', *Film Quarterly*, 46:3, Spring, pp. 9–21.

CHAPTER 8

Hesitant Journeys: Fugitive and Migrant Narratives in the New Romanian Cinema

László Strausz

Since the mid-2000s, Romanian cinema has been recognised by critics and international festival audiences as an original and coherent cinematic mode of expression that engages with the difficult task of trying to come to terms with the State's socialist past and articulating transformations in contemporary society. Films such as *Moartea domnului Lăzărescu/ The Death of Mr. Lazarescu* (Cristi Puiu, 2005), *A fost sau n-a fost?/12:08 East of Bucharest* (Corneliu Porumboiu, 2006) and *4 luni, 3 săptămâni și 2 zile/4 Months, 3 Weeks and 2 Days* (Cristian Mungiu 2007) each address the problems of the legacy of the country's history and the ways in which its reverberations impact post-socialist society. Recently, several filmmakers associated with the cycle have turned to genre formulas and thereby contributed to the heterogenisation of the new Romanian cinema, but the key element is still intact: 'the creation of a spectatorial subject position that constantly moves back and forth between often contradictory or ambiguous interpretations [of the social] offered by the texts' (Strausz 2017: 149). While most accounts of the film cycle in question approach the works from the vantage point of realism and transparency,[1] I argue that the films do not so much reveal a certain social world as they depict the mobile, hesitant ways in which the depicted social institutions and in turn the films' audiences *produce a reality* in post-socialist society.[2] In order to illustrate the historical-interpretive advantages of the concept of hesitation, this essay will focus on three fugitive and migrant narratives of new Romanian cinema, *Aurora* (Cristi Puiu 2010), *Morgen* (Marian Crișan 2010) and *Periferic/Outbound* (George Bogdan Apetri 2010), in which the characters physically move back and forth between various institutions such as the prison, the State foster home, the police and the immigration authorities. This physical movement, however, becomes a reflexive, modernist gesture about the ways in which social space is produced. By shifting and moving their characters in between these institutions and the social spaces they occupy, the films depict disorientation and hesitation as the fundamental element in the identity of the post-socialist subject.

Writing now, when the migration crisis all over Europe has reached critical dimensions, Marian Crişan's 2010 film *Morgen* seems prophetic. The film provides not only a humanitarian response to the large-scale crisis that hit Europe several years later, namely solidarity between fleeing refugees and the locals, but also effectively criticises the populist rhetoric of xenophobia that surfaced widely across the continent. While *Morgen* introduces a Kurdish man who wants to cross the continent to get to his family, the other films that I will discuss here do not explicitly thematise international migration. Movement throughout this chapter refers also to the seemingly aimless roaming through cityscapes (*Aurora*) and to the panicked fleeing of fugitives across indifferent urban spaces (*Outbound*). In this sense, mobility is understood as a text, which I will approach here using a discursive apparatus.

In the interpretation of new Romanian cinema's hesitant rhetoric, Henri Lefebvre's ideas about the performative production of social space (Lefebvre 1991) play a central role. Space accordingly becomes an arena in which contested social identities are battled out through the dialectical relationship of the panoptical forces of social control and the everyday practices of the users of space. This point can also be teased out via Certeau's formulation of crossing space as an enunciative act: '[t]he act of walking is to the urban system what the act of speaking, the *Speech Act*, is to the language [. . .] A first definition of walking seems to be the space of uttering' (Certeau 1999: 106). The model of the social production of space needs to be specified through the context of social and institutional changes in the former Eastern bloc. Thus, in the context of post-socialism, we have to pay attention to the constant transformation of the top-down forces which Lefebvre has called the representation of space, referring to the geometrical-objectifying practices 'tied to the relations of production and to the "order" which those relations impose, and hence to knowledge, to signs, to codes' (Lefebvre 1991: 33). With the anticipated top-down control gone, the transitionality of space is pushed into the foreground more forcefully. Therefore, the peripheral characters in the three films discussed – a criminally insane man, a former prostitute and a refugee – who plan their own routes and thus performatively produce their social identity through spatial means, cannot identify the top-down strategies of panoptical control. The schemes of the regulatory mechanisms alienating and reifying quotidian spatial performances are shifting and unknown: their apparatus can only be recognised in practice on a trial-and-error basis.[3] This experimental, errant mobility of the films' characters constitutes the specificity of the post-socialist production of space throughout new Romanian cinema.

Cristi Puiu's 2010 film *Aurora* highlights this tendency to depict character movement that seemingly has no goals. The three-hour-long, monotonous work revolves around Viorel, whose existential frame has entirely disintegrated. After rising from a woman's bed in the evening, the slow-paced narrative finds him again in the suburbs of the city at dawn crossing a pair of train tracks. Hiding in between truck trailers, he secretly observes a woman with two kids. Later, he is shown in a factory hall talking briefly to some workers, then in an office space making a call only to hang up immediately. Before he arrives at his dilapidated apartment he stops at a chemist's and hides between the aisles when he spots someone. Frequently, in between these episodes Puiu shows the silent Viorel in his car sitting in traffic, waiting at red lights. The trembling frame adds a nervous quality to the images. When coupled with the obscurity of his motivations and the remarkably long, hesitant takes – almost every scene consists of a single, uninterrupted shot – the sequences diffuse the conventional, causal expectations of the viewer. Puiu is capable of injecting these contemporary urban spaces with a disturbingly detached quality: they do not really help to establish hypotheses about the psychological embeddedness of Viorel's actions, but rather function as cold externalisations of his unhinged internal world. Even though Viorel is constantly moving, his mobility expresses a radical narrative stasis through his character's impenetrability, which is further intensified by the director enclosing his figure in frames within the frame in a large majority of the film's scenes.

This tension between movement and immobility becomes a reflexive device that emphasises the epistemological limits of the viewer's capacity to project and establish a coherent world behind the story. Monica Filimon notes that '[i]t is in the negotiation between film and spectator' that Puiu is interested. For the director, film is 'a tool for the investigation of reality, rather than its reproduction, and [he] emphatically underscore[s] its perceptual and expressive limits and biases' (Filimon 2014: 171). This phenomenological account of Puiu's art is thrown into strong relief by his insistence on constantly visually reminding the viewer of their distance from Viorel's inner world. In almost every scene, the depth composition of the shots isolates Viorel in space by recording his elusive actions through doorframes. Puiu makes the frame-within-the-frame aesthetic the compositional cornerstone of his version of hesitation. This strategy establishes and isolates spatial layers in front of and behind his character that we hope will include some information about the actions we witness, but instead their emptiness reflects back our attempts to impose coherence on the narrative. Whether we spot him in the lover's apartment smoking by himself, wedged between the trailers peeping at the family he lost, displaying his inability to maintain social bonds with former co-workers in the factory offices, milling around in his half-renovated apartment, taking a shower, waiting for the movers to finish emptying some rooms etc., each of these shots are blocked both from the left and the right side by doorframes, partitions, walls or pieces of furniture. This visual gesture on the one hand diminishes the 'active' part of the screen occupied by the protagonist by reducing it often to as little as one-third of its overall surface. On the other hand, these partitions remain perceptual obstacles that thwart our attempt to get through to Viorel and understand his actions. This impossibility concerns the opaqueness of Viorel's character, the unavailability of his motivations, but more importantly, our role in attempting to fill in these blanks and consider divergent contexts in our interpretations of the protagonist's actions (Figure 8.1).

From the early scenes onwards, Viorel's seemingly random mobility signals to audiences the possibility that his visits to various spaces of the city and other activities will connect later on. This expectation is met in the sense that the preparations do culminate in the killing of several people, but other than signalling the general deprivation of the character in his collapsed life, the film does not outline Viorel's incentives. Importantly, we do not find out why he chooses to kill his wife's notary and a woman at the notary's side, or his own mother-in-law and her husband. If, as we suspect, it was his divorce and the loss of his job that turned his life upside-down, then we would expect him to take revenge on those directly responsible. *Aurora*, however, suppresses the question of causality and responsibility entirely.

The ways in which Puiu depicts Viorel interacting with his physical surroundings map his quotidian spatial (non-)strategies. By isolating the character in space, *Aurora* reveals how Viorel's performance lacks continuity and cohesion, which shuts off the familiarity necessary for the navigation of social life. The character's disjointed performances produce the social space he is part of, but of course this relationship is a mutual one: the post-socialist spaces of contemporary Romania delineate the limited performative repertoire available for Viorel as well. The patterns of this common dependency show an aimlessness that is different from the carefree perambulatory strolling of Benjamin's middle-class flâneur (Benjamin 2006). Puiu's film depicts a set of performances that are enveloped by a transitional social disorder, in which the strategies and practices of panoptical-regulative institutions remain unclear. The crisis of the panoptical is effectively illustrated by the paralysed police officers, who

Figure 8.1 Blocked transparency: visual barriers emphasise the viewer's activity.

possess absolutely no vocabulary to summarise and report Viorel's actions. As Viorel sits with the two civilian-clothed officers at the police station, the assumed power imbalance between them begins to fade. Arranged around a table, the triangular distribution of the characters in the frame suggests a commensurability of the two sides. Puiu further emphasises this visually by equating the detective's character compositionally to Viorel. When the disbelieving investigator calls to get confirmation of the protagonist's confessed murders, he is framed the same way as Viorel throughout the entire film, behind a doorframe in the background. This spatial rhetoric shows how the dialectic between the panoptical and the quotidian use of space is interrupted. During the interrogation, Viorel lists all the factual data about himself, his wife, their children, and each of the murdered characters as well: their names, addresses, occupation, relationship status, and so on. However, these data do not explain the complex and uncertain factors that made him commit the murders. As he mistrustfully remarks to the officers: '[d]on't get me wrong, but I've listened to you and seen the way you think you know and understand and are perceiving me, and I'm getting scared. I don't know if you understand me.' This comment succinctly reveals the interplay between the disoriented quotidian practices of Viorel, and the equally confused strategies of the authorities to measure and control social space. According to Lefebvre, the workings of the panoptic institutions correspond with geometrical-objectifying practices generally imperceptible to the quotidian. The abstract representation of space erases the traces of everyday routines, and needs to be understood as a regulatory mechanism alienating and reifying those performances. It is this interrupted dialectical relationship of the social production of space that is articulated by the protagonist's sentence in the final scene of *Aurora*. Mobility and lived space in the film entail the disorientation of the outcast character, and the ineffectuality and blindness of top-down social control across the post-socialist spaces of contemporary Romania. The visual strategies of the film, most importantly the unsteady frame combined with the estranging framing practices, constitute for audiences a subject position that foregrounds their own attempts to make sense of the events. Puiu invites viewers to confront the epistemological boundaries of filmic, and consequently the limits of social, construction.

A different type of fugitive character, Matilda, the protagonist of *Outbound*, draws distinctive paths with her movements in the urban spaces of Bucharest. The aimless mobility of Viorel here gives way to a flight with well-defined destinations. Matilda is released from prison for twenty-four hours to attend her mother's funeral. The film follows her throughout the day, during which she attempts to reconnect with her brother, collect a debt and run away from the remaining three years of her prison sentence with her son. According to her plan, she will be smuggled out of the country in a container on a freight ship, which clearly refers to the protagonist's futile attempt to escape physical and social constraints in a prison-like metal box. The various stops that punctuate her hectic movement through Bucharest demarcate the different social contexts that have failed to assimilate Matilda: her family, which has stigmatised her, the criminals with whom she made a living before she was sentenced and finally the official authorities sanctioning her freedom. Restricted to Matilda, the film's narrative takes us along on her journey, during which nothing goes according to plan.

After being released early in the morning from prison, Matilda visits three men (or rather two men and a boy), and the film is divided into three chapters bearing their names. Apetri announces the beginning of the chapters with high-angle extreme long shots showing the city from above. A subsequent cut takes the viewer from bird's-eye perspective into the beds of three male characters: her brother Andrei, the pimp Paul she used to work for and her son Toma (Figure 8.2).

These cuts are significant because they illustrate the Lefebvrian thesis about the social production of space, which he describes as the dialectic interplay between the geometric-panoptic and everyday practices. The detached high-angle shots that open the chapters of the film are replaced by medium shots or close-ups of the men who have the capacity to help the protagonist. Changing the perspective of the viewer so swiftly, the shift from the impersonal-geometric perspective to the quotidian-personal sphere carries the promise that Matilda will find support, which throughout the course of the film is denied her. Andrei could embrace his sister despite her troubled past but ultimately does not; Paul could pay her the money he owes her but does not; and Toma could choose not to take off with all of his mother's money but decides to leave her behind. Thus, the impersonality of the social institutions the film introduces (family, prison, orphanage) is reinforced by the indifference of the individuals who could choose to make a difference.

Matilda passes through various settings throughout the day, which function as a kaleidoscopic image of the various social frames she has fallen out of. The first part depicts the indifference of her family towards her life. After she shows up at Andrei's apartment and they travel to a suburb to attend the funeral, each of the relatives she comes into contact with disowns her. Matilda's character is measured, described and regulated from an unexpected direction: the institution of the family. As the mourning members gather for the burial lunch in the garden of the mother's

Figure 8.2 Changing the narrative's scale.

house, the various relatives look at the stigmatised protagonist with barely concealed contempt and disgust. Consolidating the affective impact of the protagonist's exclusion, Apetri uses shallow-focus close-ups that isolate Matilda's character in depth. Her only ally, Andrei, also sides with the family and denounces the bond that connects them. Social exclusion expressed through visual objectification ultimately chases her away.

In the second part of *Outbound*, we follow the protagonist on her visit to Paul, her former pimp. It transpires from the slow trickle of information that Matilda went to jail after cutting up the face of a client who abused her. She took full responsibility, made a deal with Paul to serve the sentence and remain silent about the man's role in exchange for ten thousand euros. However, Paul refuses to pay the full amount as she has shown up for the money before the end of her full prison term. The sequence unfolds in the transitional spaces of cars, hotel rooms and corridors, but also around the Lacul Morii, a mostly deserted empty area on the outskirts of the city with decrepit industrial structures. Apetri's preference for decayed urban spaces that do not carry any identifiable social coordinates recalls Augé's concept of the non-place (Augé 1995: 75–115) devoid of an identity or historical relations. However, it is more accurate to describe *Outbound*'s settings as the cold spaces of the business transactions they envelop. Each of them is in fact overdetermined by its economic function: the exchange of human bodies for money. Matilda is described in this environment via her former role as a prostitute working for Paul. In the last segment of the film her son, Toma, is also introduced in this no-man's land as a young prostitute. Matilda's erratic movement through the desolate spaces operates as a desperate rebellion against the confining social frames that overdetermine her life. Apetri's film visualises this disobedience through the persistently trembling, lengthy handheld shots that follow the protagonist. Consistently, the film positions audiences slightly behind Matilda as she leaves both the family's suburban house at the end of the first episode and the crashed car of Paul at the end of the second episode. In the last segment of the film she furiously chases away the client of her eight-year-old son, which *Outbound* depicts in similar mobile following shots. As Matilda runs towards the client's car, the wildly shaking handheld camera pins us to her figure racing through the dilapidated urban desert with only some tall prefab housing estate buildings looking on indifferently in the background. Similarly to the earlier scene where Paul sells the young Selena's body to an older man at the Lacul Morii, these events take place on a dilapidated former construction site, but this time in the middle of Bucharest. In the area between the boulevards Nerva Traian, Unirii, Octavian Goga and Mircea Voda, Ceauşescu started a colossal construction project, razing the local neighborhood, which was never to be completed. Today only the crumbling foundations of the planned buildings are visible, and vegetation is starting to take over the area, the space which provides the setting for prostitution in the film. These central but at the same time peripheral enclosures of the city effectively point to the transformed dialectics of the social production of space. Tracing the disappearance of the once-existing, but now disintegrated panoptical control within the realities of the contemporary narrative, Matilda has to confront the traumatic present in which her young son could not escape his mother's destiny: prostitution. The outlines of the deteriorated social order (symbolised by the ruins of the foundations of the socialist State's building project) accommodate, and lead to the terrifying present of youth-hustling. In this sense the ruins serve as cartographic reminders of a collapsed socialist regime, and thereby of the disillusioned and unsettling present.

Visually, each sequence links the audience to the protagonist, who desperately attempts to escape her past. Matilda's constant physical movement throughout the film's scenes stems from her need to start over. After both her relatives and her former pimp disown her, she constructs the idyllic idea of escaping with Toma towards the unknown. As they travel by train towards the port town of Constanta, her young son, socialised in the harsh realities of State foster care, takes off with all the money Matilda grabbed from Paul in the second episode. The ability and freedom to move, the direct antithesis of her prison confinement, has functioned throughout the film as a promise for the protagonist. In the last shot of the film, the elusive dream of freedom and movement is visually denied her: standing on the pier in Constanta looking out towards the Black Sea, she realises that her escape routes have closed. The wide-open space of the water does not affirm the individual's ability to move. Instead, the film turns open space into a visual signifier of enclosure and disillusionment. Matilda's performativity consists of identifying and moving through social spaces she hopes will be able to shelter her. Spatial mobility as the visual marker of *Outbound* is anchored in these inquisitive, hesitant gestures of Matilda. She is a much more active character than Viorel in *Aurora*: her mobility always targets some kind of destination. However, these objectives turn out to be illusionary. By visually attaching the viewer to Matilda, the restricted, self-conscious narration simultaneously exhibits to the audience the protagonist's hesitant mission to restart her life, a struggle surrounded by the total indifference of her environment, and the crisis of the various social institutions that demarcate her journey.

In *Morgen*, the praxis of mobility in the border zone between two nation states, Romania and Hungary, is turned into a display of the performative production of social reality. On the one hand, the film reveals how the dialectics between the authorities and the quotidian subjects, whose lives these institutions regulate, is thrown out of balance: the officers in *Morgen* quite openly display their lack of interest in protecting the national borders. On the other hand, the film also exhibits how the quotidian characters, faced with a migrant/refugee in their personal sphere, reformulate their opinion after these face-to-face encounters. Nelu, *Morgen*'s protagonist, is a security guard in a local supermarket in the small border town of Salonta. Crișan's decision to make a security guard out of his leading character immediately displays the permeability of the two sides of the institutions and the sphere of the everyday. Nelu is charged with upholding security in a store where he not only personally knows each of the customers, but is good friends with most of them. In the film's first scenes he jovially helps shoppers but also assists colleagues in stacking the shelves. This shift in the roles of the supposedly controlling authorities will be confirmed towards the end of the film, when border patrol officers are depicted on similarly disoriented missions.

As we are introduced to Nelu, the film makes it clear that the regulations these institutions are supposed to uphold are increasingly meaningless: in the store, the need for security seems ridiculous in a place where people call each other by their first names. The first scenes of the film also effectively display this central theme through the protagonist's hobby: his fishing trips regularly take him across the Romanian–Hungarian border. The small canals zigzagging across the border offer him the opportunity to fish without any regard for the territorial regulations imposed on people on both sides. As Nelu tries to cross the border on his way home from such a trip with a live fish in a bucket, the border patrol officer makes him throw out the fish as he has no official permit for the transportation of live animals. By fictionalising the hollow and ridiculous regulations, and by depicting Nelu's perplexed reaction to them, his character is placed between the panoptic and the quotidian, a position very similar to the physical location of his house in the national border zone between the two countries. During the episode, the empty place in the motorcycle's sidecar foreshadows the security guard's solidarity by appearing to be waiting for Behran, a Kurdish man from Turkey on his way to his family in Germany (Figure 8.3).

The stasis of Nelu's secluded and in many ways idyllic life is interrupted by the arrival of Behran. Crișan withholds all information about Behran's life or his motivations for crossing the continent. It is not clear whether he left Turkey as a result of being a persecuted member of an

Figure 8.3 Waiting for Behran: the space of solidarity.

ethnic minority, or whether he is heading for Germany in hope of a better life. In the former scenario, he is a refugee, while in the latter case he could be described as an economic migrant. These differences are not simply technical distinctions of terminology, especially when we consider the ongoing humanitarian crisis on Europe's eastern borders that erupted in the summer of 2015. Various nationalist-populist politicians deliberately mix the two above categories by labelling Syrian refugees fleeing the destruction of the civil war in Syria economic migrants who attempt to take the jobs of the locals. Crişan's refusal to allow insight into Behran's background suggests to the viewer that it is increasingly hard and politically dangerous to determine the identities of the migrants or refugees when looking from the economically much more prosperous centres of Europe (even if the centre in the film's narrative is Romania, itself a peripheral country in Europe). *Morgen*'s social progressiveness first of all consists in its refusal to speculate on the exact classification of Behran's situation: whether political refugee or economic migrant, Nelu helps him, and thus displays undifferentiated solidarity towards the Kurdish man. By attempting to cross the continent and its several national borders on foot, Behran embodies a threat to the monocular logic of the nation state; an idea displayed as increasingly problematic through the various conflicts in *Morgen*.

The fabric of Nelu's everyday habits and praxis is produced through his quotidian relations with friends, co-workers, neighbours and even the authorities, who largely turn a blind eye to his technically illegal fishing trips across the border. This world based on interpersonal relations and acquaintance is interrupted when Nelu takes in Behran: he starts to worry about the consequences of these actions, and is visibly detached at work and at home as well. The pressing question of how his solidarity with the Kurdish man will influence his well-functioning network of quotidian relationships is effectively shifted onto the viewer of the film, who is positioned across the scenes in handheld shots wobbling behind Nelu. However, the full and medium following shots create character alignment both with Nelu and Behran. This throws into relief not simply the protagonist's support of the migrant man, and his actions' repercussions within the small community of Salonta, but also powerfully communicates to audiences the state of total displacement in which Behran finds himself. While for Nelu, solidarity with the troubled migrant is evident (he is worried about the effects of his solidarity but does not question whether he should help or not), the changes that the acts of solidarity effect in their world are emphasised throughout the film via his and Florica's characters. Nelu's bossy wife is initially irritated when she finds Behran in their house. Importantly, Crişan hints at the manipulative power of media representations when Florica attacks his husband for taking the Kurdish man in: 'he could be a terrorist, he could have diseases, don't you watch TV?' After spending some days under one roof with Behran, Florica becomes entirely comfortable with his presence. The scene with Nelu and Behran playing cards while Florica is already in bed humorously depicts the gradual transformation of the initially hostile relations between them. Subsequently, Behran turns out to be a helpful person to have around the house: he chops wood, peels potatoes and after a while gets a job at the bread-slicing machine in the supermarket. After their shifts are over, the three of them return to the farm as a family: 'let's go home!' Nelu says.[4] While these adjustments in Florica's attitude are not foregrounded, they are noticeable through their capacity of pointing towards her growing sense of solidarity.

The football game episode of the film highlights a similar adjustment in the community's attitude. Behran travels with the other Salonta men to a neighbouring Hungarian town to a football game. Their bus is full of fans singing and drinking, and the border police do not check them each individually. Behran easily makes it across the border to Hungary. Getting out of the bus, he and Nelu hug and the migrant walks free, now one country closer to his destination: Germany. However, in the next scene he spots a police car, turns back right away and makes his way back to Nelu, who is already at the local football field watching the game. After the protagonist and migrant unite, a player on the field commits a foul and a fight breaks out, in which the fans participate as well. Crişan mocks the fans' seemingly nationalistic rage by having Behran, the ultimate outsider, join their brawl: he has no stake in the fight whatsoever. Ultimately, however, his participation integrates him into the community of the Romanian fans, and the team end up paying for the medical treatment of Behran's injuries. The solidarity that Nelu and Florica show in varying degrees towards him is echoed by the larger quotidian community of the football fans.

While the community's stereotypes are resolved by the face-to-face encounters between Behran and the locals, the authorities are clueless as to how to deal with the escalating situation at the border. Officers arrest Behran at Nelu's house for having no identification papers, but they let him go again at the border zone: they have no idea what to do with him and all the other migrants sitting and waiting for a chance to cross. 'We could catch them, but what's the point? More will come tomorrow. We are just a couple of guys here . . .' – a border patrol officer tells Nelu. This last sentence shows that Crişan alleviates the two individual officers from responsibility and is interested in demonstrating the cynical futility of the national authorities in general. The officer goes on to demonstrate to Nelu the high-tech night vision binoculars they use to spot the hiding migrants on the border. 'These things can see through walls' – he says, hinting at his awareness that Nelu has been hiding Behran in the cellar of his house. The scene illustrates the official authorities' attempts to monitor and control space, which nonetheless turn out to be unsuccessful: despite their sophisticated gear, their 4x4 vehicles and their helicopters, the border patrol remains ineffective. Importantly, the authorities are depicted as even more ill-prepared for the arrival of so many underprivileged migrants than the individual members of the Salonta community. For example, the local people do not possess any language skills (*Morgen* creates an inter-linguistic space where Romanian, Turkish and Kurdish, Hungarian, German and English words mix), but find ways to communicate with Behran in an act of solidarity.

As a visual device, hesitation connects both the everyday characters such as Nelu and Florica and the representatives of the institutions: the signature handheld camera equates the two sides by capturing their actions using a similar visual style. However, their articulations of social space could not be more different: Nelu's confusion brings about a reaction of solidarity, while the ill-prepared authorities decide not to notice or deal with the problem. In an argument towards the end of the film an officer uses the idea of national sovereignty and security to justify the authorities' actions, which he himself is visibly sceptical about. His arguments are, however, easily refuted by Nelu, who stresses that ethical-humanistic imperatives overrule the abstract and limiting idea of the nation. Nelu tries to dissuade the border officers from arresting Behran:

- The man has to find his family in Germany!
- This is not a joke, but a national border! Let me remind you that unjustifiable presence in the border zone is punishable by law. And acting as an accomplice to an illegal crossing is also punishable.
- Do you think I care about your law? What has this man done to you?
- Haven't you heard about national security?
- National security? There are no more borders!

This conversation is an effective summary of the ways in which Crişan's film contrasts the hollow institutions and regulatory authorities with the quotidian maxim of solidarity.[5] According to *Morgen* the space of the nation, which is delineated by abstract lines on the cartographic map, proves to be an empty space if it is not filled by the cooperative actions of individuals. Nelu's activities disregard the fictional and imaginary space of the nation. What matters instead are the efforts of community members to fill these empty contact zones with action based on the encounter with the Other. While Nelu, Florica, or the manager of the supermarket all visibly lack the skills and means to help Behran, and vacillate when it comes to the question of how to assist the Kurdish man, their actions are firmly grounded in the ethical imperative of unconditional solidarity. *Morgen*'s importance then lies in the process of making visible the process of emerging solidarity: the face-to-face encounter with the Other produces this reaction in the characters of the film, who recognise that the ethical constitution of the Self reveals itself via these performances (Levinas 1969). Audiences of the film recognise the shifting position of Nelu and the other community members, and are confronted with how their actions effect change in the world. This is exactly the function that Homi Bhabha attaches to discursive processes that open up the so-called enunciative split: the making visible of the structure of enunciation and the performative display of the articulation of social meaning (Bhabha 1994: 36–7). In *Morgen*, audiences are faced with the production of solidarity by the members of the Salonta community. This is set against the ineffective and detached activities of the authorities, against the social institutions in crisis.

The equilibrium between the panoptic and the quotidian is disturbed by the crisis of the social institutions in the transitional spaces of post-socialist Eastern Europe: their conflict produces the permeable border zone, where individuals are left on their own to hesitantly move around in an attempt to design new patterns of social construction. *Aurora* displays how the authorities are incapable or unmotivated with regard to conceptualising and thus controlling social space: the police officers record the factual circumstances of Viorel's movements and crimes without attempting to create causal links between motivations and actions. In *Outbound*, the panoptic has become untraceable, leaving behind only signs of the once-existing control of social space: Matilda errs between these spaces by tracing the outlines of empty social frames such as the family, the criminal sphere and the institutions of the prison and of foster care. Lastly, in *Morgen* the border patrol officers are incapable of controlling the flow of refugees and migrants, and cynically withdraw from sanctioning and controlling the national border while upholding the empty rhetoric of the nation. In these contact zones the individuals have to negotiate their way through space on a trial-and-error basis: when the panoptic has become unmotivated, invisible or cynically passive, the paths of quotidian movements are necessarily experimental. The errant movements of the protagonists in the three films display these disoriented, hesitant attempts to map lived space in the transitional setting of post-socialist Eastern Europe. The hesitant movement of the films' characters through physical space becomes a performance through which the shifting social norms are negotiated. I have argued that the main goal of the language of hesitation across the discussed films is to reflexively emphasise for the viewers their own performative involvement in these social processes by occupying a position from which the semantic shifts in the constitution and the identity of authorities, migrants or refugees and institutions become visible.

Notes

1 Nasta (2013) and Pop (2014) each emphasise the capacity of new Romanian cinema to open up the historical past and contemporary social change for the viewer, and these approaches express the general tone in academic discourses on the films in question. Some exceptions to this dominant approach are Parvulescu (2009) and Filimon (2010), both of whom stress the capacity of the films to produce social realities.
2 The argument is more fully developed in my monograph *Hesitant Histories on the Romanian Screen* (Palgrave-Macmillan 2017). This essay is an adapted and rewritten version of the book's Chapter Six.
3 This aspect of post-socialist transitional societies in East–Central Europe puts Foucault's concept of the panoptic society (Foucault 1985) in a new light. Each protagonist in the films discussed assumes that the disciplinary mechanisms familiar from State socialism are still in place. A key momentum in the analysed films is the characters' gradual recognition of the transforming, institutional apparatus of social control in post-socialist societies.
4 In the subsequent shot, Crişan pays tribute to the history of cinema when he arranges his characters exiting the supermarket just like the workers leaving the Lumière factory in the eponymous 1895 film.
5 Parvulescu and Nitu describe Nelu's actions through the concepts of *transnational* and *cosmopolitan solidarity* (2014).

Works Cited

Augé, Marc (1995), *Non-Places: Introduction to an Anthropology of Supermodernity*, trans. John Howe, London and New York: Verso.
Benjamin, Walter (2006), *The Writer of Modern Life: Essays on Charles Baudelaire*, Cambridge, MA: Harvard University Press.
Bhabha, Homi K. (1994), 'The commitment to theory', in *The Location of Culture*, London and New York: Routledge, pp. 19–39.
Certeau, Michel de (1999), 'Walking in the City', in G. Ward (ed.), *The Certeau Reader*, Oxford: Wiley-Blackwell, pp. 101–9.
Filimon, Monica (2014), 'Incommunicable experiences: ambiguity and perceptual realism in Cristi Puiu's Aurora (2010)', *Studies in Eastern European Cinema*, 5:2, pp. 169–84.

Foucault, Michel (1985), *Discipline and Punish*, Harmondsworth: Penguin.
Lefebvre, Henri (1991), *The Production of Space*, London: Wiley-Blackwell.
Lévinas, Emmanuel (1969), *Totality and Infinity: An Essay on Exteriority*, Pittsburgh: Duquesne University Press.
Nasta, Dominique (2013), *Contemporary Romanian Cinema: History of an Unexpected Miracle*, London: Wallflower Press.
Parvulescu, Constantin (2009), 'Cold world behind the window: *4 Months, 3 Weeks and 2 Days* and Romanian cinema's return to real-existing communism', *Jump Cut 51*, <https://www.ejumpcut.org/archive/jc51.2009/4months/> (last accessed 30 April 2018).
Parvulescu, Constantin and Ciprian Nitu (2014), 'Challenging Communities of Values: The Peripheral Cosmopolitanism of Marian Crişan's *Morgen*', *Iluminace* 26:2, pp. 99–118.
Pop, Doru (2014), *Romanian New Wave Cinema: An Introduction*, Jefferson, NC: McFarland.
Strausz, László (2017), 'Realism under Construction', *Short Film Studies* 7:2, pp. 149–52.

CHAPTER 9

Women on the Road: Representing Female Mobility in Contemporary Hungarian–Romanian Co-productions

Hajnal Király

Introduction

In the past ten years or so, Hungarian and Romanian films have attracted considerable attention at international festivals as representatives of postnational cinemas. These co-productions accurately depict, even down to their production process, a socio-economic crisis that characterises the two countries ever since the fall of the communist régimes. Intriguingly, the arthouse cinemas of the two countries adhere to different film historical paradigms: while New Romanian Cinema (also called the Romanian New Wave) starts from a neo-realist background and has in the last few years moved towards a taste for experimentation and conceptualisation (represented most eloquently by the films of Corneliu Porumboiu),[1] Hungarian films seem to continue the modernist tradition with their preference for a poetic figurative quality. However, despite their stylistic differences, contemporary Hungarian and Romanian films show striking similarities in representing journeys that are aborted, delayed, interrupted, with protagonists ending up in situations of entrapment. Films depicting female mobility enrich the topic of the impossible journey with further meanings that call for a gendered, cultural interpretation of this phenomenon that would contribute to the discourse on films representing transnational mobility and various types of border crossings – either geopolitical or social – triggered by three major sociopolitical events: the change of régime in 1989, the two countries' joining of the EU in 2004 and 2007 respectively, and the economic crisis beginning in 2008. Relying on recent debates on the cinematic representation of European mobility,[2] I propose to reveal some socio-cultural specificities of Eastern European female journeys through an analysis of three films – *Iszka utazása / Iska's Journey* (Csaba Bollók, 2007), *Varga Katalin balladája / Katalin Varga* (Peter Strickland, 2009) and *Bibliothèque Pascal* (Szabolcs Hajdu, 2010). Each of these films represents the incomplete, fragmented journey of a female protagonist of a different age, but with similarities that enable them to be taken together as a single, representative narrative of a quest for a home and identity, endangered by betrayal and physical or psychological aggression. Moreover, the three films appear as variations of the topic of female victimisation, involving a second-wave feminist critical discourse on a traditional, patriarchal society on the one hand and a post-colonial approach to Eastern European (female) subjectivity, affected by a Western colonising gaze, on the other. Accordingly, *Iska's Journey*, the story of a teenage girl raised first by a dysfunctional family, then at an orphanage[3] in a former Romanian mining area, who is kidnapped by a sex-trafficking organisation, could be seen as providing the child's point of view to the story of Mona in *Bibliothèque Pascal*: Mona ends up as an exquisite prostitute in a brothel disguised as a library in Liverpool, leaving behind a little girl. Similarly, the rape-revenge narrative of *Katalin Varga* represents a development of Mona's story, enriched with fantastic elements of a desired female empowerment. Although only *Bibliothèque* provides specific time and space coordinates (its story starts a few years before and finishes a bit after Romania joined the EU, in full economic crisis), the films are set in a Transylvania affected by the post-communist transition, at some time during the 2000s. The setting of Transylvania is a melting pot of ethnic identities, and gains further significance as the name of the region itself refers to transition, meaning 'across the forest'.

All three films are Hungarian–Romanian co-productions, an aspect opening the topic of mobility towards new figurative, meta-narrative interpretations: shot in Romania, with both Hungarian and Romanian actors (mainly ethnic Hungarians) as protagonists, these films also thematise the limits and limitations of intercultural exchange. Although familiar with both cultures and languages (all protagonists speak Hungarian and Romanian), in neither community can one identify female agency in these journeys animated by loss (of a home, of 'honour', of the family and of a child, respectively). Instead of supporting them, both communities reject or turn down their female protagonists at some point, so they end up in places in-between: a forest, a boat and a supermarket. According to Ewa Mazierska, co-productions are also productions of heterotopias: they are in a reflexive relationship with all the other sites and institutions of both countries involved in the filmmaking process (Mazierska 2012: 484). The three co-productions involve a merger of the above-mentioned different cinematic paradigms, detectable in acting, narration and visual styles, that at times reflect on each other ironically. With the identical name of the protagonist and the type of female mobility she represents,

Hajdu's film evokes Agnès Varda's *Sans toit ni loi/Vagabond* (1985) and with it a more formalist modernist tradition characterising contemporary Hungarian films, contrasted with the micro-realism specific to New Romanian Cinema. Moreover, these films also configure the process of co-production when representing female journeys connecting different cultures and languages, epitomising what Hamid Naficy terms 'accented cinema' (Naficy 2001): films in which accent becomes figurative not only of a transnational and intercultural movement, but also of sexual, ethnic and cinematic 'otherness'.

In this essay I propose to analyse the relevant aspects of an Eastern European female journey that signifies both sexual and cultural transgression. Following a discussion of the revaluation of home in these films, I will attempt to realise a typology of these female travellers and journey patterns, highlighting (Western) cultural stereotypes related to (Eastern) female mobility. I will also focus on central heterotopias of these films as figurations of the intercultural encounters between the two countries and East and West, respectively (for instance, the boat, the train, the brothel, the orphanage). In Foucault's definition, heterotopias are 'in relation with all [. . .] other sites, but in such a way as to suspect, neutralise, or invert the set of relations that they happen to designate, mirror, or reflect' (Foucault 1986: 24).

In this respect I consider the given co-productions as heterotopias reflecting on cultural relations modelled by the filmmaking process itself: all three films are set in Transylvania, Romania, where Hungarian and Romanian communities live side by side. With the exception of British director Peter Strickland (located in Hungary at that time) the directors are Hungarian, while the professional or non-professional actors are either Romanian or ethnic Hungarians from Romania. The production and distribution companies involved are Hungarian, Romanian, other European and from the US.[4] In each film the body of the female actresses itself becomes a site of intercultural encounter.

Far and Away from Home

The classic opposition between mobility and stability naturally involves a negative perception of displacement that can be partly accounted for by what Thomas Nail considers an incorrect perspective in the definition of the migrant. He argues that the migrant has been predominantly understood from the perspective of *stasis* and perceived as a secondary or derivative figure with respect to a place-bound existence. In his view, 'the migrant is the one least defined by its being and place and more by its becoming and displacement: by its *movement*', thus becoming 'the true motive force of social history' (Nail 2015: 2–3, 7). In an era of intense social and transnational mobility, this change of perspective is reflected in a revaluation and devaluation of the concept of home, traditionally conceived of as a place of origin and return and represented as a feminine space performed by the mother. Gaston Bachelard defines it as a house that is a 'psychic state', a site and bringer-into-being of deep feelings of value and caring (1969: 72). What Mazierska and Rascaroli in their book call the 'feminisation of migration' (2006: 140), in the East European context goes hand in hand with a changed or missing image of a home that increasingly becomes an 'unlivable' place that needs to be left behind due to aggression or lack of authentic familial bonds. As I have argued elsewhere, in contemporary Hungarian films there is often only an imitation of home; missing, dysfunctional, incomplete families deeply mark the protagonist's quest for identity that takes the form of a journey narrative (Király 2015: 178). For, if we accept with Marc Augé that 'The sign of being at home is the ability to make oneself understood without too much difficulty, and to follow the reasoning of others without any need for long explanations' (Augé 2009: 179), we must realise that in the three films under analysis, the protagonists' banishment from Paradise starts with or is related to a misunderstanding, betrayal or rejection at home. Katalin is banned from home when her husband finds out about her being raped years ago, Iska's situation becomes unbearable after she is not able to make enough money for her alcoholic parents and Mona (at least according to her initial narrative) is forced into sex slavery after being entrapped by her own father. In this respect, the alleged home (of which we do not see any image in *Bibliothèque*) does not differ in any respect from the other places they encounter along their journey, in the sense that in these places 'the reasons they give for their deeds and actions are no longer understood, nor the criticisms they make or the enthusiasms they display' (Augé 2009: 179). In the case of Iska and Mona, misunderstanding also finds a linguistic figuration. They both speak both languages (Hungarian and Romanian, respectively), but while Mona speaks Romanian with a Hungarian accent (thus preserving her ethnic Hungarian identity), Iska speaks her native Hungarian with a strong Romanian accent. The loss of the mother tongue becomes a figuration of her difficult bonding with her mother and her subsequent problematic ethnic identity.

In line with the categories set up by Mazierska and Rascaroli, since they have no home to go back to, all three female protagonists qualify as 'travellers' (2006: 148), 'drifting between inconvenience and incapacitation'

(Nail 2015: 15). Home appears as a utopia that cannot be achieved or (as we shall see in the respective section) a heterotopia that can be achieved anywhere. In the three films home appears either as non-existent (*Bibliothèque*), provisory (*Iska*), or short-lived, as if dreamed and not deserved (*Katalin Varga*). Visually, in *Bibliothèque* and *Iska* the space where the protagonists start off is a post-communist (post-industrial, in the case of Iska) space, bleak and deteriorated, risking, as Alice Bardan argues in her analysis of *Lilya 4-ever* (Lukas Moodysson, 2003), merely perpetuating the abjection of the post-communist space in the Western imaginary (Bardan 2007: 100). However, the sombre imagery serves as a signifier of the complete exclusion of a nostalgic image of a welcoming, organised home. This idyllic image finds its paradigmatic representation in the seventeenth-century Dutch paintings (of Pieter de Hooch, for example) showing interiors lit by warm lights, with women and children, as if in a postcard addressed to the fathers, the seamen travelling around the world. As Ernst Bloch argues, in contrast with the functional architecture represented by gloomy blockhouse interiors,

> Nothing sick, nothing wild, nothing noisy, nothing disturbing can be seen in this lovely format. Nor does it seem that any trouble could peek in. The room and the window facing the street are painted in a way as if there were no disturbance in the world. The grandfather's clock always strikes the evening hour. There is nothing that people could not cope with. Nothing is urgent. (1996: 280)

While in *Katalin Varga* the lost home appears as an idyllic (rural) place of a happy family, in the other two films the image of home does not encourage return. What Svetlana Boym considers a Russian phenomenon, the films of the 'return of the prodigal son be it an émigré or an international prostitute who comes back to the motherland after many misadventures abroad' appears in *Bibliothèque* and is meant to thematise the encounter between the East and the West (Boym 2001: 65). The figure of the foreigner (somebody coming back from abroad) in literature and film is used to defamiliarise the local culture, to give an alternative perspective on it. However, *Bibliothèque* does not allow the native to fall back in love with his own homeland, to rediscover the pleasure of the familiar, as Boym points out about Russian films. In *Bibliothèque*, the return does not necessarily imply the existence of a home: in the closing scene we see Mona and her daughter in a furniture superstore, Kika, offering an imitation or a globalised simulacrum of a home. It is a non-place affordable, in Marc Augé's view, only to middle-class citizens, tourists, whose contract with non-places is guaranteed by their credit card (Augé 2009).

Journey Patterns

Upon leaving their homes, the three protagonists irretrievably become vagabonds, who move, according to Zygmunt Bauman, 'Because they have no other bearable choice' (Bauman 1996: 93) and no assurance of a place they can return to. However, despite the absence of a place where the desired stasis can be achieved, in all three cases there is a person who ties them to a certain place and fuels the intention to return. There is always somebody left behind: in *Iska* a sibling, in *Bibliothèque* a daughter and in *Katalin Varga* a husband. In *Iska* this personal tie facilitates repeated returns (first to the family house, then to the orphanage/hospital) and in *Bibliothèque* it leads to the final return to Romania, while distanciation between Katalin and her husband remains definitive despite her repeated efforts to call him and thus maintain, through 'the final return'[5] of the voice on the mobile phone, a connection with him. The rejection and betrayal of an emotionally significant male character appears also in Mona's confabulated story, in which a journey which was promised to be that of a tourist (acompanying her father to Germany for surgery) turns into a traumatic journey of sex-slavery. In a Romanian version of *Lilya 4-ever*, Iska's trust in adults is definitively annihilated when she is abducted and taken to a ship, traditionally a heterotopia of civilising mobility, turned into a site of barbaric deeds. Iska's story clearly falls into what Aga Skrodzka calls the official discourses of social control and anti-trafficking, that 'insist on framing the migrant experience connected to sex-affective labour well within the vocabulary of criminality and modern-day slavery, completely removing agency from the women involved, often portraying them as victims of international organised crime syndicates'[6] (Skrodzka 2015: 119). However, as Skrodzka argues, in the case of *Bibliothèque*, the magical-realist account of events delivered by Mona disqualifies Mona's journey as victimisation, showing her repeatedly as agent of the presented events, thus pointing out the complexity of female mobility in contemporary Europe (2015: 120). Furthermore, the figure of the officer does not fit into the pattern of a post-communist, hierarchical, patriarchal society, as he is the one who apparently helps Mona get back her child. And ironically he does so under the influence of her surrealistic story. Hajdu's film manages to transcend the discourse of second wave feminism by avoiding generalisations about 'men' and 'women' as well as of contemporary female mobility in the context of an authoritarian society, by showing the unique story of one woman, mixing all the characteristics of fragility and empowerment. The same is true for *Katalin Varga*, where the rape-revenge narrative is at times torn by moments of hesitation and emotion. In both cases, the journey takes a circular pattern, as the protagonists are returning to where the story has started, diegetically and non-diegetically respectively: Mona to her hometown and Katalin to the scene of her rape, depicted later in her account of the events. This pattern is paired in both films with a descending trajectory, traumatising and purifying at the same time, a descent to Hell – configured by the repeated images of tunnels and corridors in *Bibliothèque* and by the journey towards the valley and the name of the non-existent village Katalin is looking for, The Fair of the Hell (Miercurea Iadului, Jádszereda) – that proves to be, in the end, a Purgatory. They both emerge from this journey with a changed consciousness: Mona is ready to raise her daughter, Katalin reunites her son with his father, the profoundly repenting rapist. Of the three characters, it is only Katalin who does not travel alone: she is taking her teenage son along on her revenge trip by horse-drawn carriage, in an act that mixes the intention of protection with involuntary parentification (Figure 9.1).

Iska's Journey remains open, as we lose track of her on the boat, in the middle of the sea. Her wanderings preceding the kidnapping are circular and evoke the 'cinema of walking', that, as a representative of 'slow cinema', configures the 'time of hope', identified by András Bálint Kovács in Béla Tarr's films:[7] the hope that she will find enough recyclable ironware, that her mother will finally provide her with a home, that her sister will get better and finally, that she will see the sea. While of the three journeys only that of Mona is clearly transnational, all characters cross a

Figure 9.1 An unlikely couple travelling by horse-drawn carriage in *Katalin Varga*.

variety of other borders: geographic, geopolitical, ethnic and sexual ones that become, together with the repeated language shifts, signifiers of a multifaceted Eastern European female identity.

Border Crossings: Accent and Language Shifts

Iska wanders between institutions that fail to serve the purpose they are established for, and as such her journey is figurative of a post-communist Romanian society with chaotic administrative and bureaucratic structures. This is a recurrent topic of the New Romanian Cinema since *Moartea domnului Lăzărescu/The Death of Mr. Lazarescu* (Cristi Puiu, 2006), often showing individuals who fall between the institutional gaps and become irretrievably marginalised and isolated. Iska's figure is also marked by a disturbing in-betweenness: she is neither Hungarian nor Romanian, and is somewhere between childhood and teenagerhood, an androgynous character in constant movement. Her 'borderline' position is emphasised by her puzzling name, which could be that of either a girl or a boy: her sexual identity is repeatedly interrogated in her discussions with the adults she meets. After being kidnapped, on the boat she playfully puts on a girly scarf with blonde curls, a gesture foreshadowing her forced sexualisation (Figure 9.2).

As mentioned above, Iska's language, a Hungarian contaminated with Romanian lexical and grammatical elements and accent, becomes a powerful signifier of her problematic, insecure ethnic identity, and her

Figure 9.2 The scarf with the curls foreshadowing the forced sexualisation of Iska.

social insecurity and powerlessness. Due to her grammatical mistakes she often risks being misunderstood. In contrast, in the case of Mona and Katalin, the easy switch between languages, paired with geographical and national border crossing, is clearly a sign of empowerment: when Mona travels from her partly ethnic Hungarian hometown to the Romanian seaside, she switches without effort to Romanian and is even able to defend her ethnic Hungarian identity and then to get back her child by fluently speaking official Romanian. In England she speaks English with Pascal, the owner of the exclusive brothel and speaker of many languages, before, in a metaphoric act of castration and female empowerment, she bites Pascal's tongue. Similarly, upon reaching the valley and the Romanian-speaking communities, Katalin speaks Romanian with the villagers in order to get shelter from her pursuers and take revenge on her rapists.

As representatives of female power, both Mona and Katalin correspond to what Naficy calls 'a shifter': an 'operator' in the sense of being dishonest, evasive and expedient (2001: 32), or even being a 'mimic', 'a producer of critical excess, irony, and sly civility' (Bhabha 1994). As Naficy argues, in the context of so-called 'border filmmaking', 'shifters are characters who exhibit some or all of these registers of understanding and performativity. As such, they occupy a powerful position in the political economy of both actual and diegetic border crossings' (Naficy 2001: 32). They both gain their power, 'from their situationist existence, their familiarity with the cultural and legal codes of interacting cultures, and the way in which they manipulate identity and the asymmetrical power situations in which they find themselves' (2001: 32). Extra-diegetically the creators (directors, producers, actors) of these co-productions can also be considered shifters, mimics adapting to and manipulating cultural codes in order to critically reflect upon transnational communication and the authorities orchestrating this communication.

As Balázs Varga points out, in Hajdu's films linguistic hibridity and miscommunication only emphasise the sense of being lost or in-between. In these linguistically charged situations the capacity to translate is crucial: travelling characters manage to get out of a pressing situation as a result of their ability to switch between languages (Varga 2015: 8). This great adaptability of the travelling/migrating Eastern European individual to the demands of the Western market is best represented by the character of Mona in *Bibliothèque*: she switches without effort between languages (Hungarian, Romanian, English), depending on location and situation. However, her speech is always 'accented': her Romanian has a Hungarian accent, her Hungarian bears the trace of ethnic Hungarians from Romania and her English has an Eastern European accent. In all three films spoken language, either Hungarian or Romanian, often bears imperfections, detectable in pronunciation and omission of cultural nuances. Accented language becomes a signifier of a cultural discourse different from the official one.

As Katalin Sándor argues in her analysis of *Bibliothèque*, 'Mona defines herself as "jumi-juma" ("fifty-fifty") as Romanian–Hungarian, her identity being negotiated in-between languages, cultures, ethnicities'. As such, 'the ethnic–linguistic hybridity is not only manifest in a discursive–conceptual but also in a corporeal way', manifest in Mona's accent: 'while being completely fluent in Romanian, her body, the organs of speech remember and reproduce the sonorous memory of another language' (Sándor 2014: 89). Mona's statement, uttered in Romanian ('You speak as if there were only Romanians on the Earth, but there are Hungarians, too. And some are fifty-fifty'), however, goes beyond a simple statement of her nationality, revealing a clear irritation regarding the official language or as it were, official (Romanian national, patriarchal) discourse (Figure 9.3). In a similar vein, although they speak the same language, at first Mona apparently fails to understand the adoption officer's intention to help her with a lie that seems realistic instead of the truth, which appears surreal. And conversely the officer, though he understands Mona well, fails to detect the trauma that ultimately lies behind the fantastic details of Mona's narration. Accent becomes an unmistakable trace of identity in these films, both of the character and of the actor, a sign of home even in

Figure 9.3 'Some are fifty-fifty' – Mona and Viorel in *Bibliothèque Pascal*.

circumstances of displacement such as migration, exile, or work-related journeys. According to Hamid Naficy 'it is impossible to speak without an accent'. Consequently, accent can be one of the most distinguishing traits of personality:

> Depending on their accents, some speakers may be considered regional, local yokel, vulgar, ugly, or comic, whereas others may be thought of as educated, upper-class, sophisticated, beautiful, and proper. As a result, accent is one of the most intimate and powerful markers of group identity and solidarity, as well as of individual difference and personality. (Naficy 2001: 23)

Naficy terms exilic and diasporic cinema as 'accented cinema' not only due to the regular accented speech of the protagonists they represent. The syntagm rather refers to a cinema that 'derives its accent from its artisanal and collective production modes and from the filmmakers' and audiences' deterritorialised locations' (2001: 23). Although the films under analysis don't belong to the exilic and diasporic cinema in its more restricted sense (involving a permanently dislocated director and topics related to various aspects of life in diaspora), I contend that they still fulfil the most specific requirements of accented cinema as described by Naficy. They are low-budget, multilingual films, often characterised by a convoluted production process, multisource funding and collective production. The three main traits of accented cinema – interstitial, partial, multiple – also apply to most aspects of these films: they are interstitial (a production mode that articulates difference) in terms of their topics, choice of characters, actors and sometimes a mixture of genres and cinematic traditions (Naficy 2001: 46). In concordance with this, they are only partially adapted to any cinematic paradigm and alternatively choose a multiplicity of styles and cultural voices.

The interstitiality of accented cinema is defined by Naficy as the ability

> to operate both within and astride the cracks of the system, benefiting from its contradictions, anomalies, and heterogeneity. It also means being located at the intersection of the local and the global, mediating between the two contrary categories, which in syllogism are called 'subalternity' and 'superalternity'. (2001: 46)

The preference for settings at geopolitical borders and the topic of border crossings involving issues of ethnic, national and sexual identity defines the three films as 'border films' (2001: 239) rich in heterotopia that appear as 'portal places charged with intense emotions, involving fearful escapes, tearful departures, sudden entrapments, devastating rejections, joyful arrivals, and a euphoric sense of liberation that cannot be recuperated easily' (2001: 238).

Additionally, their directors and actors are often crossing borders, just like their characters who are involved in a wide variety of journey narratives, including homecoming scenarios. Peter Strickland is a British director living in Hungary making a film in Transylvania, Romania, while Hungarian director Csaba Bollók works with both Hungarian and Romanian actors in the same location. In the case of the films of Szabolcs Hajdu, the female characters are played by his preferred actress, who happens to be his wife, Orsolya Török-Illyés, an ethnic Hungarian from Transylvania, Romania. In *Bibliothèque* her bodily presence mediates between Hungarian and Romanian cultures not only on a diegetic, but also a metadiegetic level of the co-production process, due to her ability to translate between the two cultures and even to catalyse the eventual tensions and miscommunications.

In these films bodies are not only objects of exchange between countries, but often appear as heterotopias themselves, become meeting 'sites' between East and West or the Romanian and ethnic Hungarian community. The bodies of Mona, Katalin and Iska function both as 'containers of memories' of their home regions and surfaces onto which Western cultural stereotypes and prejudices can be projected. Their bodies negotiate, on an extra-diegetic level, the meeting between Hungarian and Romanian cultures, resulting in the heterotopia of the films themselves.

Heterotopias as Scenes of Intercultural Dynamics

According to Naficy, the preoccupation with territoriality, rootedness and geography is a distinct feature of accented films. He argues: 'Because they are deterritorialised, these films are deeply concerned with territory and territoriality. Their preoccupation with place is expressed in their open and closed space-time (chronotopical) representations' (2001: 5). Besides chronotopes (of which the most prominent is the road and the house), heterotopias are basic ingredients of an accented cinematic discourse on identity and cultural and economic interaction, as well as power relationships.

The fair, the train station, the police station, the brothel, the boat, the orphanage are all localisable places, whose in-betweenness, transitory and/or liminal character contributes to a figurative discourse on the cultural implications of mobility and immigration, as well as on Eastern European identity. These places function as what Foucault calls 'other places' that are in a metaphorical, reflexive relationship with society while gathering more than one aspect of it.

The film *Bibliothèque Pascal*, a Hungarian–Romanian–German–British co-production casting both Hungarian and Romanian actors, creates a brothel-library heterotopia and so reflects on the Western gaze on the Eastern European body, both that of the actor and of the protagonist, as an affordable and exotic product. The train station, the train itself and the brothel disguised as library are heterotopias that, as Mazierska would argue, exist outside the normal political, cultural and sometimes physical order (2012: 502). They are places of transition that illustrate the issues of: increased mobility in Europe; transnationalism and cultural communication (of which co-productions have become the most compelling examples); and the way that other places themselves facilitate the meeting of distant, sometimes incompatible places and cultures.

The whole post-industrial mining area in *Iska*, as well as the landfill site and the orphanage, are heterotopias reflecting on a series of aspects of post-communist Romanian society, including precarity, the isolation of the individual and institutional dysfunctionality. The orphanage, as a site of the crisis of the under-18s, can be seen as a heterotopia that figurates the necessity of surveillance of children in a period of increased, uncontrollable mobility of adults. It also becomes a trading site of the children's future, as it mediates adoption processes with Western customers. But while in this film the orphanage is a potential catalyst preparing children for a better future and a promising transnational, East–West journey (a touching figuration of which are the 'dry' swimming lessons in the yard), the boat loses its positive intercultural signification emphasised by Foucault thus:

> a floating piece of space, a place without a place, that exists by itself, that is closed in on itself and at the same time is given over to the infinity of the sea and that, from port to port, from tack to tack, from brothel to brothel, it goes as far as the colonies in search of the most precious treasures they conceal in their gardens. (Foucault 1986: 27)

As such, it has not only been the great instrument of economic development but 'has been simultaneously the greatest reserve of the imagination' (Foucault 1986: 27). Instead of being represented as a means of liberating mobility, in *Iska* the boat becomes an image of hopeless entrapment. Instead of ensuring intercultural communication, it is the scene of unspeakable events beyond all imagination as itself a floating brothel, reinforcing the discourse on the socio-political dangers of the mobility of Eastern Europeans. The representation recurrent in contemporary Romanian cinema of uninhabitable industrial zones and dysfunctional institutions unable to control this mobility, participates in Hungarian–Romanian co-productions in a cinematic trade of cultural images.

Co-productions: Filmmaking 'On the Road'

In her article on Eastern European co-productions Ewa Mazierska argues that international collaboration is reflected in the diegesis of such films, revolving around cross-cultural communication and actions that take place in or generate heterotopias (2012: 484). As we have seen, the co-productions discussed above often thematise the cultural interactions required by the production process in their very diegesis, through their 'accented' characters involved in situations of translation, miscommunication, various types of journey and return narratives, as well as the preference for places of transition, borders and other liminal spaces.

As Naficy puts it, 'accented filmmakers are not just textual structures or fictions within their films; they also are empirical subjects, situated in the interstices of cultures and film practices, who exist outside and prior to their films' (2001: 4). Beyond exilic cinema, both the terms 'accented' filmmaker and 'shifter' describe an artistic mode that characterises what Nicolas Bourriaud terms the artistic 'superrrealism' of our times (2009: 22). The case of the directors referred to above epitomises the definition of the 'radicant', travelling artist who adapts freely to different conditions of production, acting styles, language, as well as to the different stylistic paradigms of cinematic traditions involved. As Bourriaud argues,

> To be a radicant means setting one's roots in motion, staging them in heterogeneous contexts and formats, denying them the power to completely define one's identity, translating ideas, transcoding images, transplanting behaviours, exchanging rather than imposing the figure of the wanderer at the heart of contemporary artistic creation, accompanied by a domain of forms, the journey form, as well as an ethical mode, translation. (2009: 22)

In light of these definitions, all three films referred to above present 'radicant artists' (both directors and actors), who move and translate freely between cultures and languages. As Romanian–Hungarian co-productions, they intriguingly thematise cultural, ethnic relationships between the two countries, doubling, in an ironic way, the transnational dynamics of co-production. Besides an evident reflection on a multifaceted European identity, constantly replanned due to border shifts and crossings, linguistic diversity often figurates the economic exchange between Hungary and Romania. These films fulfil what Bourriaud calls the surest criteria by which to judge an artwork today: the capacity of displacement and the figuration of a productive dialogue with different contexts and cultures (2009: 105) ensures their dislocation from a provincial, Eastern

European context. As such they find their place in the global discourse of mobility and identity, in which Eastern European female journeys become complex signifiers of cultural interactions and feminisms ranging from the discourse of victimisation to that of empowerment.

This work was supported by the Hungarian Scientific Research Fund OTKA, project NN112700, titled 'Space-ing Otherness: Cultural Images of Space, Contact Zones in Contemporary Hungarian and Romanian Film and Literature'.

Notes

1 According to Andrei Gorzo, the second refers to a series of stylistic features shared by a number of internationally acclaimed films that became a mainstream style in contemporary Romanian cinematography, while the first defines simply a generation of successful directors. The Puiu-Mungiu-Muntean line does not completely fulfil the conditions of a New Wave in the sense consecrated by the French New Wave, for example, that developed on the ground of a theoretical reflection on film (Gorzo 2012, 266–7). For a more detailed discussion of the process leading from neo-realism to experimentation and conceptualisation see Andrei State (2014).
2 Started by Ewa Mazierska and Laura Rascaroli in their *Crossing New Europe: Postmodern Travel and the European Road Movie* (2006), given a feminist focus in *Transnational Feminism* (Marciniak et al. 2007) and recently enriched with new insights in *East, West, and Centre* (Gott and Herzog 2015).
3 This orphanage is clearly an allusion to the homes founded by Franciscan priest Csaba Böjte in the Transylvanian mining area.
4 Additional co-production and distribution data: *Iska's Journey*: Merkelfilm (Hungary) – production, WonderPhil Productions (US) – distribution; *Katalin Varga*: Libra Film (Romania), Ross Sanders Production Company (Great Britain), The Romanian National Centre for Cinematography – production, distributed in Hungary, the Netherlands, France, Portugal and Greece. *Bibliothèque Pascal*: various production companies, A + C Reuter new Cinema (Germany), Filmpartners, Sparks, Katapult (Hungary). Distribution: Camino Filmverleih (Germany), GoDigital Media Group (US).
5 This term, used by Michel Chion after Dennis Vassal, describes a nurturing connection that undercuts the autonomy of the subject, often represented by phone call scenes in cinema (Chion 1999: 62).
6 Mónika Dánél comes to a similar conclusion when analysing the thematisation of a Western, colonising male gaze, producer of stereotypes, in *Bibliothèque* (2012).
7 In his book *The Circle Closes*, Kovács argues that in Tarr's films endless walking opens a 'time for hope' (2013: 5).

Works Cited

Augé, Marc (2009), *Non-Places: An Introduction to Supermodernity*, London: Verso.
Bachelard, Gaston (1969), *Poetics of Space*, Boston: Beacon Press.
Bardan, Alice Mihaela (2007), '"Enter Freely, and of Your Own Will:" Cinematic Representations of Post-Socialist Transnational Journeys', in Katarzyna Marciniak, Anikó Imre and Áine O'Healy (eds), *Transnational Feminism in Film and Media*, New York and Basingstoke: Palgrave Macmillan, pp. 93–110.
Bauman, Zygmund (1996), 'From pilgrim to tourist – a short history of identity', in Stuart Hall and Paul du Gay (eds), *Questions of Cultural Identity*, London: Sage, pp. 18–37.
Bhabha, Homi K. (1994), 'Of Mimicry and Man: The Ambivalence of Colonial Discourse', *The Location of Culture*, London and New York: Routledge, pp. 85–92.
Bloch, Ernst (1996), *The Utopian Functon of Art and Literature: Selected Essays (Studies in Contemporary German Social Thought)*, Cambridge, MA: The MIT Press.
Bourriaud, Nicolas (2009), *The Radicant*, New York: Lucas & Sternberg.
Boym, Svetlana (2001), *The Future of Nostalgia*, New York: Basic Books.
Chion, M. (1999), *The Voice in the Cinema*, New York: Columbia University Press.
Dánél, Mónika (2012), 'Surrogate Nature, Culture, Women – Inner Colonies. Postcolonial Readings of Contemporary Hungarian Films', *Acta Universitatis Transilvaniae, Film and Media Studies*, 5, pp. 107–28.
Foucault, Michel (1986), 'Of Other Spaces', *Diacritics*, 16:1, pp. 22–7.
Gorzo, Andrei (2012), *Lucruri care nu pot fi spuse altfel: un mod de a gândi cinemaul, de la André Bazin la Cristi Puiu* (Things That Cannot Be Said in a Different Way: A Way of Thinking Cinema, from André Bazin to Cristi Puiu), Bucharest: Humanitas.
Gott, Michael and Todd Herzog (eds) (2014), *East, West and Centre: Reframing Post-1989 European Cinema*, Edinburgh: Edinburgh University Press.
Király, Hajnal (2015), 'Leave to live? Placeless people in contemporary Hungarian and Romanian films of return', *Studies in Eastern European Cinema*, 6:2, pp. 169–83.
Kovács, András Bálint (2013), *The Cinema of Béla Tarr: The Circle Closes*, New York: Columbia University Press.
Marciniak, Katarzyna, Anikó Imre and Áine O'Healy (eds) (2007), *Transnational Feminism in Film and Media*, New York and Basingstoke: Palgrave Macmillan.
Mazierska, Ewa (2012), 'International Co-productions as Productions of Heterotopias', in Anikó Imre (ed.), *A Companion to Eastern European Cinemas*, Oxford: Wiley-Blackwell, pp. 483–503.
Mazierska, Ewa and Laura Rascaroli (2006), *Crossing New Europe: Postmodern Travel and the European Road Movie*, New York and London: Wallflower Press.

Naficy, Hamid (2001), *An Accented Cinema: Exilic and Diasporic Filmmaking*, Princeton and Oxford: Princeton University Press.

Nail, Thomas (2015), *The Figure of the Migrant*, Stanford: Stanford University Press.

Sándor, Katalin (2014), 'Heterotopias of/and "Living Images" in Szabolcs Hajdu's *Bibliothèque Pascal* (2010)', *Ekphrasis. Images, Cinema, Theory and Media*, 12:2, pp. 79–92.

Skrodzka, Aga (2015), 'Cinematic Fairy Tales of Female Mobility in Post-Wall Europe: Hanna v. Mona', in Michael Gott and Todd Herzog (eds), *East, West and Centre: Reframing Post-1989 European Cinema*, Edinburgh: Edinburgh University Press, pp. 109–24.

State, Andrei (2014), 'Realismele lui Corneliu Porumboiu' (The Realisms of Corneliu Porumboiu), in Andrei Gorzo and Andrei State (eds), *Politicile filmului. Contribuții la interpretarea cinemaului românesc contemporan* (The Politics of Film. Contributions to the Interpretation of Contemporary Romanian Cinema), Cluj-Napoca: Tact, pp. 74–87.

Varga, Balázs (2015), 'Terek és szerepek: Tér és identitás Hajdu Szabolcs filmjeiben' (Spaces and Roles: Space and Identity in the Films of Szabolcs Hajdu), *Prizma: Film & Kult*, 13, pp. 4–13.

Part 2a

Form and Narrative in Journey Genres

CHAPTER 10

The Sense of an Ending: Music, Time and Romance in *Before Sunrise*

Carlo Cenciarelli

> The director's movies are full of the sense of what it's like to walk down a safe, empty street at 4 a.m., the only soul awake for miles. When you are young, such an hour means having nostalgia for the way you feel, even as you feel it. (von Busack 1997: 13)

One of the cultural functions of fictions, Frank Kermode (1966) famously argued, is eschatological: the stories we share provide ways of making sense of the temporary nature of existence. In *The Sense of an Ending*, Kermode was primarily concerned with post-apocalyptic eschatology, but his insight has wider applications, some of which we can explore here by focusing on a much more local and secular context: the end of a trip to Vienna in the 1995 romantic film *Before Sunrise*, the first instalment of Richard Linklater's so-called 'Before' trilogy.[1]

Cinematic journeys are a fertile context for thinking about time. Most things come to an end, of course, but films and trips typically have conspicuous temporal brackets. In this sense, the cinematic setting of a journey is twice subject to the pressures of time, with the significance of the trip constantly tested against the film's own termination. This is particularly evident when the end of the journey coincides with the end of the film, a formal pattern that is common in Linklater's work. Scholars including David Johnson, Rob Stone (2013) and Thomas Christie have noted that many of Linklater's films combine a recurring 'theme of journeying' (Christie 2011: 184–95) with a 'fascination with temporality' (Johnson 2012: 7) that typically involves both a commitment to sensitive representations of the characters' experience of time and an exploration of the temporal boundaries of film. Here, though, I want to focus on *Before Sunrise* as a way of thinking through some of the less explored eschatological implications of cinematic time. In particular, I want to make theoretical inroads into the relatively unexamined role that music plays in negotiating the sense of endings, both at plot-level and at meta-level. My wider argument will be that a closer look at the film's soundtrack can advance our understanding of the audiovisual nature of cinematic time and of the role that music has at the intersection between genre, form and broader cultural logics for making sense of passage.

The Pact with Time

Right from the start, *Before Sunrise* presents us with the problem of its ending. Linklater's film is a character piece about Jesse and Celine, who meet on a train through central Europe and agree to spend a day and night together in Vienna before continuing their respective journeys back to the US and Paris. The circumstances of Jesse and Celine's meeting display some common features of cinematic romance: the train, the chance encounter and the mindset of travel, the European backdrop, the intercultural element and, as we shall see in detail, the use of Western art music.[2] Yet, after opening credits set to the French overture of Purcell's *Dido and Aeneas*, with its heroic and tragic *telos*, the first exchange between the film's protagonists, prompted by an arguing couple, also immediately suggests a playful revision of the cultural script of romance. 'Have you ever heard that, as couples get older, men lose their ability to hear higher-pitched sounds, and women eventually lose hearing in the low end?' asks Celine. 'Nature's way of allowing couples to grow old together without killing each other . . .', Jesse replies with a charming sneer. Whereas the typical 'Hollywood romantic film' – as argued by Dowd and Pallotta – 'perpetuates the myth of romance as an ideal form of intimacy and one that need never be extinguished' (2000: 565), *Before Sunrise*, in keeping with its indie credentials, immediately exposes the illusion of permanence that lies at the core of the ideology of romance.[3]

In this sense, the joke about couples has two functions. First, it anticipates the film's scepticism about the happily-ever-after, or what writers such as James MacDowell, Rick Altman and David Shumway have described as a model of closure characterised by the convention of the 'final couple' and the 'denial of the temporality of satisfaction': the standard happy ending where the two heterosexual lovers come together and time seems to stop, 'change forever banished from their life together' (see Altman cited in MacDowell 2013: 115). Second, in performing scepticism, the joke paradoxically opens up the space for the on-the-road romance.

The sense in which the critique of romance brings the lovers together becomes even clearer a few minutes of screen time after this exchange, when Jesse convinces Celine to get off the train in Vienna with him. With the silent assent of the viewer, who has already agreed to the time-bound nature of the cinematic experience, the two protagonists explicitly trade the idea of a 'happily-ever-after' for the possibility of experiencing a moment together. 'No illusions and no delusions,' they tell each other, 'we'll just make the night great.'

In a way, the temporal bracketing aligns *Before Sunrise* with canonic examples of the genre such as *Brief Encounter* (David Lean, 1945) and *Roman Holiday* (William Wyler, 1953), passing by *Casablanca* (Michael Curtiz, 1942). Indeed, the very fact that the separation is announced from the start is in keeping with a melodramatic aesthetic. In this sense, the emphasis on the momentary is another complex way in which Linklater's film knowingly acknowledges the tropes of classical cinema and an example of how – as is often the case with indiewood – the self-conscious foregrounding of Hollywood's formulas can lead to a re-formulation and re-styling of well-established patterns, rather than to any sense of radical critique.

Yet in *Before Sunrise* the departure is significant and the re-formulation seems to imply a genuine rethinking of the dialectic between the permanent and the momentary. Whereas classical romance typically pits the ideal of eternal love against practical obstacles, Jesse and Celine commit to the idea that emotions are themselves fleeting. In *Before Sunrise*, love shares the ontological make-up of time and travel.

In this sense, the film's discourse of romance is coterminous with a discourse of time and experience. Jesse and Celine's desire for romance goes hand in hand with a desire to seize the moment. Because time and feelings pass, it is through a discontinuity, a temporal parenthesis (the impromptu visit to Vienna) that the characters can rescue a possibility of romance at a specific *point* in time. And yet for this very reason their moment together is inseparable from the awareness of the approaching farewell. This is where the film's approach to romance most suggestively resonates with the category of the moment as theorised in late modernity; and where it shows most clearly its debt to the intellectual ambitions of international art cinema. As Jesse and Celine are well aware while strolling in Vienna, the problem of the moment is that it is always already about to finish. It is always on the verge of being defined negatively by the feeling of its termination, and this threatens the experiential immediacy it was meant to recuperate in the first place.[4]

If during the night Jesse and Celine can (just about) keep this temporal anxiety at bay, renewing the focus on their time together, when the sun finally rises – about ten minutes of screen time from the end – they have to face the consequences of their investment in the momentary. It is at this point, when protagonists, filmmakers and viewers are faced with the various formal, institutional and ideological pressures of bringing the cinematic journey to an end, that music comes to the fore. After eighty minutes characterised by a very minimal underscore, dialogue becomes much sparser and two works by Bach, heard in close succession, take characters and viewers through the temporal boundary of the title and bring *Before Sunrise* to a close. Music is used to solve the film's conundrum: how can the characters' romance be sustained beyond the boundary of the title, without contradicting the very premises on which the romance is based, without giving in to notions of love and time as permanent? The answer depends on music's ability to mobilise broader ideas about time and travel and to offer two provisional tactics for making sense of passage.

Eschatological Expedient #1: The Audio-visual Photograph

The first expedient occurs at dawn. The previous scene left Jesse and Celine in a park, preparing to spend the night together. A temporal elision then takes us to the early hours of the morning. We see a shot of the sky from what would have been the characters' point-of-view had they still been in the park. In the background we hear birds and, very quietly, the sound of a harpsichord. It is one of the G-minor movements from Bach's *Goldberg Variations*, a slow-moving, stylised and highly ornate Sarabande, with a chromatic descending bass line and a melody embellished by wide expressive leaps.

A close reading of this moment is necessary if we want to attend to its capacity to offer a particular musical articulation of and solution to the film's concerns. After a view of rooftops, the sun still below the skyline, we cut to Jesse and Celine holding hands while walking through a side street, stepping into a nondescript *mise en scène* scattered with a few commercial billboards, road signs and electric meters. The music becomes even quieter in the mixing level. Jesse asks Celine about her return to Paris, and the conversation falters, failing to be illuminated by the personal and the perceptive, standard qualities for the characters' interaction inside the temporal boundary. Just after Jesse spells this out by saying that 'we are back in real time', they hear something: the sound of the harpsichord that we, as viewers, have so far experienced as underscore. They walk towards the sound source and lean over the basement window of a house to listen to it briefly. Jesse then invites Celine to 'dance to the harpsichord'. They do so for an instant. When Celine completes an underarm turn, Jesse stops, as if freshly hit by the significance of it all, and decides to take an imaginary picture of her, so as 'never to forget you, or all this'. They stare into each other's eyes, sutured by a series of over-the-shoulder shots, then kiss and embrace, before slowly resuming walking and vacating the street.

The scene presents us with a particular instantiation of the relationship between memory, music and images often found in cinematic romance. Typically, photographs and records are favourite ways in which lovers, in cinema's fictions, access their memories. Here, in keeping with Jesse and Celine's temporal anxiety, we see memory in the making. Rather than triggering the intense memory of a past encounter (what we might call the '*Casablanca* model'), invisible music and imaginary photographs serve to record the moment for a future act of remembering.[5]

Jesse's imaginary act draws on the particular temporality of picture-taking and more precisely on the way in which photographs, to use Sylviane Agacinski's phrase, have an ability to speak 'to us of presence and absence at the same time – "as much the contact of loss as the loss of contact"': 'The photograph presents something different from its object, locating the one who takes it between the *not yet* and the *already no more* of the visible – thus producing the anachronism' (Agacinski 2003: 91, emphasis in original).

This 'gap with itself' is what makes the photograph a perfect emblem for the moment and the momentary. It is the 'intractable' presence, the '"that-has-been"', the 'superimposition of reality and past' that famously evaded Barthes's analysis and fuelled his '"ontological" desire' (Barthes 1981).[6] It is why, for Barthes and Agacinski, and for many writers before and after, modernity not just is but also *has* the 'time' of images. To the extent that, as Agacinski puts it, the act of picture-taking locates the one who takes the photo between the 'not yet' and the 'already no more' of the visible, the action speaks not just of Jesse's desire to seize the ephemeral, but also of the way his time with Celine is inseparable from the feeling of its termination.

But the temporality of the photograph is only part of this scene's romantic expedient. It is, one might recall, the sound of the harpsichord that inspires Jesse to frame the moment forever. At the very start, the music's entry marks night turning into day – the crossing of the metaphorical boundary of the title. Because of *Before Sunrise*'s extremely sparse underscore, the G minor variation acts as a notable marker, indicating the scene's crucial position in the film's structure and emotional trajectory. In this sense, the use of a slow-moving Sarabande, with its mournful tone, conforms to an understanding of film music as immediately available expressive material: it sounds how the end of the night is meant to feel.[7]

Then, immediately after having sanctioned the return to real time, Jesse hears the harpsichord, and the music's function and status quickly change. Approached amidst furtive hushes and curious smiles and visualised as a solitary performance in a concealed space filled with past artefacts, hearing the music is now dramatised as the encounter with an archaic object that belongs to the foreign city. It is one of the objects that, as Eva Illouz has suggested, are typically used in the representation of romance to mark the crossing of 'symbolic boundaries' of a temporal, emotional and spatial kind.[8] Indeed, the music redefines the space around the characters. It cleans the road of all the ordinary elements present at the beginning of the scene, erasing the ads, the electricity box and the signpost to which the return of 'real time' was bound. The characters are now placed in front of a simple background with two clearly defined textures: a wall and the adorned, patterned basement window. Orange light coming from the harpsichord room tinges the paleness of the characters' skin and accents the yellows and browns of Celine's hair and dress. It is inside this space, indirectly infused with the material qualities of the music, that Jesse and Celine dance briefly.

If at the outset the music signalled the crossing of the temporal boundary, now it seems to draw the characters back into the boundary. The past object – made present by the performance and the dance – opens up another little corner of Vienna for Jesse and Celine to experience one last moment in full. Positioned within the diegesis by Jesse's off-screen look, the music thus changes identity. It turns from being treated as second nature, a 'classical' musical utterance that can function as narrative commentary and accentuation, to serving as a diegetic object whose 'pastness', materiality and mediation are marked visually and narratively.

The music's pastness complicates things further. The harpsichord music is here both embodied and self-consciously 'bracketed'. The bracketing is performed verbally, via Jesse's playful labelling of their moves ('we dance to the harpsichord?') and physically, through the stylisation of the underarm turn, which is performed by Celine with a smile. This bracketing is a way of 'quoting' that is in keeping with the characters' attitude to the signifiers of romance – one of the ways in which (in this film) such codes are both genuinely adopted and playfully critiqued. Together with the transgression of time, the harpsichord presupposes finitude and change. Its sound, while surviving the passage of time, makes that traversed distance audible. In other words, differently from the past-ness of 'classical music', with its associated idea of universality, the past-ness of anachronism can accommodate the film's split attitude to romance.[9] In this sense, as is the case with the imaginary picture-taking, listening and dancing to the harpsichord is in a gap with itself; it places the characters at once inside and outside the temporal boundary. To paraphrase Agacinski, it speaks both of the loss of contact and of the contact of loss.

Yet the music also does something that the photograph alone could not do. Whereas the act of picture-taking, as a manifestation of the characters'

Figure 10.1 After dancing to the harpsichord and some imaginary picture-taking, Jesse and Celine hold each other tightly. *Before Sunrise*, film still.

temporal anxiety, pre-emptively risks turning into memory a moment that is still unfolding, the music offers a way of remaining inside the moment via the feeling of the moment's termination. This circular, performative logic is epitomised by the final embrace (Figure 10.1). Because of the characters' split relationship to the music, embracing to the sound of the harpsichord is both a moment of closeness and a preview of their imminent goodbye. These meanings are fused into a single feeling. What we see, as the characters hold each other in front of the basement window, is a visualisation of the emotive substance that keeps them inside the moment. Music has offered an opportunity to channel the intensity of the characters' sorrow for the end of the moment into the experience of one more 'intensified present'. In this sense, Bach's music does not just motivate a moment that is *about* the characters' split attitude to time and love but – by turning the end of the moment into the experience of a new moment – it epitomises the film's attempt to carve the possibility of romance out of an awareness of romance's fleetingness.

Eschatological Expedient #2: Travelling with the *Andante*

The second temporal tactic is attempted at the very end of the film, about ten minutes of screen time after the harpsichord scene. At the moment of saying farewell, Jesse and Celine officially break their pact with time ('this is our only night') and agree to meet in six months. Yet, as the characters part, what becomes significant is not so much the verbal agreement, which leaves us and the protagonists with no certainty as to whether they will actually meet again, but how the ending is meant to feel, which is to say the emotional and conceptual framework provided to make sense of their separation.[10]

Once again, the details of this sequence are crucial if we want to explore its eschatological implications. After one final kiss, Celine steps onto the train. As Jesse slowly walks away, the music enters and runs parallel to the film, aurally foregrounded, until its final shot. We now hear the E minor *Andante* from Bach's first Sonata for Viola da Gamba and Harpsichord, a slow-moving piece with regular pulse and wandering harmonies over a walking bass. Images of the characters leaving the station are followed by a *temps mort* sequence of Vienna in the early hours of the morning: a montage of the places Jesse and Celine visited, emptied of their presence. Two shots of the characters travelling in opposite directions close the film: Jesse on a bus, looking over his shoulder as if still feeling Celine's presence, and a long take of Celine on the train, her eyes tired with tears, looking out of the window. Finally, the camera gently tracks in and draws attention to a faint smile appearing on Celine's lips (Figure 10.2). She closes her eyes, the music ends, the shot fades to dark.

If the harpsichord scene had to do with fixing time, the final sequence is about thematising movement. In both cases, the eschatological framework

Figure 10.2 On the train, facing forward, a tearful Celine seems to smile at the memory of her time in Vienna. *Before Sunrise*, film still.

is encapsulated by a visual paradigm. Whereas the first one revolved around the temporality of the (imaginary) photograph, the latter revolves around the figure of the train as a vantage point from which to see things pass by, a recurring motif in Linklater's films.[11] In *Before Sunrise*, the 'blurred' view from the window – a painterly surface of greens and browns created by the forward movement of the train – epitomises a concern with the fleeting. The *temps mort* too – by showing locations that were traversed by the characters and are now slowly seeing the light of a new day – plays into the thematisation of time as movement. Indeed, while the sequence of visited locations is not literally what the characters see from the train, the placement of this montage between shots of the characters travelling suggest that memories of the day and night in Vienna are resurfacing in Jesse and Celine's minds, as they leave the city. In this sense, the montage provides us with a particular cinematic version of what Wolfgang Schivelbusch, in his discussion of early train cultures, has called the 'imaginary surrogate landscape' of the traveller's gaze: a relocation of the gaze from the blurred visions of the train window to an internalised, fictional space (2014).[12]

Still, while the motif of the train journey puts movement at the centre of the sequence, it is the music's own temporal journey, I want to suggest, that turns this final stretch of time into a meaningful expressive gesture. In particular, music here is essential in putting forward an understanding of time that is in direct opposition with the harpsichord scene and, instead, comes close to a Bergsonian notion of duration.

Bergson's *durée* has already been used productively to theorise the narrative style and emotional tone of Linklater's films, with David Johnson discussing the director's interest in a 'subjective, more "pliable" experience of temporality', and Rob Stone noticing that some of Linklater's characters seem epitomes of the French philosopher's influential idea of time as a 'pure, unadulterated inner continuity', a paradoxical force 'that is always departing and always arriving' (2013: 11).[13] The audiovisual dimension of this, however, deserves more attention. In the case of *Before Sunrise*, the idea of movement is written into the etymology of the *Andante*, an Italian word that literally translates as 'that which goes', or 'that which is going'. The term is primarily an indication of musical tempo, suggesting that the piece be performed at a moderate pace. In this sonata, the *Andante* is also characterised by a musical texture unfolding at a steady pulse. The basic continuity provided by the music's presence, together with these style-specific features, helps emphasise the linearity of time and train travel. These features also have the potential to reinforce the sense in which the protagonists in this scene surrender to the inexorability of time, and to everything that comes with it: the resumption of the train journey; the inevitable goodbye; the end of the film.

What concerns us here, however, is that music also has the ability to shape the experience of this forward movement. Typically, works from the common practice of tonal music start from a point of harmonic stability, move to a different area, and go back to the home key. The *Andante* follows this scheme, but with a few departures that are key to the scene's performance of time.

At the start, as the characters separate, a series of arpeggios are slowly exchanged between the harpsichord and the cello, with the latter playing in its middle range.[14] The musical phrase defines the minor mode tonal area and anchors the heartbreak of the goodbye. Then, just as Celine sits down and the train starts moving, the *Andante* gradually leaves the home key and moves in new directions. The audiovisual synchronisation is as subtle as it is precise and deliberate: it suggests that the scene is being cut to music, and, more broadly, that on-screen movement is here subordinated to musical time.

Here is where the *Andante*'s style of travel becomes apparent. In a 'migratory' fashion that is characteristic of much of Bach's music, the *Andante* passes through various adjacent tonal areas without settling for any of them, constantly deferring points of rest.[15] What's more, the music's harmonic migrations are characterised by an oscillation between (implied) major and minor tonal areas.[16] This has the effect of opening up the affective range of the *temps mort*, complicating its (traditional) association with loss and mourning.[17] The music's ability to re-colour the connotations of the *temps mort* becomes clearest when the *Andante* eventually lands on a major mode plateau. Here its more affirmative tone appears in conjunction with a cut to one of the vacated locations, the edit happening exactly on the beat as the cello soars above the harpsichord. One of the consequences of this audiovisual counterpoint is that the music keeps Jesse and Celine at the centre of the system of representation. During the *temps mort*, Vienna is emptied of the characters' on-screen presence but filled with music that sustains the emotional significance of their encounter.

The music's constant shift of inflections becomes particularly significant in the final shot. Instead of tracing a circular journey back to the opening key and chord, the *Andante* remains open-ended. In keeping with tonal conventions, the final close is marked by a familiar pattern of chords. But the music never gets there, and the pattern remains incomplete, stopping just before the final chord, in what is typically called a 'half cadence'. As a smile gently materialises on Celine's tired face and she drifts into sleep, giving herself to the forward movement of the train, the last sound we hear is a major chord suspended over the implication of a minor mode resolution.

The modal and syntactical ambiguity of this half cadence becomes emblematic of the ending's affective inbetweenness and narrative openness, and thus of the film's broader revision of generic conventions: its refusal to embrace a predetermined trajectory (be it tragedy or reunion). In other words, the music serves to construct an ending that is emotionally under-determined. It contributes to shaping the emotional trajectory of the scene, landing on a conclusion that is both dramatic and understated; dramatic precisely because understated.

The way the music shapes the sequence's emotional trajectory has broader implications for the film's representation of time and travel. If the regularity of pulse emphasises the inevitability of the scene's forward progression, the piece's migratory style contributes to representing the passage of time as a field of possibilities.[18] The *Andante*, with its moment-by-moment major/minor shifts, its multiple, overlapping harmonic implications and constant deferral of cadential points, serves to thematise movement, continuity and a sense of flow, both at plot level and at meta-level.

The music's harmonic migrations also ensure that the scene's flow is tied to a subjective experience of space and time. One of the consequences of the *Andante*'s constant shifts of inflection is that the representation of time and movement appears to be filtered through the characters' subjectivity. Whether by 'filling in' the *temps mort* or by drawing attention to minimal modulations in Celine's behaviour, the music is invested with the role of representing the characters' experience of passage while also guiding the viewer's own experience of the sequence's unfolding, providing a concrete example of what cinematic 'duration' may sound like.

Temporary Endings

In *The Sense of an Ending*, one of Kermode's central intuitions is that the relationship between fictions and broader narrative archetypes needs to be constantly updated for the fictions to serve their eschatological purpose. With its efforts to both fix and mobilise the moment, *Before Sunrise* evokes a dialectic of time that has a long and illustrious pedigree in the history of ideas, and that is also subject to constant cinematic 'troping'. In this sense, the film provides an example of how revising the generic conventions of cinematic romance entails re-thinking the way we make sense of time and passage. More specifically, it acts as a reminder that cinema's performance of time is audiovisual, and so are the associated eschatological frameworks.

As we have seen, the photograph and the train window are tied to the music's function as source or underscore and to mixed conceptions of Western art music as 'classical' and 'anachronistic'. Bach is suitable both to being used as a universalising force – a material that survives, unchanged, the passing of time – and as an ancient object, found by accident in a foreign city, that stands at an audible distance from the characters' and the film's cultural and generational identity. These temporal tactics also imply alternative listening paradigms. During the last ten or so minutes of the film, similar musics but different temporalities of listening are invoked to make sense of passage. Dancing to the harpsichord is presented as a complex temporal verticality, its significance located in its power to mark and bracket a spatiotemporal moment. The *Andante* on the other hand is significant for its moment-by-moment unfolding, which heightens the level of significant detail and the density and importance of every flicker of light seen from the train window.

In keeping with the relative inertia and openness of indie forms, the unfolding of harmonies is used to instil time's inexorable forward movement with a sense of flow and possibility. And, in keeping with the temporal anxieties and self-reflexivity of indie cinema, Linklater's film draws on music's ability to re-purpose and re-channel feelings of loss and separation so that the cinematic moment can be extended by means of generating more and more 'moments about the end of the moment'.

The solutions provided by music are thus 'temporary' not just in the sense that they are about time and that they supersede one another within the context of the film, but also in the sense that they are part of a narrative economy that is still unfolding. Open endings and cinematic snapshots have very material consequences when it comes to the cinema. The gentle drifting at the end of *Before Sunrise* opened up the possibility for a sequel, which materialised nine years later, in Linklater's *Before Sunset* (2004), where – just before Celine and Jesse again bump into each other in Paris – the harpsichord moment is used as a flashback to recapitulate the previous instalment.[19] In this practical sense, if in no others, the various eschatological frameworks mobilised by *Before Sunrise* have become productive. As a matter of fact, with *Before Midnight* (the third, Greek, instalment) released nine years after *Before Sunset*, and no clear suggestion that the on-the-road sequence is now complete, the original effort of generating romance out of a critique of romance's ideology of permanence has succeeded. In this sense, the overarching eschatological expedient of Linklater's 'Before' project seems to be that of thematising the inevitability of passage while also deferring, as far as possible, the ultimate deadline. The pact with time stipulated in Vienna is undergoing a constant re-negotiation, the problem of the final goodbye keeps being postponed, and *Before Sunrise*, drawing on music's performative powers, has turned the end of the journey into more opportunities for cinematic travelling.

Notes

1 So far, the series includes *Before Sunrise* (1995), *Before Sunset* (2004) and *Before Midnight* (2013).
2 A number of commentators have talked about these elements in relation to the film's (partial) adherence to the classic Hollywood romance. See, for example, Adrian Martin (2006).
3 On indiewood and romance, see James MacDowell (2013: 133–90). At the time of its release, a number of critics celebrated *Before Sunrise* for departing from genre conventions. The film's approach to time was seen by some as a way of resisting 'the standard litany of [cinematic] clichés' (Marjorie Baumgarten 1995), dramatising 'the transience of feeling', and articulating a 'realistic acknowledgement of uncertainty' (Robin Wood 1996: 8). In particular, this critical reception focused on the characters' final separation, which was seen as the emblem of the film's resistance to romance's ideology of permanence.
4 The modern moment thus becomes at once the locus of immediacy and retrospection; the site of a presence that is perceived in the moment of its disappearance. Leo Charney sums up the theorisation of the moment that I am outlining here, referring in particular to Pater, Benjamin, Heidegger and Epstein: 'The concept of the moment provided a means to fix an instant of feeling, yet this effort at stability had to confront the inescapable fact that no moment could stay still. This dilemma led . . . towards the two interlocking concepts that defined the modern as momentary: the evacuation of stable presence by movement and the resulting split between sensation, which feels the moment in the moment, and cognition, which recognises the moment only after the moment' (Charney 1995: 279).
5 Eva Illouz has discussed the value of photographs as prosthetic devices and 'symbolic "snapshots"', 'in which romantic feelings can be recapitulated and communicated' (1997: 5–6). For a discussion of the prosthetic value of photographs, see also Celia Lury (1998: 82).
6 Much of Barthes's essay could be seen as a reflection on the temporality of photographs, but the expressions I quote above can be found in particular on pages 3, 12, 76 and 77.
7 This is what Caryl Flinn famously calls the 'classical' understanding of film music (1992: 14). The reason I am not using this term here is to avoid lexical confusion between the classical understanding of film music, and the use of classical music as film music.
8 For a discussion of the interdependence of 'four kinds of symbolic boundaries', 'temporal, emotional, spatial, and artifactual', and of the way unusual,

ritual objects can 'transport the lover back to the "sacred" moment of their first meeting' see Illouz 1997: 113–17.

9   The difference between the permanence of universalism and the permanence of anachronism is discussed by Agacinski 2003: 105–36. In literature, a similar tension between the timelessness of the Classics and the alterity of the past is discussed by Murray McGillivray (1994).

10 Various commentators have celebrated this ending as the most explicit figure of *Before Sunrise*'s subtle approach to the cultural script of romance. For Peter Hanson 'the ambiguous note on which the film ends . . . accentuates and deepens [its] poignancy' (2002: 87). Erik Syngle professes to 'know of no ending to any film more graceful – formally, emotionally, or physically – than of Celine and Jesse, alone once again on their separate coaches and drifting off to sleep to the strains of Bach's Sonata No. 1 for Viola da Gamba' (2004). Glen Norton argues that 'the seductive secret in *Before Sunrise* . . . is the hidden emotional state of each character, rendered through stunning ambiguity in [the] final two shots' (2000: 72).

11 Johnson calls this 'the motif of passing landscapes', drawing attention in particular to 'repetitions of landscape passing by outside the window in *It's Impossible to Learn to Plow by Reading Books* and *Slacker*'. See Johnson 2012: 17.

12 Schivelbusch (2014) talks about this 'imaginary surrogate landscape' in relation to the historical practice of reading novels alongside train travel.

13 See also p. 79 in the same book (Stone 2013).

14 The film uses a performance by Kenneth Cooper and Yo-Yo Ma, with the latter playing the Gamba part on the modern cello, an instrument whose sound is much fuller and more lyrical in the upper range.

15 In the language of music theory, we would say that what we have here is a series of passing modulations, none of which finds a root-position tonic. A chromatic descent in the bass line takes the harmonic progression to diatonically adjacent tonal areas (E minor, F sharp minor, E minor, D minor) and prepares each of these steps via the dominant of the relative major (in other words, $V^{4/2}$ of A major prepares F sharp minor, $V^{4/2}$ of G major prepares E minor, $V^{4/2}$ of F major prepares D minor).

16 This is an example of what theorists have named 'bifocal tonality': progressions characterised by a major/minor axis where, as LaRue puts it 'only the slightest inflection is required to change the focus' (2001: 292).

17 While not commenting explicitly on the music's contribution to this finale, Robin Wood has drawn attention to the way the film offers a variation on the *temps mort*, arguing that 'the sequence evokes the ending of Antonioni's *L'Eclisse*, but without its sense of desolation and finality: rather, the feeling is of sadness and happiness inextricably intermingled, regret for the separation and the uncertainty but a deep satisfaction in the degree of mutual understanding and intimacy two human beings have achieved in a few hours' (1996: 13).

18. In this sense, the musicalisation of this scene emphasises the sense in which, as Dimitris Eleftheriotis has discussed, in the travel film 'activity and passivity are bound in a dialectic rather than exclusive relationship: the active traveller is simultaneously passive in his/her openness to the experience of the journey' (2012: 55).
19. The two-re-encounter in a Parisian bookstore where Jesse, now provided with a surname and a job as a writer, is presenting his first book, 'This Time', a fictional version of that day of romance he had with Celine in Vienna. For an instant, glimpses of the harpsichord moment serve to recapitulate the characters' day in Vienna and to stage the vision of Celine as a juxtaposition of past and present.

Works Cited

Agacinski, Sylviane [1995] (2003), *Time Passing: Modernity and Nostalgia*, New York: Columbia University Press.

Barthes, Roland (1981), *Camera Lucida*, trans. Richard Howard, New York: Hill & Wang.

Baumgarten, Marjorie (1995), 'Before Sunrise', *The Austin Chronicle*, 27 January, <https://www.austinchronicle.com/events/film/1995-01-27/138341/> (last accessed 15 May 2017).

Charney, Leo (1995), 'In a Moment: Film and the Philosophy of Modernity', in Leo Charney and Vanessa Schwartz (eds), *Cinema and the Invention of Modern Life*, Berkeley: University of California Press, pp. 279–94.

Christie, Thomas A. (2011), *The Cinema of Richard Linklater*, Maidstone: Crescent Moon.

Dowd, James and Nicole Pallotta (2000), 'The End of Romance: The Demystification of Love in the Postmodern Age', *Sociological Perspectives*, 43:4, pp. 549–80.

Eleftheriotis, Dimitris (2012), *Cinematic Journeys: Film and Movement*, Edinburgh: Edinburgh University Press.

Flinn, Caryl (1992), *Strains of Utopia: Gender, Nostalgia, and Hollywood Film Music*, Princeton: Princeton University Press.

Hanson, Peter (2002), *The Cinema of Generation X*, Jefferson: McFarland.

Illouz, Eva (1997), *Consuming the Romantic Utopia*, Berkeley and Los Angeles: University of California Press.

Johnson, David T. (2012), *Richard Linklater*, Chicago: University of Illinois Press.

Kermode, Frank (1966), *The Sense of an Ending*, Oxford: Oxford University Press.

LaRue, Jan (2001), 'Bifocal Tonalities: An Explanation for Ambiguous Baroque Cadences', *Journal of Musicology*, 18:2, pp. 283–94.

Lury, Celia (1998), *Prosthetic Culture: Photography, Memory and Identity*, London: Routledge.

MacDowell, James (2013), *Happy Endings in Hollywood Cinema: Cliché, Convention and the Final Couple*, Edinburgh: Edinburgh University Press.

Martin, Adrian (2006), 'Love's Moment: *Before Sunrise* and *Before Sunset*', *Cinemascope*, 4, January–April, pp. 1–6.

McGillivray, Murray (1994), 'Creative Anachronism: Marx's Problem with Homer, Gadamer's Discussion of "the Classical," and Our Understanding of Older Literatures', *New Literary History*, 25:2, Spring, pp. 399–413.

Norton, Glen (2000), 'The Seductive Slack of *Before Sunrise*', *Post Script: Essays in Film and the Humanities*, 19:2, pp. 62–72.

Schivelbusch, Wolfgang (2014), *The Railway Journey: The Industrialization of Time and Space in the Nineteenth Century*, Berkeley: University of California Press.

Stone, Rob (2013), *The Cinema of Richard Linklater: Walk, Don't Run*, New York: Wallflower Press.

Syngle, Erik (2004), 'Love Me Tonight', *Reverse Shot*, 21, 25 June, <http://reverseshot.org/archive/entry/203/before_sunrise> (last accessed 1 May 2017).

von Busack, Richard (1997), 'Waiting for the Sun', *Metro*, February. pp. 13–19.

Wood, Robin (1996), 'The Little Space in Between: Preliminary Notes on *Before Sunrise*', *Cineaction*, 41, pp. 4–13.

CHAPTER 11

Moving in Circles:
Kinetic Elite and Kinetic Proletariat in 'End of the World' Films

Ewa Mazierska

After road movies, science fiction is the fictional genre in which journeys play the greatest role. Arguably the first SF film and a noted example from the first years of cinema, Georges Méliès' *Le voyage dans la lune/ A Trip to the Moon* (1902) concerns a group of astronauts travelling from the Earth to the Moon. The film testifies to the ambition to transcend the borders of human existence through the development of technology, of which both the cine camera and the spaceship became potent symbols in various cultural contexts. During the period of the Cold War the moon was 'conquered' by humans, hence trips to the moon were relegated (or upgraded) to the documentary genre, but journeys to faraway planets and galaxies remained a staple diet of SF films, produced in the capitalist West and the socialist East. The ability to represent such journeys testified primarily to the technological and colonial ambitions of the respective political orders, capitalism and state socialism. During the Cold War outer space, both in reality and in filmic representations, was seen as a place where new technologies could be tested to ensure the hegemony of one or the other political order. Another common motif, especially at the peak of the Cold War, was the invasion of Earth by aliens. It was particularly common in Hollywood films, but there were also a number of Soviet and Eastern European films which used it, such as *Stalker* (1979) by Andrei Tarkovsky. Usually this was regarded as a metaphor for the threat posed by a hostile political order.

In most research devoted to SF films with the motif of interplanetary journeys made during the Cold War period, a class aspect is omitted. This is not without reason, because even when the trips are undertaken by a tiny minority of the bravest and fittest (the elite), the travellers act on behalf of the whole of humanity, rather than to advance the position of a specific social class. Similarly, when aliens invade the Earth, they are regarded as a threat to the entire population rather than a specific stratum. The issue of how aliens were chosen to come to Earth, and the class structure of the populations of distant planets, is also usually omitted from the narrative. Such obfuscation of the class character of journeys is not the case, however, in more recent, post-Cold War SF films, such as *Gattaca* (1997) by Andrew Niccol, where the chance to travel to outer space is linked to having a particular genetic make-up, which can be compared to belonging to the 'blue- blooded' aristocracy. Still, in *Gattaca*, the futuristic journey brings the promise of both physical escape and transcending one's class position; the Earth in this film is not a limit for the brave, even if they come from the 'wrong' class.

The two films I consider in this chapter, *Elysium* (2013) by Neill Blomkamp and *Snowpiercer* (2013) by Joon-ho Bong, also use the motif of a journey and take us to the near future, when class matters more than any other aspect of identity, such as nationality or age. What is also specific about them is that in the future they present, there is practically no escape from our planet, as if by this point there were nothing new to discover or conquer.

Travelling in the End of Times

In my investigation I will draw on two ideas which are in tension with each other. One concerns the importance of movement under modernism and postmodernism; the second that we have reached the end of history. The most famous thinker who put movement at the centre of the modern world was undoubtedly Karl Marx. Marx described the class of capitalists and capital itself as being always on the move, pressing forward and destroying everything in its way in a relentless pursuit of surplus value, as stated in this famous fragment: 'All fixed, fast-frozen relations, with their train of ancient and venerable prejudices and opinions, are swept away, all new-formed ones become antiquated before they can ossify. All that is solid melts into air' (Marx and Engels 2008: 38).

In this scheme of things the fate of the bourgeoisie and the proletariat are intertwined, as capitalism cannot develop without the work of the proletariat in the production of commodities. The proletariat trails behind the bourgeoisie, having to adjust to the rules of capital. Such a situation, according to Marx, would last until the victory of the proletarian revolution, which would abolish all classes and class antagonism. However, when describing the lives of real workers in *Capital*, Marx presents them as sedentary, toiling in factories, where machines move faster than them. Moreover, they come across as so exhausted from work that they barely have a chance to ponder their identity. Revolution is the only opportunity to transcend it.

By contrast, the postmodern thinkers Ulrich Beck and Elisabeth Beck-Gernsheim emphasise mobility as a universal condition, which takes many shapes and is linked to creating or projecting a specific identity. In their take on 'the globalization of biography' they declare that,

> In the global age, one's life is no longer sedentary or tied to a particular place. It is a travelling life, both literally and metaphorically, a nomadic life . . . spent in cars, aeroplanes and trains, on the telephone or the internet, supported by mass media, a transnational life stretching across frontiers. The multilocal transnationality of the life of one's own is a further reason for the hollowing out of national sovereignty and the obsolescence of nation-based sociology. The association of place and community or society is coming unstuck. (2002: 25)

As people take control of their own lives in the global community, everything 'is acted out in the personalised costumes of the individual – independently' in 'all the glitter of the campaign for their own lives' (2002: 22). Physical mobility is a marker of freedom, including freedom to appropriate different masks, be one person in one place and a different one in another.

Zygmunt Bauman also links the problem of mobility with that of identity, claiming that the goal of people living under the postmodern condition is to avoid having a stable, fixed identity:

> Not to get tied to the place. Not to wed one's life to one vocation only. Not to swear consistency and loyalty to anything and anybody. Not to *control* the future, but to *refuse to mortgage it* . . . To forbid the past to bear on the present. In short: to cut the present off at both ends, to sever the present from history, to abolish time in any other form but a flat collection or an arbitrary sequence of present moments; a *continuous present* . . . The hub of postmodern life strategy is not identity building, but avoidance of fixation. (1996: 24)

Bauman argues that while the figure capturing the time of modernity was that of a pilgrim trying to reach a specific goal, in the postmodern era that of a stroller, a vagabond, a tourist or a player is more suitable (1996: 26–32). All these figures indicate a movement without any specific direction and with variable speed. They also emphasise the agency of the traveller. S/he decides where to go and whom to be rather than allowing the circumstances (most importantly economic ones) to decide it.

These texts by the Becks and Bauman reflect a certain optimism pertaining to the earlier stage of neoliberalism and postmodernism, fuelled by the fall of the Berlin Wall and a widespread fascination with advances in transportation and communication, to which many authors attributed the potential to democratise societies. They suggest that a pleasurable nomadic life is available to almost everybody and there is not much difference in the way it is experienced by people from different regions and classes. They present the situation of an affluent traveller as a universal condition, playing down the cases when mobility results from colonisation, pauperisation or war and is resisted by those on the move.

By the time Blomkamp and Joon-ho Bong completed their films, this optimism had all but evaporated, with the world financial crisis of 2008 being a crucial factor in its disappearance. This crisis had largely to do with mis-sold and defaulted mortgages and more widely with the impossibility of escape from the past. The crisis showed that it is not up to individuals to refuse to mortgage one's future; it is often mortgaged before they are born, given that most people are born with a significant debt which increases as years go by (Lazzarato 2012).

In later works theorising mobility, the focus is on mobility as something that divides rather than connects people. Kevin Hannam, Mimi Sheller and John Urry (2006), use terms such as the 'fast and slow lanes of social life' and 'aeromobile elite', who travel fast, in comfort and with ease, in contrast to the low-speed majority, who often travel against their will. The kinetic elite also differs from the proletariat in their access to technology. The former can use it to allow them to reach places; the rest are not able to reach or even to slow the pace of their movements. 'There is a proliferation of places, technologies and "gates" that enhance the mobilizations of some while reinforcing the immobility, or demobilization of others', they summarise (Hannam, Sheller and Urry 2006: 11). Mobility, from this perspective, reflects existing inequalities and accelerates them.

The second idea that informs my investigation is that we live in the 'end times', marked by the demise of state socialism in the late 1980s to early 1990s, and the hegemony of neoliberalism. While some authors, most importantly Francis Fukuyama (1992), see this as a positive outcome of history, others, such as Mark Fisher (2009) and Slavoj Žižek (2011) view it negatively. Žižek summarises this end aptly:

> The global capitalist system is approaching an apocalyptic zero-point. Its 'four riders of the apocalypse' are comprised by the ecological crisis, the consequences of the biogenetic revolution, imbalances within the system itself (problems with intellectual property; forthcoming struggles over raw materials, food and water), and the explosive growth of social divisions and exclusions. (2011: x)

An additional aspect of living in the end times is a 'crisis of imagination'. As Fisher puts it: 'For most people under twenty in Europe and North America, the lack of alternatives to capitalism is no longer even an issue. Capitalism seamlessly occupies the horizons of the thinkable' (Fisher 2009: 8).

While accepting the premise that we live in the 'end times', I argue that in the films under discussion this end is not really marked by an acceleration of capitalism, but by its exhaustion. Capitalism in the two films considered here reached its limit, and is neither able nor willing to expand. Producing a surplus value is no longer an objective of the capitalist elite, and even if it would be possible to keep producing, there are no markets able to absorb the production. Colonisation, which in the past was an answer to the crisis of over-production and over-accumulation, is no longer an option. For this reason I suggest labelling the reality depicted in them as postcapitalist rather than capitalist-realist or neoliberal.

The concept of the 'end times' brings association with stasis rather than movement, hence the question of how to reconcile the idea of the end (of capitalism, of civilisation, of humanity) with the conviction that contemporary people move faster than their antecedents. In the subsequent part of my chapter I will show how this dilemma is solved in the two films under examination.

Vertical and Horizontal Journeys in *Elysium*

In her recent examination of digital cinema, Kristen Whissel suggests a link between what she calls the 'new verticality' of the Hollywood blockbuster, achieved by using digital special effects and the hegemony of neoliberalism (Whissel 2014: 21–58).

> Because verticality lends itself so well to the dynamic elaboration of conflict between opposed forces, it seems remarkably suitable for an area defined by economic polarization and new forms of political, religious, and military extremism, all of which seem to have had [the] effect [...] of evacuating previously available middle grounds. (2014: 26)

She adds that verticality allows the films

> simultaneously to acknowledge extremism, economic polarization, and thwarted upward mobility as significant aspects of their global audience's condition of existence and to charge these crises with new visual pleasures and imaginary resolutions ... Precisely by defying verisimilitude, the new verticality lends these films a different sort of emblematic truth able to resonate – strongly and broadly – within the historical context of the late twentieth and early twenty-first centuries. (2014: 26)

Paul Dave, drawing on Whissel's research, argues that the

> delirious freedoms, the defiance of the laws of time and space, captured by "new verticality", stands for the neoliberal capitalist class whose dominance has led to the

stretching of the social structure, such that a distant, cocooned elite floats in all the magnificence of its material and symbolic power above a disregarded human mess whose abandonment is now seen as a given. (2016)

In this context it is also worth quoting Žižek again, who observes that the true evil of our times is not capitalist dynamics as such, but the attempts of the privileged to extricate themselves from the conditions they created, by carving out self-enclosed communal spaces, from 'gated communities' to exclusive racial or religious groups.

> The exemplary figures of evil today are not ordinary consumers who pollute the environment and live in a violent world of disintegrating social links, but those who, while fully engaged in creating conditions for such universal devastation and pollution, buy their way out of their own activity, living in gated communities, eating organic food, taking holidays in wildlife preserves, etc. (2008: 27)

From the perspective of the relationship between the capitalist class and working class this is a new situation, because under capitalism these two classes were always dependent on each other. Capitalists could not afford to abandon the proletariat, at best they could move from one location to another in search of cheaper labour. As Antonio Negri puts it,

> Neither the concept of capital nor its historical variants would exist in the absence of a proletariat which, whilst being exploited by capital, is always the living labour that produces it. Class struggle is the power relation between the boss and the worker: this relation invests exploitation and capitalist command and is established in the institutions that organize the production and circulation of profit. (2010: 155–6)

By contrast, what Whissel, Dave and Žižek allude to is a situation in which capitalists have accumulated enough capital to afford them comfortable living till the end of times and prefer to enjoy it rather than to engage in a struggle to get the proletariat to create more surplus value, risking their wellbeing and security. However, this scenario raises a number of questions, for example whether capital itself allows for comfortable living or indeed has any value at all in the absence of the proletariat. According to Marx in *The Communist Manifesto* and *Capital*, this is not the case – to have any advantage for a capitalist, capital has to be put in motion by the workers, employed to multiply it and ensure a comfortable life for the capitalist. However, in his *Grundrisse*, in what is known as the 'Fragment of the Machine', Marx envisages the world in which the 'general intellect', embodied by advanced machines, does the labour previously undertaken by humans (Marx 1973: 690–5).

Such questions can be raised in relation to the situation presented in *Elysium*. The film was directed by a South African director, whose main source of fame prior to making this film was *District 9*, a low-budget mockumentary concerning the plight of aliens in Johannesburg (Mazierska and Suppia 2016: 127–40). *District 9* acted as Blomkamp's pass to Hollywood, which rewarded him for his success with a production budget of US$115 million and two 'heavyweight' stars in the main parts: Matt Damon, in the leading role of Max, and Jodie Foster, cast as his main antagonist, Delacourt; but it also, as I will argue in due course, constrained him, reducing his complex take on the issue of emigration and human rights to a typical Hollywood story, where a lonely hero wins over the powerful bad guys.

Elysium is set in Los Angeles of the year 2154. By this point the Earth has become overpopulated, polluted and practically barren due to people's failure to take proper care of their habitus. The film begins with a panorama showing burnt-out and empty skyscrapers. Skyscrapers used to signify human ambition to reach the sky – their despicable state in this film is a testimony to the ultimate failure of such aspiration. Later we see that the remainder of the population (I will call them Earthlings) live largely in shanty towns, bungalows and cellars, near the ground. The Earth in *Elysium* thus comes across as a gigantic shanty town, whose inhabitants are trapped by poverty. This state suggests a reversal of human history and a return to some primitive state when humans lived in caves and shacks.

The wealthy have found a solution to ecological and social disaster by emigrating to the eponymous Elysium, a space station the size of the moon that orbits the Earth, as in the scheme described by Žižek. This location of the space station is a reference to Greek mythology, where Elysium or the Elysian Fields were located at the edge of the Earth. Those chosen by the gods were destined to spend their afterlife there.

The fact that Elysium is not located in a far-away galaxy is a recognition that, even in its imperfect state, the Earth is ultimately the only possible source of life known to humans, therefore one cannot separate oneself from it completely. Unlike the space ships in earlier science-fiction films, which are usually enclosed and claustrophobic places, Elysium is an open space. Neither is it a temporary abode used by travellers to reach a more permanent home, but a stable home for those able to afford it. It gives the impression of a luxurious holiday resort, complete with swimming pools and palms. The houses of the inhabitants of this artificial miniplanet are furnished with a med bay, a device which treats any imaginable disease or accident, in this way affording the Elysians if not an immortal existence, then at least semi-immortality. It can thus be seen as a perfect solution to the modern and postmodern desire for mobility with that of having a home. This paradise is governed by Delacourt, Elysium's female Minister of Defence, whose behaviour brings to mind British Prime Minister Margaret Thatcher, with her open support of inequality and protection of the privileges of the rich. Delacourt's objective is to ensure that Elysium remains safe, namely free from any intrusions from the Earth. For this purpose any spaceship that appears near Elysium is shot down. Delacourt implements such a policy not out of mindless cruelty, but sheer pragmatism. She is aware that Elysium, like every space ship (and ultimately every habitable planet) has limited capacity to carry humans. Overcrowding brings a distinct risk of destroying the vehicle, which has practically happened to Earth by this point in time.

Dave implies that the new Hollywood films promote and normalise a situation in which the rich and powerful detach themselves from social reality and history, finding a place in the universe where they cannot be affected either by the laws of history or gravity. In *Elysium* this is only partially the case. The escape of the rich from history indeed takes place there, as Elysium is situated outside Earth. However, in a sense it reflects on what happens on Earth, as demonstrated by the fact that security is its primary concern, and for this purpose the inhabitants of the Earth are constantly spied upon. The poor, on the other hand, attempt to join the elite and participate in their luxurious lifestyle, which can be regarded as an allegory of the economic migration from the poorer to the richer regions. Neither does the film normalise this status quo of extreme polarisation, but presents it as highly immoral. In this sense, it follows in the footsteps of Blomkamp's *District 9*, where the poor aliens try to be integrated into South African society, while the indigenous population wants them to leave. However, there are also differences between these two films, reflecting the different circumstances of their production. In *District 9* South Africa is not a holiday resort, where everybody enjoys its luxuries. Rather, true to its historical reality, the bulk of its society come across as poor and suffering from high unemployment, which partly explains their hostility towards the aliens, seen as a threat to their already difficult position. In *Elysium*, by contrast, the Elysians appear to belong to one homogeneous and self-contained group. Unemployment is of no concern because (perhaps with the exception of politicians) nobody there works. The rich do not even need servants as this function is fulfilled by robots.

Work is also scarce among the Earthlings. Production of goods to be used by the planet's inhabitants or sell at a profit to each other has practically ceased. The only people occupied by what can be termed 'work' belong to three categories: those who work in essential services, such as overcrowded and poorly equipped hospitals, those engaged in criminal activity, organising trafficking operations to Elysium and those working in a military factory, producing equipment whose purpose is ensuring the security of Elysium. None of these types of work allows for social development, but the first type ensures that humanity is preserved or, read negatively, that its agony is prolonged. The organisation of work affects the mobility of its citizens. Work has always been the main stimulus of mobility. People travel to work and for tourism/holidaying, but the latter is possible only when they have the means to travel, which usually come from work. By contrast, on Earth as presented in *Elysium*, we see no tourists and travel to/from work and inside the workplace is heavily curtailed. In the only factory depicted in the film, there is a reversal of roles between humans and the machines. People there perform menial and sedentary jobs, while the robots hold managerial positions, ensuring that the human employees produce commodities at the required speed and with the right attitude and move freely around the factory. Any transgression by the employees of the rules imposed by the robots is severely punished by beatings and a worsening of the conditions of labour. Not only are workers not allowed to rebel, but they are forbidden to have rebellious thoughts. The surveillance of workers is extended to the road to the factory, where their belongings are searched before they board a bus and the smallest misdemeanour results in a severe beating, bringing to mind the treatment of slaves or of inmates of concentration camps.

The prevailing means of transport on Earth are people's own feet. Few people in the middle of the twenty-second century possess cars, the most common means of transportation in the previous century. Cars are now used only in exceptional circumstances. They are all battered, no doubt because few new cars are built at a time when natural resources are all but exhausted. Freedom of movement is also limited by legal means. The majority of the population thus moves in the narrow vicinity of their neighbourhood. The Earth as depicted in Elysium comes across as a collection of shanty towns, whose inhabitants are trapped by their poverty. Although overpopulation is stated as a reason why the elite left Earth, it is not reflected in the type of movement we observe in the film. Most importantly, there are no crowds. This might reflect the individualistic logic of capitalism, which the poor have internalised to their own disadvantage, or the demise of factory work, where collective action was designed and put into practice, or it might be a conscious strategy of the elite, which uses robots to prevent people from communicating and collaborating with each other. Of course, in their old buses and cars the Earthlings have no chance to catch up with Elysians.

While Elysium has an efficient government, the Earth comes across as leaderless and chaotic. The greatest power is wielded by some computer hackers-cum-mechanics (and criminals from the perspective of Elysians), who specialise in transporting the desperate Earthlings to Elysium, like traffickers who ship refugees and economic migrants from the global South to the global North in real life. They use battered, most likely unsafe space ships, bringing to mind the old boats and dinghies in which migrants are smuggled across the Mediterranean Sea. By contrast to the Earthlings, who have to negotiate bumpy roads in unsafe vehicles, the kinetic elite travel in a space station the size of the moon that floats calmly across the stratosphere. The beauty of travelling this way is that it does not feel like travelling at all, because the movements of the ship are not reflected on the surface of the space station. The perfectly circular shape of the orbit symbolises their quasi-immortal life. Elysium can be seen as an answer to the question of how to reconcile a desire to travel and have a stable home. The circular shape of Elysium can also be seen as a symbol of the end of history, when there is nothing else to conquer, as in the scheme described by Fukuyama. The film thus presents two versions of history's end – positive (on Elysium) and negative (on Earth).

Although *Elysium* concerns space travel, journeys in this film are very short. Even going from Earth to Elysium in a dilapidated shuttle lasts only nineteen minutes. The problem concerns not the distance or physical difficulty of travelling in outer space, but overcoming security barriers, which reflect class boundaries. The sky is not the limit for humans any longer, but the Earth is. The fact that the paradise created by the elite is close to the Earth rather than on a distant planet, points to the nurturing function of the Solar System and even Earth itself, and the end of utopian dreams associated with exploring outer space. Physical travel in *Elysium* is accompanied by virtual travel, thanks to the Earth and Elysium being connected by new technologies. However, the traffic is one-way only. The government of Elysium can send messages to Earth, and spy on it, but Earthlings cannot reciprocate. To reach Elysium and its luxuries, they have to go there physically. This adds to the imbalance of power between the kinetic elite and the proletariat, and illustrates the view of Hannam, Sheller and Urry (2006) that access to communication is an important factor in the stratification of travellers.

This situation is interrupted when Max, an ex-convict severely injured at the factory where he works and at risk of losing his life, decides to travel illegally to Elysium to get treatment from a med bay. However, being in the possession of a code for rebooting Elysium, which in practice means that he can programme it so that it would welcome travellers from the Earth, he decides to sacrifice his life so that Earthlings, including the daughter of his childhood love, can go to Elysium. The film finishes there, with hordes of people boarding space ships to Elysium, leaving out the question of what happens if Elysium becomes overcrowded, like Earth itself. We can presume that it would collapse, annihilating the kinetic elite and most likely further damaging the Earth. As I mentioned earlier, this question was broached by Delacourt, who said that she could not accept any 'visitors' from Earth, because it would jeopardise the future of their children. Her argument, which represents what Fisher describes as 'capitalist realism', namely a conviction that the current system is deeply immoral, but there is no alternative to it, is rejected not only by the Earthlings, but even by some members of Elysium's authorities. The film's reviewers, including ordinary viewers posting their reviews on the IMDb website, expressed their dissatisfaction with the ending of the film. For example, one reviewer wrote: 'Last but certainly not least: the ending. Apparently everyone is going to live happily ever after on Elysium now? Every rich person on Elysium just wanted all those poor people on earth to suffer! But now the world is sugar plums and everyone lives happily! Yay!'

The ending of the film can also be regarded as representing a happy moment before the catastrophe. The fact that the catastrophe itself is not represented might be seen as a reflection of the position of a left-leaning filmmaker working in the neoliberal economy of Hollywood, who is torn between showing solidarity with the underprivileged and avoiding the question of how to change their position without destroying the privileges of the wealthy and deepening the ecological crisis.

There are numerous similarities between *Elysium* and Fritz Lang's *Metropolis* (1927), as both films show an extremely polarised world with the masses suffering numerous deprivations contrasted with the privileges of the elite. In both films class and progress are represented in terms of verticality – the workers toil beneath the city; the rich live at the top of Metropolis. In both, the conflict is around the poor transcending their position and reaching the elite. Both films show that this is possible, largely thanks to brave individuals who reject such a polarised world. However, *Metropolis* is different in that it was made at a time when there was literally and figuratively plenty of space at the top. In *Elysium* this is no longer the case, and the film oscillates between acknowledging and disavowing this fact. By contrast, the next film in my investigation takes issue with the lack of the room at the top and, indeed, any place left for humans.

Snowpiercer: All Together on the Same Train

In common with *Elysium*, *Snowpiercer* is a product of international collaboration, but with more countries involved in its production. The film is based on a French graphic novel and was shot in the Czech Republic and Austria. Its director is South Korean and the cast is truly multinational, with American and English actors in the principal roles. It was made on a budget of about US$40 million, roughly one-third that of *Elysium*. Although this is a crude measure, we can assume that the smaller involvement of American capital and creative personnel in *Snowpiercer*, and the smaller budget in comparison with *Elysium*, might explain some differences in their treatment of problems afflicting post-capitalist society in the respective films.

The film is set in 2031, when following an experiment that took place seventeen years earlier and whose purpose was to reverse global warming, the whole of Earth became frozen and uninhabitable. Importantly, the first image of the film shows planes 'piercing' the sky and followed by a white trail. Most likely such planes carried a substance which was meant to lower the temperature, but whose effect was catastrophic. The image of the planes can also be regarded as a sign of a failed project of 'verticality', of humans' desire to escape the Earth, which not only was ultimately unsuccessful, but led to the destruction of the atmosphere. Not unlike *Elysium*, the catastrophe is also signified by images of cities reduced to ruins.

The lucky few people who survived the ecological disaster did so thanks to boarding a train, the eponymous Snowpiercer. Those who managed to reach this safe haven came from different places, races and classes, bringing to mind the variety of species on Noah's Ark. The presence of both the low and high classes makes Snowpiercer a more egalitarian vehicle than Elysium, where there is no room for the poor. However, the class structure existing before the ecological disaster is recreated and enhanced inside the train. The society in *Snowpiercer* is polarised between the super-rich and the very poor, with the middle class practically non-existent.

It takes a year for the train to circle the whole of Earth. This renders it similar to spaceships. Yet Snowpiercer moves on the ground, being unable either literally or metaphorically to escape the physical and economic conditions of the Earth. By the same token, the film metaphorises the idea of the end of history, when movement does not bring progress, only reinforces the status quo. Snowpiercer survives in the harsh, post-apocalyptic climate thanks to its technological advancement, most importantly its sustainability; it uses only as much energy as it is able to produce. Rather than producing surplus product and surplus value which creates capital and allows for colonial expansion, the rule governing the operations of this mini-universe is recycling. In recognition of this fact, Vlad Dima describes the system as end-of-the-world capitalism (Dima 2016: 162).

However, there are different rules for the rich and the poor: the poor have to recycle and scale down; the rich can use as many resources as they wish. Those occupying the front of the train live in luxury, eat natural food, such as fruit, vegetables and meat, and enjoy freedom; including the freedom to proliferate, as signalled by the image of a pregnant teacher working in a class full of children. Those living at the back live in overcrowded compartments, eat disgusting processed 'protein blocks' made of cockroaches and are heavily policed, randomly harassed and punished for the smallest misdemeanours. Moreover, to fulfil the requirement of sustainability, the population of Snowpiercer has to be restricted, because the train has no capacity for expansion. Too many people on the train means that it will be unable to pierce the snow, resulting in everybody freezing to death. The stability of the population on Snowpiercer is achieved by culling the surplus of the proletariat, largely through instigating in-fighting. Although the film is coy about it, we can conjecture that this objective is also achieved by limiting the sexual activity of the lower class passengers. This is suggested by a low proportion of children in the tail of the train and the fact that they do not attend any school. Children there are thus seen as not worthy of investing in – they are not the future, but remnants of the past. The existence of this kinetic underclass reminds us of the prisoners of concentration camps. This connotation is reinforced by the narrative, *mise en scène* and casting. In one episode children are measured and separated from their parents, as happened in the concentration camps, where children were subjects of Nazi eugenics, with Jewish and Gypsy children being sent to the gas chambers, and blue-eyed Slavic children being spared, to serve the Reich. We also see heavy barrel-like objects being pushed by the people of the lowest class, although it is difficult to establish what purpose this serves, except to keep the passengers constantly occupied. Again, engaging the proletariat in labour for the sake of keeping it moving, rather than any productive activity, brings to mind concentration camps, where prisoners were required to work irrespective of whether their work was needed or not and it was not unusual for them to push or pull something for the enjoyment of their sadistic supervisors. The most important work is performed by children, who are employed in the engine section of the train, effectively acting as its spare parts.

The film begins when the proletariat, led by a man called Curtis, rebels against his fate and decides to move to the head of the train, not unlike the Earthlings trying to reach Elysium. We observe two physical movements:

one circular (of the train) and one linear (on the train). In this case belonging to the kinetic elite does not mean moving faster or being able to reach a destination which is denied to the poor, but only travelling in luxurious conditions, which is a privilege which the rich are not anxious to give up. As in *Elysium*, the rich are confined even more than the poor, as the poor can still press forward, while the rich have reached the limits of their movement.

To the physical movements we can add the metaphorical movements through social classes, because through negotiating the compartments the people from the bottom move to the top. This involves class struggle – fighting with those who guard higher positions, till they reach the head of the train and finally the engine. The 'engine', which is a term of particular importance for communist discourse, features extensively in the dialogue. We hear statements such as 'Who controls the engine, controls the world' and 'All past revolutions failed, because people did not reach the engine'. 'Engine' here functions as a metaphor of a centre of power and the means of production of the capitalist economy. Engine ensures movement. The fact that in the film the adjective 'sacred' is added to it suggests that movement is idolised – it is a source of life. Indeed, if the engine is stopped, the train will stop too, being unable to penetrate the snow anymore.

Curtis and his followers move forward only to learn that the train's owner and manager, Wilford, is in fact happy to pass his power to Curtis. He even praises Curtis for inducing the proletarian revolution, as this allows a reduction of the train's population, which is a necessary condition for the 'train-system' to work smoothly, as previously mentioned. Wilford's decision to give his place to Curtis shows that he realises the supremacy of the system over the people. Individuals can change their place in the society, but this does not change its organisation; there will always be an elite at the head of the train and the poor at the train's tail. Wilford plays down the difference between the kinetic elite and the kinetic proletariat, saying that 'we are all stuck in this train' and 'this train is a closed ecosystem'. 'Being stuck' goes against the idea of capitalism, as capitalism is about conquering new territories for the purpose of selling surplus product and creating more surplus value and capital. What we get is thus again the situation of 'post-capitalism', when the polarised class structure pertaining to the capitalist order has survived or even solidified, but the main purpose of capitalism, namely producing more capital, has been abandoned due to the combination of ecological disaster and possibly a lack of interest on the part of the elites to get wealthier. The second point is suggested by emphasising the decadent lifestyle of the elite, complete with using night clubs, high-class brothels and hot tubs.

However, rather than taking the baton from Wilford and accepting the cruel logic of post-capitalism, Curtis prefers to halt the train. If we see the situation as a metaphor for the current social and political order, then it seems as if the poor have only two choices: accept that only a small proportion of them can change their status quo, those who are most gifted or ruthless, or those who fight it and make the world perish. Such a scenario is typically presented by those in favour of 'capitalist realism', claiming that the current system is far from perfect, but its alternative would lead to disaster. The end of capitalism equals the end of the world. But *Snowpiercer* suggests that it is better to end the world than continue post-capitalism.

Conclusion

In this chapter I argued that in the films under consideration travelling has lost most of the functions attributed to it by modernist and postmodernist thinkers, such as ensuring economic or social progress and personal fulfilment. At the end of history, or perhaps after its end, there is nothing to discover and conquer and identities are already fixed. This is conveyed by the prevalence of circular movements over linear ones, with characters returning to the same point. Yet, paradoxically, movement is more important than in earlier periods, because abandoning it equals metaphorical and physical death. At the same time, the films suggest that such movement is pointless; it might be better to die than to move in circles.

Works Cited

Bauman, Zygmunt (1996), 'From Pilgrim to Tourist – or a Short History of Identity', in Stuart Hall and Paul du Gay (eds), *Questions of Cultural Identity*, London: Sage, pp. 18–35.

Beck, Ulrich and Elisabeth Beck-Gernsheim (2002), *Individualization: Institutionalized Individualism and its Social and Political Consequences*, London: Sage.

Dave, Paul (2016), 'Contemporary British Social Realist Film: *Bypass*, Obscure Forces and Ontological Unrest', paper presented at conference 'British Social Realism', Teesside.

Dima, Vlad (2016), 'Man within machines: *Snowpiercer* from *bande dessineé* to film', *Journal of Graphic Novels and Comics*, 7:2, pp. 156–66.

Fisher, Mark (2009), *Capitalist Realism: Is There No Alternative?*, Winchester: Zero Books.

Fukuyama, Francis (1992), *The End of History and the Last Man*, London: Penguin.
Hannam, Kevin, Mimi Sheller and John Urry (2006), 'Editorial: Mobilities, Immobilities and Moorings', *Mobilities*, 1, pp. 1–21.
Lazzarato, Maurizio (2012), *The Making of the Indebted Man: An Essay on the Neoliberal Condition*, Los Angeles: Semiotext(e).
Marx, Karl [1857–8] (1973), *Grundrisse: Foundations of the Critique of Political Economy*, trans. Martin Nicolaus, London: Penguin.
Marx, Karl and Friedrich Engels [1848] (2008), *The Communist Manifesto*, London: Pluto Press.
Mazierska, Ewa and Alfredo Suppia (2016), 'Capitalism and Wasted Lives in *District 9* and *Elysium*', in Ewa Mazierska and Alfredo Suppia (eds), *Red Alert: Marxist Approaches to Science Fiction Cinema*, Detroit: Wayne State University Press, pp. 121–48.
Negri, Antonio (2010), 'Communism: Some Thoughts on the Concept and Practice', in Costas Douzinas and Slavoj Žižek (eds), *The Idea of Communism*, London: Verso, pp. 155–65.
Whissel, Kristen (2014), *Spectacular Digital Effects: CGI and Contemporary Cinema*, Durham, NC and London: Duke University Press.
Žižek, Slavoj (2008), *Violence*, London: Picador.
Žižek, Slavoj (2011), *Living in the End Times*, London: Verso.

CHAPTER 12

Gothic Journeys: Travel and Transportation in the Films of Terence Fisher

Chris Fujiwara

Introduction

The journey appears as a regular trope in Gothic literature and cinema. Such classic Gothic novels as Ann Radcliffe's *The Mysteries of Udolpho*, Matthew G. Lewis's *The Monk*, Mary Shelley's *Frankenstein*, and Charles Robert Maturin's *Melmoth the Wanderer* are, in part, journey narratives that trade in a kind of exoticism, enabling the reader to travel to wild, unknown regions haunted by the constant proximity of death. In Emma McEvoy's view, 'early literary Gothic, with its depictions of abbeys and castles, of ruins and wild landscapes', can be regarded 'as a kind of vicarious tourism', reflecting 'a time when domestic tourism was becoming increasingly affordable for, and popular with, a middle-class public' (2014: 479).

The prototypical Gothic journey takes the form of the displacement of a traveller from a safe and familiar home to an enigmatic and unpredictable space. Such journeys often have, no doubt, strong nationalist underpinnings, and, according to Justin D. Edwards, Gothic literature draws on the British tradition of travel writing in order to distinguish 'the homely place of the nation [. . .] from] the unhomely spaces of foreignness, which are by contrast seen as mysterious, enigmatic and shrouded in darkness' (Edwards 2014: 57–8). Nevertheless, the Gothic journey tends to lead to the erosion of this demarcation and the subversion of established patterns of self-identity, family, nation and empire. Thus Stephen D. Arata finds in the journey of Jonathan Harker as recounted in Bram Stoker's novel *Dracula* a critique of the narrator's Orientalism (1990: 635), while William Beckford's *Vathek*, Justin D. Edwards writes, charts a Gothic journey that 'subverts the Enlightenment principles of discovery, reason, logic and rationality' (2014: 57).

The work of Terence Fisher, who directed most of the best known horror films made by Britain's Hammer Films in the 1950s and 1960s, reconfigures the Gothic journey in cinema. As Fisher's characters make their way across the vividly rendered geographies of his films, the initial polarity between home and away progressively loses its organising power. At the same time, the films ground their fantasies of mortal peril and the transformation of human beings in mundane aspects of the experience of travel, including such problems as collisions, roadblocks, jostling, loss of luggage and recalcitrant drivers.

By foregrounding such difficulties, Fisher's films suggest the extent to which the modernity they depict is an insufficient one, still bearing the traces of a past that it seeks unsuccessfully to deny. In *Dracula: Prince of Darkness* (1966), a pair of British tourists in Transylvania insist that since Castle Dracula, from which they have just been warned away by a local priest, does not appear on their map, it must not exist. The map offers a comforting fictional view that collapses in the face of a reality that contradicts the mapmakers' project of the inscription of a rational geographic space. The absence of Castle Dracula from the map signifies an irrational existence, the survival of an earlier reality that has been incompletely superseded by the new one. The geography of *So Long at the Fair* (1950, co-directed by Antony Darnborough) is organised by two poles: one is the newly completed Eiffel Tower, symbol of progress; the other is a hotel room that mysteriously vanishes along with its last occupant, another unfortunate British traveller who is found to have succumbed to plague, a disease whose very name carries connotations from the age of European feudalism. As with the travellers' map in *Dracula: Prince of Darkness*, the site of an unwholesome survival of the past is simply expunged from the spatial order.

The space of Fisher's films is thus an incomplete and partial one, a mixture of the familiar and the uncanny, the present and the past. In navigating this space, his protagonists find themselves enacting, or reenacting (since many of the films are repetitions of literary models, or sequels), the unnatural transformations and mysterious displacements that are familiar from Gothic literature, notably from Stoker's *Dracula* and Shelley's *Frankenstein*, each of which inspired a series of Hammer films, the best of them directed by Fisher. The director gives these Gothic themes expressive visual, temporal and spatial form through images of transportation. Moreover, Fisher's films extend the function of the Gothic as 'vicarious tourism' by mobilising narrative elements that metaphorically represent the cinematic apparatus and the specificity of the viewing situation. Through these procedures, Fisher restructures the field of the Gothic.

Embodiment and Transportation

To define this field, it may be useful to cite Irving Malin's account of New American Gothic literature as concerned with a dichotomy of spatial confinement and movement. 'The voyage,' Malin writes, '[. . .] represents movement, exploration, not cruel confinement. But the voyage is also horrifying because the movement is usually erratic, circular, violent, or distorted' (1962: 106). These two poles – confinement and violent movement – structure Fisher's work while locating its narrative events in an atmosphere charged with transgression. Though it would be pointless to catalogue all the moments of confinement in Fisher's films, a few of the more memorable and significant can be mentioned: Frankenstein's various creations and patients (in five films directed by Fisher) strapped down, shackled or caged after undergoing surgical operations; Kharis trapped alive in a sarcophagus in *The Mummy* (1959); Baron Meinster shackled by the ankle in *The Brides of Dracula* (1960); the imprisonment of Leon in *The Curse of the Werewolf* (1961). Inevitably, each of these moments of entrapment is followed by a liberation that leads to terror and disaster.

Fisher's Gothic is a mode of relentless embodiment, in which the supernatural is compelled to assume stable material form, and in which the triumph of good over evil is effected through the activation of the physical and spatial limitations to which the representatives of evil are subject. Resolutely faithful to the material and the visible, Fisher's cinema insists not only on representing indecorous or taboo practices and objects (an insistence for which his early horror films were routinely criticised at the time of their release), but on giving external form to the inconspicuous and the inherently unrepresentable. In *The Gorgon* (1964), a man who is turning to stone writes a description of the process as he feels it internally, and Fisher's camera shows his writing. Even the soul becomes manifest in *Frankenstein Created Woman* (1967). Fisher's cinema adapts metaphysical concepts and themes from Gothic and Romantic literature to a context that is recognisable and mundane, if also stylised through dialogue, set design and performance.

Fisher's three vampire films all emphasise restrictions on the vampire's mobility. In *Dracula* (1958), Van Helsing declares the belief that vampires can transform themselves into bats or wolves to be 'a common fallacy'. When it comes to long-distance travel, Dracula is subject to the same limitations as ordinary mortals and must rely on the same means to overcome them. The curtailment of Dracula's supernatural powers, together with Van Helsing's understanding of vampirism as a 'contagion' or disease 'similar to addiction', signals an insistence on material reality that affects all aspects of the film, including its depiction of technology (Van Helsing uses a phonograph to record his research notes; the blood transfusion from Holmwood to Mina is shown in detail) and travel. In this insistence, as in the director's characteristic measured pacing and dry, geometrical *mise en scène*, Fisher's cinema can be seen to constitute an exception to the 'general opposition to realist aesthetics' in which David Punter identifies the criterion according to which 'a unitary "Gothic tradition"' might be most simply defined (1996: 182).

The conditions of the vampire's physical existence are peculiar and arbitrary. By highlighting these conditions, Fisher evokes a more general arbitrariness, which any of us may feel characterise the rules that govern our own lives as bodies. 'During the day, a vampire must rest in his native soil,' Van Helsing announces in *Dracula*, explaining a requirement that will figure importantly in the narrative action. 'He's got to come back here before cockcrow,' says Greta of Baron Meinster in *The Brides of Dracula*. In *Dracula: Prince of Darkness*, a further limitation is introduced: 'A vampire cannot cross a threshold unless he's invited by someone already inside,' as Father Sandor explains. The litany of these restrictions, and their importance in the narratives of the films, serves to underline the inherently limited nature of embodied existence.

As a corollary to the law of embodiment in Fisher's cinema, and as if to make their stories more readily accessible to the viewer, his films constantly emphasise the practical difficulties of getting from one place to another. 'There's an excellent train service to and from London,' Holmes remarks while visiting Dartmoor in *The Hound of the Baskervilles* (1959), but few of Fisher's characters are so fortunate as to obtain unclouded enjoyment of the comforts of modern transportation. Mishaps of carriage are a persistent occurrence in Fisher's films. 'Not so fast,' Marianne implores the coachman at the beginning of *The Brides of Dracula*, but he pays her no notice as he speeds through the Transylvanian woods, causing Marianne to be jostled about. In *Dracula*, *The Brides of Dracula*, and *Dracula: Prince of Darkness*, characters are inconvenienced by being abandoned mid-journey by their drivers. In *Frankenstein Created Woman*, a sudden bump during a coach ride, which the driver attributes to one of the horses throwing its shoe, causes the two passengers to disembark and continue their journey on foot through the woods. In *The Mummy*, two drunken hauliers, terrified at having to pass an insane asylum on their route, drive too fast, causing the crate they are carrying (which contains the mummified Kharis) to fall into a swamp. Early in *Dracula: Prince of Darkness*, a pair of coach horses take four travellers against their will to

Castle Dracula; near the end of the film, a rifle shot causes the horses to start off on their own, and again they head towards the castle; when the coach careens around a corner, Dracula's coffin slides out of the back of the coach onto the frozen castle moat.

Two of Fisher's most remarkable films, *To the Public Danger* (1948) and *The Earth Dies Screaming* (1964), make clear the structural function of mobility in his cinema by representing crashes of transportation vehicles. Both films are set in England in the mid-twentieth century (the time of their production), and if they are deemed to belong to the Gothic genre, it must be according to a definition of that genre considerably expanded from its origins in a body of British fiction from the late eighteenth and early nineteenth centuries. Such an expansion has long been customary in scholarly studies of the Gothic, and it is unnecessary to make elaborate justifications for it here. It will be sufficient, and pertinent, to recall David Punter's claim that, at whatever place and period, 'it is in its concern with paranoia, with barbarism and with taboo that the vital effort of Gothic fiction resides; these are the aspects of the terrifying to which Gothic constantly, and hauntedly, returns' (1996: 184).

An early directorial effort by Fisher, *To the Public Danger*, mobilises all three of these aspects with panache, translating them into the visual and spatial terms of automotion. Based on a radio play by Patrick Hamilton, the medium-length film (less than fifty minutes) takes place over a single evening, as the selfish, amoral Captain Cole, seeking to impress a girl he has met in a roadside inn, drives at high speed across the countryside. Becoming increasingly drunk and reckless, the Captain crashes the car into a tree, apparently killing himself and two companions. The Gothic quality of the film lies in the exposure of the barbarism behind the civilised veneer of the Captain, ready to use force to achieve his desires and avoid the law. In *To the Public Danger*, travel is presented as mere pointless forward motion; Captain Cole's journey is nihilistic and suicidal, and the dramatic tension of the film arises from the efforts of the other characters to resist being caught up in this movement, even though one of them, Nancy, is also attracted to it.

A paranoid film par excellence, *The Earth Dies Screaming* opens with a sequence in which independent and geographically dispersed breakdowns in transportation (crashes of a train, a car and an aeroplane) signal a catastrophe that its survivors will come to ascribe to an alien invasion of Earth. The control or loss of control of vehicles of transportation becomes a crucial issue in the film. Two of the main characters are introduced lying seemingly inert in the front seat of a wrecked car. Only by his ability to take command of a jeep and, in the final shot of the film, an aeroplane, does the hero gain a measure of control over the situation that confronts him and the other survivors.

One of the most startling moments of the film is a single continuous take that is filmed through the front windshield of a jeep as the vehicle approaches and runs down an alien. The destructive movement in which this exceptional shot unites the jeep and the film camera not only destroys the alien but also threatens to destroy the film's illusion of reality, since the alien, who in previous shots was incarnated by a costumed and helmeted actor, is now all too evidently a somewhat makeshift dummy that has been propped up in the road. Because of this counter-illusion – one that violates a taboo of narrative cinema through an excessively materialist presentation – the power invested in the moving vehicle as an instrument identified with the camera becomes diminished.

The theme of destructive transportation enters Fisher's films in ways other than the conveyance of people and objects from place to place. Transportation is also central to Fisher's Frankenstein series, in which not only body parts, most crucially brains, but also the soul, are moved from one body to another. The geographical displacements of Baron Frankenstein – for example, from Germany to England at the end of *The Revenge of Frankenstein* (1958) – are metaphors of this transplantation of identity, just as the Baron's freedom of movement asserts his pretension to dominate not only physical but also metaphysical limits, a pretension that the films usually end by thwarting (significantly, Frankenstein's sole successful experiment in the entirety of the series is that with which *The Revenge of Frankenstein* concludes, in which he himself is the patient).

The ancestral curse that threatens Sir Henry in *The Hound of the Baskervilles* is another kind of transportation, as is the curse, apparently brought on by the reduction of a beggar to a beast-like state through prolonged incarceration, that dooms Leon in *The Curse of the Werewolf*. In both these films, evil originates in the depravity of the aristocracy. The spread of vampirism is similar. In *The Brides of Dracula*, Baron Meinster is said to have been turned into a vampire by one of his friends, a fellow participant in what the family servant darkly calls 'wicked games'. Dracula's servant, Klove, informs the travellers in *Dracula: Prince of Darkness*, 'My master died without issue, in the accepted sense of the term.' Klove's remark can be taken to mean that the persistence of the vampire's life after death is a form of unacceptable issue, or perhaps Dracula's 'issue' could be understood to encompass those whom he has turned into vampires by infecting them with his bite. Called a 'vile contagion' in *Dracula*, vampirism has similarities to the plague that dooms the heroine's brother in *So Long at the Fair*, which is not a horror film but which, David Pirie claims, 'could easily have been re-shot, sequence for sequence, as a vampire movie without making any difference to its basic mechanics' (1973: 55).

Tourists and Spectators

Telling similar stories, both set in the late nineteenth century, about English travellers on holiday in Europe, *So Long at the Fair* and *Dracula: Prince of Darkness* set up contrasting attitudes among their tourist characters. In *So Long at the Fair*, on a trip to Paris, Johnny seeks vainly to master his new surroundings while also keeping them at arm's length with his ironic and dismissive attitude, while his sister, Vicky, is enraptured. 'You never know with foreigners,' he says (by way of warning his sister to take her valuables along with her rather than leave them in the hotel); Vicky says almost the same thing, but with a different meaning: 'Anything could happen in Paris,' she remarks excitedly. In *Dracula: Prince of Darkness*, four English tourists are in Transylvania: Charles is ready for any adventure, but his sister-in-law, Helen, insists on sticking to their itinerary and their map and becomes peevish when plans are deviated from ('Two miles outside London and nothing's ever right' is how Charles characterises her attitude). Helen becomes the victim of Dracula, just as Johnny succumbs to plague; if Helen is transformed into one of the undead, Johnny is spirited away and suffers the indignity of being erased from the hotel records as if he had not existed.

The dangers of travelling, an activity intended to 'broaden the mind' (the phrase constitutes an ironic refrain in *Dracula: Prince of Darkness*, placing travel in an Enlightenment context that the figure of Dracula disrupts), are illustrated by the fate of the mad Ludwig (a character equivalent to the Renfield of Stoker's novel), as recounted by Father Sandor: 'He was a traveller like yourself. I found him one night near Castle Dracula. Something he had seen or heard unhinged his mind. He lost his memory completely.' Later in the film, Sandor again shows himself able to analyse the possible effects of the events of the narrative on the spectator: 'If you wish to see the destruction of the horror spawned by Count Dracula, come with me. But I warn you, it is not a sight for the squeamish.' *Dracula: Prince of Darkness*, a film about tourists, thus becomes a horror film that explicitly addresses itself to horror-film spectatorship and evokes the paranoiac dimension of film spectatorship.

Landscape and Place; The Inn

The process, characteristic of Gothic narratives, by which, as Benjamin A. Brabon writes, 'the monstrous Other is repelled and geographically displaced, while simultaneously revealing that it already inhabits the central ground of an English national sense of identity' (2014: 99), is made spectacularly evident in the way Fisher's *Dracula* telescopes the geography of Stoker's novel. In the film, the relocation of the action and the main British characters from England to Central Europe reverses the displacement of the novel (Dracula moving from Transylvania to London). We might suppose that the borders of Britain have been imaginatively extended and that Dracula, instead of invading Britain, is already in some sense inside Britain. As Peter Hutchings notes, if the shifting of the scene of the story was motivated by budgetary reasons (which necessitated eliminating Stoker's sea journey), 'the space of the film is also an imaginative fantasy space, one that is not fully bound by notions of the real. So far as the film's broader geography is concerned, the closeness of the castle to the Holmwood house serves . . . a thematic function – Dracula is "closer to home" than ever before' (2003: 62). To be sure, a border separates Dracula's realm from that of the Holmwoods, but it is a ludicrous one, ineptly guarded and easily crossed.

The topography of Fisher's Dracula films is a quintessentially Gothic one, in which the vampire's remote, forbidding castle can be reached only by journey through a forest. These settings represent, for the non-undead protagonists of the films, a dangerous realm, an exoticised middle Europe where the restrictions that govern behaviour in the domestic sphere are thrown off. Thus, in *Dracula*, Harker appears quite willing to let himself be seduced by the nameless vampire woman who appears before him in Castle Dracula, begging for his help; and in *Dracula: Prince of Darkness*, Helen, the most prim and repressed of the four British travellers, is the one who is transformed by Dracula into a vampire, a transformation that appears to liberate her sexuality, as her choice of a daringly décolleté nightgown and her new-found interest in her sister-in-law indicate.

In a highly economical manner, through the repetitive inscription of movements and landmarks, Fisher's films generate a strong sense of place, of where things are in relation to one another. The narrative action of both *Dracula* and *Dracula: Prince of Darkness* oscillates between two geographical poles: one is Castle Dracula; the other, in the first film, is the Holmwood house; in the second film, it is a monastery. The action of each film follows the same tripartite pattern: first, visitors enter the castle; second, Dracula tries to gain access to the opposite site; third, the protagonists pursue

Dracula back to his castle. In both films, the intermediate space between the two sites is largely a *terra incognita*. Similarly, in *The Hound of the Baskervilles*, the moor of Dartmoor constitutes a sprawling, inexplicable zone where unwary travellers risk losing their way and getting sucked into Grimpen Mire. In *Frankenstein Created Woman*, the guillotine where Hans's father is executed in the opening sequence serves as a landmark for the expeditions of various characters for the rest of the film. Standing at the edge between the town and the country, the guillotine marks the symbolic limit of established social definitions and the beginning of a zone of dissolution of identity, as is seen in the climactic scene of the film, set outside the town limits, in which Christina (in whose body Frankenstein has transplanted the dead Hans's soul) speaks in Hans's voice.

The inn is an important setting in several Fisher films, from *To the Public Danger* and *Stolen Face* (1952) to *Frankenstein Created Woman* and *Night of the Big Heat* (1967). The essential characteristics of the inn are defined in *To the Public Danger*: a space of leisure and alcoholic refreshment, the inn is constituted in relation to the road and mobility, and thus it also bears and records the pressure of social and historical changes, as is clear from Nancy's lament for the inn during its wartime heyday, when it was frequented by friendly Americans and the parking lot was full of Buicks, Packards and jeeps.

In *Dracula* and *The Brides of Dracula*, the inn functions as a kind of museum of local beliefs (the garlands of garlic flowers strewn not for decoration but for protection against vampires), serves as a site for the transmission of knowledge (in the form of Harker's diary, passed on to Van Helsing by a sympathetic barmaid) and permits the local community to come together in rituals and exclusions (leaving en masse at a signal from a mysterious visitor in *The Brides of Dracula*; casting suspicious looks at strangers) that affirm the shared fear of a surrounding monstrous evil. In *The Brides of Dracula*, the inn is also a place where the aristocracy (represented by Baroness Meinster) can meet the common people, although it seems clear that their interactions must be constrained, and furthermore, the Baroness's intentions are purely exploitative (she seeks to obtain victims for her vampire son). Similarly, in *Frankenstein Created Woman*, the inn enables three aristocratic young men to interact with the innkeeper and his disabled, disfigured daughter, but the purpose of the former group in doing so is to make abusive fun of the latter.

In *The Revenge of Frankenstein* and *The Mummy*, the inn is a meeting place for working men and criminals. In *Night of the Big Heat*, the inn is the primary setting, a space where social cohesion is desperately maintained in the face of rising temperatures and the intrusions of an aloof scientist, a sexually predatory woman and marauding alien life forms. In all its functions, the regular features of the inn in Fisher's films are the opportunistic nature of the social interactions it facilitates, its receptivity to all sorts of people and (to name the feature that makes possible the previous two) its close proximity to the road (or, in urban settings, the street). Being close to the road, the inn belongs to the chronotope of travel.

Three Films

I will now examine three Fisher films (*Stolen Face*, *The Stranglers of Bombay* (1959), *The Devil Rides Out* (1968)) that, though they stand apart from the 'Gothic' core of his work as narrowly defined in terms of narratives of supernatural terror set in nineteenth-century Europe, fully belong to the Gothic in the expanded sense set out above, characterised by Punter in terms of paranoia, barbarism and taboo. Each of these films demonstrates Fisher's creative use of the close connection of the Gothic with travel and transportation.

Stolen Face

The smoothly directed melodrama *Stolen Face* can be read as a Gothic narrative whose mainsprings are obsessive love and a doomed experiment in human transformation. On holiday, Philip Ritter, a plastic surgeon, meets and falls in love with Alice, a concert pianist, but she leaves him to return to her fiancé. The loss of his beloved drives Ritter to try (with plastic surgery) to recreate her in another woman, Lily, a convicted thief whose face was badly scarred in the Blitz. Ritter gives Lily the face of Alice and marries her, but his new wife soon proves her unsuitability for the role in which he has cast her, reverting to her previous criminality and carrying on with another man.

The relevance of *Stolen Face* to Fisher's later work is obvious (and has been commented on by Peter Hutchings in his study of Fisher's films, 2001: 63–6). Ritter is a Frankenstein figure, crossing class boundaries (as Frankenstein does in *The Revenge of Frankenstein*, tending to wealthy patients while also running a clinic for the poor) and giving beauty to a disfigured woman (as Frankenstein does in *Frankenstein Created Woman*). What is also significant for my purposes is the key role played by journeys throughout the narrative of *Stolen Face*. Ritter's driving holiday enables him to meet Alice when a rainstorm causes him to turn off the road to seek shelter in the country inn where she happens to be staying. Their growing involvement with each other is shown through a montage of short rural excursions by car, on horseback, and in a horsedrawn carriage. Alice's European concert tour is the immediate pretext for her separation from Ritter.

The film reaches its climax in the compartment of a train travelling from London to Plymouth, in which Lily, accompanied by her husband, becomes progressively drunker. This leads to a Hitchcockian situation in which the hero, having every motive to rid himself of his tormentor and offered the opportunity to do so, is briefly suspected by the audience of being about to do just that: in a shot from outside the compartment, Ritter lowers the shades, blocking the interior of the compartment from the audience's view, whereupon Lily's scream is heard off-camera. A cut to inside the compartment reveals, however, that Lily has merely spilled her drink over her dress; and instead of trying to kill her, Ritter saves her from falling out of the speeding train when she drunkenly opens the outside door.

The train compartment is, like the car in *To the Public Danger*, both a space in rapid motion and one that provides a maximum of constriction. The paradoxical tension created by the quasi-public nature of the compartment leads to the catastrophe. Lily initially asserts her exclusive possession of the space, driving away the other occupants, an elderly couple, with her bad manners; later, Alice unexpectedly enters the compartment, having hurried after the train by car in order to catch and board it. Lily attacks Alice in a fit of rage and, struggling with Ritter, who tries to separate her from Alice, falls from the train to her death. Lily is doomed by the taboo nature of her dual relationship with Alice, here brought to a paroxysm by their presence, for the first time in the film, in the same space at once.

The Stranglers of Bombay

The ambivalence of the close relationship of the Gothic with empire and colonialism has been widely recognised. 'Gothic writing about foreign lands,' writes Justin D. Edwards, 'can serve as a tool of colonial expansion, reinforcing colonial rule by instituting the imaginary borders separating savagery from gentility, brutality from civilisation. Within this process, though, the foreign always presses against the borders and an invasion seems imminent' (2014: 58). In view of this relationship and its significance with regard to the theme of the journey, *The Stranglers of Bombay* (1959), one of two Fisher films (with *The Mummy*) that deal explicitly with imperialism, deserves special attention. In *The Stranglers of Bombay*, set in the early nineteenth century, merchants in India are alarmed by a wave of mysterious losses of caravans. These disappearances prove to be the work of a Thuggee sect working in complicity with a village leader. Lewis, an officer of the East India Company, uncovers and defeats the sect.

As Marcia Landy points out, *The Stranglers of Bombay* differs from typical 'empire films' such as Zoltan Korda's *Sanders of the River* (1935) in directly linking commerce and imperialism. 'The violence and destruction [of the Thuggees] is not supernatural or fortuitous,' Landy writes,

> but linked to the desire for profit. The Indians are portrayed as seeking to reappropriate what has been expropriated from them, and the violence of their methods, when read against the grain, is a distorted mirror of the methods of the expropriator [...] The film opens up the terrifying world of the colonial Other in such a way as to implicate the British characters as well as the external spectator, casting doubts in 1959 on any lingering notions of reviving the glories of the British Empire. (1991: 420)

The Stranglers of Bombay thus becomes, rather than a celebration or defence of imperialism, an examination of the problems imperialism creates, which are mainly problems of transportation – that of Indian resources outside India and of British soldiers and administrators within India.

The ending of *The Stranglers of Bombay* is devoid of comfort: Lewis, refusing any momentary complacency over his defeat of the Thuggees and a promised promotion, looks off-screen into the jungle and tells his wife (a notably undeveloped character, and the more haunting for that, as if she were an actor with no clear idea of the film she was appearing in): 'She's out there, Kali the murderess, with her murdering sons. This is only the beginning.' With the film viewer, the Lewises remain suspended in a place where they cannot comfortably make a home, waiting for a further manifestation of an annihilating threat that has only temporarily been vanquished. There follows a short succession of ending titles, culminating in a rueful summation ascribed to Major General Sir William Sleeman, the historical figure credited with the capture of the Thuggees: 'If we have done nothing else for India, we have done this good thing.'

As a spectacle, *The Stranglers of Bombay* draws its power from the forbidden nature of what it shows. The camera observes the rituals of the cult with a strangely impersonal sense of shock and with a sort of calm indifference that mirrors the placidity of Karim, a female cult member who has no dialogue but who is visible on the margins of scenes, most notably at the ordeal of the captured Lewis, spread-eagled on the ground and tied to stakes. (Marcia Landy calls Karim a 'surrogate' for the film spectator, 1991: 420.) Cinematic transportation in *The Stranglers of Bombay*, Fisher's *mise en scène* seems to assert, poses a situation that we can only endure in full consciousness that it is *wrong* – a wrongness that some viewers may identify as the racism of the film (one commentator accuses the film of manifesting 'the peak of racist paranoia', Izhar 2011: 111), but it can be argued that the film does not espouse this racism but merely makes it visible.

The Devil Rides Out

From beginning to end, *The Devil Rides Out* (1968) is Fisher's major statement on transportation. The first scene shows an aeroplane landing in a field; the pilot, Rex, disembarks and joins his waiting friend, the Duc de Richleau, and the two drive off together in the latter's car. The film is concerned with direction ('time itself has been reversed for us', the Duc announces near the end), with supernatural obstacles to travel (the fogging of the windshield of a car in which Rex pursues his beloved, Tanith), and with comings and goings, some of them ritualised or repetitious: the black magician Mocata returning de Richleau's car; Rex arriving at the house of his friends, the Eatons, only to leave again immediately; the arrival and departure of the Angel of Death (who, once summoned, cannot return empty-handed); the repeated emergence of Rex and Tanith from the woods. The car is a key object in this film set in the 1930s, when the motorcar was still a sign of wealth and status (asked for the loan of a car, the Duc replies with sublime nonchalance, 'take any of 'em'). It functions not only as a vehicle of transportation but as a source of light, when Rex and de Richleau disrupt the black sabbath in the woods.

Instead of back projection, still commonly used in driving scenes at the time when *The Devil Rides Out* was made, Fisher's film rather oddly employs matte shots, notably for scenes in which Rex and Tanith drive cars. Matting is used again later in the special-effects-laden climaxes: the scene in which the protagonists take refuge inside a magic circle, and the scene in which Mocata tries to make a human sacrifice of the Eatons' young daughter, Peggy. The matte itself is a form of transportation, putting a body in front of a foreign background. To accomplish this, the matte dematerialises the body, reducing it to a flat image that seems to threaten to disappear from the film and that perhaps needs to be held down to keep it from flying away, the way Tanith is constantly trying to fly away from Rex.

Like Fisher's Dracula and Frankenstein films, *The Devil Rides Out* is structured on the repetition of images of bodies being carried from one place to another: the Duc and Rex overpower Simon and carry him out of his house; Rex carries Tanith from the woods. With the arrival of Simon and Tanith (bodies partially emptied out and subject to Mocata's will) into the Eatons' home, not just the supernatural also enters there, but the narrative itself as something extraordinary and difficult to believe is transported into a calm and reasonable domestic space.

* * *

What is Gothic about acts of transportation would appear to be their forbidden nature, their violation of a taboo: this is the theme of Fisher's Frankenstein and Dracula films, and it also surfaces in *Stolen Face*, *The Stranglers of Bombay* and *The Devil Rides Out*. The cultural conservatism implied by the terms in which Fisher's films state this theme is undercut not by making evil attractive (that interpretation would be the clichéd argument for Fisher's films from a liberal, enlightened perspective) but by exposing that very attractiveness as an effect of historical and social forces (such as global imperialist capitalism in *The Stranglers of Bombay* and the post-war malaise of Britain in *To the Public Danger*) and revealing the scope such conditions allow to predators (such as Dracula, Mocata and Captain Cole) and to obsessional neurotics in positions of authority (Ritter in *Stolen Face*).

The Devil Rides Out reveals transportation to be a metaphor not only of the Gothic, but of cinema. De Richleau's magic circle is undoubtedly a paranoid construction, but as it is also a metaphor of the film experience (with the central characters assaulted by successive visual tricks and illusions), Fisher is able to make the point that the cinema – *his* cinema at least – derives value from the protective nature of its fantasies. The dangerous travels of the heroic characters end in a comforting, satisfying return to the English domestic space of the Eatons' house – a rare achievement of bliss in a body of work that most often remains (as the clipped and desolate ending of *The Stranglers of Bombay* reminds us, and it is hardly exceptional among Fisher's endings) unsettled even in its moments of stasis.

Conclusion

Given the ontological basis of cinema in the photographic depiction of movement and the affinity of the medium for bodily and geographical materiality, it is hardly surprising that filmmakers, in taking over Gothic themes from literature, should emphasise space and movement. I have sought to show that Terence Fisher's work constitutes not merely a typical case of an emphasis that must result automatically from the inherent properties and biases of the medium but a precise and far-reaching restructuring of the Gothic elements of paranoia, barbarism and the taboo in cinematic terms.

Numerous Fisher films explore the theme of destructive, illicit or cursed transportation. Fisher's emphasis on visible, material embodiment serves to ground the Gothic elements of his narratives in a realistic context, in which the insistence on practical difficulties and mishaps of transportation and on the corporeal limitations to which even the supernatural characters are subject evoke the embodied experience of the viewer. If Fisher's topography is, in general, characteristic of the Gothic mode, his distinctive use of the space of the inn highlights the richness of his work and the centrality of mobility to his films. At the opposite pole from the violent movement that is characteristic of the Gothic (exemplified in the furious climaxes of several Fisher films), confinement serves as a regular motif in Fisher's work, creating an emotionally turbulent atmosphere.

Fisher's work is embedded within the context of British modernity of the second half of the twentieth century. His depiction of the breakdown of society and the danger of barbarism in such contemporary-set films as *To the Public Danger*, *The Earth Dies Screaming* and *Night of the Big Heat* both reflect and comment on that context. So, in a different way, does his evocation of paranoid spectatorship in several films, including *The Devil Rides Out*. If Fisher remains, stylistically, an artist of the classical cinema, his treatment of Gothic themes leads his work to the limits of that classicism, confirming the deep association of the Gothic with transgression while demonstrating the director's commitment to an aesthetic of balance and containment.

Works Cited

Arata, Stephen D. (1990), 'The Occidental Tourist: *Dracula* and the Anxiety of Reverse Colonization', *Victorian Studies*, 33:4, Summer, pp. 621–45.

Brabon, Benjamin A. (2014), 'Gothic Geography, 1760–1830', in Glennis Byron and Dale Townshend (eds), *The Gothic World*, London: Routledge, pp. 98–109.

Byron, Glennis, and Dale Townshend (eds) (2014), *The Gothic World*, London: Routledge.

Edwards, Justin D. (2014), 'British Gothic Nationhood, 1760–1830', in Glennis Byron and Dale Townshend (eds), *The Gothic World*, London: Routledge, pp. 51–61.

Hutchings, Peter (2001), *Terence Fisher*, Manchester: Manchester University Press.

Hutchings, Peter (2003), *Dracula*, The British Film Guides 7, London: I. B. Tauris.

Izhar, Dror (2011), *'Quit India': The Image of the Indian Patriot on Commercial British Film and Television, 1956–1985*, Newcastle upon Tyne: Cambridge Scholars Publishing.

Landy, Marcia (1991), *British Genres: Cinema and Society, 1930–1960*, Princeton: Princeton University Press.

Malin, Irving (1962), *New American Gothic*, Carbondale: Southern Illinois University Press.

McEvoy, Emma (2014), 'Gothic Tourism', in Glennis Byron and Dale Townshend (eds), *The Gothic World*, London: Routledge, pp. 476–86.

Pirie, David (1973), *A Heritage of Horror: The English Gothic Cinema, 1946–1972*, London: Gordon Fraser.

Punter, David (1996), *The Literature of Terror: A History of Gothic Fictions from 1765 to the Present Day. Volume 1: The Gothic Tradition; Volume 2: The Modern Gothic*, 2nd edn, London: Longman.

CHAPTER 13

Transnational Productions and Regional Funding: Border-crossing, European Locations and the Case of Contemporary Horror

Stefano Baschiera

The new millennium has seen a flourishing of horror cinema production in Europe. This is a phenomenon involving different media, national cinematographies, international partnerships, and the development of niche subgenres. Countries such as Germany, Greece, Norway, the Republic of Ireland, Russia, Spain, France, the UK and Hungary have witnessed a new proliferation of the genre across a range of films, directors and co-production agreements that can compete in number with the rich genre landscape of the 1970s. I argue that the tension between the national and regional settings of the films on the one hand, and the transnational context of their production and distribution on the other, can suggest how popular cinema is the site for a new mapping of Europe. As seen through the prism of the horror genre, this mapping reveals recent trends in the industry, as well as an innovative cultural representation of European journeys. The idea is to consider the different policies which form the backbone of the contemporary film industry on the continent, so as to portray a European space that goes beyond touristic postcard cities, engaging with backward regionalisms in place of cosmopolitan realities.[1]

The close relationship between travel and cinema has been at the centre of several scholarly investigations (see for instance Eleftheriotis 2010) and of course it is at the basis of genres such as road movies and travelogues. Horror cinema often uses the trope of the journey as dangerous trespass in a hostile environment, facing alterity and uncanny dislocations. The discovery of exotic locations and the feeling of danger at the unknown have been exploited in hundreds of films from *King Kong* (Merian C. Cooper and Ernest B. Schoedsack, 1933) to *An American Werewolf in London* (John Landis, 1981), from the Italian *mondo* films to the cannibal series. I argue that the flourishing location business favours a rediscovery of the so-called 'rural horror cinema' (see Clover 1992: 124–37; Bernard 2014: 168), also defined as the 'road horror movie' or 'travel horror cinema' (see Ballard

2008), a subgenre traditionally characterised by border crossing, touristic activities and more or less exotic locations.

Rural horror is understood as the subgenre whose most significant representatives are Tobe Hooper's *Texan Chainsaw Massacre* (1974) and Wes Craven's *The Hills Have Eyes* (1977), and whose plot line can be summarised by a group of city dwellers travelling into an unknown location who face backward and ultimately murderous and/or monstrous locals. At the core of the rural horror there is the meeting of the middle-class protagonists with places 'where the rules of civilization do not obtain' (Clover 1992: 124) and the emphasis is often on the isolation and remoteness of the deadly stage of the journey. Rural horror films include both journeys within the nation and border crossing, with the latter further emphasising the dislocation of the protagonists.

The 'rural' can be either a paradisiac remote place which was the intended destination of the journey but which hides a secret, or the unexpected detour, the wrong turn from the safety of points A and B. The subgenre had a revival in the US at the start of the millennium, thanks to films such as *Jeepers Creepers* (Victor Salva, 2001), *Wrong Turn* (Rob Schmidt, 2003) and *The House of 1000 Corpses* (Rob Zombie, 2003), soon followed by a series of remakes of 1970s productions.[2]

Recent developments in film exhibition, distribution and production have contributed to the resurgence of horror in Europe and to defining its new features in a period when the genre rediscovered the travel horror narratives. In the last decade, digital disruption and the consequent proliferation of different online platforms and business models have had a clear impact on the availability of horror, in particular at the low-budget end of the market, where 'long-tail straight-to-DVD, download services and free video-hosting sites like YouTube are making more content available to international cult audiences than ever before' (Lobato and Ryan 2011: 200). Looking, for instance, at the catalogue of SVOD platforms such the ubiquitous Netflix and Amazon Prime Video, it is easy to grasp how horror, along with crime, is one of the most successful genres in crossing national borders, and populating the online catalogues. The online presence of international and foreign-language horror productions happens 'because of the predominance of low-budget productions, the minor impact of language differences and because of the thriving of subgenres on the long tail markets' (Baschiera 2014). European horror cinema, having historically had a significant presence in the international home video market (see Olney 2013: 16) has found a new distribution platform that can make the niche profitable.

While streaming distribution has created a new international market, and consequently demand, for horror, European production of the genre has started to benefit from new forms of financial aid through the development of regional funding and policies. Such aid shifts the 'cultural' accent from the artistic quality of the filmic text to the health of the cultural industry, thanks to the financial repercussions of screen activities in the area. As Marco Cucco and Giuseppe Richeri point out in their investigation into the location market (Cucco and Richeri 2013), local administrations no longer consider the film industry an artistic area in need of support as a matter of regional or national prestige, but a strategic economic area able to help the local economy and generate employment and territorial marketing. In doing so, they mirror European regional development policies with the goal of boosting the economy in areas of industrial and agricultural decline by encouraging skills development and inter-state collaborations (see Hunter 2016). The regional development funds do indeed have a main objective of attracting film production to the territory, with the consequence of bringing financial benefits to the local economy, promoting its visibility and developing its infrastructure and local employability. This economic-driven system, originating in northern European countries, often does not include any consideration of quality in order to access the financial contribution. In fact, to access these funds one production may need to spend 120–150 per cent of the financial aid received in the location or to shoot a given percentage of scenes in the territory.

The new role played by the screen industries as a possible means of regeneration of a particular area is also manifested in the increased numbers of film commissions, film funds and fiscal advantages which contribute to a portfolio of film-friendly policies. As of 2016, sub-national funds equal 60.8 per cent of the funding body population, while the total resources they make available is inferior to those of national/federal funding (€473 million yearly average versus €1.9 billion) which makes them more significant for medium- and low-budget productions (Talavera Milla, Fontaine and Kanzler 2016: 10–13).

Nevertheless, regional funding may work alongside existing national incentives, creating in this way a competitive film-friendly offer and a further territorialisation of the policies in place. Sub-national funds have a clear scope dedicated to the economic development of the area. Looking, for instance, at the funds for TV and film production offered by the Ile-de-France film commission to promote shooting in the Paris region, it is possible to grasp how the requirements to access the financial contribution are clearly oriented towards local employment. In order to be considered for the funding, the projects need to employ a France-based executive producer, to have a minimum of 50 per cent of the shooting time in Ile-de-France (with a minimum of twenty shooting days in the region), and to complete at least two technical services (among: set and costumes; equipment; editing and sound engineering; laboratory and post-production) in the location, with at least 80 per cent of the cost located in the Ile-de-France from each service. Similarly, the funding offered by British Screen Yorkshire requests that the project be based in the region and 'managed by a registered company located in Yorkshire and Humber', stressing again the goal to create a viable regional industry.[3]

National funding, instead, generally has more sets of criteria featuring cultural characteristics alongside economic ones. These may include a 'cultural test' to affirm proof of nationality where the background of directors, actors and members of crew come into play alongside the 'heritage' quality of the story shot, the language used, etc.[4] These criteria come into play in particular in cases of co-productions where proofs of national belonging are at the basis of the agreements and of public contributions.

Among the support available at national and sub-national level, fiscal incentive schemes are those which developed most strongly over the past decade, rising from twelve to twenty-six between 2008 and 2014. They have become a crucial (albeit controversial) feature attracting inward investment and guaranteeing the competitiveness of a territory on the global production market (Talavera Milla, Fontaine and Kanzler 2016: 71). The film commissions play a beneficial role in managing funding and tax incentives as well as in the development and management of locally based production facilities and locations of interest. In 2005 the European Film Commission Network was officially instituted, which now features eighty film commissions from twenty-four countries. These are impressive numbers if one thinks that at the start of the 1990s only England and France had film commissions and their development moved from a national context and a focus on urban areas to a more capillary regional landscape (see Cucco and Richeri 2013).

These policies shift attention towards a territorialisation of films, with the 'location business' playing an increasingly important role. Russ Hunter (2016) has recently addressed the impact of regional funding on contemporary horror cinema, framing it within the genre history of international collaboration and co-production agreements, which Tim Bergfelder has defined as the 'Genre Factory' (Bergfelder 2005b). Hunter argues that recent changes in the scope of funding promote 'a proliferation of films that combine more traditional co-production agreements with the use of both regional and intra-regional funding sources'

(Hunter 2016: 70) in order to gain access to new markets while receiving funding at a local level.

Overall, we can grasp how questions of mobility, territorial development and internationalisation are central to the policies of European film commissions as well as to the mode of production of contemporary horror films which increasingly rely on these forms of localised support. Free from the specifications of 'artistic quality', horror film production is quick to look out for these incentives, relying also on the genre's wider international appeal and low-budget status to offer a return on investment for the film commission while at the same time showcasing the local territory. Therefore, it is not surprising that representatives of the genre are constantly present among the funded projects of different bodies and institutions from supranational to regional level.

If we look at a particular supranational funding body such as the Nordisk Film and TV fund, we can note not only the creation of development support for genre production entitled 'Nordic Genre Boost' but also that the majority of funded projects in 2016 and 2017 feature horror elements. At a national level, the example of Luxembourg demonstrates how the formation of film commissions and the offer of different incentives to shoot in the territory led to a recurring (and overall new) presence of horror films, in particular through co-production agreements involving several nations. I am thinking of the UK/Germany/Luxembourg/USA/Canada co-production *Feardotcom* (William Malone, 2002) and the horror fantasy *Minotaur* (Jonathan English, 2006), which is the result of a seven-party co-production (UK/Luxembourg/Germany/France/Spain/Italy/USA). Both films received support from Film Fund Luxembourg and were partially shot in the small nation. Looking at regional support, we can take British Screen Yorkshire as a seminal example. It received support from the European Regional Development Fund and it contributed to financing several horror productions in the territory such as *The Cottage* (Paul Andrew Williams, 2008), *Hush* (Mark Tonderai, 2008), and *Kill List* (Ben Wheatley, 2011) aiming to help local employability in the film industry and reach a return on investments (see Hunter 2016 and Walker 2016).

The cases where European horror films manage to access supra-national, national and regional support are not uncommon and, as previously mentioned, they ideally merge the international and transnational scope of the production with a regional development approach. A very recent case is the 2016 co-production between France and Belgium *Grave/Raw* (Julia Ducournau, 2016) which managed to secure support from the European Media Programme, the French Centre national du cinéma et de l'image animée, the regional support of Centre du Cinéma et de l'Audiovisuel de la Fédération Wallonie-Bruxelles, and of Bruxelles Capitale; and tax shelters in Belgium like the Tax Shelter du Gouvernement Fédéral de Belgique. The film received international theatrical distribution (not very common with contemporary horror films) and a presence on the film festival circuits, including Toronto, Cannes and London.

I suggest that this tension between the internationalisation of contemporary European horror cinema – through its distribution, supra-national support and co-production agreements – and its regional dimension, thanks in particular to the work of film commissions and the location market, needs to be addressed by looking at the question of the journey both as an industrial framework and as a thematic feature.

The (Trans)national Dimension of Contemporary Euro-horror

We can consider how production mobility, international collaboration, and the aim for a global – albeit niche – market further problematise the question of the 'national' label within the genre, if not of the European label overall.[5] This is the case, for instance, with American runaway productions being shot in European territories, often receiving a series of local incentives and support. One such example from the horror genre is *Resident Evil* (Paul W. S. Anderson, 2002), which despite being shot mainly in Europe (Germany) by a British director with numerous European cast and crew, is not perceived as European (see Hutchings 2012). Peter Hutchings points out as much when he argues that contextualising Eurohorror films

> does not [. . .] involve simply addressing the question of whether such films are American or European, one thing or the other, but rather involves thinking about the often complex international relations in place within and around the films in question. (2012: 21)

European rural horror cinema, because of its economic and thematic relationship with the territory, is a good example of the attempt to make films that can appeal to an international audience, following in the footsteps of American horror while also displaying some national/local features. Nevertheless, it is not uncommon for European horror productions to be shot outside European borders, significantly in North America, so as to appeal to a wider market. I am thinking for instance of the French low-budget film *Dead End* (Jean-Baptiste Andrea and Fabrice Canepa, 2003), shot very cheaply in California in English with an American cast, which received a wide home-video distribution. As I shall discuss later, *Dead End* is also among the films whose narratives embody the question of travel and dislocation, being a story of a road trip taking the wrong shortcut.

European locations can also double for American spaces, as is the case with the British *The Descent* (Neil Marshall, 2005) shot in UK but set in the Appalachian mountains, and again embodying a travel/touristic narrative. As Johnny Walker, among others, notes: 'Setting the action in America gave the film more market scope than otherwise provincial horror films of the period – a case in point being Marshall's own *Dog Soldiers*, in which a group of British squaddies are attacked by werewolves in Scotland' (Walker 2016: 26). The question of a certain degree of hiding of national belonging to attract an international audience is not new, and was the case, for instance, during the heyday of Italian horror cinema. However, the new online markets for the genre led to a textual customisation consisting in 'the industrial construction of genre at the point of distribution, feeding back into production and textual form' (Lobato and Ryan 2011: 195) where national features may be part of the brand, or may need to be hidden.

This process of a loop between distribution and production involves a particular configuration of national identity and branding, where the cultural specificities of a given country can be more or less determining for the successful marketability of the film. Ramon Lobato and Mark Ryan use the example of Australian horror as a brand where the appeal to an international market derives from the national specificity present in the film, which 'operates as a marker of difference' (Lobato and Ryan 2011: 197; see also Ryan 2009).

Despite internal national differences, the branding of Euro horror has derived mainly from the American understanding that groups together the continent's different national productions without discrimination. However, in the contemporary landscape, issues of national cultural specificities are at play with the promotion of differentiation. In France, for instance, horror production of the new millennium is often linked to national characteristics, present more or less in background. Some examples include *Frontière(s) / Frontier(s)* (Xavier Gens, 2007) and *À l'intérieur / Inside* (Alexandre Bustillo, Julien Maury, 2007) which on the one hand contain common horror plots, while, on the other hand, refer to national social issues and events, such as the 2005 riots in the Parisian *banlieues*. In fact, it can be argued that French horror films generally carry some important points of contact with other aspects of French national cinema.

First of all, they are part of the so-called New French Extreme cinema, or *Cinéma du corps* (see Palmer 2011) a definition which includes works by Claire Denis, Bruno Dumont and Catherine Breillat. Even though the explicit depiction of sexuality is mostly absent from French horror, and surely the understanding of those films is not framed by the auteur cinema canon, their constant and shocking provocations through realistic and gory depictions of the body mean that these films can also be listed under this same label. Linked to this idea of the effective depiction of gore is the broad use of digital effects, which has made some critics relate these films to the *cinéma du look*. We should also remember how Luc Besson's EuropaCorp produced *Haute Tension/Switchblade Romance* (Alexandre Aja, 2003) and that a film like *Frontier(s)* lists the special effects company BR Films among its producers.

However, the third and most important influence of national cinema on the authors of the French New Horror film comes from *le jeune cinéma*, also known as new-realism. At first sight, it seems quite awkward to seek similarities between French horrors and films such as *Y'aura t'il de la neige à Noël?/Will It Snow for Christmas?* (Sandrine Veysett, 1996), Erick Zonca's *La vie rêvée des anges/The Dreamlife of Angels* (1998) or Jean-Pierre and Luc Dardenne's *Rosetta* (1999). Nevertheless, if we agree with Guy Austin that 'what defines the genre even more clearly than its semantics (regional settings, handheld cameras, lack of music, alienated characters) is its socially-conscious syntax' (Austin 2009: 222), we can also see that recent French horror often represents stories of social exclusion, local struggles, despairing plotlines and migrations (whether in the foreground or as background elements). Therefore, if *le jeune cinéma* focuses on 'the fragments left behind once globalization has passed through the social terrain', it represents 'the local struggles of small groups of individuals, usually with no viable collective, political language to name the wrongs done to them' (O'Shaughnessy 2005: 77). We can easily find traces of this social consciousness in many French horror films, where the characters' exclusion is often represented in spatial terms with their persistent dislocation and the challenging of any idyllic depiction of the countryside.

The dominance of co-production agreements at the backbone of European horror cinema further complicates issues of national branding and identity because of the need to assess the national contribution of the different partners involved in the production in order to be considered eligible for the agreement. Such national contribution may rely on the nationality of above and beyond the line crew, to the topics addressed by the film, and the use of location and settings. To further complicate national branding, several of the directors involved in European horror cinema have become 'transnational auteurs' (for the Spanish case see Lázaro-Reboll 2012) as they tend to go to work in the US and their national belonging becomes important for the co-production agreement.

At a thematic level the renegotiation of national characteristics, co-production agreements, supranational and regional support for production, and the new competitive nature of the locations market are embodied in the consistent emergence of travel narratives which address issues surrounding European identity through a genre heavily contaminated by American influences, in particular in its 'rural horror' form.

Rural Horror Cinema and European Travel

It can be argued that the rural horror subgenre, understood within a travel narrative, enjoyed a new popularity with the mobility of film production and the global competitiveness of the location markets, local incentives and the representation of touristic destinations. Films such as *A Perfect Getaway* (David Twohy, 2009), set in Hawaii and shot in Hawaii and Puerto Rico; the American, German, Australian co-production *The Ruins* (Carter Smith, 2008), shot in the Gold Coast of Australia; and the American *Turistas/Paradise Lost* (John Stockwell, 2006) shot entirely in Brazil, are just a few significant examples of this trend and of the implications of using global locations for travel horror narratives. In these cases, the exotic locations are the background for the dislocation of American tourists facing a dangerous 'other'.

The subgenre is also present in different national cinematographies in the attempt to appeal to an international market already familiar with the key features of the subgenre. For instance, the Filipino *The Road* (Yam Laranas, 2011), the Israeli *Rabies/Kalevet* (Aharon Keshales, Navot Papushado, 2010), the Singapore and Indonesia co-production *Macabre* (Kimo Stamboel and Timo Tjahjanto, 2009) and the Australian *Wolf Creek* (Greg McLean, 2005) achieved international distribution presenting horror stories that play with national features and landscapes.

It is easy to find a significant number of representatives of rural horror cinema across Europe with different budgets and ambitions: the British *This is Not a Love Song* (Bille Eltringham, 2002), *Straightheads* (Dan Reed, 2007), *Devils Bridge* (Chris Crow, 2010), *Splintered* (Simeon Halligan 2010), *The Cottage*, *Truth or Dare* (Robert Heath, 2012); the Belgian *Calvaire* (Fabrice du Welz, 2004) and *Cub/Welp* (Jonas Govaerts, 2014); the French *Promenons-nous dans le bois/Deep in the Woods* (Lionel Delplanque, 2000), *Dans ton sommeil/In Their Sleep* (Caroline du Potet, Éric du Potet, 2010), *Aux yeux des vivants/Among the Living* (Alexandre Bustillo, Julien Maury, 2014) as well as the aforementioned *Switchblade Romance* and *Frontier(s)* from 2006; the Norwegian *Rovdyr/Manhunt* (Patrik Syversen

2008), *Død snø/Dead Snow* (Tommy Wirkola, 2009), *Troll Hunter* (André Øvredal, 2009), *Fritt vilt/Cold Prey* (Roar Uthaug, 2006); the Spanish and Mexican co-production *Atrocious* (Fernando Barreda Luna, 2010); the Spanish, UK, Bulgarian co-production *Los abandonados/The Abandoned* (Nacho Cerdà, 2006); the Austrian *Blutgletscher/Blood Glacier* (Marvin Kren, 2013); the Irish, UK, US co-production *Isolation* (Billy O'Brien, 2005); and the German *Bela Kiss: Prologue/The Kiss of a Killer* (Lucien Förstner, 2013).

This is just a very small selection, which offers an idea not only of the variety of productions but also of how horror cinema, which can be shot with a low budget and find a home video international distribution, is present in very different national contexts. It also shows how horror cinema can result in an interesting mapping of European locations thanks to the production incentives underlined earlier in the chapter. They not only benefit from the development of locally based film commissions but also from different kinds of regional and national support. That is the case, for instance, with *Blood Glacier*, which tells the story of an international group of researchers studying global warming in the Alps. The film received support at national and regional level (the Austrian Film Commission, the BLS Südtirol-Alto Adige and the Vienna Film Financing Fund) to promote film activity in the territory.[6]

From a thematic perspective, the journey in European rural films is often bound up with the issue of European identity, of which migration and travelling are important components. As Ewa Mazierska and Laura Rascaroli point out when addressing the European road movie:

> road cinema provides an excellent opportunity to explore [...] the variety and differences of European national and regional cultures; the common 'European identity', of which migration and travelling are often regarded as an important component; and the areas of potential conflict and domains of cooperation. It also offers the opportunity to re-examine and re-negotiate the relationship between the centre of Europe and its margins, which seems to us a crucial prerequisite for any meaningful discussion concerning a new, united Europe. (2006: 201)

This re-negotiation is potentially central in rural horror films as they often represent marginal European locations as settings for the horrific plot and the encounter with the unknown. Moreover, financially, they are offered the opportunity to shoot in territories which do not appeal to mainstream productions, finding in this way less competition for the attention of film commissions and regional funds. For these reasons, European rural horror films investigate the abandonment of a countryside that seems unable to be productive or even to maintain its heritage value.

Films such as the already mentioned *Frontiers*, *Calvaire*, *Isolation*, *The Abandoned* and *The Cottage* engage at different stages with the ideas of identity and social consciousness, with the failure of what could be defined as the 'rural utopia' and the demise of peripheral post-production areas in the global economy, dwelling on the landmarks of abandoned production activities and commercial routes. Of course, the narrative trope of the shortcut, the detour, the abandonment of the main road and the failure to reach a recognisable destination are central in many of these productions. Disused factories, mines, and isolated rural communities are clearly defined as marginal and as the 'dark Europe' that tourists, as well as viewers, seldom come across. The reason for travel or migration is not important – tourism, escape, etc. – since the encounter with the socio-economical 'other' happens by mistake. The detour also implies the problematic mapping of the territory, making it almost impossible to determine the location of the territory except for some national traits (language, food, etc.). Often we know only that it is a European rural 'other'. Films belonging to the subgenre represent spaces that show an economic and social post-apocalypse with no hope for the future and with the cumbersome remnants of a recent productive past.[7]

* * *

A trend that has emerged in the mapping of European borders through horror cinema is the attention towards Eastern Europe in rural films. It can be argued that Eli Roth's *Hostel* (2005) was a watershed for the subgenre, achieving global success with representation of the countries of the ex-Soviet bloc as places with hidden violence, where anything can happen. In fact, it was soon followed by several European co-productions set in Central–Eastern Europe, which offered a fresh background for their films and a financially convenient place to shoot, in particular considering the 2004 enlargement of the European Union. Films such as *The Abandoned*, *Severance* (Christopher Smith, UK/Germany/Hungary, 2006), *Them/Ils* (David Moreau, Xavier Palud, France/Romania, 2006) have not only been shot in Bulgaria, Hungary and Romania, but set the stories in an Eastern Europe still haunted by war, social issues and problematic pasts in a portrayal not dissimilar from the 'otherness' described by Clover (1992).

As Stojanova argues, there is a sort of outsourcing of evil in a series of films 'where Eastern Europe is constructed as a continuous source of dread from without, a site of an abject, horrifying Other' (Stojanova 2012: 225). To grasp the international appeal of the Eastern European setting and the question of the national belonging of the production, we can look at *The Abandoned*, which tells the story of an American film producer travelling to rural Russia to receive the family house she inherited. As Antonio Lázaro-Reboll points out, the film 'was destined to the international marketplace; it was shot in English with an international cast, set in the Eastern European backwoods (Bulgaria standing in for Russia) and presented a narrative that crossed national borders and temporalities' (Lázaro-Reboll 2012: 243). The film received a wide theatrical distribution, debuting in the US before Spain and was 'the second Spanish film to have more copies in the US market (1,250) (only surpassed by *The Others*)' (2012: 243).

What is interesting are the reasons for the protagonists' ill-fated journeys, which go beyond tourism to highlight the permeability of European borders. They can span from a team-building white-collar exercise on the Hungarian mountains (*Severance*), to a journey to the wilderness of Russia by an adopted woman living in California (*The Abandoned*) and the move to Romania to teach French in a school (*Them*). The indiscriminate use of generic Eastern European settings for rural horror films and references to the Balkan war to fuel the plot is exemplified in Western European productions that recreate the space in local rural areas, such as *Captifs/ Caged* (2010), shot in Alsace, and *The Seasoning House* (Paul Hyett, 2012), shot in Britain.[8]

Although the subgenre is characterised by co-production agreements and travel narratives, 'on-screen' border crossing is a rare event. The horror journeys develop mainly in a national context, which (despite its real connotations) is mostly isolated from a European geography. The travel is mainly embodied in the dislocation of the protagonists, who are often foreigners and unfamiliar with the area. The actual on-screen journey is usually by car, and accentuates, on the one hand, the distance between the origin and the destination, while on the other hand it presents all the connotations of freedom offered by the driving in a way not dissimilar from traditional road horror movies. Nevertheless, the journey does not offer any sense of a unified Europe that is easy to cross. *Frontiers* is one of the few exceptions: the characters decide to travel to the Netherlands to find safety and start a new life, escaping the violence of the Parisian suburbs and chased by the police because of an armed robbery. However, as the title suggests, their journey stops violently at an inn on the borders with Belgium, where they have to deal with a Nazi patriarch and his incestuous, cannibalistic and murderous family. This reminds us of the strong American imprint even on the films that do play more strongly on the connotations of their European settings.

Conclusion:
Framing *The Pack* as a European Rural Horror

An example of a rural horror film which employs more traditional modes of production finance with supranational, national, regional funding, and tax incentives is the French Belgian co-production *La meute/The Pack* (Franck Richard, 2010). The film was shot with a budget of €3,546,307, which is at the high end of European productions of the genre. It received the support of the French broadcasters Canal+ and TPS Star, underlining the financing role of television companies in the new wave of European horror films, and from the supranational body MEDIA with a small contribution as part of the 2009 i2i Audiovisual scheme, helping access to financing by subsidising part of the financial costs related to the production. At a national level, *The Pack* was supported by the French Centre national du cinéma et de l'image animée, and by the Belgian Tax Shelter. It is noteworthy to point out that the tax shelters differ from other tax incentives as the 'provider of funds [. . .] receives a profit share in the project' (Talavera Milla, Fontaine and Kanzler 2016: 72) and the funds are normally provided during production, so the financial support acts in a way not dissimilar from a minority co-producer, as the contribution is considered an investment. Access to tax incentives was also achieved thanks to the collaboration with a regional body, the Pôle Image de Liège (PIL), which coordinates screen infrastructures and support to production in the area. In fact, their website states:

> Via Tax Shelter services partners, the PIL pledges a euro for each euro spent, thus funding a large part of the services linked to Sound and Image. This subsidy helps to create jobs and exerts a structuring impact on the region. One of the essential conditions to access this support is for the executive producer to earmark an amount of expenditure among the member companies. (http://www.lepole.be/tax-shelter.php)

Interestingly, the French co-producer, La Fabrique 2, was also involved in a series of ambitious European horror productions such as *Livide/Livid* (Alexandre Bustillo, Julien Maury, 2011), *Secuestrados/Kidnapped* (Miguel Ángel Vivas, 2010), and the drama *Balada triste de trompeta/The Last Circus* (Álex de la Iglesia, 2010). Similarly to *The Pack*, the latter two films apply a 'hybrid' production involving co-production agreements and support from the local broadcaster as well as national and regional supports.

The Pack was presented at the Cannes Film Festival in May 2010 and had a very limited theatrical release in Europe, clearly making it a film for home video consumption. The plot of the film is very derivative of the American subgenre, presenting a series of recognisable tropes and twists which could make the film internationally accessible despite the French language and the regional settings. It tells the story of a young woman who travels aimlessly across Europe to heal her broken heart. Her only plan is to travel until she listens to all of the CDs in her car. However, after being harassed by a gang of bikers, she decides to offer a lift to a hitchhiker 'for protection' and together they stop in a desolate American-themed saloon in the middle of a relatively ill-defined countryside. There the horror begins, involving a mysterious matriarch, a semi-abandoned farm, cannibalism and undead/underground creatures.

While the film clearly develops in a European setting and the reason for travel is the kind of personal introspection that one may expect to find in a European road movie, *The Pack* borrows heavily from an American cinematic culture. The *mise en scène* features a wealth of Americana, including bikers, the big station wagon driven by the protagonist, the ranch-like saloon showcasing Texan flags and one-dollar bills on the walls, the cowboy hats, an American tourist named 'John Wayne', and so on. Interestingly, these elements are completely dislocated into the middle of a countryside where it is impossible to imagine any existing tourist route. There are signs of a forgotten productivity, if not prosperity, mainly through references to mining as part of a remote industrial era. However, the locations are not well determined and one could assume that this is one of the cases where expenditure in the territory and in the auxiliary services to the production located in the region was more important than showcasing the local area.

To some extent, *The Pack* summarises the opportunities and the limits of contemporary European rural horror cinema, trying to strike the balance between territory-linked support, the use of the familiar tropes of American horror, and an ambition towards a global home video distribution. However, in this case local/global negotiation does not lead to a reflection of the marginal sides of Europe other than in a stereotypical 'white-poor' rural context. It is sufficient to look at a film like the Norwegian *Manhunt* to see similar tropes appear again, in an attempt to mimic and re-present the American road horror settings, this time, however, with greater links to regional characteristics. Nevertheless, the possibility of engaging with the question of border crossing and European identity disappears, making the territorialisation and international collaboration of the production context almost irrelevant. I would argue that rural horror films need to renegotiate not only national features but European ones, grasping the opportunity offered by the variety of territorial financial support in order to present and reflect on borders, margins, and transnational identities, while finding a balance between the tensions emerging from the territoriality of their production and the global influences. The new 'Genre Factory' can create an opportunity to reframe locally based features of the Euro horror in order to negotiate a brand that can attract international attention for its transnational features – a quality increasingly important to differentiate the subgenre in the massive choice offered in the online catalogue of Subscription Video On Demand players.

Notes

1 On the impact of supranational policies in contemporary European cinema, see Mariana Liz, in particular with reference to the touristic postcard representation of cities (2016: 108–27).
2 On post-millennial road horror movies, see Ballard 2008.
3 See <http://www.screenyorkshire.co.uk/investment/faqs/>.
4 However, it is noteworthy that some fiscal incentives schemes offered by some European nations are aimed exclusively at foreign productions, in order to attract inward investment. That is the case, for instance, for Croatia.
5 On the role of mode of production and distribution in problematising the national aspect of European cinema see Bergfelder (2005a).
6 *Troll Hunter* is another excellent example of several regional contributions to production (see Hunter 2016).
7 On the presence of abandoned factories and backward rural locations in French horror cinema see Denis Mellier (2010).
8 There are also several North American productions with rural horror storylines set in Eastern Europe. An example is the Canadian *The Shrine* (Jon Knautz, 2010) entirely shot in Ontario but set in a Polish village.

Works Cited

Austin, Guy (2009), *Contemporary French Cinema: An Introduction*, Manchester: Manchester University Press.
Ballard, Finn (2008), 'No Trespassing: The post-millennial road-horror movie', in *The Irish Journal of Gothic and Horror Studies*, 4, 8 June, <https://irishgothichorror.files.wordpress.com/2018/03/finn-ballard.pdf> (last accessed January 2018).
Baschiera, Stefano (2014), 'Streaming World Genre Cinema', *Frames Cinema Journal*, 6, December, <http://framescinemajournal.com/article/streaming-world-genre-cinema/> (last accessed May 2015).
Bergfelder, Tim (2005a), 'National, transnational or supranational cinema? Rethinking European film studies', *Media, Culture & Society*, 27, pp. 315–31.

Bergfelder, Tim (2005b), *International Adventures: German Popular Cinema and European Co-productions in the 1960s*, Oxford: Berghahn Books.

Bernard, Mark (2014), *Selling the Splat Pack: The DVD Revolution and the American Horror Film*, Edinburgh: Edinburgh University Press.

Clover, Carol (1992), *Men, Women and Chainsaws: Gender in the Modern Horror Film*, Princeton: Princeton University Press.

Cucco, Marco and Giuseppe Richeri (2013), *Il mercato delle location cinematografiche*, Venice: Marsilio.

Eleftheriotis, Dimitris (2010), *Cinematic Journeys*, Edinburgh: Edinburgh University Press.

Hunter, Russ (2016), 'Horrifically Local? European Horror and Regional Funding Initiatives', *Film Studies*, 15:1, Autumn, pp. 66–80.

Hutchings, Peter (2012), 'Resident Evil? The Limits of European Horror: *Resident Evil* versus *Suspiria*', in Patricia Allmer, Emily Brick and David Huxley (eds), *European Nightmares: Horror Cinema in Europe Since 1945*, London: Wallflower Press, pp. 13–24.

Lázaro-Reboll, Antonio (2012), *Spanish Horror Film*, Edinburgh: Edinburgh University Press.

Liz, Mariana (2016), *Euro-visions: Europe in Contemporary Cinema*, London and New York: Bloomsbury Academic.

Lobato, Ramon and Mark David Ryan (2011), 'Rethinking Genre Studies Through Distribution Analysis: Issues in International Horror Movie Circuits', *New Review of Film and Television Studies*, 9:2 (June), pp. 188–203.

Mazierska, Ewa and Laura Rascaroli (eds) (2006), *Crossing New Europe: Postmodern Travel and The European Road Movie*, London: Wallflower Press.

Mellier, Denis (2010), 'Sur la dépouille des genres. Néohorreur dans le cinéma français (2003–2009)', *Cinémas: revue d'études cinématographiques/Journal of Film Studies*, 20:2–3, pp. 143–64.

Olney, Ian (2013), *Euro Horror*, Bloomington: Indiana University Press.

O'Shaughnessy, Martin (2005), 'Eloquent Fragments: French Fiction Film and Globalization', *French Politics, Culture & Society*, 23:3, Winter, Special Issue: French Cinema and Globalization, pp. 75–88.

Palmer, Tim (2011), *Brutal Intimacy: Analyzing French Cinema*, Middletown: Wesleyan University Press.

Pôle Image de Liège (PIL) (n.d.), <http://www.lepole.be/tax-shelter.php> (last accessed May 2018)

Ryan, Mark David (2009), 'Whither Culture? Australian Horror Films and the Limitations of Cultural Policy', *Media International Australia, Incorporating Culture and Policy*, 133, pp. 43–55.

Screen Yorkshire (n.d.), <http://www.screenyorkshire.co.uk/investment/faqs/> (last accessed January 2017).

Stojanova, Christina (2012), 'A Gaze From Hell: Eastern European Horror Cinema Revisited', in Patricia Allmer, Emily Brick and David Huxley (eds), *European Nightmares*, London: Wallflower Press, pp. 225–37.

Talavera Milla, Julio, Gilles Fontaine and Martin Kanzler (2016), *Public Financing for Film and Television Content: The State of Soft Money in Europe*, Strasbourg: European Audiovisual Observatory (Council of Europe).

Walker, Johnny (2016), *Contemporary British Horror Cinema*, Edinburgh: Edinburgh University Press.

Part 2b

The Politics of the Road Movie

CHAPTER 14

Colonialism in Latin American Road Movies

Natália Pinazza

Introduction

The leap to prominence of the Latin American road movie within film studies over the past five years (Brandellero 2013; Pinazza 2014; Garibotto and Pérez 2016; Lie 2017) has testified to the rethinking of the road movie as a global film category instead of a quintessentially US genre (Berry 2016). Such a reframing foregrounds the diversity of Latin American road movies and their contribution to global film production, and refutes the notion that these films are mere attempts to copy Hollywood. Clearly, treating film production from different parts of the world as Hollywood's 'other' is not a problem exclusive to the road movie genre or to Latin American cinema. In this respect, Lúcia Nagib, writing on world cinema, argues that 'in multicultural, multi-ethnic societies like ours, cinematic expressions from various origins cannot be seen as "the other" for the simple reason that they are us' (2011: 1). In a similar vein, this chapter will argue that Latin American road movies are integral to the development of the genre, and examine the way in which some of these films have dialogued with transnational aesthetics and themes.

This chapter's approach to Latin American road movies draws on Ella Shohat and Robert Stam's notion of 'polycentric multiculturalism', which is 'reciprocal, dialogical' and 'sees all acts of verbal and cultural exchange as taking place not between discrete bounded individuals or cultures but rather between permeable, changing individuals and communities' (1994: 49). Indeed, the increasing number of Latin American films in the road movie genre is particularly significant in relation to the transnational cultural exchanges and sociopolitical challenges faced by Latin American countries in the past twenty years. Road movies such as *Historias mínimas/Intimate Stories* (Carlos Sorín, 2002), *Y Tu Mamá También* (Alfonso Cuarón, 2001) and *Central do Brasil/Central Station* (Walter Salles, 1998) were milestones for the consolidation of national cinemas in Argentina,

Brazil and Mexico at the turn of the century. The national and international appraisal of Latin American road movies was accompanied by the success of transnational Latin American auteurs, including Cuarón, Campanella, Iñárritu, Salles and Padilha. As a result, such a globalisation of Latin American cinema has raised questions about its specificities when adopting internationally recognised genres such as the road movie.

The specificities of Latin American cinema will be teased out with reference to texts and films of the region's cinematic tradition in my examination of the road movie's global situatedness. Here the theme of colonialism, both physical and cultural, is particularly instrumental in identifying tropes and predominant concerns in cinematic journeys set in Latin American countries, whose historical experience of a 'third world' and 'underdeveloped' status is negotiated in the context of a changing global economic order. The second part of this chapter will pay particular attention to the ways in which *El Abrazo de serpiente / Embrace of the Serpent* (Ciro Guerra, 2015) uses journeys to denounce historical colonialism and engage with more contemporary and global discourses on eco-criticism. The film's explicit postcolonial critique and its subversion of road movie genre conventions will be analysed in light of Homi Bhabha's 'temporality of the in-between' (1994). It is worth noting that the all-encompassing term 'Latin America' is employed in this chapter for practical purposes, as there are mentions of films from Argentina, Brazil, Colombia and Mexico. The chapter maintains, however, that the diversity within the region is a compelling factor of journey narratives set in Latin America.

Latin American Road Movies: Aesthetics of Precarity

At the heart of the aesthetics of precarity in the Latin American road movie is a pervading sense of underachievement and inferiority, which also resonates with how films from the region have been discursively framed as Hollywood's 'other'. Such an 'othering' process, which has impacted the analysis of genre films from different parts of the world, is even more pertinent in discussions of the road movie genre, whose origins and iconography remain strongly associated with Hollywood. The notion that the road movie is a 'Hollywood genre that catches peculiarly American dreams, tensions and anxieties even when imported by the motion picture industries of other nations' (Cohan and Hark 1997: 2) tends to overlook the significant contribution by filmmakers from different nationalities in the development of the genre both at home and abroad. For instance, Walter Salles' cross-border collaborations and preoccupation with mobility are present in internationally well-known films such as *Diarios de*

Motocicleta / The Motorcycle Diaries (2004) and *On the Road* (2011), a film adaptation of Jack Kerouac's novel with the same title. Significantly, the influence on Salles' road movie *Central Station*, one of the key films of the Brazilian *retomada*,[1] is not attributed to a US film, but to the German film *Alice in den Städten / Alice in the Cities* (1974), which alongside *Falsche Bewegung / The Wrong Move* (1975) and *Im Lauf der Zeit / Kings of the Road* (1976) form Wim Wenders' road movies trilogy. Nonetheless, despite the numerous successful manifestations of the genre across the globe, the widespread understanding of the road movie as a US genre persists, as illustrated in Guy Lodge's review of *Paris, Texas* (Wim Wenders, 1984) for *The Guardian* (2015). In the same text, Lodge acknowledges *Paris, Texas*'s 'transatlantic identity', mentions Wenders' German road movie trilogy, but surprisingly, ends up defining the road movie as the 'most essentially American of genres'.

The debate on cultural legitimacy and standards established by a hegemonic culture, more precisely US cinema, harks back to the early days of Brazilian cinema. If on the one hand Brazilian cinema's 'incapacity of copying',[2] to use Paulo Emílio Salles Gomes' well-known phrase, has resulted in the marginalisation of some movie genres made in the region, as is the case with Brazilian sci-fi films (Suppia 2016), on the other, it paved the way for the emergence of other unique genres such as the *chanchadas*, Brazilian musical comedies produced in the 1930s and 1940s. In defining *chanchada* as a national genre, Lisa Shaw and Stephanie Dennison pose the following question:

> Without doubt similar cinematic traditions or genres emerged in other national contexts, such as tango films in Argentina, *fado* films in Portugal, and the *ranchera* musical comedies in Mexico, each with its own particular relationship to Hollywood paradigms, so can it, in fact, be argued that the *chanchada* had culturally specific elements that differentiated it from its foreign cousins? (2007: 76)

The question of genre and Hollywood paradigms has been widely reconsidered in the context of the boom in Latin American film production in the mid-1990s and 2000s. For instance, Tamara Falicov addresses how the Argentine action film *Comodines / Cops* (Jorge Nisco, 1997) was 'billed the "first Hollywood-style movie in Spanish"' (2007: 97), whereas Deborah Shaw draws on García Canclini's argument that: 'popular culture is not suppressed by modernity and globalization but takes new hybrid forms' (Canclini in Shaw 2007: 71) to argue that Argentine blockbuster *Nueve Reinas / Nine Queens* (Fabián Bielinsky, 2000), which was remade in English, plays 'Hollywood at its own game'. Niamh Thornton draws on cultural theorist Ángel Rama's transculturation to examine how the Latin American films

El Viaje (Fernando Solanas, 1992), *Y tu mamá también* and *The Motorcycle Diaries* have re-signified or re-inscribed the US road movie genre.[3]

Establishing a dialogical relationship between the road movie as a US genre and national cinemas is not exclusive to the Latin American context. For instance, in their study of the Australian road movie, Murphy, Venkatasawmy, Simpson and Visosevic (2009) explore bushranger and drover films and claim that the 'Australian road movie constitutes a form of liberation from nostalgia – from the vestiges of colonialism associated with the bush as well as from narratives of Hollywood' (2009: 83). They identify local markers of 'Australianness' combined with Hollywood on well-known films such as *Mad Max* (George Miller, 1979) and *The Adventures of Priscilla, Queen of the Desert* (Stephen Elliott, 1994). The authors draw on Schaber's argument that hybridity is 'contemporary to the road movie genre' to argue that 'Australian cinema takes this notion of hybridity even further in the way it indigenises Hollywood formats and styles while telling specifically Australian stories' (2009: 75).

The road movie genre becomes a powerful tool in the exploration of Latin America's social problems and the nations' uneven experiences of modernity. Latin American cinema has a marked history of self-consciously incorporating its own lack of resources as per the manifestos 'For an Imperfect Cinema' (Espinosa [1969] 1997) and 'An Esthetic of Hunger'[4] (Rocha [1965] 1997) that informed the revolutionary filmmaking of the 1960s and 1970s. However, in road movies made in the past twenty years such as *The Motorcycle Diaries*, *Y Tu mamá también*, *Central Station* and *Cinema, Aspirins and Vultures*, 'precarity' plays out in markedly different ways from the ideals of Espinosa's 'imperfection' and Rocha's 'hunger'. These road movies chart the individual experiences of 'precarity' and their journey is portrayed in a more aestheticised way; there are music, colour and easily recognised road movie conventions such as 'buddy ethics', which actively encourage identification with the characters' struggles from audiences across the globe. Social problems and impediments found on the road affect the characters' individual journey, retaining the most oblique relationship with the social and political impetus of a cinematic tradition that adopts 'precarity' as both mode of production and aesthetics.

Nonetheless, Espinosa's argument that 'the real tragedy of the contemporary artist lies in the impossibility of practising art as minority activity' (1997: 75) remains relevant to the present day. Limited resources continue to provide little choice to independent filmmakers but to embrace self-consciously or not the glitches and imperfections that are symptomatic of precarious filmmaking conditions. In fact, any consideration of Latin American cinema's contribution to a global film category should take into account the asymmetries of transnational cultural exchanges, which prevent many other films from having greater visibility due to production and distribution obstacles. However, for the purpose of this chapter, my critical focus is on globally distributed and commercially successful Latin American road movies so as to identify recurring motifs and examine the ways in which these films establish a close dialogue with genre conventions.

Through its very synecdochical relation to the nation, the Latin American road movie frequently incorporates local concerns such as the 'precarity' of the journeys, thereby resemanticising conventions of the genre. The precarious means of transportation, which invariably signal the economic situation of the characters, emerge as a recurrent motif in Latin American road movies. In cutting up the forward progression of the journey and suggesting the economic immobility of the characters, precarious transporation subverts dominant codes of the road movie genre from within. While transportation is seen as a means of speed and empowerment in canonical road movies, including for instance *Easy Rider* (Dennis Hopper, 1969), Latin American road movies problematise the traditional filmic status of the motorised vehicle. At times this occurs consciously and humorously, as in *The Motorcycle Diaries*, where the motorcycle ironically named 'La poderosa' (the powerful) breaks down and the protagonists have to continue their journey on foot. In one of the most emblematic scenes of *Familia Rodante/Rolling Family* (Pablo Trapero, 2004), an Argentine family road movie, the old van breaks down and the family members have to push it in a collective effort that unites them (Figure 14.1). In the Brazilian, French and Uruguayan film co-production *El Baño del Papa/The Pope's Toilet* (César Charlone, Enrique Fernández, 2007), the protagonist's precarious bicycle is central to the narrative as he depends on it to make a living as a petty smuggler on the border between Brazil and Uruguay. Significantly, these three films, *The Motorcycle Diaries*, *Rolling Family* and *The Pope's Toilet*, show borders within the Southern Cone,

Figure 14.1 Family pushing the broken trailer in *The Rolling Family* and close-up of the motorcycle, ironically named 'La poderosa' in *The Motorcycle Diaries*.

which is an illustration of the link I am suggesting between the increase in Latin American road movies and globalisation in South America. Globalisation is interlinked with the regionalisation processes, which has prompted the formation of Mercosur (Common Market of the South) in the aftermath of democracy. However, as Grimson and Kessler point out

> current regionalisation and globalisation processes have not erased frontiers between countries but instead altered the way they function and the meaning ascribed to them [. . .] stigmas and prejudices persist on both sides of the border, so any analysis of the sociocultural dimensions of Mercosur 'integration projects' must take them into account. (2005: 22)

Within this understanding, the choice to set filmic journeys on the borders between countries brings to the fore notions of 'us' and 'them' while showcasing the region's diversity.

As another motif of precarious transportation, hitchhiking also comes into play in a number of Latin American road movies, including for instance *Las Acacias* (Pablo Georgelli, 2011) and *Cinema, Aspirinas e Urubus/Cinema, Aspirins and Vultures* (Marcelo Gomes, 2005). At times characters on the road are vulnerable to the driver of the motorised vehicle, as in *O Caminho das Nuvens/The Middle of the World* (Vicente Amorim, 2003). Through an emphasis on the mode of transportation, filmmakers like Salles comment on the socio-economic situation of the characters, which relates to a broader political and historical background. This was a strategy adopted in *Terra Estrangeira/Foreign Land* (Walter Salles, Daniela Thomas, 1995), *Central Station* and *The Motorcycle Diaries* (listed here in chronological order). *Central Station*, as already indicated by the title, puts great emphasis on transportation. The journey is shaped by Dora's internal transformation and she is framed taking different methods of transportation. Firstly, Dora takes an overcrowded train at Central Station in Rio de Janeiro (Figure 14.2a, 14.2b), she then embarks on a journey by bus to help a boy find his father in the north-east of Brazil (Figure 14.2c). She feels attracted to a truck driver, who gives them a lift, and nearer the destination, she is framed with the boy on the back of a deteriorating pickup truck with other passengers singing religious songs, which the boy sings along with, but to which she clearly does not relate.

In those films, the motorised vehicle operates according to a completely different agenda than the 'phallic frisson' (Hark 1997: 214) that characterises it in road movies. Although it is not the main focus of this chapter (see for example Anna Cooper's chapter (15) in this book), literature on the road movie is very much preoccupied with gender and the connections between male subjectivity and the motorised vehicle. Hayward contends

Figure 14.2 Journeys in *Central Station* are characterised by various precarious means of transportation: hitchhiking and overcrowded trains and buses.

that 'the codes and conventions of a road movie have meant that until fairly recently this genre has predominantly been a gendered one' (2004: 335–6). In this regard, Corrigan argues that 'as an explicitly desperate genre, the contemporary road movie (and its first cousin, the buddy movie) responds specifically to the recent historical fracturing of the male subject, who has traditionally been the main support of those institutional walls of a dominant cinema' (1991: 138). It is worth noting that films like *The Motorcycle Diaries* and *Cinema, Aspirins and Vultures* channel 'buddy films' (Williams 1982: 9). However, Latin American road movies in general are more preoccupied with the economic struggles of the characters than with the construction of modern masculinity, which according to Connell relates to 'conquistadores' and is exemplified by 'men of the frontier' (2002: 246).

Instead of highlighting the characters' mobility, the means of transport in these films often draws attention to the characters' stasis. 'With all their speed forward, they may be a step backward in civilisation', says Eugene Morgan (played by Joseph Cotton) in reference to the automobile in *The Magnificent Ambersons* (Orson Welles, 1942), providing an early critique of the relationship between civilisation, linearity, forwardness and speed. Such critiques have increasingly gained force with environmental awareness, a trend observed across the globe with the span of documentaries and fiction films addressing environmental disasters, which I will analyse in the next section.

Roadless Journeys: Eco-criticism and Postcolonial Critique

Cinema's engagement with eco-criticism through the reconstruction of the experience of colonialism and the denunciation of its legacies has gained international relevance given the rise of global environmental awareness. The Academy Award for Best Picture at the 2016 Oscars for *Mad Max: Fury Road* (George Miller, 2015) and Best Actor for environmental activist Leonardo Di Caprio in *The Revenant* (2015) directed by Mexican filmmaker Alejandro Iñárritu can be attributed to this sensibility, as can the nomination of *Embrace of the Serpent* in the Best Foreign Language Film for the same year. The extraordinary success of Iñárritu has also raised an array of questions around national identity, genre and the relationship between Hollywood and Latin American cinema (see Shaw 2007; Tierney 2009). The interweaving of environmental concerns and journey narratives, present both in *Mad Max: Fury Road* and *The Revenant* also provides material for more experimental endeavours, including *Embrace of the Serpent*, Ciro Guerra's third film.

Embrace of the Serpent, a very timely and sophisticated contribution to eco-criticism, maintains the director's preoccupation with issues of displacement, which were present both in his directorial debut, *La sombra del caminante / The Wandering Shadows* (2004) and his second film *Los Viajes del Viento / The Wind Journeys* (2009). If the journey of *Embrace of the Serpent* is informed by encounters in the heart of the Amazon forest, *The Wind Journeys* centres on the journey of a musician and a young man through the Colombian countryside, supplying the spectator with a survey of local communities and traditions. *The Wind Journeys*' focus on two characters with a considerable age difference, whose journey to a remote part of the nation is imbued with representations of rural communities, evokes Salles' emblematic *Central Station*, made ten years earlier. In their geographical exploration of the nation, Colombia and Brazil respectively, both *The Wind Journeys* and *Central Station* explore the travellers' encounters with locals in a number of sequences that appear to be improvised with the use of non-actors. Salles sees improvisation as integral to the road movie genre: 'I believe that a defining aspect of this narrative form is its unpredictability. You simply cannot (and should not) anticipate what you will find on the road – even if you scouted a dozen times the territory you will cross. You have to work in synchronicity with the elements. If it snows, incorporate snow. If it rains, incorporate rain' (2007). His argument is reminiscent of Bazin's famous analysis of De Sica's *Bicycle Thieves* (1948). For Bazin, the broader location and the 'fortuitous character of chance' (Bazin 1971: 68) shape the narrative as opposed to the contrived actions that characterised Hollywood film conventions up to that time.

Together with the anthropological value inherent in the documentation provided by the film's geographical exploration of remote parts of the nation, *The Wind Journeys* introduces other crucial ingredients that characterise *Embrace of the Serpent*, most notably the blurring of superstition and reality and the emphasis on the ambient sounds of nature. *Embrace of the Serpent*'s narrative trajectory is shaped by the bewildering journey across the Amazon, undertaken by a shaman and two different scientists, each in search of a rare sacred plant, at different moments set thirty years apart. The film uses the road movie's metaphor of quest (Corrigan 1991) to denounce the exploitation of the environment and indigenous people. The quest here is for indigenous traditional knowledge, which is on the verge of extinction and contains vital information for the explorer's health as the yakruna flower is the only remedy that could cure him.

Inspired by the writings of German ethnologist Theodor Koch-Grünberg and American biologist Richard Evans Schultes and its black-and-white cinematography, Guerra's inclusion of biographical information through the use of intertitles showing excerpts of the explorers' journals would appear to establish a more realistic framework. Yet the viewer quickly realises that *Embrace of the Serpent* is not an anthropological or ethnographic film; rather, it repeatedly brings into focus dreams and imaginings that disrupt linearity.

Embrace of the Serpent uses narrative devices like intertitles alongside passages from diaries and letters, evoking the motifs that characterise colonial literature only to challenge their very narration of history. On the one hand the black-and-white cinematography combined with intertitles of western writings appears to generate a historical distance between spectator and story. On the other, *Embrace of the Serpent*'s representation of the colonial past is in tandem with recent trends in ecocriticism. This link resides in a challenge to western linear notions of progress while speaking to present ecological concerns. The way that it does this means that in order to grasp the complexities of *Embrace of the Serpent*'s representation of the colonial past, its readings need to be anchored in the neocolonial present.

This was a strategy notably adopted by the Brazilian allegorical film *Como Era Gostoso o Meu Francês/How Tasty Was My Little Frenchman* (Nelson Pereira dos Santos, 1971), which portrays the colonial past and cannibalism in order to denounce political repression during the dictatorship in the early 1970s. Like *Embrace of the Serpent*, *How Tasty Was My Little Frenchman* was also loosely based on the journal of a German adventurer, namely Hans Staden. In *How Tasty Was My Little Frenchman*, the first-person voiceover creates a contrast between what the spectator sees and what the adventurer says, which deliberately generates comic effect and undermines the credibility of Western storytelling. In *Embrace of the Serpent*, there is an arbitrary distinction between the Western telling of history underpinned by intertitles, and what we see within the scene, creating a disjunction between the journey's trajectory and Western narration, as is in line with Guerra's intention:

> The film is an attempt to build a bridge between Western and Amazonian storytelling, because if you read Amazonian mythology, it has a completely different narrative logic [. . .] Time is also non-linear. At first I wanted to make a very Amazonian narrative, but I soon realised it would be incomprehensible to other audiences. I needed to fuse the two styles of storytelling. Anthropological fact became less important; dream and imagination became central to the narrative. (Graham 2016: 43)

In a magical realist fashion, the fusion of fact and fantasy is immediately evident in the narrative construction as the dreams of the characters and the juxtaposition of two different journeys continuously derails the linearity of the story, disrupting identification.

There are two 'main' journeys in the film, Grünberg's and Schultes', both of which are guided by the same shaman in his younger and elder years, respectively. However, the distinction between the journeys is not respected through the film and this blurring serves to demonstrate the non-linearity of the narrative. Such is also the effect created by the montage, which disrupts the coherence of the narrative with fantastical images, evoking 'the forgotten'. The linearity of the quest is rendered even more problematic by the fact that the guide on the journey has forgotten his knowledge. The film denounces the loss of traditional knowledge, and its impacts are vocalised by Karamakate's fears of becoming '*chullachaqui*', which means empty, or having no memories. The images of dreams that disrupt the narrative fill these gaps in history as the 'forgotten', a discourse that is refracted by indigenous oral tradition and the fluidity of the river. Drawing on Renan's concept of the 'syntax of forgetting', Bhabha argues that '[t]o be obliged to forget – in the construction of the national present – is not a question of historical memory; it is the construction of a discourse on society that *performs* the problem of totalizing the people and unifying the national will' (1994: 230; emphasis in original). Within this understanding, the 'syntax of forgetting' relates directly to the violence that marked the colonising mission, and the film is implicated in the manifold task of reconstructing the colonial past and celebrating what is now endangered or even gone. This understanding finds echo in Guerra's statement that 'we Latin Americans are the result of this violent clash. We have this dual heritage, but the indigenous heritage is one we have denied.'

Embrace of the Serpent draws attention to what remains unrepresented and even 'forgotten' or 'forgotten to be remembered'. There is a marked absence of the road and motorised vehicles, and arguably this is due to the fact that, like Western narratives, the iconography and conventions of the road movie genre are informed by a sense of linearity: 'Generally speaking, the road movie goes from A to B in a finite and chronological time' (Hayward 2004: 336). In her study of indigenous road movies, Wendy Pearsons argues that 'Roads go somewhere. They seem, by their very nature and purpose, to be linear, narrative and teleological and thus indicative of Western ideologies of history and progress' (2011: 150). An intriguing comparison holds itself out with the US film *Apocalypse Now* (Francis Ford Coppola, 1979) as somewhere in between the two poles of Western and non-Western narratives, since its trip down the Mekong Delta may progress towards a particular destination – the 'heart of darkness' of General Kurtz's lair – but only so as to find confusion, a dissolution of stable subjectivities and eventually madness.

Through a series of bird's-eye shots *Embrace of the Serpent* signifies the river as a locus for articulation of difference, the 'in-between space' (Bhabha 1994) that refuses the linearity of stories and journeys. In his sustained analysis of 'the trope of the highway' in Brazilian cinema, José Carlos Avellar (1995) focuses on films that address Western notions of progress and ecological disaster in the Amazon, including the semi-documentary road movie *Iracema, Uma Transa Amazônica / Iracema* (1975) by Jorge Bodanzky and Orlando Senna. *Iracema* inhabits an interstitial space between fictive construct and documentary; as Salles contends, 'it is virtually impossible to know who is merely representing a reality and who is truly living it' (2007). Bondanzky and Senna do not fail to ridicule the 'civilised' positivist discourses behind the capitalist exploitation of nature. The film is set during the construction of the Trans-Amazon Highway, which caused the deforestation of the Amazon region and exposed indigenous populations to outsiders. At the beginning of the film the truck driver, who introduces himself as Tião Brasil Grande (translated as 'Sebastian Great Brazil') dismisses indigenous approaches to the environment by claiming that 'nature is the road' (a natureza é a estrada). This is clear when Tião relates the Trans-Amazon Project to development, by claiming 'this place is improving, they are now building roads here'.[5] For the indigenous female character, on the other hand, being on the road means prostituting herself. According to Avellar, the film engages with a neocolonial critique where the 'highway provides a privileged setting for the "free investment" of distant capital (from southern Brazil and abroad) that organizes an intensified exploitation of the labor force, illegal land seizures, contraband in precious hardwoods, and new circulations of goods and human beings' (Avellar 1995: 329).

If the traditionally exalted status of the highway in the road movie genre as locus of progress is overtly problematised in *Iracema*, it is the absence of the motif that aligns *Embrace of the Serpent* with postcolonial discourses that refute Western notions of progress. Here the river plays a significant role in postcolonial readings of *Embrace of the Serpent*. This is not only because indigenous characters refer to it as 'Anaconda's son', an allusion to the 'Serpent' in the title, but also because the cinematography and sound effects put great emphasis on the river flow and how it shapes the characters' journeys. *The Embrace of the Serpent* channels some of the 'buddy ethic' that informs a number of road movies, but the protagonists' relationship is based on mistrust and betrayal because of the context of colonialism. Diversions in storytelling and perceptions of time and space also resonate with Western and indigenous characters' divergent approaches to nature, and more specifically, to the river. For the scientist, the river has two angles, whereas the indigenous characters emphasise the intermittent and fluid nature of the river by claiming it has many angles. Indeed, the river causes a disturbance of direction and a restless movement that forces the scientist to leave some of his luggage aside in order to continue the journey (Figures 14.3a–c). This suggests that to embrace indigenous traditional knowledge he has to detach himself from Western 'baggage'. This notion is epitomised by the sequence in which Schultes is reluctant to get rid of his gramophone player, which he sees as a connection to his own ancestry. The sequence is a filmic reference to Werner Herzog's *Fitzcarraldo* (1982), which centres on an Irish adventurer who

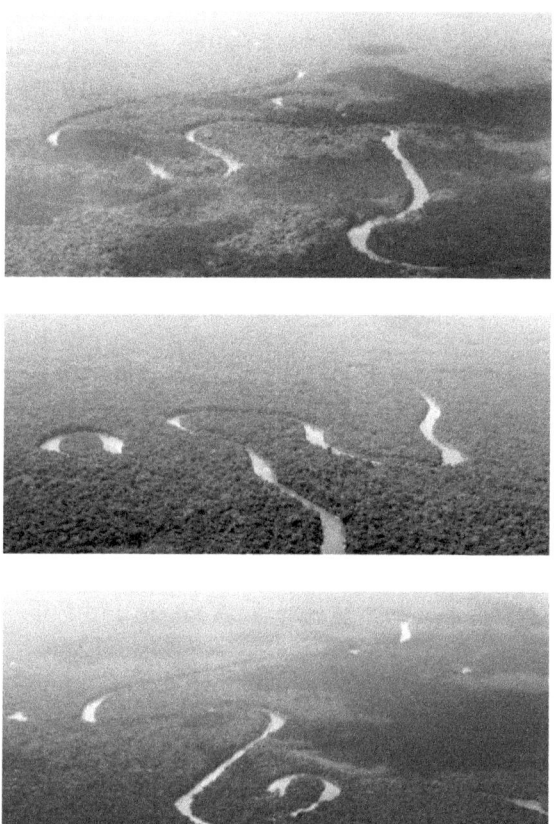

Figure 14.3 A series of bird's-eye shots of the Amazon forest emphasises the curves of the river, which guides the character's journey and undermines the linearity that informs Western storytelling, including history books and the highway in the road movie genre.

wants to build an opera house in the Amazon forest. Like *Embrace of the Serpent*, Herzog's classic is also set during the rubber boom in the early twentieth century.

It could be argued that to consider a roadless film set in the middle of the Amazon jungle with no motor vehicle a road movie is farfetched. However, *Embrace of the Serpent*'s critique of the historical achievements of modernity lies in the way the road movie 'self-consciously explores the relationship between the spatial and temporal displacement of the journey and the discourse of film itself' (Everett 2004: 19). It is precisely this displacement that allows other temporalities to emerge, thereby opening cracks in dominant discourses and denouncing what has been conveniently 'forgotten'.

Conclusion

In order to make a case for the Latin American contribution to the road movie genre, to use solely Hollywood paradigms for the analysis of the films would be out of kilter with understandings of the genre as a global film category. For this reason, my argument drew parallels between Latin American road movies from the region to demonstrate how these films marked a strategic exploration of the nation's geographical space and a rearticulation of neocolonial critique. Latin American film production pertinent to the theme 'journeys and colonialism' is by no means confined to films that broke into the global market. For instance, filmmakers Silvina Cuman and Javier Orrade's film project 'De Tierras y de Utopías', which is funded by the Argentine National Institute of Cinema and Audiovisual Arts (INCA), draws on Eduardo Galeano's seminal work *Open Veins of Latin America* ([1971] (1997)) to travel across Latin America in search of its roots, which are associated with the native population ('pueblos originarios'). Similarly, recent Brazilian documentary films like *Amazônia desconhecida/Unknown Amazon* (Daniel Augusto and Eduardo Rajabally, 2013) and *Coração do Brasil/Heart of Brazil* (Daniel Solá Santiago, 2013) combine indigenous and environmental matters with journey narratives. My approach to *Embrace of the Serpent* as a 'roadless' road movie was determined by the film's presentation of itself as a journey of quest and conscious engagement with important characteristics of the genre. Journey narratives and, more precisely, the road movie, are fruitful for postcolonial readings and questions involving historical progress.

Salles argues that 'the first documentary filmmakers, like Robert Flaherty, the creator of the landmark 1922 film *Nanook of the North*, were the founding fathers of this narrative form' (2007). Others, such as Shari Roberts, attribute the origins of the road movie to the Western and in this transference 'the frontier becomes the road, the horse becomes the car, and the hero becomes a desire' (1997: 66). The well-known iconography of the road movie genre consists of symbols of modernity such as highways and motor vehicles, allowing films to overtly and consciously refute the genre's iconography when trying to problematise Western notions of progress. This defining feature of the genre was central to identifying precarious transportation as a recurrent motif in Latin American road movies such as *Central Station*, *The Motorcycle Diaries* and *Rolling Family* and to analyse *Embrace of the Serpent*'s postcolonial critique through its refusal of the road. In its refusal of the linearity of both the road and Western storytelling, *Embrace of the Serpent* adheres to a strongly global agenda because the experience of violence and inequality as colonial legacies not only presents an insurmountable obstacle for the region's development, but also a disaster for humanity.

Notes

1 *Retomada* is the term used to refer to the re-emergence of Brazilian cinema in the mid-1990s after almost twenty years of stagnation in national film production. See Pinazza 2013.
2 'We are neither Europeans nor North Americans. Lacking an original culture, nothing is foreign to us because everything is. The painful construction of ourselves develops within the rarefied dialectic of not being or being someone else. Brazilian film participates in this mechanism and alters it through our creative incapacity of copying' (Salles Gomes in Johnson and Stam 1995: 245).
3 Within the theoretical framework of transculturation, Thornton applies three elements of transculturation in her analysis of the road movie: 'the use of local situational language; experimental changes, which result in a move away from conventional narrative structures; and the reflection of a fractured worldview' (2007: 32).
4 Also frequently referred to as 'Aesthetics of Hunger'.
5 'aqui está melhorando, agora eles estão construindo estradas'.

Works Cited

Avellar, José Carlos (1995), 'Seeing, Hearing, Filming: Notes on the Brazilian Documentary', in Robert Stam and Randal Johnson (eds), *Brazilian Cinema*, New York: Columbia University Press, pp. 328–39.
Bazin, André (1971), *What is Cinema?*, Berkeley and Los Angeles: University of California Press.
Berry, Chris (2016), 'Introducing the Chinese Road Movie: Rethinking Journey Films and the Transformation of the Chinese Film Industry', keynote at *Screen Conference 2016* (24 June).
Bhabha, Homi. K (1994), *The Location of Culture*, London and New York: Routledge.
Brandellero, Sara (ed.) (2013), *The Brazilian Road Movie: Journeys of (Self) Discovery*, Cardiff: University of Wales Press.
Cohan, Steven and Ina Rae Hark (eds) (1997), *The Road Movie Book*, London: Routledge.
Connell, Raewyn (2002), 'The History of Masculinity', in Rachel Adams and David Savran (eds), *The Masculinity Studies Reader*, Oxford: Wiley-Blackwell, pp. 242–52.
Corrigan, Timothy (1991), *A Cinema without Walls: Movies and Culture After Vietnam*, New Brunswick, NJ: Rutgers University Press.
Espinosa, Julio García [1969] (1997), 'For an Imperfect Cinema', in Michael T. Martin (ed.), *New Latin American Cinema: Theory, Practices, and*

Transcontinental Articulations, Vol. 1, Detroit: Wayne State University Press, pp. 71–82.

Everett, Wendy (2004), 'Leaving Home: Exile and Displacement in Contemporary European Cinema', in Wendy Everett and Peter Wagstaff (eds), *Cultures of Exile: Images of Displacement*, London: Berghahn Books, pp. 17–32.

Falicov, Tamara (2007), *The Cinematic Tango: Contemporary Argentine Film*, New York: Wallflower Press.

Galeano, Eduardo [1971] (1997), *Open Veins of Latin America: Five Centuries of the Pillage of a Continent*, New York: Monthly Review Press

Garibotto, Verónica and Jorge Pérez (eds) (2016), *The Latin American Road Movie*, New York: Palgrave Macmillan.

Graham, Tom (2016), 'Jungle Fever', *Sight & Sound*, July, pp. 42–3.

Grimson, Alejandro and Gabriel Kessler (2005), *On Argentina and the Southern Cone: Neoliberalism and National Imaginations*, New York: Routledge.

Hark, Ina Rae (1997), 'Fear of Flying: Yuppie Critique and the Buddy-road Movie in the 1980s', in Steven Cohan and Ina Rae Hark (eds), *The Road Movie Book*, London: Routledge, pp. 204–33.

Hayward, Susan (2004), *Cinema Studies: The Key Concepts*, New York: Routledge.

Johnson, Randal and Robert Stam (eds) (1995), *Brazilian Cinema*, New York: Columbia University Press.

Lie, Nadia (2017), *The Latin American (Counter-) Road Movie and Ambivalent Modernity*, Cham: Springer Nature.

Lodge, Guy (2015), 'My Favourite Cannes Winner: *Paris, Texas*', *The Guardian*, 27 April, <https://www.theguardian.com/film/filmblog/2015/apr/27/my-favourite-cannes-winner-paris-texas> (last accessed 24 February 2017).

Murphy, Ffion, Rama Venkatasawmy, Catherine Simpson and Tanja Visosevic (2001), 'From Sand to Bitumen, from Bushrangers to "Bogans": Mapping the Australian Road Movie', *Journal of Australian Studies*, 25:70, pp. 73–84.

Nagib, Lúcia (2011), 'Realism, Presentation, Respresentation Presentational Ethics', in Lúcia Nagib (ed.), *World Cinema and the Ethics of Realism*, London: Continuum, pp. 1–15.

Pearson, Wendy (2011), 'Detours Homeward: Indigenous Uses of the Road Movie', *The Canadian Journal of Native Studies*, 31:1, Autumn, pp. 139–59.

Pinazza, Natália (2013), 'The Re-emergence of Brazilian Cinema: A Brief History', in Louis Bayman and Natália Pinazza (eds), *Directory of World Cinema: Brazil*, Bristol: Intellect, pp. 32–3.

Pinazza, Natália (2014), *Journeys in Argentine and Brazilian Cinema: Road Movies in a Global Era*, New York: Palgrave Macmillan.

Renan, Ernest (1990), 'What is a nation?', in Homi K. Bhabha (ed.), *Nation and Narration*, New York: Routledge, pp. 8–22.

Roberts, Shari (1997) 'Western Meets Eastwood: Genre and Gender on the Road', in Steven Cohan and Ina Rae Hark (eds), *The Road Movie Book*, London: Routledge, pp. 45–70.

Rocha, Glauber [1965] (1997), 'An Esthetic of Hunger', in Michael T. Martin (ed.), *New Latin American Cinema: Theory, Practices, and Transcontinental Articulations*, Vol. 1, Detroit: Wayne State University Press, pp. 59–61.
Salles Gomes, P. E. (1995), 'Cinema: A Trajectory within Underdevelopment', in Randal Johnson and Robert Stam (eds), *Brazilian Cinema*, New York: Columbia University Press, pp. 245–55.
Salles, Walter (2007), 'Notes for a Theory of the Road Movie', *The New York Times Magazine*, 11 November, <http://www.nytimes.com/2007/11/11/magazine/11roadtrip-t.html?_r=0> (last accessed 24 February 2017).
Shaw, Deborah (2007), 'Playing Hollywood at its own Game? Bielinsky's *Nine Queens*', in Deborah Shaw (ed.), *Contemporary Latin American Cinema: Breaking into the Global Market*, Lanham: Rowman and Littlefield, pp. 65–85.
Shaw, Lisa and Stephanie Dennison (2007), *Brazilian National Cinema*, Oxford: Routledge.
Shohat, Ella and Robert Stam (1994), *Unthinking Eurocentrism: Multiculturalism and the Media*, London: Routledge.
Suppia, Alfredo (2016), 'Science Fiction in Brazilian Cinema', in Natália Pinazza (ed.), *New Approaches to Lusophone Culture*, New York: Cambria Press, pp. 141–73.
Thornton, Niamh (2007), 'Travelling tales: Mobility and Transculturation in Contemporary Latin American Film', *Film and Film Culture*, 4, pp. 30–40.
Tierney, Dolores (2009), 'Alejandro Gonzalez Iñárritu: director without borders', *New Cinemas*, 7:2, pp. 101–17
Williams, Mark (1982), *Road Movies*, London: Proteus Publishing Company.

CHAPTER 15

Spaces of Failure:
The Gendering of Neoliberal Mobilities in the US Indie Road Movie

Anna Cooper

In *The Queer Art of Failure*, Judith/Jack Halberstam proposes failure as a mode of existence defined in radical opposition to the 'punishing norms' of success in neoliberal capitalism (2011: 3). Contrary to how failure is defined in dominant culture – i.e. as a lack, defeat, disaster or inadequacy – they[1] explore the creative potential of failure as a mode of resistance, particularly for queers and for women, to a neoliberal culture which seems to have few other outs. In this article, I aim to answer the question of what such *spaces* of failure might look like, examining failure's oppositional potential for, in particular, poor American women through the lens of space, mobility and landscape. I do this by analysing a contemporary cycle of women-directed US independent and Indiewood films that belong to the road movie genre or are significantly in dialogue with it, including *Gas Food Lodging* (Allison Anders, 1992), *Little Miss Sunshine* (Jonathan Dayton and Valerie Faris, 2006), *Frozen River* (Courtney Hunt, 2008), *Wendy and Lucy* (Kelly Reichardt, 2008), *Seeking a Friend for the End of the World* (Lorene Scafaria, 2012), *The Guilt Trip* (Anne Fletcher, 2012) and *American Honey* (Andrea Arnold, 2016). If the road movie has long functioned as a locus for the depiction of mostly-male rebels and their alternative modes of inhabiting space outside the norms of American society (Cohan and Hark: 1997), these women-centred road movies depict a separate, feminised mode of opposition that, I argue, can be interpreted as a form of resistant failure within US neoliberal disciplinary regimes of space and mobility.

The term 'neoliberalism' first came into use as a general label for the rise of the post-welfare state and the reassertion of free market principles in both the economic and political spheres; previous scholarship on neoliberalism and cinema has tended to focus on film as a global industry (Kapur and Wagner 2011). However, it has also been increasingly understood as a form of governmentality in the Foucauldian sense: it seeks to subject not only economic activity but all institutions, individuals and social action to the principles of the free market (Larner 2000: 12). As Wendy Brown has shown, through its capacity to normatively 'construct and interpellate individuals as entrepreneurial actors in every sphere of life' (Brown 2003: n.p.), neoliberalism asserts a new disciplinary regime in which individuals are always conceived as responsible for their success or failure, no matter how severe the constraints they face. This means that people in oppressed circumstances – the poor, people of colour, women and so on – are blamed for 'mismanaging' their lives. Combined with a normative conception of individuals as in a constant state of competition with each other, this functions to shift attention away from social and economic power, and to imbue the subject with passivity and political complacency (2003: n.p.), as desire for a better life is redirected towards discourses of self-improvement rather than fighting for social change.

Even political movements aimed squarely at dismantling oppressions have themselves become subject to market values under neoliberalism. As Catherine Rottenberg shows, feminism itself has been harnessed and redirected towards buttressing neoliberal hegemonies. For example, the Lean-In movement, started by Sheryl Sandberg's book of the same name (Sandberg 2013), aims to inspire women to work harder to fulfil their leadership potential in the business world. According to Rottenberg, this movement 'forges a feminist subject who is not only individualised but entrepreneurial in the sense that she is oriented towards optimising her resources through incessant calculation, personal initiative and innovation' (Rottenberg 2014: 422). As women seek to succeed in their careers and to create work–life balance for themselves, 'the question of social justice is recast in personal, individualized terms' (2014: 422) in which women who don't make it to the upper echelons of business are castigated for having insufficient ambition or drive, while (mostly quite privileged) women's success in business is centred as the sole measure of feminist triumph. Meanwhile, Rottenberg argues, neoliberal feminism (along with increasing LGBT rights) becomes 'the latest discursive modality to (re)produce the USA as the bastion of liberal democracy' (2014: 433) and is thus recuperated for neoliberal neocolonialist ideologies that justify US interventionism. In a political universe where even anti-oppressive movements have been turned around to serve free-market logic and colonial ideology while heaping further blame on the oppressed for their own oppression, it is not immediately clear what genuine opposition to such an order might look like. Through hipsterism, too, the material cultures of various once-oppositional subcultures (notably punk and queer subcultures) have been appropriated by a voracious free-market consumer culture: thus a traditional avenue for delineating an outsider status to capitalism is neutralised through its conversion to a consumer vanguard. This is why Halberstam's identification of failure as a mode of resistance to neoliberalism has such significance: perhaps only by embracing one's status as a 'loser' in this system – despite or perhaps because of the various miseries almost certain to result from such a status – can one hope to escape neoliberal governmentality or implement any kind of alternative.

Yet I believe Halberstam misses a crucial opportunity when they fail to account for space and mobility in their explorations of failure. Anna Minton's riveting study *Ground Control* argues that the reorganisation of public and private space in cities and towns is key to understanding neoliberal shifts in social discipline. As the high street gave way to the shopping mall in the 1980s under Thatcherite land-use policies in Britain, Minton argues, activities traditionally allowed in public space, like begging, protesting or even simply being idle in public, became increasingly policed and surveilled, often by private security firms (2012). Minton shows how these new privatised public spaces, part and parcel of 'urban renewal' efforts, have contributed to the securitisation and stratification of society, as outsiders of any kind – whether marked by raced, classed or other subcultural identities – are systematically harassed and barred from 'clean and safe' places to shop and live, particularly if they are not buying anything. Thus consumer behaviour is enforced, those who can't afford or don't want to participate are excluded, and the 'winners' and 'losers' in the neoliberal order become physically segregated in an increasingly totalising reorganisation of society. In light of these trends, my central question in this chapter – what do the spaces of failure look like? – seems critical to an understanding of failure as an alternative to neoliberal disciplinary regimes.

The road movie may be a particularly fruitful place to begin answering this question. This is of course partly because of its longstanding and well-documented interest in outsider spaces; Barbara Klinger, for example, shows us how *Easy Rider* (Dennis Hopper, 1969), the road movie which established the genre, reimagines US geography through a countercultural lens, depicting hippie protagonists who feel most at home in empty or otherwise marginal locales (1997). But perhaps even more importantly, the road movie's rise as a genre coincides with the advent of neoliberal reconfigurations of space and landscape. To show this, some historical contextualisation is first needed. In *The Condition of Postmodernity*, David Harvey argues that in capitalist societies, 'the intersecting command of money, time, and space forms a substantial nexus of social power' (1990: 226). (He has since revised his terminology and now calls these shifts under the name neoliberalism rather than postmodernity;

see Harvey 2005: 3–4.) Harvey traces what he calls an unprecedented compression of space and time from the Enlightenment onwards, which both was caused by and aided the development of capitalism: as European merchants brought goods from ever further afield, both distance and the time it took for goods to travel across it became indexed to money, and the three – space, time, and money – became complexly intertwined. This process developed in stages throughout the periods of the industrial revolution and modernism, as time and space became progressively smaller/cheaper. The period from roughly 1970 onwards, Harvey argues, has constituted a new phase of accelerated time–space compression (1990: 284); time and space began to shrink relative to money so rapidly in this period that it vastly increased volatility and ephemerality in nearly every area of the economy and culture, including 'fashion, products, production techniques, labor processes, ideas and ideologies, values and established practices' (1990: 285), as well as communication and images of all kinds. Viewed in light of these changes, the road movie, arising right around when this new phase began circa 1970, can be reread as a nostalgic genre. Just as the movement of goods becomes so smooth and ubiquitous as to be almost invisible, we witness a genre of films which features the car as a manual, physically grounded mode of travel which fetishises the journey itself, with all its coarse unevenness, its disruptions and detours and dust. Despite its obsession with speed, the road movie enacts a slowing-down compared with the accelerating globalisation of neoliberal capitalism. Effacing this newly globalised world, the road movie genre concentrates on the physical beauty of the national landscape, memorialising the Western's mapping of the (white male) soul across the wide open spaces of the frontier. The rebel/outlaw figure so central to the road movie, read in light of these neoliberal changes to space and time, foments chaos and a paradoxical slowness (despite the car chases) in a world turned over to speed and smoothness. Yet, as I shall argue, the male rebel/outlaw figure of the typical road movie, like Lean-In feminism, constitutes a false mode of resistance that actually ends up buttressing the very ideologies it appears to counteract – a move which, as I'll show, also has significant implications for the road movie's imagined geography.

The Patriarchal and Colonial Politics of the Road Movie: *Little Miss Sunshine* and *Thelma and Louise*

A discussion of *Little Miss Sunshine* will illustrate this point as well as highlight the significance of space, mobility, and landscape to a conception of radical failure. Halberstam argues that *Little Miss Sunshine* depicts a family who, at first beholden to neoliberal concepts of success (the father, played by Greg Kinnear, is a motivational speaker flogging a nine-step 'Refuse to Lose' programme), ultimately comes to reject this disciplinary regime and become 'ecstatic losers' who reject 'the contradictions of a society obsessed with meaningless competition' (2011: 5). Through the daughter Olive's (Abigail Breslin) spectacular failure in the Little Miss Sunshine beauty contest,

> [a] new kind of optimism is born. Not an optimism that relies on positive thinking as an explanatory engine for social order, nor one that insists upon the bright side at all costs; rather this is a little ray of sunshine that produces shade and light in equal measure and knows that the meaning of one always depends upon the meaning of the other. (2011: 5)

While this analysis has much to commend it and seems true to the film's understanding of itself, as it were, the film's spatial politics tells a conflicting story. Olive's brother Dwayne (Paul Dano) is intensely focused on his goal of flying planes in the Air Force, working towards this with great discipline. When he abruptly discovers that he is colourblind and therefore ineligible, he is devastated. In a later moment of reflection, Dwayne says to his uncle,

> Fuck beauty contests. Life is one fucking beauty contest after another. School, then college, then work – fuck that, and fuck the Air Force Academy. If I want to fly, I'll find a way to fly. You do what you love, and fuck the rest.

This seems to function as a kind of moral for the film: not to be beholden to the mindless goalsetting and endless competition of life in neoliberalism. The trouble is that air travel represents a colonial and gendered understanding of what such freedom looks like. Seeing far into the distance, looking down upon the landscape from above, moving frictionlessly across the Earth: Mary Louise Pratt (1992), Christine Battersby (2007), Wolfgang Schivelbusch (1977), Lynne Kirby (1997), Giuliana Bruno (2002) and others have led a forceful thread of scholarship connecting the spatial positionings enabled by colonial exploration, particularly via various Western technologies of transit (railways, automobiles, aeroplanes), to hegemonies of race and gender. These technologies, and the changes in visual culture to which they gave rise, ultimately both enabled and justified colonial-capitalist expansion as well as a racist, masculinist understanding of the Earth as there-for-the-exploiting by white men. Seen in this light, Dwayne's – and the film's – vision of 'ecstatic failure' through flight appears perilously close to standard colonialist/capitalist/patriarchal visions of success. And this extends back to the road-movie aspects of the film more generally: the Hoover family, though struggling financially, still has the racial, economic and gendered privilege to move across the landscape, symbolically conquering it. In some ways this ability is marginal, as their old van gets increasingly decrepit as they go; yet in other ways their privilege of mobility is quite secure, as when they are stopped by a policeman who laughs awkwardly at the pornography in the trunk and then lets them go without so much as a ticket. (The film was made several years prior to the advent of the Black Lives Matter movement, but with hindsight it is infuriating to think about how different the outcome would have to be if this family were not white.)

What this all means is that finding your own path to your goals (note the typical repetition of metaphors of travel) might make you a maverick or rebel of some sort, but not the sort that truly calls into question the established order of the world. In other words, in a film culture as full of mavericks and rebels as American cinema is – the vast majority of them male and white – we need to find a way to distinguish between those mythologies of rebellion that ultimately play into the hands of reigning hegemonies, versus those (often feminine/queer/people of colour) figures who offer bona fide resistance. Halberstam acknowledges the need for such a distinction in their analysis of Irvine Welsh's novel *Trainspotting*, which they call 'far too hetero-masculine in its simple reversals of masculine authority, its antifemale fraternity, and its unpredictable bursts of violence', thus constituting a form of 'unqueer failure' (2011: 92) which ultimately reinforces the very status quo that it appears to criticise.

The road movie, with its investments in outsider-ness, can tell us a lot about the differences between queer and unqueer failure. Going at least as far back as the 1930s with films like *You Only Live Once* (Fritz Lang, 1937), the road and the automobile in Hollywood cinema have been associated with the white male outlaw. Going even further back, to historian Frederick Jackson Turner's eulogisation of the American West, the heroic white male pioneer, constantly on the move to explore and conquer new landscapes, was theorised as straddling the divide between wild and civilised; this mode of mobility has for a very long time in American culture been associated with the maverick figure (1976). Given the entwined histories of the road movie and the Western, it is not hard to see how the road movie's white male maverick reabsorbs colonialist and sexist logics of domination; despite the theme of rebellion, this character-type actually seems central to the US's understanding of itself as a culture. Indeed, as Steven Cohan has shown (1997), the figure of the psychopath is integral to the principal configuration of white American masculinity in the twentieth century, constituting one half of a split male self in which the civilised, responsible, family-oriented half is constantly repressing and modulating a second, more violent, barbarian half which otherwise threatens to erupt. The psychopath, the imagined embodiment of the savage white male self, is a central figure in the road movie, going back at least to films like *Bonnie and Clyde* (Arthur Penn, 1967), *Vanishing Point* (Richard C. Sarafian, 1971), *Two-Lane Blacktop* (Monte Hellman, 1971), *Badlands* (Terrence Malick, 1973), and *Taxi Driver* (Martin Scorsese, 1976), if not all the way back to *You Only Live Once*. Additionally, there seems to have been a second wave of road movies in this psychopathic vein in the early 1990s, including *Natural Born Killers* (Oliver Stone, 1994), *Kalifornia* (Dominic Sena, 1993), *True Romance* (Tony Scott, 1993) and *Wild at Heart* (David Lynch, 1990), and perhaps even a third wave very recently, in films like *Drive* (Nicolas Winding Refn, 2011), *Nocturnal Animals* (Tom Ford, 2016) and, more self-reflexively, *American Honey* in the figure of the Shia LaBeouf character. In all these cases, I would argue, the psychopathic figure must be understood as a variant on an empowered subjectivity, ostensibly a rebel but in fact compellingly buttressing dominant ideologies of gender and race. (Although not a fully-fledged psychopath, Dwayne in *Little Miss Sunshine* does refer to this tradition with his obsessive reading of Nietzsche and his refusal to participate in the civilised niceties of speech.)

But what about when women inhabit the road? Does simply being a woman in the outsider space of the road make it a space of queer failure? *Thelma and Louise* (Ridley Scott, 1991) is of course the archetype here. Although much has been written, and not wrongly, of Thelma and Louise as feminist and queer icons, I ultimately read them as, in essence, female variants on the psychopath. Although their death at the end of the film points to the impossibility of the existence of the female psychopath and thus to the essential otherness of Woman in patriarchy, still, Thelma and Louise are briefly empowered in terms of how they inhabit space: travelling across the landscape, speeding in a machine, deriving pleasure from the feelings of freedom that arise from this newfound mobility after a lifetime of gendered imprisonment. In essence, they become like white men in terms of their mobility and their violent (colonial) relationship to the landscape; they thus function, however briefly and impossibly, to turn patriarchy against itself, like Mulvey using the patriarchal tools of psychoanalysis to commit acts of violence against patriarchy (1989). (*Monster* (Patty Jenkins, 2003) enacts an even more explicit reuse of patriarchal violence by a woman taking revenge on men, and a more explicit punishment for such a gendered transgression.)

Little Miss Sunshine and *Thelma and Louise*, then, produce a form of false or un-queer failure that is borrowed from the white male maverick figure. They are a sort of limiting case: examples of road movies that, although made by women (at least in part) and featuring women characters, do not ultimately challenge the dominant neoliberal order. Two other films in the corpus for this chapter also fall into this category. *The Guilt Trip* is a flop of a comedy about an aging mother (Barbra Streisand) who embarks on a road trip with her son (Seth Rogen), a failing businessman; in *Seeking a Friend for the End of the World*, Keira Knightley plays a Manic Pixie Dream Girl whose love transforms bumbling insurance salesman Steve Carell against the backdrop of the apocalypse – the ultimate failure. Both films, though they address situations of failure and feature 'loser' characters, depict women solely in terms of their relationships to men. Their mobility – for in these films, as in *Little Miss Sunshine* and *Thelma and Louise*, the women do actually go somewhere – remains tied to and defined by a man's mobility.

But what do women do when they don't have a man to travel with, nor the resources available to become like men – when they simply do what they have always done as women? What relations do women qua women have with the open road in US culture? The remainder of the films in my corpus, I argue, do something radically different: they depict spaces of failure, or what we might call women's counter-space (riffing off Claire Johnston's concept of counter-cinema (1999)). Women's counter-space is a space of poverty, lack, nothingness, located in the cracks of neoliberal culture or at its outer margins; indeed, these films significantly appear to be failed road movies, as despite their proximity to the open road, the women in them are largely unable to get anywhere at all. Rather, these women use what few resources and what little self-determination they have, in a culture defined by a seemingly irrevocable conspiracy of patriarchy with neocolonial technologies of transit and surveillance, to eke out a life for themselves as best they can. Taking *Gas Food Lodging* and *Wendy and Lucy* as primary examples, I show how 'loser' women, and the counterspaces they inhabit, poignantly illustrate the shape of neoliberal culture, depicting the destruction it wreaks on its subjects and yet giving at least a glimmer of hope for true resistance.

Failure as Radical Femme Aesthetics: *Gas Food Lodging*

Gas Food Lodging is, fittingly, about a girl named Shade (Fairuza Balk). Shade lives with her sister and mother in a single-wide trailer in Laramie, New Mexico, a small, decaying town sitting aside a two-lane highway in the dusty high desert. The film opens with a long take evidently shot from the front of a vehicle as it rolls down the highway and enters Laramie – the film thus immediately raising an expectation that it will be a road movie, where, one supposes, this little town might be but one pit-stop of many. We see several stationary shots of Laramie's features, like postcards but in sad reverse: an abandoned trailer in a vacant lot, the decaying marquee of an old theatre on a crumbling main street. Yet rather than passing by on the way elsewhere, it soon becomes clear that the film will linger here, exploring the lives of residents largely rooted here by circumstances outside their control, as the drivers of the world pass on through. This is a territory of failure: overlooked, half-dead and – crucially – immobile.

The film is almost entirely about women and girls; men inhabit the margins of their lives, although in most films it would be these women who inhabit the margins of men's lives: waitresses, one-night conquests, abandoned daughters. The men in the film are all headed somewhere: they come in and out of Laramie, whether to run away and come back again, like Shade's absentee father (James Brolin), or to explore from a different world, like the British geologist (Robert Knepper) who impregnates Shade's sister Trudi (Ione Skye). Indeed, white men in this film are virtually the only people who own cars, and we see them more often in their cars than outside them. Shade's mother Nora (Brooke Adams) is the exception, as she owns a beat-up old sedan, but even this functions repetitively as a site for her interactions with men – most of whom are trying to sleep with her. Nora also works as a waitress in a truck stop, spending long days serving travelling men who doubtless see her as sexually available as well. Cars and roads are masculine spaces in this film, and mobility is largely the prerogative of white men, a function of their power over women (and, as we'll see, people of colour too). This gendered access to mobility – men move, women stay put – has a long tradition in American cinema. Tania Modleski has shown how, in the woman's film, the female protagonist often has a repetitive, 'hysterical' relationship to both time and space, characterised by endless returns to the same places over and over again rather than moving forward or outward (Modleski 1987, 330). Thomas Elsaesser also discussed the contrast between the Western and what he called the family melodrama,[2] in which women are confined to elaborate and stifling indoor spaces:

> The family melodrama . . . records the failure of the protagonist to act in a way that could shape events and influence the emotional environment, let alone change the stifling social milieu. The world is closed, and the characters are acted upon. (Elsaesser 1987: 55–6)

In the Western, on the other hand – a genre largely concerned with men – male protagonists move the drama forward through decisive action that often involves traversing space and (symbolically or literally) conquering the land. *Gas Food Lodging* inherits this tradition of gendered mobilities, with men on the move *across* the landscape, while women are rather situated as *part of* the landscape, immobile and devalued by the men passing through.

The two sisters deal with these spatial conditions of oppression quite differently, however. Trudi, the older, rebellious sister, does more or less what a lot of young women in a lot of Hollywood films do: she inhabits the world of men the best she can, hoping that men's sexual attention will convert into a source of power for herself. She plays by the rules of teenage femininity in a man's world, starving herself to look good for a date and skipping high school to be more sexually available. The sex she has with various men happens almost entirely in and near cars, often as payment for a lift. As if signifying her fealty to the reigning geo-patriarchal structures of power, she wears a driving jacket covered in car-related branding. She longs to get out of Laramie, rejoicing when she finds a man who she believes will take her away. When he disappears and she realises she is pregnant, she at last gets out, taking a Greyhound bus to Dallas to give birth; afterwards, she plans to become a model, once again hoping for salvation through submission to the male gaze. This world is fraught with danger for Trudi; indeed, we learn that her promiscuous behaviour began with her gang-rape by male classmates, and it sees her abused and slut-shamed terribly.

Shade does something quite different with her gendered marginality, constructing alongside her mother a feminine – as well as, to a degree, queer and indigenous – world largely apart from and invisible to white men. She has an affinity for woman's films, delighting in the resplendently histrionic films of a (fictional) Mexican movie star named Elvia Rivero (Nina Belanger). Indeed Shade herself repetitively prowls the shabby cinema where Rivero's films play; in this and other ways she seems prone to finding unexpected delights within the enforced stasis of her life. Her clothing contrasts starkly with Trudi's: while the older sister's clothes are tight, short and with clean modern lines, Shade wears fanciful and dramatically femme ensembles made of lace and chiffon and lamé, often accessorised with vintage jewellery and outlandish shoes. Nora, the mother, has similar taste in clothing and seems to be a more jaded version of Shade; the interior décor of their trailer is characterised by elaborate wallpaper and ornate clutter. Rosalind Galt has written of the radical political potential of the decorative, or the 'pretty,' as an aesthetics that resists 'high culture' and its normative insistence on clean lines (2011). She traces a longstanding suspicion of decoration and detail in Western culture as a modality for enforcing misogynist, heteronormative, and colonialist hegemonies, demonstrating how the 'pretty' can function as a means of resistance countering each of these. In *Gas Food Lodging*, Shade's world is alive with a kind of radical femme aesthetics that is devalued by if not invisible to white men, both in her world and in ours: it is a counter-space, showing what ecstatic, creative failure can look like within the passed-over cracks of patriarchal culture.

The two men Shade does allow into her world are both Others to heteronormative white masculinity; they enrich rather than do violence to her fragile counter-space. One is Darius (Donovan Leitch), a beautiful queer goth in a velvet jacket and flaming eye-makeup who seems imbued with trans-feminine energy (though in 1992 trans consciousness may not have been available to most viewers). The wizard behind the curtains of Shade's sartorial tastes, Darius runs a fabulous second-hand clothing store on a semi-abandoned street in downtown Laramie, bringing to her life a queer exuberance which they bond over, and which she experiences as sexual attraction (unrequited by Darius, however). The space of the second-hand store, with its dusty discarded objects displayed for decorative pleasure – sold cheaply and locally, devalued by and of no benefit to global capital – itself seems a prime territory of queer failure, and it certainly plays a crucial function in giving Shade's life its queer femme texture.

The other man is Javier (Jacob Vargas), a young Mexican-American whose family has been in Laramie for five generations (i.e. since the land was part of Mexico). Although most white people in the film read him as a *cholo* (gangster) and call him racist slurs, he too inhabits an invisibly, impossibly rich culture which comes into a subtle yet powerful alliance with Shade's femme aesthetics. Javier, Shade discovers, is a projectionist in the cinema where she watches Elvia Rivero films. He lives with his deaf mother in an old adobe home of the sort that might now be reclaimed as 'rustic' and made over by yuppies, but is here devalued as indigenous – except by Javier and Shade. As they fall in love, they bond over a shared vision of the desert around them as a glowingly beautiful and magical space which, they realise, most people cannot see; most who pass through see only dust and tumbleweeds. Through her alliances with these two men, the film proclaims the queer and indigenous energies of Shade's radical aesthetics of failure.

As we might expect of a film about failure, by the end of the narrative, Shade and her magical counter-space face grave losses. She loses her sister, who decides to stay in Dallas, as well as her baby niece, who is given up for adoption, and who, Shade reflects in voiceover, 'will never know where any of her features came from . . . or the desert where she was conceived'. Even the magical, private beauty of the New Mexico desert is up for sale by the end of the film: she sees a roadside stand selling the Day-Glo rocks that are emblematic of her family's private, matriarchal relationship to the landscape. Shade's ecstatic femme world, it turns out, is being ravaged by the encroachment of white patriarchal capitalism. In hindsight, it seems prescient on the part of the film that the three places most precious to Shade – the second-hand shop, the decaying cinema and the old adobe house – represent the quintessential aesthetic properties of what would soon become neoliberal hipsterism: vintage, rustic, handmade, local, ripe for reclamation. This oppositional aesthetics of failure would itself become subject to commodification in the years following the film's release, valued by the US bourgeoisie perhaps due to its very capacity to obscure the violent functioning of global capital.

'This machine's gonna kill me': *Wendy and Lucy*

Not all failure can be ecstatic or productive; it can also be, and often is, simply miserable. *Wendy and Lucy* exemplifies a bleak hopelessness, an affect that must also be considered in relation to failure, I believe, if we are to do full justice to the subject. If *Gas Food Lodging* depicts a counter-space that is fragile and under assault, *Wendy and Lucy* depicts its last gasps: it shows Wendy (Michelle Williams), a woman whose entire domain – all the security and community she has in the world – consists of the interior of her car and her one companion, her dog Lucy. And she soon loses both, fighting with all she can muster to keep them, but failing in the face of an indifferent and dehumanising system. Although there is little room for revolutionary creativity within the failures presented here, the film does teach us about another facet of failure that is largely ignored by Halberstam: its complex relationship to information technology, which in turn shapes and is shaped by neoliberal spatial politics.

Halberstam's primary corpus consists of films by Pixar; a move which leaves them, to my mind, uncomfortably beholden to dominant myths about the maverick dropouts who became tech pioneers and built the Pixar empire (2011: 7), whom they apparently see as exemplars of creative failure. Unfortunately, I think this credulousness towards the figure of the white male 'geek' makes Halberstam myopic towards the enormous significance of information technologies in neoliberal economics and culture. Harvey discusses how the acceleration in technological change in recent centuries, often developed with the explicit aim of making human labour less necessary and/or easier to control, has come to such a crisis point that it is collectively functioning to make workers' wages low enough to suppress demand for consumer goods, and therefore to hurt profits (2014: 103–104). There has been much talk in the past couple of years about the possibility of creating a universal basic income in a 'post-work' society, due to the sheer number of once-human jobs now being relegated to machines (see, for example, Srnicek and Williams 2015; Mason 2016) – a situation which clearly contributes to the neoliberal disempowerment of workers. This is one major way in which technology informs neoliberal culture, but there are many others too: access to and proficiency in information technologies like personal computers and the internet is also commonly seen as a necessary facet of participation in the contemporary labour force, and the lack of such access/skills is often discussed as a failure on the part of the poor and/or a crucial hole to fill in order to charitably lift them out of poverty (Eubanks 2011).

Information technologies are profoundly entangled with questions of neoliberal space, the connections between which are depicted at the most intimate individual levels in *Wendy and Lucy*. For example, information technology plays a pivotal role in globalised trade, which it both causes and is caused by (as Harvey addresses at length in his discussion of the annihilation of space and time, discussed previously). Such shifts in the geography of labour trickle down to Wendy, who is on this road trip not for pleasure nor to express her nature as an outsider, but to reach the Alaskan fisheries where she has heard there is ample work. There are a couple of paradoxes at work here: although she heads west towards the frontier and thus follows the standard colonial trajectory of movement, she does so in an astoundingly disempowered way. Like the Joads in *The Grapes of Wrath*, she is forced to increase the flexibility of her labour at great personal cost. And the other paradox is that although this is normally a heteromasculine trajectory – picking up stakes and heading into the entrepreneurial west – the fact that she is a woman doing this makes her a queer figure and thus doubly an outsider. (Her androgynous hairstyle, clothes and mannerisms confirm this sense of her queerness, though we know nothing of her sexual orientation.)

Another connection between technology and space lies in how devices such as the mobile phone and satellite navigation, as well as companies like Airbnb, are changing patterns of mobility for individuals through instantaneous access to information and communications. In *Wendy and Lucy* this is depicted not so much through the presence of such devices as through their absence: she has no phone, no digital camera, no computer, no internet access, no bank account or credit card. In a world where these items are expected even amongst the poor, her lack puts her at a grave disadvantage, scrambling for change to use the payphone and guarding her cash – all the money she has in the world – in a pouch underneath her clothes. Indeed, nearly all her access to technology is mediated through male gatekeepers (a point to which we shall return). Her lack of technology has spatial implications, not just in increasing the difficulty and expense of her road trip, but in forcing her to trek around town in circles to gather and disseminate information about her car and her dog, and compelling her to wait in a car park for hours until the kindly security guard (Walter Dalton) returns with his mobile phone.

Information technologies are also at the centre of the surveillance boom described by Minton, which has largely been enabled by digital CCTV and which, as we saw, has functioned to divide cities into spaces for the haves and the have-nots. In this regard, too, Wendy finds herself on the losing side. First, she is ejected from a drugstore car park on the grounds that she is not buying anything. Later she is caught shoplifting by a blond, prosperous-looking and rather sadistic teenage clerk. Unable to afford a hotel room, she sleeps in her car and then in a thicket near the train tracks, both transgressions against neoliberal spatial order which leave her highly vulnerable and frightened. Much of the texture of the film derives from the barren hopelessness of this spatial outsider-ness, its pathos enhanced by a cool palette of blues, long sequences of lonely silence and a chillingly beautiful bass flute solo on the soundtrack.

Being on the losing end of technology – surveilled and excluded rather than empowered by it – also leads to further spatially oriented humiliations for Wendy. Squad cars, jail cells, waiting rooms and long queues all become her lot, as she must wait patiently for various agents of the system – mostly men – to 'process' her according to the protocols they are paid to enforce. The kinder of these agents are at least vaguely apologetic, as when the security guard shrugs repeatedly that 'those are the rules', echoing a refrain that has become in recent years a kind of sad *non mea culpa* for many corporate employees enforcing infuriating and arbitrary regulations over which they have no control. The man who takes fingerprints at the jail also displays a modicum of solidarity with her through an assumed shared hatred of machines, apologetically proclaiming, 'This machine's gonna kill me. We've gotta do it all again.' Others, like the mechanic now in charge of her car, are coldly indifferent.

Virginia Eubanks' accomplished book, *Digital Dead End*, explores how such differences in technological access are deeply gendered. Against the predominating 'levelling the playing field' paradigm in which the poor are viewed as hindered by a lack of access to technology that must be redressed through policy, she argues that information technologies are embedded within pre-existing systems of oppression (2011). As most hardware and software is designed by economically privileged white men, Eubanks argues, such systems tend to reduce the often complex needs of the poor, people of colour, and women to simplistic and inflexible schema that many such users find vexatious and hostile rather than helpful or empowering. When the system in question is, say, a system which a government bureaucracy uses for determining housing benefits, the results can be catastrophic to the lives of the oppressed, but regardless, such systems are often – and rightly, Eubanks argues – seen as intrusive, hostile and dangerous, countering the dominant narrative of technology as liberating. Moreover, Eubanks shows that the lives of poor women of colour are often saturated with technology, but in ways that tend to be erased – for example, they are employed by the thousands in low-paid, unpleasant tech work like call centres and data entry, where, too, technology functions as a force of surveillance and control. *Wendy and Lucy* very poignantly depicts precisely this gendered and classed technological universe, where poor women continually inhabit the losing end of 'the system'.

What the film shows us, extending Eubanks' analysis, is how this technological state of affairs affects the gendered organisation of neoliberal space, impelling disempowered women further into spirals of spatial exclusion that make things worse and worse for them. Such a reorganisation of space in turn affects social interactions and patterns of emotion, as agents of the system are discouraged through architectural and interior design from feeling sympathy for those they process: separated by glass, tall desks or simply by a physically superior position looking out over a car park, the humanity of those caught within such arrangements is more easily disregarded. Neoliberal space, as Minton demonstrates, is segregated space, and *Wendy and Lucy* powerfully portrays the perspective of a poor queer woman caught on the failing side of the neoliberal divide between 'winners' and 'losers'.

Women's counter-space here is fraught with danger, suffering and loneliness, and Wendy sees little hope of escape except through continued capitalist striving, as she heads for Alaska via freight train. One wonders if, in her newly minted life as a hobo, she might eventually give up on her crusade for neoliberal success, and instead find community in the hardscrabble tribe of wandering 'losers' she met around the campfire near the start of the film – or whether her status as a woman excludes her even from communities of the homeless.

Conclusion

In answer to the question, 'what do the spaces of failure look like?', *Gas Food Lodging* and *Wendy and Lucy* give distinct but linked answers. Anders' film depicts a radical counter-space characterised by femme aesthetics and alliances with the queer and indigenous, all functioning together as Others to a technologised, globalised white heteropatriarchal culture. Reichardt's film depicts what's left when even these marginalised femme counter-spaces break down, ravaged by a voracious neoliberal machine that devours attempts to resist it, until all that's left is loneliness and suffering for the 'losers' of neoliberal society.

The remaining two films in my corpus function in a similar vein, delineating women's counter-spaces on the margins of neoliberal culture. *Frozen River* returns to the indigenous – in this case, the Mohawk reservation in northern New York state – as a space for community amongst women. At first a fragile alliance forms between Ray (Melissa Leo), a poor white mother trying desperately to provide for her children while working a minimum-wage job in a dollar store, and Lila (Misty Upham), also a poor mother living on the reservation. The two women band together smuggling migrants across the border with Canada in Ray's car, and their solidarity – both with each other and with the women migrants they encounter – grows, strengthening as a counter-space to the ravages of global capital in whose detritus they live. In *American Honey*, Star (Sasha Lane) travels the country with a band of other working-class youth, who go door-to-door to flog a magazine scam. They are already excluded from neoliberal society in various ways due to their visible poverty, but Star is marked through her blackness as separate even from this group; in a climactic night-time swimming scene in a lake, she becomes conscious of her distance from them and resolves to follow her own path.

These films, in depicting poor women who are failures in neoliberal disciplinary regimes, move us away from the white male 'maverick' with his neocolonial relationship to US and world geography and his participation in patriarchal power structures. In depicting poor women – some queer, some of colour – and the counter-spaces they inhabit, these films show their characters' irreducible Otherness to neoliberal culture. Though fragile and under attack from free-market forces, these counter-spaces depict failure as a mode of resistance which quietly but fundamentally challenges neoliberal governmentality and its spatial regimes.

Notes

1. 'They,' 'them,' and 'their' are used throughout this chapter as singular gender-neutral pronouns to refer to Halberstam.
2. This term has been largely discredited by Steve Neale (1993) and others, who have shown that melodrama should be understood as a cross-generic mode applying at least as much to 'masculine' genres like the Western and the gangster film as to the woman's film.

Works Cited

Battersby, Christine (2007), *The Sublime, Terror, and Human Difference*, London: Routledge.
Brown, Wendy (2003), 'Neo-liberalism and the End of Liberal Democracy', *Theory & Event* 7:1, n.p.
Bruno, Giuliana (2002), *Atlas of Emotion: Journeys in Art, Architecture, and Film*, London: Verso.
Cohan, Steven (1997), *Masked Men: Masculinity and the Movies in the Fifties*, Bloomington: Indiana University Press.
Cohan, Steven, and Ina Rae Hark (1997), 'Introduction', *The Road Movie Book*, London: Routledge.
Elsaesser, Thomas (1987), 'Tales of Sound and Fury: Observations on the Family Melodrama', in Christine Gledhill (ed.), *Home Is Where the Heart Is: Studies in Melodrama and the Woman's Film*, London: BFI.
Eubanks, Virginia (2011), *Digital Dead End: Fighting for Social Justice in the Information Age*, Cambridge, MA: The MIT Press.
Galt, Rosalind (2011), *Pretty: Film and the Decorative Image*, New York: Columbia University Press.
Halberstam, Judith/Jack (2011), *The Queer Art of Failure*, Durham, NC: Duke University Press.
Harvey, David (1990), *The Condition of Postmodernity: An Enquiry into the Origins of Cultural Change*, Oxford: Blackwell.
Harvey, David (2005), *A Brief History of Neoliberalism*, Oxford: Oxford University Press.
Harvey, David (2014), *Seventeen Contradictions and the End of Capitalism*, Oxford: Oxford University Press.
Johnston, Claire (1999), 'Women's Cinema as Counter-Cinema', in Sue Thornham (ed.), *Feminist Film Theory: A Reader*, New York: New York University Press, pp. 31–40.
Kapur Jyostna and Keith B. Wagner (2011), *Neoliberalism and Global Cinema: Capital, Culture, and Marxist Critique*, London: Routledge.
Kirby, Lynne (1997), *Parallel Tracks: The Railroad and Silent Cinema*, Durham, NC: Duke University Press.

Klinger, Barbara (1997), 'The Road to Dystopia: Landscaping the Nation in *Easy Rider*', in Steven Cohan and Ina Rae Hark (ed.), *The Road Movie Book*, London: Routledge, pp. 179–203.

Larner, Wendy (2000), 'Neo-liberalism: Policy, Ideology, Governmentality', *Studies in Political Economy*, 63:1, pp. 5–25.

Mason, Paul (2016), *Postcapitalism: A Guide to Our Future*, London: Penguin.

Minton, Anna (2012), *Ground Control: Fear and Happiness in the Twenty-First Century City*, 2nd edn, London: Penguin.

Modleski, Tania (1987), 'Time and Desire in the Woman's Film', in Christine Gledhill (ed.), *Home Is Where the Heart Is: Studies in Melodrama and the Woman's Film*, London: BFI, pp. 326–39.

Mulvey, Laura (1989), 'Visual Pleasure and Narrative Cinema', in *Visual and Other Pleasures*, London: Macmillan, pp. 14–30.

Neale, Steve (1993), 'Melo Talk: On the Meaning and Use of the Term "Melodrama" in the American Trade Press', *Velvet Light Trap*, 32, pp. 66–89.

Pratt, Mary Louise (1992), *Imperial Eyes: Travel Writing and Transculturation*, London: Routledge.

Rottenberg, Catherine (2014), 'The Rise of Neoliberal Feminism', *Cultural Studies*, 28:3, pp. 418–37.

Sandberg, Sheryl (2013), *Lean In: Women, Work, and the Will to Lead*, New York: Knopf.

Schivelbusch, Wolfgang (1977), *The Railway Journey: The Industrialization of Time and Space in the Nineteenth Century*, Oakland: University of California Press.

Srnicek, Nick, and Alex Williams (2015), *Inventing the Future: Postcapitalism and a World Without Work*, London: Verso.

Turner, Frederick Jackson [1893] (1976), *The Significance of the Frontier in American History*, ed. Harold P. Simonson, New York: Ungar.

CHAPTER 16

Sic transit:
The Serial Killer Road Movie

Louis Bayman

This chapter identifies the category of the serial killer road movie, which it finds to be less a genre and more an encounter of two phenomena – killer and road – both subject to modern mythology. Their encounter offers, however, an opportunity to understand the function of mobility to such mythology, for not only is mobility a common characteristic in establishing a serial killer's existence beyond normal society, its importance derives from the very centrality of mobility to that society. Mobility is thus a vehicle of both commonality and aberrance, a paradox I have chosen to illustrate through a comparison of *Henry: Portrait of a Serial Killer* (John McNaughton, 1986) and *Sightseers* (Ben Wheatley, 2012). These somewhat atypical serial killer road movies seek not so much the thrill of the road as to destroy its romance, by engaging a critical awareness of the cultural meanings of mobility in the diverse contexts respectively of American independent cinema and British comedy. Such critical awareness helps put into relief a poetics of automobility, and the three main aims of this chapter: to demonstrate mobility as a bearer of broad significance which, secondly, is determined by the particularities of convention (as illustrated here in the contrast between the UK and the USA), alighting finally on a general cultural property of mobility, that is, *how* it assumes this significance. This how, I conclude, lies in the special narrational position that mobility offers, one of simultaneous involvement and remove with respect to the characters who undertake it.[1]

The Mobility of the Movie Killer

The wider corpus of the serial killer road movie is a varied one, and can point to a hypothesis that the road movie is an inherently hybrid form. It includes the 'rural horror' movies Stefano Baschiera discusses in this volume, whose travellers get lost in the savage wilderness of a gothic pre-modernity (see also Ballard 2008). It can provide a vehicle for the slasher film or torture porn to meet the older traditions of the cinematic thrill-ride, injecting horror into the action-adventure of the 'car-chase film' (Romao 1994). Other examples, like *Duel* (Steven Spielberg, 1971), *The Hitcher* (Robert Harmon, 1986) and *Spoorloos/The Vanishing* (George Sluizer 1988 and 1993), focus less on graphic violence than the frisson of an antagonistic male duo, thereby also inverting the central relationship of the road movie's 'first cousin', the buddy movie (Corrigan 1991: 138). Ritual sacrifice films like *Race with the Devil* (Jack Starrett, 1975), *Le porte del silenzio/Door to Silence* (Lucio Fulci, 1991) and *Dust Devil* (Richard Stanley, 1992), edge instead towards the supernatural. Meanwhile a counter-cultural burst of unrestricted energy characterises the spree film (Sargeant 1999). Alternatively, the American 'psychokiller cinema' identified by Martin Rubin (1992) as beginning with *The Honeymoon Killers* (Leonard Kastle, 1970) and including *Badlands* (Terrence Malick, 1973) and *Henry: Portrait of a Serial Killer* evokes the 'numb [. . .] anti-expressiveness' of prolonged transit within the ambiguity of the arthouse (Rubin 1992: 55–6). *Henry* also contributes a serial killer entry in the 'postmodern road movie' (see Laderman 2002), inspiring the later films *Kalifornia* (Dominic Sena, 1993) and *Natural Born Killers* (Oliver Stone, 1994), although one may place it alongside *Taxi Driver* (Martin Scorsese, 1976) as a 'confined' road movie because the protagonist spends the duration of the film on the road without leaving the city.

The corpus draws, however, upon a much longer tradition, endowing mobility with the notion of going beyond normal existence, one which has artistic and intellectual significance in representations of the serial killer. In this regard, the first significance of mobility, at least within the cinema, is that it provides mechanisms that propel the narrative and invite emotional engagement. This is most obviously so in the elusiveness of the classic movie killer, a clear aid to the plot of films that concern criminals and their capture. The surreptitious ease with which the serial killer evades systems of detection (see Willis 2006) feeds into people's insecurities regarding their potential proximity to danger in everyday life. This general threat produces city-wide hysteria in the classic example *M* (Fritz Lang, 1931), and challenges the complacency of systems of public protection, as when Hannibal Lecter calls Clarice Starling from a tropical location in a final taunt to the police before slipping away at the end of *The Silence of the Lambs* (Jonathan Demme, 1991). In both cases, the killer-at-large inspires dread at danger's random, unfixed presence: it is out there somewhere, but no one knows where.

The serial killer's elusiveness pertains to more than his[2] capacity for surprise. Cinematically, the screen killer often assumes a presence beyond physical form (see Hantke 2002), in contrast to the inert matter to which he reduces his victims. In *Die Büchse der Pandora/Pandora's Box* (G. W. Pabst, 1929) the Ripper appears as if an element of the night's darkness, taking shape out of the fog into which he merges back at the film's close; the murderer in *M* first appears as a disembodied whistle and a shadow cast against a poster; the opening sequence of *Strangers on a Train* (Alfred Hitchcock, 1951) presents an extended montage of close-ups of the killer's elegantly shod foot encroaching on the legroom of a passenger. The serial killer in these representations is not all there, yet exceeds the frame of representation. Nor can he be contained by moral or legal values, which he transgresses as he also slips between charm and violence, assumes different identities and disrupts sexual norms. Such instabilities befit the spectator of violence's oscillation between horror and pleasure, and volatile identification between victim and attacker.

Mobility is thus a factor of narrative and formal excitement, as it is also related to the killer's disruption of the integrity of the body, the self or the social order in ways that are intrinsic to the production of horror. Mobility is also more straightforwardly present in the serial killer's access to travel and transport. The serial killer narrative often begins with the unanticipated arrival of a gentleman from out of town, or the movements of an accidental globetrotter, as in the Ripley series. The panic around the 'Jack the Ripper' case of 1888 elicited contemporary fears of mobility, as suspicion alternately fell on immigrants to the East End or a wealthy day-tripper exploiting the degraded poor (Walkowitz 1992). The Ripper's place as the first serial killer[3] links the serial killer to modernity, a period in which transport systems enable unprecedented criminal reach and whose media networks diffuse the killer's fame. Furthermore, the anonymity, disposability and sensation of modern cities may even be what produce the desire to serially kill in the first place (see Seltzer 1998).

One dimension of the mobility acquired by the screen killer then lies in an essential elusiveness; a second is a propensity to travel, incorporating an affinity with mechanised technology in an age characterised by transience or impermanence; but, classically, a third reveals him as somehow fixed in place. At one point, the train-driver protagonist of *La Bête humaine* (Jean Renoir, 1938) walks down the night-time tracks, prey to a hereditary propensity to murder in a spatial rendition of how he is unable to deviate from the destiny set by his bloodline of killer ancestors. Thus, a Mephistophelean ability to traverse the universe is tempered by limitations of either fate, birth, environment or nature. Limitation aids the classical tendency to give the killer pathos, or at least subjectivity: he is mobile but trapped, if not by the law then by compulsion. The Victorian misery of the East End of London and the febrile licence of interwar Berlin appear not only to house but to produce a killer.

It is notable, however, that motorcars do not play a significant role in the examples just mentioned, whose familiarity gives them the status of classic cinematic exemplars. The idea of putting a compulsion killer onto the road is already present in James Hogg's *doppelgänger* narrative, *The Private Memoirs and Confessions of a Justified Sinner* of 1824, and has cinematic antecedents in 1947's *The Devil Thumbs a Ride* (Felix E. Feist) and *The Hitch-Hiker* (Ida Lupino) in 1953, but as a category the serial killer road movie only really takes shape around several clusters of low-budget, independent filmmaking appearing since the 1970s (see Morton 1999), as the examples at the top of this section show. Prior to this, the private mobility of the motorcar was, primarily, associated first with the glamour of the leisure class and a dangerous yet exciting urban modernity, and then the spread of post-war prosperity, so much as to make it unsuitable as a site of horror. For while the 'auto' in automotive indicates only that cars run independently of rails, its suggestion of autonomy is part of what is known as the 'myth of automobility', created around 'powerful cultural dreams of adventure and freedom: the capacity to go anywhere, to move and dwell without asking permission, the self-directed life free from the surveillance of the authorities' (Featherstone 2005:2). What the serial killer road movie does is turn this myth around, to express late capitalist fears either of rural desolation, or an aggressively unrestrained individualism. It performs, then, an anti-humanist inversion of the road movie, in which the turbo-charge of abandon amidst nature's vastness becomes the relentless pursuit of a killer whose identification with his vehicle makes him both superior to, and deficient in, humanity (in *Duel* the antagonist apparently simply *is* the truck, whose driver remains unseen but whose headlights, windscreen and grill create a monstrous metal face). The importance of the elusiveness outlined in the examples above is to show that the association of the serial killer with properties of mobility is a general one. The association of cars with horror, however, is a historically specific one, propelled by the changing fears of the societies that produce it: the dark interior of a horse-drawn cab may put us into a lost world of Victorian melodrama, but the classic serial killer films of the 1920s to 1960s remain more concerned with questions of civic life and public space than the ideal of self-realisation indicated by the car. It is not until cinematic anxieties focus more specifically upon a commodified, post-industrial landscape that the car develops its more negative meanings, as *Henry, Portrait of a Serial Killer* will demonstrate.

Henry, Portrait of a Serial Killer

The negative – indeed, nihilistic – principle that tends to underlie the combination of road and serial killer is especially present in the '*cause célèbre*' (Rubin 1992) of X-rated fame, *Henry, Portrait of a Serial Killer*. The film presents a fairly episodic series of reflections on mobility, which in some ways characterises the social environment, in others primarily regards feeling and perception, but is always grounded in a particular vision of post-Fordist, postmodern experience. It is inspired by the confessions of Henry Lee Lucas, who was convicted of a trail of rape, robbery, assault and murder carried out with Ottis Toole (named Otis in the film). Lucas offered police the opportunity to clear 213 unsolved cases from their books, but despite his own increasingly extravagant claims he was found guilty of only eleven. The film achieved an official designation of 'disturbing' by the Motion Picture Association of America (MPAA) when initially holding back its release. 'Disturbing' is a spatial metaphor that means to be moved out of place, like two other epithets applied to the film, unsettling (Hantke 2001: 32) and upsetting (Simpson 2000: 139), and the film employs the destabilising tendencies of the killer's elusiveness by incorporating uncertainty, already present in the lack of established facts about the real-life case, as a radical artistic principle. It variously skirts horror, satire, documentary, exploitation and art cinema without ever finally settling into any of them. Unlike other 'video nasties' of its era, it does not revel in his violence but nor does it shy away from it, for brutality simply happens, and goes on happening.

'Motivation' cannot be said to structure *Henry*, if by this we mean the conventional dramatic dynamic of a progressive understanding of the protagonist's interior life. It is, however, the main narrative dynamic insofar as it expresses instead a plainly physical fact of inertia, with Henry in continual motion and those around him in stasis. This is established in an opening montage that represents a kind of murderous play on artistic 'still lives': four tableaux present bodies after violent death intercut with Henry leaving a diner, putting the car radio on, driving down a freeway and arriving at a mall. The camera gracefully moves across the corpses, which only the associative editing links to Henry, while reverberating screams on the soundtrack of a struggle long past further emphasise their present stillness. Such physical dynamics remain throughout the film, whose conclusion returns to the deadly stillness of the opening. Henry strikes up a relationship with Otis's sister Becky (it is unclear whether they consummate it) and eventually kills Otis when he finds the latter trying to rape her. On their drive out of Chicago Becky says 'I love you' and he responds 'I guess I love you too', before turning on the car radio and continuing to drive in silence. Alone the following day he packs a suitcase and drives away from the motel, to stop at a roadside. Cars speed past indistinctly and he discards the bloodstained case, to drive out of frame as the camera tracks towards it and the reverberating screams return to the soundtrack. Becky is dead weight, baggage, ditched, but Henry moves on. Mobility equals indifference, and stasis, mortality.

Movement thus replaces intimacy with or between characters, though it remains Henry's only identifiable characteristic: he makes and dispatches friends without apparent reflection, tells inconsistent stories about his upbringing and explains his *modus operandi*: never to repeat a method of killing twice. Automobility crowds out closeness, as characters are shown separated by gear sticks, seats or windows, but it also governs Henry's perception (see Figure 16.1). The film is set in Chicago, one of the centres of the US auto industry and synonymous with the governing rationality of the assembly line.

Mark Seltzer (1998) uses *Henry* to argue for an equivalence between the serially repetitive activities of the serial killer and a technologised society that empties out the subject's interiority and replaces intimacy between human beings with an intimacy with machines. According to Seltzer, this process produces '*assemblages* of bodies and technologies' (1998: 74, emphasis in original). A bleakly comic example of such an assemblage occurs in one scene, when Henry and Otis go to a fence[4] to replace their broken television; he is rude to them, and they stick soldering plugs into his hand and smash a television screen-first onto his head, the electric current animating his dying body and lighting him up. As a vision of the stupefaction of televisual culture it also provides a literalised image of the 'fantasy of dismemberment' that Seltzer claims the assemblage of man and machine involves; a fantasy expressed by Henry Ford's own idle calculations in his autobiography of how many of the 7,882 separate operations required to make a Model T Ford could be done by legless, one-legged, one-armed or blind men (Seltzer 1998: 69). Henry Ford's application of Taylor's Principles of Scientific Management provided the model for organising twentieth-century production, consumption and sub/urban planning, and its equation of human progress to the rationalising principles of machine technology was celebrated in visions like the 1939–40 World's Fair exhibitions of General Motors' Futurama and Democracity, and the 1950s Disneyworld exhibit of Autopia, Tomorrowland (see Avila 2014). It is striking, then, that the architects of actually existing 'Autopia' shared Ford's fantasies of dismemberment: Le Corbusier proclaimed 'we must kill the city street' (cited in Berman 1983: 168) and Robert Moses boasted that 'when you operate in an overbuilt metropolis, you have to hack your way with a meat ax' (also cited in Berman 1983: 290), echoing Mussolini's so-called *sventramento* (gutting) of working-class neighbourhoods to rebuild Rome.

While Henry Ford's dismemberments were imagined and Henry Lee Lucas's real, the film identifies cars and violence as the two omnipresent components of this society. Otis works at 'Bob's Gas Station' selling drugs and pornography to passing motorists, as we first see occurring before a cut to an anonymous woman dead on a sofa as a cartoon about cop cars plays on TV. Henry's first victim is a hitchhiker, and he introduces Otis to killing by breaking the necks of two prostitutes in his vehicle. This rusty, dented car is appropriate to the post-industrial decay of the Chicago Henry traverses, which is a dominating but impermanent environment of tarnished prefab housing and containers. Mobility here is shorn of vitality and has no link to progress, and Henry's nomadic impulse is directionless: he tells Otis when driving on a freeway that he is going to pack up and move soon. 'Where you going?' 'Nowhere. Wanna come?' (Otis's parole conditions won't allow him to leave the state.) Both mobile and trapped, Henry's movement is literally to no particular end.

Life is certainly devalued in *Henry*, but the resulting reduction to mere objects does not so much equate humanity with the status of the machine as render it as trash; a term commonly applied to the impoverished white population of America in the desolate, unproductive, wastelands at its social margins (Isenberg 2016). Otis in particular is played as a stereotypical dolt and uncontrolled, sexually motivated voyeur. However, the film's association of people with trash transcends social class to become a more general vision of a post-Fordist environment, as the viewer sees from the opening montage which associates Henry's victims with the disposable objects of mass production. The image of the first body cuts to Henry stubbing out his cigarette, then a couple lying dead next to rows of bottles, and a third victim with an empty Coke bottle through her face, before Henry throws a cigarette stub out of the car window in a graphic match to a plastic container drifting past a body in the water. In this environment, Henry stands out as different. He embodies health, functional efficiency, and manual ability, shown when he saws Otis's head off in the bathroom and packs it into a case with his bag of tools. Placing his navy-coloured shirt over the vest that displays the strength of his arms, he is the well-kept and literally blue-collar Fordist ideal of working manhood. He is thus distinct from the transience that reduces the value of human life to trash, occupying the position mentioned at the outset of this essay, of being at odds with a setting that simultaneously determines his frame of reference.

Figure 16.1 Automotive perception.

Henry is different from the film's other characters, but as spectators we occupy a position analogous to his. The film in fact produces the effect of being a *passenger* accompanying Henry, as the spectator is denied absorption into his inner life but closely allied with the perceptual processes connected to his mobility (see Figure 16.1). It employs many point-of-view shots, and continually reflects Henry's expressionless, occasionally distorted gaze from the windscreen or rear-view mirror. Filmed on a grainy 16mm, its observational camerawork mimics stalking, which we see Henry do from his car at the start of the film (before losing his target). The road is first shown from several low, oblique angles as Henry walks to his car, presenting a position of literally unstable ground. The mechanics of perception, so allied with those of automobility, thus underline the absence of any identifiably human intimacy. The film also draws attention to spectatorship, but only so as to commit acts of destruction upon it: Otis and Henry record a home invasion that they commit, but Henry causes the video camera they use to break, and asks incredulously why Otis wants to watch the video again. In the film's violent climax Becky stabs Otis in the eye with a metal comb. The film thereby produces a meta-spectatorial gaze, but a disengaged one, as, like us, the characters spectate, but for no fulfilling purpose.

Henry's intent stare does, however, bring to mind the ways that driving has been described as an affective state, that inculcates a 'detached involvement' (Brodsly 1981:41) with one's surroundings and an attitude of 'diffuse attentiveness and quasi-automatism' (Crary 1999:78). This attitude can describe spectatorship, and the serial killer road movie often creates a disturbing effect precisely through highlighting the commonality between the everyday technologies of both driving and spectatorship, linking them to the mental processes of the killer. As Lucy Mazdon points out regarding the serial killer films of Cédric Khan,[5] both cinema and car

> share the mechanization and standardization [. . .] [of commodities which help] to shift perception, ways of seeing, enabling as they did a mobile gaze in which the viewer does not necessarily inhabit the same space as the object perceived. It is perhaps worth noting the shared terms used in English for cinema 'screen' and car 'wind screen'. In both cases we look at an apparatus, a defined screen space to see a series of moving objects through which we travel. (2009: 46)

The systematisation of both car manufacture and the production of the feature film in fact display intriguing parallels. Edward Dimendberg has described both the construction of motorways and the sites of cinema spectatorship as interwar aesthetic projects expressing 'the will to motorization' (1995: 90). The car plant assembly line was introduced in 1911, contemporaneously to the development of narrative cinema, providing the model for the classical film studio. These historical coincidences continue as far back as their very invention: the first commercial launch of photography was in 1839 and the first patent for a two-cycle internal combustion engine in 1844, with Nicéphore Niépce involved in both, while Karl Benz's four-wheel car appeared in 1893 and the Lumières' experiments came to fruition at the end of 1895. But these inventions also coincide with the arrival of the serial killer onto the stage of modern life, for 1888 marks the Jack the Ripper case and the public sensation that greeted the simultaneous stage production of Robert Louis Stevenson's 1886 novel *The Strange Case of Dr. Jekyll and Mr. Hyde*.

These three common histories link cars, cinema and serial killing to diverse aspects of the reorganisation of experience and desires in the age of mechanisation. Though ease of use corresponds to a masking of the inner workings of both cinema and car, with the serial killer, mystery is located within the person himself. But each one establishes forms of detached involvement: the car takes passengers into surroundings from which it cocoons them (Beckman 2004:89); cinema photographs worlds whose lived moment is past; and killing offers the intensity of visceral stimulation at the expense of the victim's life. What novelist J. G. Ballard called the 'huge metallized dream' (cited in Wollen 2002:16) of car driving is then an apt description of our everyday experience of mass, standardised forms of production and consumption. Yet as theorists of alienation like Seltzer point out, such experience means killing off something human within us.

In light of the above analysis, the replacement of human intimacy with mechanical technology completes the series of disturbances that *Henry* presents: the blue-collar Henry is out of place amidst the trash and his interior life is substituted by the mechanical aspects of automobility, as is emphasised by consistent point-of-view strategies with which we as spectators closely identify, instead of with his more human, interior motivations. In further displacements, once the factories have left, Chicago's automotive society is reduced to an encompassing culture of standardised, private consumption, human life is equal to trash, killing tantamount to banality, spectatorship analogous to driving, and driving an extension of killing. Each category displaces the other yet forms an equivalent state of being.

Mobility therefore has wider meaning both to social environment, and to how we perceive the characters that travel through fictionalised versions of it. Anna Cooper notes in this volume that the road movie's nostalgia started fetishising the mechanics of journeying at the very point when the global transport of goods, finance and people was becoming ubiquitous. But we can distinguish *Henry* and the serial killer road movie in general as eschatological rather than nostalgic. Whether in the post-Fordist impermanence of *Henry*, *Natural Born Killers*, *Kalifornia* and *Monster* (Patty Jenkins, 2003), or the gothic wilderness of rural horror, the killer presents what is left behind by upward mobility, the living evidence of an existence that progress sought to eradicate (Ballard 2008). Otis tells an open-eyed Becky that Henry is on his 'way out west', and she appears to have a naïve idealisation of him as a chivalric bringer of justice. Maintaining a fantasy of the ease of white, male American travel, *Henry* nevertheless marks the distance of its protagonist from this ideal, marked instead in terms of class and positioned in relation to decline.

* * *

The above analysis demonstrates how Henry's mobility separates him from the society through which he passes, at the same time as it expresses a condition essential to it. The serial killer is presented as radically other, yet also involves an assumption that the spectator will have some level of recognition with him. He thus conforms to Mark Seltzer's description of the serial killer's '*abnormal normality*' (Seltzer 1998: 106, emphasis in original), and provides an example of what Richard Dyer notes as the desire to confer fundamental significance upon what remains an exceedingly rare figure (2015). As a type, culture thus tends to characterise the serial killer as what Georg Simmel describes as the stranger, defined as one who is 'close to us, insofar as we feel between him and ourselves common features of a national, social, occupational, or generally human, nature. He is far from us, insofar as these common features extend beyond him or us, and connect us only because they connect a great many people' ([1908] 2009: 603). This nearness and distance goes some way towards describing the common fascination with both the serial killer and the road. The killer is strange yet somehow typical, just as the road provides escape from a social world which exalts it as a model for reorganising life according to (a)utopian visions.

As Simmel mentions, identification with the stranger occurs not at an individual, but at a 'generally human' level. The ascription by *Henry* of this generally human level to an almost abstracted figure of the white male killer at its centre is itself significant. Those other than the white American male who embark upon the road tend less often to embody universal ideals, occupying instead a position defined by limitation: the female serial killers of *Monster*, *Butterfly Kiss* (Michael Winterbottom, 1995) (Mazierska and Rascaroli 2006: 186) and *Baise Moi* (Virginie Despentes, 2000) frequently meet obstacles to their passage. The Mexican *Perdita Durango* (Álex de la Iglesia, 1997) contends with roadblocks, traffic jams and poverty, and the killer couple in *Das Deutsche Kettensägen Massaker/The German Chainsaw Massacre* (Christoph Schlingensief, 1990) must negotiate travel between the newly unified East and West Berlin. As indicated in the British comedy *Sightseers*, these limitations are not a refusal of wider significance, but an acknowledgement of particularity, often commonly held, but rarely found in a US road culture that would present itself as universal.

Sightseers

Sightseers follows a caravan trip from the English midlands into the northern countryside by a couple, Chris and Tina (her full name presumably Christina), on what Chris refers to as an 'erotic odyssey'. As in *Henry*, the spectator can neither identify with, nor be completely distanced from, the protagonists, but this produces not so much disturbance as condescension. We can laugh both at the disdain of a snobby woman towards Tina's taste for 'clutter' and at the pot pourri into which Tina places her face during sex. The places they visit are quaintly ridiculous, and mismatches are a motif of the *mise en scène*: Chris broods in a campsite children's playhouse, and after an argument a distraught Tina buys a three-foot souvenir pencil from the Pencil Museum to write to her mother. They meet a cyclist, Martin, who sleeps in a self-designed contraption he calls a carapod, explaining that 'what with the growing displacement of persons due to the instability of politics I'm hoping that this will become a whole new way of living for economic migrants'. Tina remarks that 'it looks like an alien's coffin', to which Chris responds apologetically 'Tina hasn't travelled much' (in an implied gendering of the power associated with mobility, see Tyree 2016). Resenting his friendship with Chris, Tina eventually pushes the diminutive carapod off a cliff with Martin inside.

Unlike *Henry*'s unmotivated actions, the protagonists of *Sightseers* provide a surfeit of reasons for their behaviours. Chris states on their first stop, at the Crich Tramway Museum, that 'mobility is the key to personal opportunity. That's why I prefer the Abbey Oxford as a caravan, because I'm the captain of my own fate', shortly before ramming the vehicle into a visitor for dropping a crisp packet. Killing is an act of redress: Chris explains of his second victim that 'it was smug complacency that killed Ian'. When a visitor to Kimberley Stone Circle brusquely orders Tina to clean up after her dog, Chris clubs him to death, quips 'Report that to the National Trust mate', then expands upon a philosophy of killing predators and the passing of the rights of the Lordly class to ravish peasant women, concluding 'Don't thank me Tina, thank the democratic process.' To Tina's hesitation about murdering innocent people Chris points out that 'He's not innocent, he's a *Daily Mail* reader.'[6] Before committing her own first murder, Tina argues that killing reduces the population's carbon footprint, leading Chris to ponder 'So you're saying murder is green?'

The caravan in *Sightseers* is to the romance of car culture what staying in Britain is to holidaymaking: disappointing. As a place of truncated domesticity, it encourages not only ridicule, but a pang of recognition at such awkward smallness elevated into an entire way of life. Such a perception of national pettiness characterises much cultural commentary on the place of the British road, as summarised by Peter Merriman thus:

> Britain's roads are relatively short and congested, 'lacking the mystique' and expansiveness of America's highways (Picken): 'Britain seemed so notably deficient in motorway culture compared with other countries, particularly the United States.

The idea of a proper British road movie was laughable.' (Will Self) 'Now we are a rain-soaked dime of a country, shrunk by roads into an awayday island where everywhere is near everywhere else, nowhere is worth going to and the journey in between is a misery [. . .] In other countries, roads are the carriers of romance and they spawn genre movies and books [. . .]' (Stuart Jeffries) 'In Britain, the cultural status of the motorway remains [. . .] rooted, unwaveringly, in the very opposite of America's road-movie romance with the highway.' (Malcolm Bracewell) (Merriman 2007: 18–19)

We may see this distance from the romance of the road as itself what constitutes a distinct road culture, in examples from *Summer Holiday* (Peter Yates, 1963) to *The Trip* (Michael Winterbottom, 2010), *Magical Mystery Tour* (Lennon, Harrison, McCartney, Starr, 1967), *On the Buses* (Harry Booth, 1971), *Chitty Chitty Bang Bang* (Ken Hughes, 1968) to *Genevieve* (Henry Cornelius, 1953).[7] The vehicles in these films are cumbersome and slow: in *Genevieve* the vintage car plays host to a pedigree of amateur sportsmanship and nobility in defeat. Rather than anti-authoritarian revolt, the first scene of *Summer Holiday* takes care to state that the youngsters have obtained the Routemaster with the official sanction of London Buses. This culture is indeed 'laughable', but deliberately so, because it is based in a consciousness of its own stature.

Sightseers belongs then to the comic traditions informing the British road movie, in which the relationship with the passenger is both fraught and key, and the protagonists exemplify more a class or type than the abstracted individual implied in the US model. The emphasis in the British road movie tends to be on industrial heritage over the fetishisation of speed, folk over pop culture, and the boredom of the trip, while landscape passes from the slow motorway to a nature which is picturesque rather than immense, farmland rather than wilderness. The method of transport is a source of inconvenience rather than mastery, and a common motif is the sudden stop, whether as a breakdown, lunch break, for a traffic policeman or whatever else. The road itself then is more functional (Picken 1999) than romantic, and the point of the journey is the need to actually get to a specific place, which, however, remains often beyond reach. Thus the British contribution to the road movie is the dramatic – usually comedic – state of *not-quite-getting-there*, whether to an actual destination or the realisation of the protagonists' dreams (including in non-comedic examples like *Locke* (Steven Knight, 2013), the art film *Radio On* (Chris Petit, 1979), or the psychogeographic circularity of *London Orbital* (Iain Sinclair, Chris Petit, 2002)).

Such falling short occurs in *Sightseers* through the tension it establishes between abandon and restraint. Sightseeing is probably the least wildly

THE SERIAL KILLER ROAD MOVIE 283

escapist form of pleasure-seeking, subject to itinerary and the regulation of common spaces and defined by the work ethic against which tourism is defined (see John Urry on 'the tourist gaze' (2002: 2), also Simon Evans and Martin Spaul 2003). The characters' route is governed by a schedule meticulously charted over a map of northern England during the opening credits, and the visits are to improving heritage sites. Regulation is itself a source of pleasure: Chris and Tina cement a friendship with an older couple at an abbey as they gaze in lingering dismay at some small graffiti which Chris draws their attention to, reading the legend, 'ROB LOVES KERRY'. Even the killings embody structure, rising up the class scale from a yob, to professionals and then an aristocrat, and two of them regard littering and dog fouling, in other words disputes over the rules guiding the use of space.

These disciplinary pleasures indicate a culture of close personal identification with the rules. But they also contain an underlying aggression which undoes the very regulation that gives them expression. The killings are bursts of anger, their justifications incoherent and their depictions emphasise bodily ruin, as the litterer's blood splatters the wheel of the caravan and the pulpy remains of the ex-public schoolboy's head are shown in close-up. At one point Tina swerves the caravan into a passing bicyclist so as to put emphasis into an argument. Their spree is marked as a release of pent-up, wild energy: a red balloon rises skywards at the first murder, untethered from the grasp of a bystander as a discordant synth sound harmonises and the couple hug, skirting the ambiguity of horror and excitement, and associating killing with the passions. The holiday, therefore, enables a progressive loosening of constrictions, from the opening at Tina's suburban home to the penultimate sequence when the couple howl with their stolen puppy on top of a cliff as they set the caravan ablaze, to 'The Power of Love' (Figure 16.2).

But like the deficient romance of the British road, attempts at physical or emotional freedom result only in awkward embarrassment. Chris's initial motivation is to loosen his writer's block, inspiring Tina to state her aim of 'personal empowerment and thinking out of the box, and I've been in a box and don't want to go back' (again, the gendering of constriction is implied). Yet release is literally foreign to them. Chris first had the idea that Tina could be his muse when looking at her at capoeira class, although he never writes anything and his work 'sabbatical' is actually redundancy; the French acoustic song 'Amours Toujours, Tendresse, Caresses' plays as the couple first arrive at the campsite but Chris rather ruins the moment when he aggressively overtakes some surprised campers, laughing; posh couple Ian and Janice boast of their German voice-activated stereo unit;

Figure 16.2 Abandon to the passions.

and Tina's well-boiled pasta ends up slopped around the mouth of a bear-shaped plastic bin when Chris fails to return to the campsite for dinner, having immobilised himself at a pub.

One can go so far as to say that automotive prowess is itself at odds with the awkwardness sometimes ascribed to the English, not least by the English themselves. Indeed, the construction of a national motorway system was delayed until the late 1950s in part by concern that such a German or US invention was unsuitable to the national temperament (Urry 2004). Britain's uniquely restrictive speed limits began as early as the 1865 'Red Flag' Act which required all road locomotives to travel at a maximum of four miles per hour and be preceded by a man carrying a red flag. A more contemporary example resides in the permanently aggrieved attitude incarnated by the presenters of *Top Gear*, who imply a national sense of self that is defined by the awareness of being outclassed by foreign rivals. *Sightseers*' mismatch between heritage visits and serial murder is then just one example of the anxiety of physical overreaching that historically structures discourse around the road in the UK. The ultimate opening of the M1 met disquiet over the effect that previously unimaginable speeds and distance would have on otherwise law-abiding drivers, and a flurry of press reports of outbreaks of 'Motorway madness'.

At the opening of the Birmingham and St Albans Bypass in November 1959 the Conservative MP Eric Marples warned that,

> It will bring immense benefits if drivers use discipline, common sense and obey the rules. But disaster and tragedy may descend on those who drive recklessly or selfishly. For on this magnificent road the speed which can easily be reached is so great that senses may be numbed and judgment warped. (Cited in Merriman 2007: 153)

Restraint is thus in these conceptions a vigilance against one's own propensity for criminal recklessness, and common adherence to internalised codes of behaviour the measure lest civility reveal itself to be only a fragile veneer.

Throughout *Sightseers* the remnants of an archaic Englishness battle with the forces of order, as seen when police apprehend some Portsmouth shamans in the campsite's yurt field for sacrificing one of the owner's chickens to the Goddess Kali. The murder of the ex-public schoolboy at Kimberley Stone Circle plays to a recitation of Blake's 'Jerusalem', a Romantic ode to a national ideal set to Elgar, which jarringly halts midline on the words 'dark Satanic . . .' to a final whack by Chris's improvised wooden club. Unruly forces are thus indigenous to England's green and pleasant land, part of the very landscape as the protagonists pass over ley lines and stone circles, and hear at the Pencil Museum the legend of a strange, black, underground material unleashed by a storm. The point of all this, then, is that regulation does not signal an absence of passion but a necessary requirement whose removal the protagonists of *Sightseers* cannot handle, and which the film satirically presents as a national condition, put in place against the potential eruption of unruly forces. But in the end, the not-quite-getting-there of the British road enables Tina's ultimate self-realisation. She stands with Chris, who has previously accused her of witchcraft, to enact what he thinks is a suicide pact. He jumps from the Ribblehead Viaduct, a huge nineteenth-century railway structure erected, significantly, over the site of an ancient field system, to land alone with an abrupt thud.

In neither *Henry* nor *Sightseers* is the protagonists' mobility solely an aberrant monstrosity, as it bears also a marked normality, even banality, in relation to the wider world through which they pass. Henry represents the serial killer as an abstracted form of either social alienation, or evil itself. *Sightseers* instead particularises its killers' compulsions as a way of ridiculing English eccentricity. Rather than anything fundamental about the serial killer, it embodies the British road movie's generic property of not-quite-getting-there, and also has an affinity with holiday films like *Carry on Camping* (Gerald Thomas, 1969), *Nuts in May* (Mike Leigh, 1976) or even *The Italian Job* (Peter Collinson, 1969), in which individual idiosyncrasy must negotiate group belonging in a post-colonial Britain. It adds to the conception of domestic tourism in the UK as grey and constrained, other examples of which include Morrissey's 'Every Day Is Like Sunday' and Martin Parr's *Boring Postcards* (2004), in which hopes remain drearily or comically unrealised. Yet while *Henry*'s banality is disturbing, seeming to reveal the destabilising infinity of the void, in *Sightseers* it produces a deflating comedy of manners in which the abandonment of restraint remains delineated by a definitive deficiency and petty awkwardness.

Conclusion

Henry: Portrait of a Serial Killer and *Sightseers* provide contrasting cultural manifestations of the meaning associated with automotive culture, even down to their attitudes to meaningfulness itself. The nomadic existence presented in *Henry* acquires a fundamental importance, even if that is of the horror of an ultimate lack of meaning. In *Sightseers*, however, it satirises a farcical inability to live up to modest pretension. These differences are formed by context, for travel acquires an excessive significance in relation to the US, charged with the figure of the Discoverer, the frontiersman, of expansion and Manifest Destiny (see Cohan and Hark 1997: 1–2, or Anna Cooper in this volume). The UK's colonising mission spanned the globe, and yet its culture does not accord mobility quite the same role. Surely this can in part be explained by the loss of Britain's industrial pre-eminence by the age of the motorcar, and yet even in the eras of naval and railway power, there is a tendency in some travel narratives, from *Robinson Crusoe* (Defoe 1719) to *The Chronicles of Narnia* (Lewis 1950–6), to present movement as melancholic or perilous, and their protagonists as desiring a return home and the establishment of stability. We may be able then to speculate that the US conception of mobility as a universal property of individuality responds to a more diffuse, but totalising, process of imperial control and cultural hegemony, rather than the UK's geopolitical demarcations between home and colony, and its settled and territorially delineated flows of power and subservience.

This chapter's aim was to provide an analysis not only of what significance mobility brings to the serial killer road movie, but of *how* it produces this significance. The findings reveal that the connection lies in the position of being set aside, of being both at-odds-with yet arising-from a frame of reference set by the given conception of stability, as seen in both *Henry* and *Sightseers*. Figures as diverse as the outlaw, exile, or vagabond, mercenary, merchant or mendicant preacher each find their place in society to be defined by their movement through it, and while they may occupy a position anywhere from sacred to abject, their potential is to fascinate societies for whom stability is equivalent to security. This fascination is especially pronounced with regard to the serial killer, who, like the Western gunslinger, the chivalric knight or the *flâneur*, is, despite his actual historical existence, primarily a product of the creative imagination. The nearness and distance that defines such a figure is thus determined by the mechanisms of narrative drama, which give a different meaning to the category of 'motivation' within cinema: as no longer a description of a potentially sympathetic character but a literal fact of physical movement, carrying us along with the action without absorbing us into identification with those performing it. That is, their nearness-yet-distance in relation to the spectator leaves them able to define an estrangement from normality, *at the same time* as they characterise something essential to it. This ambivalence helps shed light on the imagination that the serial killer is both a general yet elusive presence, which forms only one of a series of tensions surrounding a character conceived of as mythical but modern, bizarre but banal, mobile but trapped, a grim figure of the true crime chronicles and a fantastical product of the cultural imagination. Each of these tensions results from a simultaneous nearness and distance, which gives the serial killer a particular power to represent broad truths about society, whether the post-industrial alienation of *Henry* or the disciplinary Englishness of *Sightseers*, without requiring us to actually stand in a position of identification with the characters who embody them.

Roads, then, do not only carry away, they also lead back, and so finally, the journey taken by this investigation leads us back to the starting point, the two films' titles. Sightseeing and portraiture indicate fixed objects of vision that are different from and older than the cinematic images that relay them here. This difference establishes such a position of at-odds-with yet arising-from, by indicating an absorbing visual medium and a distance from its formal means, whether in *Henry: Portrait of a Serial Killer* or *Sightseers*. Meanwhile, the cinema itself presents an illusion of movement, but to an immobile spectator (see Bruno 2002: 99). Looking beyond the cinema, the corporate-bureaucratic economies that give rise to the automobile or the film industries and that are products of capitalist modernity have eradicated nomadism as a viable form of society, at the same time as they continually tear up settled stability by compelling the migration of people in their millions, whether within or across countries. Meanwhile our melancholic human condition, our consciousness of our own mortality, condemns us to awareness of a transience on Earth that we can never fully accept. We are – as spectators, as moderns, or as human beings – mobile, at the same time as we are trapped; viewing in the imagined mobility of the cinematic serial killer the extreme predicament of a position common to us all.

Notes

1 I am grateful to Anna Cooper, Rebecca Harrison and Laura Sava for their help on earlier drafts, and retain of course every responsibility for all subsequently remaining defects.
2 Although fiction often reveals the killer to be female, the surprise this assumes is evidence that the figure is assumed to be male. Indeed, *Henry* presents the serial killer as an abstract force, and *Sightseers* as perverse romanticism (as Cameron (1996) points out, those female serial killers who do exist tend to be understood in relation to men).
3 A debatable but persistent notion ever since the original case.
4 A seller of stolen goods.
5 Which share with other French serial killer road movies a desire to question the nature of the killer's and the spectator's gaze.
6 The National Trust for Places of Historic Interest or Natural Beauty is the largest membership organisation in Britain, with over four million subscribers, and the right-wing tabloid the *Daily Mail* is (with *The Sun*) the country's highest-circulation newspaper. Their mention implies two variants of national petit-bourgeois life, the former conservationist, the latter conservative.
7 Specifically, that is, in road movies: the Bond franchise, for example, is different.

Works Cited

Avila, Eric (2014), *The Folklore of the Freeway: Race and Revolt in the Modernist City*, Minneapolis: University of Minnesota Press.

Ballard, Finn (2008), 'No Trespassing: The Post-millennial Road Horror Movie', *Irish Journal of Gothic and Horror Stories*, 4, 8 June.

Beckman, Jörg (2004), 'Mobility and Safety', *Theory, Culture and Society*, 21:4–5, pp. 81–100.

Berman, Marshall (1983), *All that is Solid Melts into Air: The Experience of Modernity*, London: Verso.

Brodsly, David (1981), *L.A. Freeway, an Appreciative Essay*, Berkeley: University of California Press.

Bruno, Giuliana (2002), *Atlas of Emotion: Journeys in Art, Architecture and Film*, New York: Verso.

Cameron, Deborah (1996), 'Wanted: The Female Serial Killer', *Trouble and Strife*, 33, pp. 21–8.

Cohan, Steven and Ina Rae Hark (eds) (1997), *The Road Movie Book*, London: Routledge.
Corrigan, Timothy (1991), *A Cinema Without Walls: Movies and Culture after Vietnam*, New Brunswick, NJ: Rutgers University Press.
Crary, Jonathan (1999), *Suspensions of Perception: Attention, Spectacle and Modern Culture*, Cambridge, MA: The MIT Press.
Defoe, Daniel (1719), *Robinson Crusoe*, London: W. Taylor.
Dimendberg, Edward (1995), 'The Will to Motorization: Cinema, Highways and Modernity', *October*, 73, Summer, pp. 90–137.
Dyer, Richard (2015), *Lethal Repetition: Serial Killing in European Cinema*, London: Palgrave.
Evans, Simon and Martin Spaul (2003), 'Straight Ways and Loss: The Tourist Encounter with Woodlands and Forests', in David Crouch and Nina Lubbren (eds), *Visual Culture and Tourism*, Oxford: Berg, pp. 205–23.
Featherstone, Mike (2005), 'Automobilities: An Introduction', in Mike Featherstone, Nigel Thrift and John Urry (eds), *Automobilities*, London: Sage, pp. 1–24.
Hantke, Steffen (2001), 'Violence Incorporated: John McNaughton's *Henry: Portrait of a Serial Killer* and the Uses of Gratuitous Violence in Popular Narrative', *College Literature*, 28:2, pp. 29–47.
Hantke, Steffen (2002), 'Monstrosity without a Body: Representational Strategies in the Popular Serial Killer Film', *Post Script*, 22:2, pp. 34–54.
Hogg, James [1824] (1997), *The Private Memoirs and Confessions of a Justified Sinner*, Ware: Wordsworth.
Isenberg, Nancy (2016), *White Trash: The 400-Year Untold History of Class in America*, New York: Viking.
Laderman, David (2002), 'The 1980s Postmodern Road Movie', in *Driving Visions Exploring the Road Movie*, Austin: University of Texas Press, pp. 132–74.
Lewis, C. S. (1950–6), *The Chronicles of Narnia*, London: Geoffrey Bles.
Mazdon, Lucy (2009), 'Masculinity on the Road in the Films of Cédric Kahn', *New Readings*, 10, pp. 42–56.
Mazierska, Ewa and Rascaroli, Laura (2006), *Crossing New Europe: Postmodern Travel and the European Road Movie*, London: Wallflower Press.
Merriman, Peter (2007), *Driving Spaces: A Cultural-Historical Geography of England's M1 Motorway*, Oxford: Blackwell.
Morton, Jim (1999), 'Horror on the Highway', in Jack Sargeant and Stephanie Watson (eds), *Lost Highways. An Illustrated History of Road Movies*, London: Creation, pp. 119–29.
Parr, Martin (2004), *Boring Postcards*, London: Phaidon.
Picken, Susan (1999), 'British Road Movies', in Jack Sargeant and Stephanie Watson (eds), *Lost Highways. An Illustrated History of Road Movies*, London: Creation, pp. 221–31.

Romao, Tico (1994), '"Guns and Gas": investigating the 1970s car chase film', in Yvonne Tasker (ed.), *Action and Adventure Cinema*, London: Routledge, pp. 130–53.

Rubin, Martin (1992), 'The Grayness of Darkness: *The Honeymoon Killers* and its impact on psychokiller cinema', *Velvet Light Trap*, 30, Autumn, pp. 48–64.

Sargeant, Jack (1999), 'Killer Couples', in Jack Sargeant and Stephanie Watson (eds), *Lost Highways: An Illustrated History of Road Movies*, London: Creation, pp. 147–69.

Sargeant, Jack and Stephanie Watson (eds) (1999), *Lost Highways. An Illustrated History of Road Movies*, London: Creation.

Seltzer, Mark (1998), *Serial Killers: Death and Life in America's Wound Culture*, New York: Routledge.

Simmel, Georg [1908] (2009), 'Excursus on the Stranger', in A. J. Blasi, A. K. Jacobs and M. Kanjirathinkal (trans. and eds), *Sociology: Inquiries into the Construction of Social Forms*, Leiden and Boston: Brill, pp. 601–5.

Simpson, Philip L. (2000), *Psycho Paths: Tracking the Serial Killer through Contemporary American Film and Fiction*, Carbondale: Southern Illinois University Press.

Stevenson, Robert Louis [1886] (2012), *Strange Case of Dr. Jekyll and Mr. Hyde*, London: Penguin.

Tyree, J. M. (2016) 'Murder, Considered as One of the Fine Arts of Women's Liberation: Notes on *Sightseers*', *Critical Quarterly*, 58:1, pp. 36–40.

Urry, John (2002), *The Tourist Gaze*, London: Sage.

Urry, John (2004), 'The "system" of automobility', *Theory, Culture and Society*, 21:4–5, October, pp. 25–39.

Walkowitz, Judith R. (1992), *City of Dreadful Delight: Narratives of Sexual Danger in Late-Victorian London*, Chicago: University of Chicago Press.

Willis, Martin (2006), 'Jack the Ripper, Sherlock Holmes and the narrative of detection', in Alexandra Warwick and Martin Willis (eds), *Jack The Ripper: Media, Culture, History*, Manchester: Manchester University Press, pp. 144–58.

Wollen, Peter (2002), 'Introduction: Cars and Culture', in Peter Wollen and Joe Kerr (eds), *Autopia: Cars and Culture*, London: Reaktion Books, pp. 10–20.

Index

4 luni, 3 săptămâni și 2 zile/*4 Months, 3 Weeks and 2 Days* (film), 130
6 Desires: DH Lawrence and Sardinia (film), 8, 86–98
12:08 East of Bucharest see *A fost sau n-a fost?*
24/7: Late Capitalism and the Ends of Sleep (book), 4
360 (film), 19
400 Blows, The see *quatrecents coups, Le*

A fost sau n-a fost?/*12:08 East of Bucharest* (film), 130
À l'intérieur/*Inside* (film), 221
abandonados, Los/*The Abandoned* (film), 224, 225, 225
Abbey Oxford caravan, 281
Abrazo de Serpiente, El/*Embrace of the Serpent* (film), 12–13, 235–51
Acacias, Las (film), 240
Academy Awards of Motion Picture Arts and Sciences, The, 242
Accented Cinema: Exilic and Diasporic Filmmaking, An (book), 5
Adams, Brooke, 260
Adventures of Priscilla, Queen of the Desert, The (film), 238
Aeneid, The (epic poem), 10
'Aesthetics of Hunger, An' see 'Esthetic of Hunger, An'
Africa, 25, 30
Agacinski, Sylviane, 171–2, 180n9
Airbnb, 264
Ajapikku unustatakse meie nimi/*Our Name Will Gradually Be Forgotten* (film), 115n3
Alaska, 264, 266
Alice in den Städten/*Alice in the Cities* (film), 237

Alighieri, Dante, 10
All that Is Solid Melts into Air: The Experience of Modernity (book), 4
Alps, 224
Alter, Nora, 88
Altman, Rick, 168
Amazon Prime Video, 216
Amazon region, 242–9
Amazônia desconhecida/*Unknown Amazon* (film), 248
America see USA
American Honey (film), 252, 258, 267
American Werewolf in London, An (film), 215
Americas, 30
  Latin America, 12–13, 235–51
  North America, 186, 220, 229n8, 249n2
  South America, 240
  Southern Cone, 240
Among the Living/*Aux yeux des vivants* (film), 223
'Amours, Toujours, Tendresse, Caresses' (song), 283
Angelopoulos, Theo, 108
Apetri, George Bogdan, 136, 138
Apocalypse Now (film), 245
Apollo, 29
Appadurai, Arjun, 52, 57, 64n4
Appalachian Mountains, 221
Arata, Stephen D., 199
Äratus/*Awakening* (film), 106
archives de la planète, Les (film series), 30
Argentina, 235–7, 248
Around the World in Eighty Days (novel), 20
Arrivée d'un train en gare de La Ciotat, L'/*The Arrival of a Train at La Ciotat* (film), 2, 7, 37, 40
Arthur, Paul, 98
Arthus-Bertrand, Yann, 19

Ashes in the Snow (film), 106
Asia, 25, 30, 64n6
Atlas of Emotion (book), 4
Atrocious (film), 224
Augé, Marc, 32, 42–3, 138, 150–1
Aurora (film), 9, 130–5, 139, 144
Auschwitz, 96, 97, 118, 126, 128
Austerlitz, 86
Austin, Guy, 222
Australia, 28, 84n1, 221, 223, 238
Austria, 31, 194, 224
Austrian Film Commission, 224
Autopia, Tomorrowland exhibit, 275
Aux yeux des vivants / Among the Living (film), 223
Avellar, José Carlos, 245–6
Awakening see *Äratus*

B Sixth Avenue, 123
B52 bomber aircraft, 91
Babel (film), 19
Bach, Johann Sebastian, 11, 170, 173–8, 180n10
Bachelard, Gaston, 150
Badlands (film), 258, 271
Baise-Moi (film), 280
Baker, Robert, 21, 23
Bakhtin, Mikhail, 7, 70–5, 112–13
Balada triste de trompeta / The Last Circus (film), 227
Balázs, Béla, 31
Balk, Fairuza, 259
Balkan war, 226
Ballard, J. G., 279
Ballyglunin station, 77, 78
Balzac, Honoré de, 33n2
Baño del Papa, El / The Pope's Toilet (film), 239–40
Barbarossa, Operation, 127
Barbican, 97
Barbican Estate, 96
Bardan, Alice, 151
Baron, Jaimie, 95
Barthes, Roland, 10, 171
Barton, Ruth, 109
Baschiera, Stefano, 12, 270
Battersby, Christine, 256
Baudelaire, Charles, 4
Bauman, Zygmunt, 5, 152, 185
Bayman, Louis, 13
Bazin, André, 3, 87–8, 243
BBC, 19, 32, 33, 42
Beautiful Planet, A (TV series), 19

Beck, Ulrich, 185
Beckford, William, 199
Beck-Gernsheim, Elisabeth, 185
Before Midnight (film), 178
Before Sunrise (film), 11, 167–82
Before Sunset (film), 178
Behdad, Ali, 63
Beinoriūtė, Giedrė, 106
Bela Kiss: Prologue / The Kiss of a Killer (film), 224
Belanger, Nina, 261
Belgium, 12, 219–20, 223, 226, 227–9
Bell, Duncan, 107
Bełżec, 126
Bend it Like Beckham (film), 64n2
Benjamin, Walter, 133
Benz, Karl, 278
Bereg, 122
Beregszász, 124
Bergfelder, Tim, 218
Bergman, Ingmar, 11
Bergson, Henri, 175–7
Berlin, 280
Berlin Express (film), 40
Berlin Wall, 185
Berman, Marshall, 4
Besse, Jean-Marc, 23, 24
Besson, Luc, 222
Bête humaine, La (film), 40, 272
Betjeman, John, 42
Bhabha, Homi, 104, 112, 114, 236, 245
Bhaji on The Beach (film), 64n2
Bibliothèque Pascal (film), 9, 147–61
Bicycle Thieves see *Ladri di biciclette*
Birkenau, 126
Birmingham and St Albans bypass, 285
Black and Tans, 76, 81
Black Lives Matter, 256
Black Sea, 139
Blake, William, 285
Bloch, Ernst, 151
Blomkamp, Neil, 11, 184, 186, 189–90
Blood Glacier see *Blutgletscher*
BLS Südtirol-Alto Adige, 224
Blutgletscher / Blood Glacier (film), 224
Bodanzky, Jorge, 245–6
Body Memory see *Kehamälu*
Bollók, Csaba, 158
Bollywood, 7, 52–69
Bollywood / Hollywood (film), 52
Bombay, 51, 56
Bond, Ward, 77, 83
Bong, Joon-ho, 11, 184, 186

INDEX   293

Bonnie and Clyde (film), 257
Border as Method, or, the Multiplication of Labor (book), 6
Boring Postcards (book), 286
Borough Park, 123, 124
Boston, 25
Boulevard des Capucines, 23
Bourriaud, Nicolas, 160
Boyle, Danny, 43
Boym, Svetlana, 151
Brabon, Benjamin A., 205
Brah, Avtar, 50, 61, 62
Brampton, 54, 61, 64
Brazil, 223, 236–7, 239, 240, 243–6, 248, 249n1, 249n2
Breillat, Catherine, 221–2
Brides of Dracula, The (film), 201, 202, 204, 207
Brief Encounter (film), 7, 36–49, 169
British Screen Yorkshire, 218, 219
Brolin, James, 260
Brooklyn, 89, 122, 123
Brown, Wendy, 253
Bruno, Giuliana, 4, 256
Brussels, 25
Bruxelles Capitale, 220
Bruzzi, Stella, 123
Bucharest, 135, 136, 138
Büchse die Pandora, Die / Pandora's Box (film), 272
Budapest, 122, 124
Bulgaria, 224, 225–6
Busk, 127
Butler, Judith, 6
Butterfly Kiss (film), 280

Caged see *Captifs*
California, 220, 226
Calvaire (film), 223, 225
Cambria boat, 81
Caminho das Nuvens, O / The Middle of the World (film), 240
Campanella, Juan José, 236
Canada, 50–3, 57–9, 61–2, 219, 229n8, 267
Canal +, 227–9
Canclini, García, 237
Cannes, 220
Cannes Film Festival, 227
Canudo, Ricciotto, 3, 31
Captifs / Caged (film), 226
Carell, Steve, 259
Carnforth station, 36, 47, 48
Carry on Camping (film), 285–6

Carter, Ian, 89
Casablanca (film), 169, 171
Casey, Edward, 38, 39
Castro, Teresa, 29
Ceaușescu (boulevard), 138
Cenciarelli, Carlo, 11
Central do Brasil / Central Station (film), 235, 237–43, 248–9
Centre du Cinéma et de l'Audiovisuel de la Fédération Wallonie-Bruxelles, 219–20
Centre national du cinéma et de l'image animée, 219, 227
Certeau, Michel de, 4, 131
Cervantes Saavedra, Miguel de, 10
Chadha, Gurinder, 64n1, 64n2
Chaplin, Joyce E., 31
Charles Urban Trading Company, 30
Chaudhuri, Shohini, 52
Chhatrapati Shivaji Terminus, 43
Chicago, 274–6, 279
Chion, Michel, 161n5
Chitty Chitty Bang Bang (film), 282
Chopra, Aditya, 64n2
Christie, Thomas, 167
Chronicles of Melanie see *Melānijas hronika*
Chronicles of Narnia, The (book series), 286
Cinema, Aspirinas e Urubus / Cinema, Aspirins and Vultures (film), 238, 240–1
Cinematic Journeys: Film and Movement (book), 3
Cinquegrani, Maurizio, 8–9
Clini, Clelia, 7
Clisby, Loressa, 19
Clover, Carol, 225
Cohan, Steven, 257–8
Cold Prey see *Fritt vilt*
Cold War, 96
Colombia, 236, 242
comédie humaine, La (book series), 33n2
Comment, Bernard, 21, 23
Como Era Gostoso o Meu Francês / How Tasty Was My Little Frenchman (film), 243
Comodines / Cops (film), 237
Condition of Postmodernity, The (book), 254–5
Cong, 70, 71, 73, 75, 76, 80, 81, 83
Conservative Party, 285
Constanta, 139
Content (film), 8, 86–98
Cooper, Anna, 13, 240, 279

Cooper, Kenneth, 180n14
Cops see *Comodines*
Coração do Brasil/Heart of Brazil (film), 248
Corrigan, Timothy, 10, 87, 241
Cosgrove, Denis, 28
Cosmorama, 7, 25
Cosmos: A Sketch of a Physical Description of the Universe (TV series), 21
Cottage, The (film), 219, 223, 225
Cotton, Joseph, 242
Coward, Noël, 44
Crary, Jonathan, 4
Craven, Wes, 216
Crişan, Marian, 131, 143, 145n4
Croatia, 229n4
Crossing New Europe: Postmodern Travel and the European Road Movie (book), 6
Cub see *Welp*
Cuarón, Alfonso, 236
Cucco, Marco, 217
Culture of Speed: The Coming of Immediacy, The (book), 4
Cultures of Exile: Images of Displacement (book), 6
Cuman, Silvana, 248
Curse of the Werewolf, The (film), 201
Czech Republic, 194

Daily Mail (newspaper), 281, 288n6
Dallas, Texas, 261, 262–3
Dalton, Walter, 265
Damon, Matt, 89
Dánél, Mónika, 161n6
Dano, Paul, 256
Dans ton sommeil/In Their Sleep (film), 223
Dardenne brothers, 222
Darnborough, Anthony, 200
Dartmoor, 202
Dave, Paul, 187–8
Davis, Colin, 74
de Hooch, Pieter, 151
de Luca, Tiago, 7
De Sica, Vittorio, 243
'De Tierras y de Utopías' (film project), 248
Dead End (film), 220–1
Dead Snow see *Død snø*
Death of Mr. Lazarescu, The see *Moartea domnului Lăzărescu*
Debord, Guy, 94
Debrecen, 124

Deep in the Woods see *Promenons-nous dans le bois*
Defoe, Daniel, 10
Delanglard, Charles, 23, 24, 25
Deleuze, Cinema and National Identity: Narrative Time in National Contexts (book), 104
Deleuze, Gilles, 104, 114
Delluc, Louis, 31
Democracity exhibit, 275
Denis, Claire, 221–2
Dennison, Stephanie, 237
Derrida, Jacques, 73, 74
Desai, Jigna, 55, 56, 64n1
Desbois, Patrick, Father, 125, 126, 127
Descent, The (film), 221
Deutsche Kettensägen Massaker, Das/The German Chainsaw Massacre (film), 280
Devil Rides Out, The (film), 207, 211–13
Devil Thumbs a Ride, The (film), 273
Devil's Bridge (film), 223
Di Caprio, Leonardo, 242
Diarios de Motocicleta/The Motorcycle Diaries (film), 237–42, 248–9
Dickens, Charles, 39
Dido and Aeneas (opera), 168
Digital Dead End (book), 265–6
Dilwale Dulhania Le Jayenge (film), 64n2
Dima, Vlad, 195
Dimanche à Pekin (film), 88
Dimendberg, Edward, 4, 11, 278
Disneyworld, 275
District 9 (film)), 189, 190
Divan (film), 8, 119, 122–5, 126, 128
Divine Comedy, The (epic poem), 10
Død snø/Dead Snow (film), 223–4
Dog Soldiers (film), 221
Dohány Street Synagogue, 124
Dombey and Son (novel), 39
Don Quixote de La Mancha (novel), 10
Door to Silence see *porte del silenzio, Le*
Douglas, Eileen, 120
Dracula (novel), 199, 200, 206
Dracula (1958 film), 201–2, 206–7
Dracula: Prince of Darkness (film), 200, 202–3, 204–5, 207
Drive (film), 258
Dude, Where's My Car? (film), 11
Duel (film), 271, 273
Dulac, Germaine, 3
Dumont, Bruno, 221–2

Dust Devil (film), 271
Dyer, Richard, 45, 46, 280

Earth, 5, 20, 22, 24, 25, 28, 29, 32, 156, 183–4, 189–96, 256, 287
Earth Dies Screaming, The (film), 203–4, 213
East Anglia, 96
East India Company, 201
Easy Rider (film), 239, 254
L'Eclisse (film), 180n17
Edwards, Justin D., 199, 209
Eiffel Tower, 200
Egyptian pyramids, 25
Einsatzgruppen, 125, 127
Ekskursantė / The Excursionist (film), 106
Elavad pildid / Living Images (film), 115n3
Eleftheriotis, Dimitris, 3, 181n18
Elgar, Edward, 285
Elmshorn, 88
Elsaesser, Thomas, 260
Elysian Fields, 189
Elysium (film), 11, 184, 187–96
Embrace of the Serpent see *Abrazo de Serpiente, El*
Engels, Friedrich, 4
England, 25, 26, 44, 94, 155, 203, 204, 206, 218, 283–7
Epstein, Jean, 179n4
Erice, Victor, 82
Espinosa, Julio García, 238
espíritu de la colmena, El / The Spirit of the Beehive (film), 82
'Esthetic of Hunger, An' (essay), 238, 249n4
Estonia, 8, 103–17, 121
Eubanks, Virginia, 265–6
Eureka: An Essay on the Material and Spiritual Universe (poem), 21
EuropaCorp, 222
Europe, 7–9, 12, 27, 30, 94, 101–63, 167, 186, 206–12, 215–31, 249n2
  East-Central, 145n3
  Eastern, 7–10, 89, 101–64, 183, 225–6, 229n8
  Western, 9, 126–8, 158, 183, 226
European Film Commission Network, 218
European Media Programme, 219
European Regional Development Fund, 219
European Union (EU), 8, 147–8, 225
Everett, Wendy, 6
'Every Day Is Like Sunday' (song), 286

Excursionist, The see *Ekskursantė*
Ezra, Elizabeth, 6

Fabrique 2, La, 227
Falicov, Tamara, 237
Falsche Bewegung / The Wrong Move (film), 237
Familia Rodante / Rolling Family (film), 239–40, 248–9
Feardotcom (film), 219
Fencer, The see *Vehkleja / Miekkailija / ENDEL – Der Fechter*
Filimon, Monica, 132, 145n1
Film Fund Luxembourg, 219
Fisher, Austin, 6
Fisher, Mark, 74, 186–7
Fisher, Terence, 11–12, 199–214
Fitzcarraldo (film), 246–7
Flaherty, Robert, 248
Flames of Passion (film), 45
Flinn, Caryl, 179n7
'For an Imperfect Cinema' (essay), 238
Ford, Henry, 274–6
Ford, John, 7, 70, 73, 77, 79–81
Foreign Land see *Terra Estrangeira*
Foster, Jodie, 189
Foucault, Michel, 5, 145n3, 149, 158–9, 252
France, 3, 12, 23, 25, 31, 42–3, 125–6, 128n3, 161n1, 161n4, 168, 175, 194, 215, 217–29, 239
Frankenstein (novel), 199, 200
Frankenstein (1931 film), 82–3
Frankenstein Created Woman (film), 201, 202, 207, 208
Freeman, Adam Ludford, 7–8
Fricke, Ron, 19
Friedrich, Caspar David, 22
Fritt vilt / Cold Prey (film), 224
From Moscow to Madrid: Postmodern Cities, European Cinema (book), 4
Frontière(s) / Frontier(s) (film), 221, 222, 223, 225, 226
Frozen River (film), 252, 267
Fujiwara, Chris, 11
Fukuyama, Francis, 186, 192
Futurama exhibit, 275

Galeano, Eduardo, 248
Galt, Rosalind, 261–2
Galway, 70, 75
Gance, Abel, 3
Gare de l'Est, 41

Gare d'Orsay, 37
Gare Montparnasse, 43
Gas Food Lodging (film), 13, 252, 259–63, 267
Gattaca (film), 184
Gazzera, Abbé, 25
General Motors, 275
Genevieve (film), 282
Georama, 7, 23, 24
German Chainsaw Massacre, The see *Deutsche Kettensägen Massaker, Das*
Germany, 88–90, 96–7, 115n3, 121, 127, 128n3, 140–3, 152, 158–9, 161n4, 204, 215, 219, 220, 223, 224, 225, 237, 243, 244, 280, 283, 284
Gestapo, 125
Global Panoramas, 24
Globalism, 31
Gluck, Pearl, 119, 122, 123, 124, 125
Goethe, Johann Wolfgang von, 22
Gold Coast, 223
Goldberg Variations (musical composition), 170–3, 178
Google Earth, 19, 32
Gorgon, The (film), 201
Gorzo, Andrei, 161n1
Grand Cairo, 25
Grand Central, 41
Grand voyage autour du Monde (exhibit), 26
Grandpa and Grandma see *Gyveno senelis ir bobutė*
Grapes of Wrath, The (novel), 264
Grave/Raw (film), 219
Gravity (film), 2
Great Britain, 12, 13, 26, 30, 38, 39, 158, 199–214, 215, 219, 220–1, 224, 226, 254, 270, 281–6
Great Globe, 25
Great Train Robbery, The (film), 2, 40
Greece, 161n4, 178, 189, 215
Greyhound Buses, 261
Griffiths, Alison, 4
Grimson, Alejandro, 240
Ground Control (book), 254
Guardian, The (newspaper), 36, 48, 237
Guerín, José Luis, 7, 70–85
Guerra, Ciro, 242–5
Guest (film), 80
Guilt Trip, The (film), 252, 259
Gunning, Tom, 27
Gyveno senelis ir bobutė/Grandpa and Grandma (film), 106

Hajdu, Szabolcs, 149, 152, 155, 158
Halberstam, Judith/Jack, 251, 254–5, 257, 263–4, 268n1
Hall, Stuart, 52
Hamburg, 88
Hamilton, Patrick, 203
Hammer Films, 199, 200
Hannam, Kevin, 186, 191
Hanoi, 91, 92
Hanover, 96
Happy Ending (film), 64n2
Harrison, Rebecca, 3
Harvey, David, 4, 254–5, 264
Haute Tension/Switchblade Romance (film), 222, 223
Havrylivna, Olga, 129n4
Hawaii, 223
Hayward, Susan, 240–1
Heart of Brazil see *Coração do Brasil*
Heaven on Earth (film), 51, 52, 53, 54, 55, 56, 58, 60, 62, 63, 64
Heidegger, Martin, 28, 179n4
Helde, Martti, 8, 103–17
Henry: Portrait of a Serial Killer (film), 13, 270, 271, 273–81, 285–7, 288n2
Herzog, Werner, 246–7
Hesitant Histories on the Romanian Screen (book), 145n2
Hills Have Eyes, The (1977 film), 216
Hindu, 58
Hirsch, Marianne, 119, 120
Historias mínimas/Intimate Stories (film), 235
Hitchcock, Alfred, 209
Hitcher, The (film), 271
Hitch-Hiker, The (film), 273
Hitler, Adolf, 105
Ho Chi Minh, 89
Hodász, 124
Hoffman, Eva, 121
Hogg, James, 273
Holocaust, 8–9, 107, 115, 118–29
Holland see Netherlands
Hollywood, 6, 51–4, 70, 76, 82, 83, 168, 169, 179n2, 183, 187, 189–90, 193, 235–8, 242–3, 248, 257, 261
Holocaust, 107, 115, 118, 119, 120, 122, 125, 126, 127, 128
Holquist, Michael, 71
Home (film), 19
Homer, 10
Honeymoon Killers, The (film), 271
Hooper, Tobe, 216

Hostel (film), 225
Hound of the Baskervilles, The (1959 film), 202, 204, 207
House of 1000 Corpses (film), 216
How Tasty Was My Little Frenchman see *Como Era Gostoso o Meu Francês*
Hugo (film), 43
Huhtamo, Erkki, 25, 26
Humboldt, Alexander von, 21
Hungary, 8, 9, 118–25, 139–40, 142–3, 147–64, 215, 225, 226
Hunter, Russ, 218–19
Hush (film), 219
Hutchings, Peter, 206, 208, 220
Huyssen, Andreas, 124
Hyde, Ralph, 26

i2i Audiovisual scheme, 227
Icard, Romain, 119, 125, 127
Ile-de-France, 217–18
Illouz, Eva, 172, 179n5
Ils/Them (film), 225–6
Im Lauf der Zeit/Kings of the Road (film), 237
IMAX, 19, 20
'Imperial Imaginary, The' (essay), 4
Impossible Voyage, The see *Voyage à travers l'impossible*
In the City of Sylvia (film), 80
In the Crosswind see *Risttuules*
In their Sleep see *Dans ton sommeil*
Iñárritu, Alejandro González, 19, 236, 242
INCA see National Institute of Cinema and Audiovisual Arts
India, 50, 51, 54, 58, 64n1, 210
Indochinese War, 92
Indonesia, 223
Ingold, Tim, 88
Inimene, keda polnud/A Man Who Never Was (film), 106
Innisfree (film), 7, 70–85
Inside see *À l'intérieur*
Internet Movie Database (IMDb), 193
Intimate Stories see *Historias mínimas*
Iracema, Uma Transa Amazônica/Iracema (film), 245–6
Ireland, 7, 70–1, 77–82, 215, 224
Irish Sea, 81
Iska's Journey see *Iszka utazása*
Island of Phyloe, 25
Isolation (film), 224, 225
Iszka utazása/Iska's Journey (film), 9, 147–54, 158, 159, 161n4

Israel, 128n2
Italian Job, The (1969 film), 286
Italian Journey (book), 22
Italy, 31, 219, 221
Ivano-Frankivsk, 125

Jack the Ripper case, 272, 278, 288n3
Jeepers Creepers (film), 216
'Jerusalem' (poem), 285
Jetée, La (film), 86, 98
Johannesburg, 189
Johar, Karan, 64n2
Johnson, David, 167, 175, 180n11
Johnston, Claire, 259
Jones, Reece, 5
Joyce, James, 10
Juzėnas, Audrius, 106

Kabhi Khushi Kabhie Gham (film), 64n2
Kahn, Albert, 30
Kairish, Viestur, 106
Kakar, Sudhir, 58
Kalavet/Rabies (film), 223
Kalifornia (film), 258, 271, 279
Kardomah, 44
Karnad, Girish, 51, 54, 58, 60, 64n5
Katalin Varga see *Varga Katalin balladája*
Kehamälu/Body Memory (film), 8, 103–17
Kensington, 94
Kermode, Frank, 167, 177
Kerouac, Jack, 237
Kessler, Gabriel, 240
Khan, Cédric, 278, 288n5
Kidnapped see *Secuestrados*
Kill List (film), 219
Kimberley Stone Circle, 281, 285
King Kong (1933 film), 215
Kings of the Road see *Im Lauf der Zeit*
Kinnear, Greg, 256
Király, Hajnal, 9
Kirby, Lynne, 39, 40, 41, 256
Kiss of a Killer, The see *Bela Kiss: Prologue*
Klinger, Barbara, 254
Knepper, Robert, 260
Knightley, Keira, 259
Koch-Grünberg, Theodor, 243–4
Korda brothers, 30, 210
Kostopil, 127
Kovács, András Bálint, 153, 161n7
Krasna, Sandor, 86, 98
Krishna, Srinivas, 64n2
Kvil, Leonid, 127

Laarse, Rob van der, 126
LaBeouf, Shia, 258
Labour Camp 325, 125
Ladegaard, Jakob, 107, 114
Ladri di biciclette/ Bicycle Thieves (film), 243
Laine, Janne, 108
Lancashire, 36
Landscape and Film (book), 4
Landy, Marcia, 210
Lanzmann, Claude, 119
Lane, Sasha, 267
Lang, Fritz, 193
Laramie, New Mexico, 259–60, 262
Last Circus, The see *Balada triste de trompeta*
Latvia, 106, 127
Lázaro-Reboll, Antonio, 226
Le Corbusier, 275–6
Lean, David, 36, 43
Lean-In movement, 253, 255
Lefebvre, Henri, 4, 131, 135–6
Lefebvre, Martin, 4
Leicester Square, 25
Leitch, Donovan, 262
Leo, Melissa, 267
Letter from Siberia (film), 87
Lewis, Matthew G., 199
Liepāja, 127
Life in a Day (film), 19
Lilya 4-ever (film), 151, 152
Lindsay, Vachel, 31
Linklater, Richard, 11, 167–82
Lithuania, 8, 86–97, 106, 118–29
Little Miss Sunshine (film), 252, 255–9
Livide/ Livid (film), 227
Living Images see *Elavad pildid*
Lobato, Ramon, 221
Locke (film), 282
Lodge, Guy, 237
London, 25, 26, 36–8, 41, 43, 81, 94, 96, 202, 205, 206, 209, 220, 272–3
London Buses, 282
London Orbital (film), 282
Lonely Planet (book series), 32
Long, Jon, 19
Los Angeles, 189
Lowenthal, David, 90, 91, 92, 122, 128
Lucas, Henry Lee, 274, 276
Lumière brothers, 2, 7, 30, 37, 40, 96, 145n4, 278
Lusiads, The (epic poem), 10
Luxembourg, 219
Lviv, 125, 126

M (film), 271–2
M1 motorway, 284
Ma, Yo-Yo, 180n14
Macabre (film), 223
MacDonald, Kevin, 19
MacDowell, James, 168
McEvoy, Emma, 199
McGillivray, Murray, 180n9
Mackenzie, John M., 38, 41, 47
McNeill, Isabelle, 95
Mad Max (film), 238
Mad Max: Fury Road (film), 13, 242
Magical Mystery Tour (film), 282
Magnificent Ambersons, The (film), 242
Malin, Irving, 201
Mammoth (film), 19
Man Who Never Was, A see *Inimene, keda polnud*
Manchester, 38
Mandel, Naomi, 118
Manet, Édouard, 39
Manhattan, 123
Manhunt see *Rovdyr*
Marker, Chris, 87, 88
Markevicius, Marius A., 106
Marples, Eric, 285
Marshall, Neil, 221
Martin, Andrew, 38
Martin-Jones, David, 104, 105, 111, 112, 114
Mazierska, Ewa, 4, 6, 10, 11, 148, 150, 159, 160, 161n2, 224
Marx, Karl, 4, 38, 184, 188
  Capital, 184, 188
  Communist Manifesto, The, 3, 188
  Grundrisse, The, 38, 188
Masala (film), 64n2
Massey, Doreen, 43, 87
Maturin, Charles Robert, 199
Mazdon, Lucy, 7, 278
MEDIA, 227
Mediterranean Sea, 191
Mehta, Deepa, 7, 50–69
Mekas, Jonas, 88, 89, 90, 91, 97
Mekong Delta, 93, 245
Melānijas hronika/ Chronicles of Melanie (film), 106
Méliès, Georges, 2, 30, 183
Melmoth the Wanderer (novel), 199
Melville, Herman, 10
Memories Denied see *Tõrjutud mälestused*
Mercosur, 240

INDEX

Meirelles, Fernando, 19
Merriman, Peter, 281–2
meute, La / The Pack (film), 12, 227–9
Metropolis (film), 193
Mexico, 224, 236–7, 242, 280
Mezőkaszony, 124
Mezzadra, Sandro, 6
Mhahabharata (religious text), 10
Middle of the World, The see *Caminho das Nuvens, O*
Milford, 48
Milford Junction, 36, 44, 47
Minatour (film), 219
Minton, Anna, 254, 266
Mirbeau, Octave, 3
Mircea Voda (boulevard), 138
Mishra, Vijay, 54, 62, 63
Mississippi Masala (1991 film), 64n2
Mitchell, Timothy, 27, 28
Moartea domnului Lăzărescu / The Death of Mr. Lazarescu (film), 9, 130, 154
Moby Dick, or, The Whale (novel), 10
Model T Ford, 275
Modleski, Tania, 260
Mohawk, 267
Monet, Claude, 39
Monk, The (novel), 199
Monster (film), 258, 279, 280
Moodysson, Lukas, 19
Moon, 183
Mooney, Nicola, 55, 56
Morgen (film), 9, 130–1, 139–45
Morii, Lacul, 138
Morris, Michael, Third Baron Killanin, 76, 77, 79
Morrissey, 286
Moses, Robert, 275–6
Motion Picture Association of America, 274
Motorcycle Diaries, The see *Diarios de Motocicleta*
Moving Pictures, Migrating Identities (book), 6
Mulvey, Laura, 258
Mummy, The (1959 film), 201, 202, 207, 209
Mungiu, Cristian, 161n1
Muntean, Radu, 161n2
Mussolini, Benito, 276
My Grandfather's House: The Journey Home (film) 8, 119–23, 125, 126, 128
Mỹ Sơn, 92

Myers, Toni, 19
Myriorama, 26
Mysteries of Udolpho (novel), 199

Nadel, Sam, 123, 128n2
Naficy, Hamid, 5, 51, 52, 53, 61, 64n3, 149, 155, 157, 158
Naga Mandala (play), 51, 60
Nagas of Indian, The, 64n6
Nagib, Lúcia, 235
Nagykálló, 124
Nair, Mira, 64n2
Namesake, The (film), 64n2
Nanook of the North (film), 248
Näripea, Eva, 8
National Institute of Cinema and Audiovisual Arts (INCA), 248
National Trust, 281, 288n6
Natural Born Killers (film), 258, 271, 279
Nazi, 37, 91, 96, 119, 120, 122, 124, 125, 127, 128n3
Neale, Steve, 268n2
Negri, Antonio, 188
Neilson, Brett, 6
neo-realism, 3, 161n1
Nerva Traian (boulevard), 138
Netflix, 216
Netherlands, 161n4, 226
New American Cinema, 3
New York, 25, 41, 88, 89, 90, 120, 122, 123, 124, 125, 267
Niagara Falls, 62
Niccol, Andrew, 184
Niépce, Nicéphore, 278
Nietzsche, Friedrich, 258
Night and Fog see *Nuit et brouillard*
Night of the Big Heat (film), 207, 213
Night Train to Munich (film), 40
Nikolayev, 125
Nitu, Ciprian, 145n5
Noah's Ark, 194
Nocturnal Animals (film), 258
Nora, Pierre, 93, 119
Nordisk Film and TV Fund, 219
Norton, Glen, 180n10
Norway, 215, 223, 228
Nouvelle Vague, 3, 161n1
Novozlatopol, 125
Nueve Reinas / Nine Queens (film), 237
Nuit et brouillard / Night and Fog (film), 127
Nuts in May (film), 286

Octavian Goga (boulevard), 138
Odyssey (epic poem), 10
Oettermann, Stephan, 21
O'Feeney brothers, 76
Oleksandriya, 127
Oleksijczuk, Denise Blake, 23, 36n4
On the Buses (film), 282
On the Road (book and film), 237
One Day on Earth (film), 19
Ontario, 229n8
Open Veins of Latin America (book), 248
Orford Ness, 96
Orgeron, David, 3
Orrade, Javier, 248
Others, The (film), 226
Our Name Will Gradually Be Forgotten see *Ajapikku unustatakse meie nimi*
Outbound see *Periferic*

Pack, The see *meute, La*
Paddington, 94
Padilha, José, 236
Paju, Imbi, 115n3
Pakistan, 64n1
Pandora's Box see *Büchse die Pandora, Die*
Paradise Lost see *Turistas*
Parikka, Jussi, 31
Paris, 23, 25, 26, 37, 41, 43, 86, 125, 168, 170, 178, 181n19, 205, 217–18, 221, 226
Paris, Texas (film), 237
Parr, Martin, 286
Parvulescu, Constantin, 145n1, 145n5
Pater, Walter, 179n4
Pathé, 30
Päts, Konstantin, 112
Patterson, John, 48
Pearsons, Wendy, 245
Pencil Museum, Derwent, 281, 285
Perdita Durango (film), 280
Perfect Getaway, A (film), 223
Periferic/Outbound (film), 9, 130–1, 135–9, 144
Petit, Chris, 94, 95, 97
Philippines, The, 223
Pigott, Michael, 7
Pikkov, Ülo, 8, 103, 104, 109, 114
Pinazza, Natália, 12
Pixar, 263
Pittsburgh, 71
Planet Earth (TV series), 19, 32
Planet Earth II (TV series), 33
Plutarch, 1

Plymouth, 38, 209
Poe, Edgar Allan, 21, 22
Poland, 126, 229n9
  Second Commonwealth of Poland, 126
Pôle Image de Liège, 227
Pollin-Galay, Hannah, 118
Poole, Charles, 26
Poole, George, 26
Pop, Doru, 145n1
Pope's Toilet, The see *Baño del Papa, El*
porte del silenzio, Le/Door to Silence (film), 271
Portsmouth, 285
Porumboiu, Corneliu, 130, 147
Portugal, 161n4, 237
Potteiger, Matthew, 87, 90
Powell, Dilys, 47
'Power of Love, The' (song), 283
Powley, Bel, 106
Prager, Brad, 118
Pratt, Mary Louise, 256
Principles of Scientific Management, 275
Private Memoirs and Confessions of a Justified Sinner (novel), 273
Production of Space, The (book), 4
Promenons-nous dans le bois/Deep in the Woods (film), 223
Puerto Rico, 223
Puhastus/Puhdistus/Purge, 115n3
Puiu, Cristi, 132–3, 135, 161n1
Punjab, 51
Punter, David, 202, 203, 208
Purcell, Henry, 168
Purge see *Puhastus*
Purinton, Jamie, 87, 90
Purrington, Caleb, 25

quatrecents coups, Les/The 400 Blows (film), 3
Queer Art of Failure, The (book), 252
Quiet Man, The (film), 7, 70–85

Rabies see *Kalavet*
Race with the Devil (film), 271
Radcliffe, Ann, 199
Radio On (film), 282
Railway Children, The (film), 40
Rain, Steam and Speed: The Great Western Railway (painting), 39
Rama, Ángel, 237–8
Ramayana (epic poem), 10, 59–60
Rascaroli, Laura, 4, 6, 10, 150, 161n2, 224

Rava-Ruska, 125, 126, 127, 128n3
Raw see *Grave*
Rawle, Steven, 6
'Red Flag' Act, 1865, 284
Regent Street, 25
Reichardt, Kelly, 267
Reminiscences of a Journey to Lithuania (film), 8, 86–98
Renaissance, 41
Renoir, Pierre-Auguste, 40
Rescued by Rover (film), 2
Resident Evil (film), 220
Resnais, Alain, 127
Revenant, The (film), 13, 242
Revenge of Frankenstein, The (film), 204, 207, 208
Ribblehead Viaduct, 285
Richards, Jeffrey, 38, 41, 47
Richeri, Giuseppe, 217
Ripley series, 272
Risttuules/In the Crosswind (film), 8, 103–17
Rivette, Jacques, 3
Rivne, 127
RKO, 30
Road, The (film), 223
Road Movies: From Muybridge and Méliès to Lynch and Kiarostami (book), 3
Roberts, Les, 92
Roberts, Shari, 248
Robinson Crusoe (novel), 10, 286
Rocha, Glauber, 238
Rogen, Seth, 259
Rohod, 122, 124
Rolling Family see *Familia Rodante*
Roman Holiday (film), 169
Romania, 8, 9, 130–46, 147–63, 225, 226
Rome, 25, 276
Rosetta (film), 222
Roth, Eli, 225
Rottenberg, Catherine, 253
Roue, La (film), 3
Routemaster, 282
Rovdyr/Manhunt (film), 223, 228
Rowden, Terry, 6
Royal Academy, 39
Rubin, Martin, 271
Ruddick, Kyle, 19
Rueschmann, Eva, 6
Ruins, The (film), 223
Ruoff, Jeffrey, 87
Russel, Catherine, 87, 89
Russell, Benjamin, 25

Russia, 107, 108, 111, 113, 151, 215, 226; see also Soviet Union (USSR)
Ryan, Mark, 221

Sachs, Lynne, 91, 92, 93
Sacred Planet (IMAX film), 19
Salles, Walter, 236–7, 242–3, 245–6, 248–9
Salles Gomes, Paulo Emílio, 237, 249n2
Salonta, 139, 141, 142, 143
Samsara (film), 19
Sandberg, Sheryl, 253
Sanders of the River (film), 210
Sans Soleil (film), 86, 98
Sans toit ni loit/Vagabond (film), 149
Sarny, 127
Schama, Simon, 88
Schivelbusch, Wolfgang, 41, 175, 180n12, 256
Schlesinger, John, 43
Schultes, Richard Evans, 243–4
Scorsese, Martin, 43
Scotland, 221
Scott, James, 42, 43, 45
Seasoning House, The (film), 226
Second World War, 37, 47, 88, 92, 96, 107, 112, 115n3
Secuestrados/Kidnapped (film), 227
Seeking a Friend for the End of the World (film), 252, 259
Seltzer, Mark, 275, 279, 280
Semeniškiai, 88, 90
Senegal, 3
Senna, Orlando, 245–6
Sense of an Ending, The (book), 167, 177
Severance (film), 225–6
Shabbat, 122
Shaw, Deborah, 6, 237
Shaw, Lisa, 237
Sheller, Mimi, 186, 191
Shelley, Mary, 199, 200
Shiva, 58, 59
Shoah par balles: l'histoire oubliée (film), 8, 119, 125–8
Shohat, Ella, 4, 27, 30, 235
Shrine, The (film), 229n9
Shumway, David, 168
Siberia, 88, 105, 106, 111, 113, 121
Sights of the World, 26
Sightseers (film), 13, 270, 280–7, 288n2
Sikh, Jat, 55
Sikhism, 59
Silence of the Lambs, The (film), 271
Sillart, Jüri, 106

Simm, Peeter, 106
Simmel, Georg, 280
Singapore, 223
Singing Revolution, 106
Shackleton, Mark, 63
Shanghai Express (film), 40
Skrodzka, Aga, 152
Sky Captain and the World of Tomorrow (film), 2
Skye, Ione, 260
Slumdog Millionaire (film), 43
Smith, George Albert, 2
Smith, Iain R., 6
Snowpiercer (film), 11, 184, 193–7
So Long at the Fair (film), 200, 205
Solnit, Rebecca, 89
sombra del caminante, La / The Wandering Shadows (film), 242
'Sonata for Viola da Gamba and Harpsichord' (musical composition), 174–8, 180n10, 180nn14–16, 180n10
Sööt, Andres, 115n3
Sortie de l'Usine Lumière à Lyon, La / Workers Leaving the Lumière Factory in Lyon (film) 2, 96
Sound and Image, 227
South Africa, 188–90
South Korea, 194
Soviet Union (USSR), 91, 103–17, 121, 127, 129n3, 183, 225; see also Russia
Spain, 70, 82–3, 215, 219, 222, 224, 226, 237
Spirit of the Beehive, The see *El espíritu de la colmena*
Spivak, Gayatri, 6
Splintered (film), 223
Spoorloos / The Vanishing (film), 271
St Pancras, 41
Staden, Hans, 243
Stalin, 105, 113
Stalker (film), 183
Stam, Robert, 4, 27, 30, 235
State, Andrei, 161n2
Steinman, Ron, 119, 120
Stepanova, Nadia, 129n4
Stepanova, Misha, 129n4
Stevenson, Robert Louis, 278
Still Life (play), 44
Stojanova, Christina, 225
Stoker, Bram, 199, 200, 205, 206
Stolen Face (film), 207, 208–9, 212

Stone, Rob, 167, 175
Stosberg, Hans, 96
Straight Heads (film), 223
Strange Case of Dr. Jekyll and Mr. Hyde (novel), 278
Strangers on a Train (film), 272
Stranglers of Bombay, The (film), 207, 209–12
Strausz, László, 9
Streisand, Barbara, 259
Strickland, Peter, 149, 158
Suffolk, 96
Summer Holiday (film), 11, 282
Sun, The (newspaper), 288n6
Switchblade Romance see *Haute Tension*
Syngle, Erik, 180n10
Syracuse, 121
Syria, 141
Szabolcs, 122
Szatmár, 122
Széchenyi Chain Bridge, 124

Tarkovsky, Andrei, 183
Tarr, Béla, 108, 153, 161n7
Taylor, Henry, 275
Tax Shelter du Gouvernement Fédéral de Belgique, 220, 227
Taxi Driver (film), 258, 271
Technicolor, 2
Terminus (film), 43
Terra Estrangeira / Foreign Land (film), 240
Texas Chainsaw Massacre, The (film), 216
TGV (French rail service), 42, 43
Thatcher, Margaret, 190, 254
Théâtre Mécanique Morieux de Paris, Le, 26
Thelma and Louise (film), 255, 258–9
Them see *Ils*
Third Reich, 128
This Is not a Love Song (film), 223
Thomson, David, 36
Thornton, Niamh, 237–8, 249n3
Time with Betjeman (TV series), 42
Titanic (film), 2
Titfield Thunderbolt, The (film), 40
To the Public Danger (film), 203, 207, 209, 212, 213
'To the World We Show: Early Travelogues as Filmed Ethnography' (essay), 4
Tölölyan, Khachig, 62

Tolstoy, Leo, 39
Tomberg, Donald, 109
Tomlinson, Jonathan, 4
Toole, Ottis, 274
Top Gear (TV series), 284
Tõrjutud mälestused / Memories Denied (film), 115n3
Török-Illyés, Orsolya, 158
Toronto, 51, 54, 55, 220
Touki Bouki (film), 3
TPS Star, 227–9
Trainspotting (novel), 257
Tramway Museum, Crich, 281
Trans-Amazon Highway, 246
Transnational Cinema: An Introduction (book), 6
Transnational Cinema: The Film Reader (book), 6
'Transnational Cinemas: A Critical Roundtable' (essay), 6
'Transnational Cinemas: Mapping a Field of Study' (essay), 6
Transylvania, 148, 149, 158, 161n3, 200, 202, 205, 206
Traveller's Guide to Planet Earth, The (book), 32
Trip, The (2010 film), 282
Trip to the Moon, A see *voyage dans la lune, Le*
Troll Hunter (film), 224, 229n6
True Romance (film), 258
Truth or Dare (film), 223
Tuchyn, 127
Turistas / Paradise Lost (film), 223
Turkey, 140
Turner, Frederick Jackson, 257
Turner, J. M. W., 39
Two-Lane Blacktop (film), 258

UK see Great Britain
Ukraine, 8, 118, 124–8
Ulysses (novel), 10
Unas fotos en la ciudad de Sylvia (film), 80
Unirii (boulevard), 138
United States Holocaust Memorial Museum, 120
Universal Studios, 30
Unkown Amazon see *Amazônia desconhecida*
Upham, Misty, 267
Urry, John, 186, 191
Uruguay, 239
US Sorrento Production, 106
USA, 1, 12, 13, 26, 27, 30, 31, 82, 89, 91, 93, 94, 120, 123, 125, 161n4, 167, 186, 194, 201, 207, 220–1, 223–4, 226, 228, 235–9, 245, 252–69, 270, 271, 275–6, 279, 281–2, 284

Vagabond see *Sans toit ni loi*
Valencia, 25
Vancouver, 55
Vanishing, The see *Spoorloos*
Vanishing Point (film), 257
Varda, Agnès, 149
Varga, Balázs, 155
Varga Katalin balladája / Katalin Varga (film), 9, 147–53, 161n4
Vargas, Jacob, 262
Vassal, Dennis, 161n5
Vathek (novel), 199
Vehkleja / Miekkailija / ENDEL – Der Fechter / The Fencer (film), 115n3
Verne, Jules, 2, 20, 21
Vežėjų Street, 122
Viaggio in Italia / Voyage to Italy (film), 3
Viaje, El (film), 238
Viajes del Viento, Los / The Wind Journeys (film), 242–3
Videsh see *Heaven on Earth*
vie rêvée des anges, La / The Dreamlife of Angels (film), 222
Vienna, 88, 91, 167–9, 172, 14, 176, 178–9, 181n19, 224
Vienna Film Financing Fund, 224
Việt Cộng, 93
Vietnam, 86, 91, 92, 93
Vietnam War, 92
Vilijampolė, 122
Vilnius, 121
Violent Borders: Refugees and the Right to Move (book), 5–6
Vishnu, 58
Volhynia, 125
Voyage à travers l'impossible / The Impossible Voyage (film), 2
voyage dans la lune, Le / A Trip to the Moon (film), 183
Voyage to Italy see *Viaggio in Italia*

Wagstaff, Peter, 6
Walker, Johnny, 221
'Walking in the City' (essay), 4
Wallström, Martin, 106
Wandering Shadows, The see *sombra del caminante, La*

Washington, 120
Waterloo Station, 43
Way Is East: Notebooks from Vietnam (film), 86
Way We Were, The (film), 123
Wehrmacht, 127
Weiss-Wendt, Anton, 107
Wells, H. G., 37
Welp / Cub (film), 223
Welsh, Irvine, 257
Wenders, Wim, 11, 237
Wendy and Lucy (film), 13, 252, 259, 263–7
Werbner, Pnina, 51
Westway, 94
Whaling Voyage Round the World (panorama), 25
Which Way Is East (film), 8, 86–98
Whissel, Kristen, 187–8
Who Sings the Nationa State?: Language, Politics, Belonging (book), 6
Wild at Heart (film), 258
Wild Colonial Boy, The (ballad) 82
Will It Snow for Christmas? see *Y'aura t'il de la neige à Noël?*
'Will to Motorization, The' (essay), 4, 290
Williams, Michelle, 263
Williamsburg, 89
Wind Journeys, The see *Viajes del Viento, Los*

Winston, Brian, 10
Wizard of Oz, The (film), 2
Wolf Creek (film), 223
Wood, Robin, 180n17
Workers Leaving the Lumière Factory in Lyon see *Sortie de l'Usine Lumière à Lyon, La*
World's Fair exhibition 1939–40, 275
Wrong Move, The see *Falsche Bewegung*
Wrong Turn (film), 216
Wyld, James, 25

Y'aura t'il de la neige à Noël?/Will It Snow for Christmas? (film), 222
Y Tu Mamá También (film), 235, 238
Yalta Conference, 107
Yeats, William Butler, 75
'Yellow Backs' (trains), 39
Yorkshire and Humber, 218
You Only Live Once (film), 257, 258
YouTube, 96, 216
Young, Victor, 83

Zaporozhye, 125
Zhovkva, 125
Zinta, Preity, 52
Žižek, Slavoj, 186, 188, 189
Zola, Émile, 39, 40
Zonca, Eric, 222

EU representative:
Easy Access System Europe
Mustamäe tee 50, 10621 Tallinn, Estonia
Gpsr.requests@easproject.com

www.ingramcontent.com/pod-product-compliance
Lightning Source LLC
Chambersburg PA
CBHW070016010526
44117CB00011B/1596